Lecture Notes of the Institute for Computer Sciences, Social Informatics and Telecommunications Engineering 332

Mahdi H. Miraz · Peter S. Excell ·
Andrew Ware · Safeeullah Soomro ·
Maaruf Ali (Eds.)

Emerging Technologies in Computing

Third EAI International Conference, iCETiC 2020
London, UK, August 19–20, 2020
Proceedings

 Springer

Editors
Mahdi H. Miraz ⓘ
CFRED
Chinese University of Hong Kong
Hong Kong, China

Peter S. Excell ⓘ
Professor Emeritus
Wrexham Glyndwr University
Bradford, UK

Andrew Ware ⓘ
Faculty of Computing, Engineering
and Science
University of South Wales
Pontypridd, Mid Glamorgan, UK

Safeeullah Soomro ⓘ
AMA International University
Salmabad, Bahrain

Maaruf Ali ⓘ
Epoka University
Tirana, Albania

ISSN 1867-8211   ISSN 1867-822X (electronic)
Lecture Notes of the Institute for Computer Sciences, Social Informatics
and Telecommunications Engineering
ISBN 978-3-030-60035-8   ISBN 978-3-030-60036-5 (eBook)
https://doi.org/10.1007/978-3-030-60036-5

This Springer imprint is published by the registered company Springer Nature Switzerland AG
The registered company address is: Gewerbestrasse 11, 6330 Cham, Switzerland

Preface

It is our great pleasure to introduce the proceedings of the Third International Conference on Emerging Technologies in Computing (iCETiC '20), held on the 19th and 20th August, 2020. As in previous years, the conference was supposed to be held at London Metropolitan University, London, UK. However, due to travel restrictions resulting from the spread of COVID-19, iCETiC 2020 was instead held online as a live interactive virtual conference, to ensure the safety, comfort and quality of experience of the attendees. All matters related to the quality, publication and indexing remained unchanged.

The theme of iCETiC 2020 was "Emerging Technologies" as outlined by the Gartner Hype Cycle for Emerging Technologies, 2019. This conference drew together international researchers and developers from both academia and industry - especially in the domains of computing, networking and communications engineering.

iCETiC 2020 was organised by the International Association for Educators and Researchers (IAER) and technically co-sponsored by the Chester and North Wales Branch of the British Computer Society (BCS). As a knowledge partner, the European Alliance for Innovation (EAI) also played a significant role in organising the conference and publishing the proceedings.

The technical programme of iCETiC 2020 consisted of 25 full papers in oral presentation sessions in the main conference tracks. The primary conference tracks were:

- Track 1 - Blockchain and Cloud Computing
- Track 2 - Security, Wireless Sensor Networks and Internet of Things (IoT)
- Track 3 - AI, Big Data and Data Analytics
- Track 4 - Emerging Technologies in Engineering Education and Sustainable Development

Apart from the high-quality technical paper presentations, the technical programme featured two keynote speeches and a keynote workshop. The keynote speakers were Andrew Ware, Professor of Computing at the University of South Wales, UK and Professor Jonathan C. Roberts from Bangor University, UK. The keynote workshop was facilitated by Professor Garfield Southall, Executive Dean for the Faculty of Science and Engineering at the University of Chester, UK. The workshop demonstrated the application of the Wolfram Programming Language (WPL), using COVID-19 data.

It was a great pleasure to work with such an excellent Organising Committee team, who put in significant effort in organising and supporting the conference. The work of the Technical Programme Committee is also much appreciated: they completed the peer-review process of technical papers culminating in a high-quality professional programme.

Yet again, iCETiC 2020 provided an excellent forum for researchers, developers and practitioners to discuss recent advancements in computing, networking and communications engineering. We will continue to strive to ensure that future iCETiC conferences will be as successful and stimulating.

August 2020

Mahdi H. Miraz
Peter S. Excell
Andrew Ware
Safeeullah Soomro
Maaruf Ali

Organisation

Steering Committee Co-chairs

Maaruf Ali	Assistant Professor, Faculty of Architecture and Engineering, Department of Computer Engineering, Epoka University, Albania
Safeeullah Soomro	Dean, School of Computer Studies, AMA International University BAHRAIN (AMAIUB), Bahrain
Mahdi H. Miraz	Postdoctoral Fellow, Centre for Financial Regulation and Economic Development (CFRED), The Chinese University of Hong Kong, Hong Kong SAR and Visiting Fellow, Wrexham Glyndwr University, UK

Organising Committee

General Co-chair

Safeeullah Soomro	Dean, School of Computer Studies, AMA International University BAHRAIN (AMAIUB), Bahrain

Advisory Board

Peter S. Excell	Professor Emeritus and Former Deputy Vice-Chancellor, Wrexham Glyndwr University, UK
Andrew Jones	School of Computer Science, University of Hertfordshire, Hatfield, Hertfordshire, UK
Garfield Southall	Associate Dean for the Faculty of Science and Engineering at the Thornton Science Park, University of Chester, UK
Andrew Ware	Professor, Faculty of Computing, Engineering and Science, University of South Wales, UK

Technical Programme Committee Co-chair

Mahdi H. Miraz	Postdoctoral Fellow, Centre for Financial Regulation and Economic Development (CFRED), The Chinese University of Hong Kong, Hong Kong SAR and Visiting Fellow, Wrexham Glyndwr University, UK

Web, Publicity and Social Media Chair

Shayma K. Miraz	Administration Officer, International Association of Educators and Researchers (IAER), London, UK

Publications Chair

Mahdi H. Miraz
Postdoctoral Fellow, Centre for Financial Regulation and Economic Development (CFRED), The Chinese University of Hong Kong, Hong Kong SAR and Visiting Fellow, Wrexham Glyndwr University, UK

Local Chairs

Anowarul Karim
Head, Logistic Support, International Association of Educators and Researchers (IAER), London, UK

Emily Thomas
PhD Researcher, Wrexham Glyndwr University, Wrexham, UK

Track Chairs

Cloud, IoT and Distributed Computing Track Chair

Virginia N. L. Franqueira
Senior Lecturer (Assistant Professor), Distributed and Intelligent Systems Centre for Research and Technology Transfer, University of Derby, Derby, UK

Software Engineering Track Chair

M. Abdullah-Al-Wadud
Associate Professor, Department of Software Engineering, College of Computer and Information Systems, King Saud University, Riyadh, KSA

Communications Engineering and Vehicular Technology Track Chair

Bhawani Shankar Chowdhry
Distinguished National Professor and Dean, Faculty of Electrical, Electronics, & Computer Engineering, Mehran University of Engineering & Technology, Pakistan

Mohab A. Mangoud
Department of Electrical and Electronics Engineering, College of Engineering, University of Bahrain, Bahrain

AI, Expert Systems and Big Data Analytics Track Chair

Christian Esposito
Department of Computer Science DI, Università degli Studi di Salerno, Italy

Web Information Systems and Applications Track Chair

Seifedine Kadry
Associate Professor, Faculty of Sciences, Beirut Arab University (UMB), Beirut, Lebanon

Security Track Chair

Aniello Castiglione   Department of Computer Science, University
                               of Salerno, Italy

Database System and Application Track Chair

Basit Shahzad   Department of Computer and Information Sciences,
                               King Saud University, KSA

Economics and Business Engineering Track Chair

Olga Angelopoulou   Senior Lecturer (Assistant Professor), School
                               of Computer Science, University of Hertfordshire,
                               Hatfield, Hertfordshire, UK

mLearning and eLearning Track Chair

Garfield Southall   Associate Dean for the Faculty of Science
                               and Engineering at the Thornton Science Park,
                               University of Chester, UK

General Track Chair

Andrew Jones   School of Computer Science, University
                               of Hertfordshire, Hatfield, Hertfordshire, UK

Technical Programme Committee

Ajith Abraham   Director, Machine Intelligence Research Labs (MIR
                               Labs), Monash University, Australia
Renaud Lambiotte   Associate Professor of Networks and Nonlinear
                               Systems, University of Oxford, UK
Ajay K. Gupta   Director, WiSe (Wireless Sensornets) Lab, Western
                               Michigan University, USA
Ljiljana Trajkovic   School of Engineering Science, Faculty of Applied
                               Sciences, Simon Fraser University, Canada
Been-Chian Chien   Department of Computer Science and Information
                               Engineering, National University of Tainan, Taiwan
Victor Preciado   Assistant Professor, Electrical and Systems Engineering
                               (ESE) University of Pennsylvania, USA
Lin Liu   Associate Professor, School of Software, Tsinghua
                               University, China
Guanghui Wen   Associate Professor and Assistant Dean of School
                               of Mathematics, Southeast University, China
Nowshad Amin   Professor of Renewable Energy and Solar Photovoltaics
                               Universiti Kebangsaan Malaysia and Head, "Solar
                               Photovoltaics Research Group", Solar Energy
                               Research Institute (SERI), Malaysia

Yalin Zheng   Senior Lecturer (Assistant Professor), University
                            of Liverpool, Liverpool, UK
AbdelRahman H. Hussein   Assistant Professor and Vice-Dean of Quality
                            Assurance, School of Computer Science
                            & Information Technology, Al-Ahliyya Amman
                            University, Al-salt, Jordan
Ali Kashif Bashir   Associate Professor, University of the Faroe Islands,
                            Faroe Islands, Denmark
Rabie Ramadan   Assistant Professor, School of Computer Science
                            & Software Engineering, University of Ha'il,
                            Ha'il, KSA
Vincenza Carchiolo   Dipartimento di Ingegneria Elettrica, elettronica
                            e informatica - Universita di Catania, Italy
Imran Mahmud   Assistant Professor & Associate Director (Research),
                            Department of Software Engineering, Daffodil
                            International University, Dhaka, Bangladesh
G. Sahoo   Professor of Computer Science and Engineering, Birla
                            Institute of Technology, Mesra, Ranchi, India
Brenda Scholtz   Head of Department, Department of Computing
                            Sciences, Nelson Mandela University,
                            Port Elizabeth, South Africa
Fabiana Zama   Associate Professor, Department of Mathematics MAT,
                            University of Bologna, Italy
Wahab Yuseni   Lecturer, Department of Industrial Computing,
                            Technical University of Malaysia Malacca (KUIM),
                            Malaysia
Jia Uddin   Assistant Professor, Department of Computer Science
                            and Engineering, BRAC University, Bangladesh
Saad Alharbi   Associate Professor, Taibah University, Madinah, KSA
Aniello Castiglione   Department of Computer Science, University
                            of Salerno, Italy
Fazal Noor   Associate Professor, Islamic University of Madinah,
                            Madinah, KSA
Bernhard Peischl   Research Associate, Technische Universität Graz,
                            Austria
Anupama Prasanth   Programme Head, School of Computer Studies, AMA
                            International University BAHRAIN (AMAIUB),
                            Bahrain
Christian Esposito   Department of Computer Science, University of
                            Salerno, Italy
Zainab Alansari   PhD Researcher, Faculty of Computer Science and
                            Information Technology, University of Malaya,
                            Kuala Lumpur, Malaysia
Ruchin Jain   Assistant Professor, School of Computer Studies, AMA
                            International University BAHRAIN (AMAIUB),
                            Bahrain

Abdul Rehman Soomrani	Head, Department of Computer Science, Sukkur Institute of Business Administration, Pakistan
Asadullah Shah	Department of Information Systems, International Islamic University, Malaysia
Arcangelo Castiglione	Postdoctoral Research Fellow, Department of Computer Science, University of Salerno, Italy
Suhail A. Molvi	Lecturer, School of Computer Science & Software Engineering, University of Ha'il, Ha'il, KSA
Zahid Hussain	Research Associate, Technical University Graz, Austria
Mohammed Riyaz Belgaum	Quality Assurance Chair, School of Computer Studies, AMA International University BAHRAIN (AMAIUB), Bahrain
Trupil Limbasiya	PhD Researcher and Associate Professor, NIIT University, India
Zahida Parveen	Lecturer, Department of Computer Science and Engineering, University of Ha'il, Ha'il, KSA
Marija Mitrovic Dankulov	Assistant Research Professor at Scientific Computing Laboratory, Institute of Physics Belgrade, Serbia
Balakrishnan K. (HoD)	Electrical & Electronics Engineering, Karpaga Vinayaga College of Engineering and Technology, India
Ahmed Ibrahim	Post Doctoral Research Fellow, Edith Cowan University, Perth, Australia
Asadullah Shaikh	Assistant Professor and Head of Research, Najran University, KSA
Ibrahim Kucukkoc	Assistant Professor and Research Fellow, Balikesir University, Turkey
Faisal Karim Shaikh	Associate Professor, Department of Telecommunication Engineering, Mehran University of Engineering and Technology, Pakistan
Cristóvão Dias	Centro de Física Teórica e Computacional, Faculdade de Ciências da Universidade de Lisboa, Portugal
Morgado Dias	Assistant Professor, Centro de Competências de Ciências Exactas e Engenharias, Universidade da Madeira, Portugal
Radoslaw Michalski	Assistant Professor, Faculty of Computer Science and Management, Wroclaw University of Science and Technology, Poland
Nor Badrul Anuar Bin Juma'at	Associate Professor, Faculty of Computer Science & Information Technology, Department of Computer System & Technology, University of Malaya, Malaysia
Samina Rajper	Assistant Professor, Department of Computer Science, Shah Abdul Latif University, Pakistan

Amirrudin Bin Kamsin	Senior Lecturer (Assistant Professor), Faculty of Computer Science & Information Technology, Department of Computer System & Technology, University of Malaya, Malaysia
Wasan Shakir Awad	Dean, College of Information Technology, Ahlia University, Bahrain
Yousuf M. Islam	Vice-chancellor, Daffodil International University, Bangladesh
Prabhat K. Mahanti	Professor, Department of Computer Science, University of New Brunswick, Canada
Massimo Ficco	Associate Professor, Department of Information Engineering (DII), Università degli Studi della Campania Luigi Vanvitelli, Italy
Rosa María Benito Zafrilla	Universidad Politécnica de Madrid, Spain
Syed Faiz Ahmed	Senior Lecturer (Assistant Professor), British Malaysian Institute, Universiti Kuala Lumpur, Malaysia
Anurag Singh	Head, Department of Computer Science & Engineering, National Institute of Technology (NIT) Delhi, India
Mohammad Siraj	Assistant Professor, College of Engineering, King Saud University, KSA
Anthony Chukwuemeka Ijeh	Assistant Professor, College of Computer Information Technology, American University in the Emirates, UAE
José Javier Ramasco	Distinguished Reseacher, Institute for Cross-Disciplinary Physics and Complex Systems (IFISC), Spain
Zi-Ke Zhang	Institute of Information Economy, Hangzhou Normal University, China
I-Hsien Ting	Dean, International Affairs; Associate Professor, Department of Information Management, National University of Kaohsiung, Taiwan
Francisco Rodrigues	Associate Professor, Institute of Mathematics and Computer Science, University of São Paulo, Brazil
Amir Rubin	Doctoral Candidate, Department of Computer Science, Ben-Gurion University, Israel
Ahmed N. Al Masri	Assistant Professor & Director of the Patent Office, College of Education, American University in the Emirates, UAE
Ahmed Bin Touq	Assistant Professor, Unit of Government, Policies and Urban Studies, United Arab Emirates University, UAE
Daniel Onah	Software Developer, UCL Institute of Neurology, Department of Molecular Neuroscience, University College London, UK
Oussama Hamid	Assistant Professor, Department of Computer Science, University of Kurdistan Hewlêr, Erbil, Iraq

Muniba Memon	Assistant Professor, Department of Computer Science, Najran University, Saudi Arabia
P. Vijaya	Head- Academic Support Services, Birla Institute of Technology-Muscat Centre, Waljat College of Applied Sciences, Oma
Mansoor Hyder Depar	Director, Information Technology Centre (ITC), Sindh Agriculture University (SAU), Pakistan
Hamid Tahaei	Faculty of Computer Science & Information Technology, University Malaya, Malaysia
Md Tanvir Arafat Khan	Senior Energy Storage System Engineer, Hanwha Q Cells America Limited, Palo Alto, CA, USA
Afaq Ahmad	Professor, Department of Electrical and Computer Engineering, College of Engineering, Sultan Qaboos University, Oman
Abhishek Shukla	Associate Professor, R.D. Engineering College, Dr A P J Abdul Kalam Technical University, Lucknow, India
Shkelqim Hajrulla	Assistant Professor, Department of Computer Engineering, Epoka University Albania
Sonia Rathee	Assistant Professor, Department of Computer Science, MSIT, India
Rezaul Azim	Professor, University of Chittagong, Bangladesh
Toufique Ahmed Soomro	Assistant Professor, Department of Electronic Engineering, Quaid-e-Awam University of Engineering and Science Technology, Pakistan
Purushottam Jadhav	Assistant Professor, Mechanical Department, Brahmavalley College of Engineering & Research Institute, India
Jinfeng Li	Postdoctoral Research Fellow, Department of Electrical and Electronic Engineering, Imperial College London and University of Southampton, UK
Abdul Baqi Khan	Faculty Computer Science and Engineering, Jubail Industrial College and Jubail University College, Kingdom of Saudi Arabia
Swati Namdev	Assistant Professor, Department of Computer Science, Career College, Bhopal, India
Muhammad Aamir	Professor, Faculty of Engineering, Sir Syed University of Engineering & Technology, Pakistan
Muhammad Saddam Khokhar	Postdoctoral Research Fellow, School of Computer Science & Information Technology, Jiangsu University, China
Man Fung Lo	Lecturer, Department of Mathematics and Information Technology, The Education University of Hong Kong, Hong Kong SAR

Amando Jr. Pimentel	IT Faculty Member/Quality Assurance Coordinator, IT Department, Higher College of Technology, Muscat, Oman
Ezendu Ariwa	Professor, Department of Business and Management Science, University of Wales Trinity Saint David, UK

Contents

**Emerging Technologies in Engineering Education
and Sustainable Development**

Blockchain and Cloud Computing

Cloud Forensic Analysis on pCloud: From Volatile Memory Perspectives

Nur Hayati Ahmad[1], Ameerah Saeedatus Syaheerah Abdul Hamid[1],
Nur Solehah Sorfina Shahidan[1], and Khairul Akram Zainol Ariffin[2](✉) (iD)

[1] Faculty Technology and Information Science, Universiti Kebangsaan Malaysia,
Bangi, Malaysia
{p95384,p98563,p98901}@siswa.ukm.edu.my
[2] Cybersecurity Center, Faculty Technology and Information Science, Universiti Kebangsaan
Malaysia, Bangi, Malaysia
k.akram@ukm.edu.my

Abstract. Cloud computing is widely used but with an undefined term for a multitude of different resources that are automatically distributed. Cloud computing can be called a double edge weapon from law enforcement and forensic investigation standpoint. Digital evidence collected from cloud sources, on the one hand, can present complex technical and cross-jurisdictional legal issues. This study explores the ability to retrieve possible data remnants for pCloud applications that can be applied in the preliminary analysis for forensic investigation. It is based on volatile memory analysis. The experiment on the retrieval involves three scenarios on pCloud; download, upload, and view the files on the cloud. The retrieval of the possible data remnants on this cloud application is the first step in introducing the indicator of cloud usage that can assist the forensic investigation at the early phase.

Keywords: Cloud computing · Cloud forensic · Digital forensic · pCloud · Memory analysis · Information retrieval

1 Introduction

Presently, cloud computing is considered as an expanded technology that replaces the traditional information technology (IT) systems. It consists of a pool of resources such as hardware, software, and applications that can be accessed through the web-based or pay-per-usage platform. Its main features are availability, accessibility, and scalability [1]. Due to these features, it can offer additional advantages when compared to the traditional IT system in terms of computing power and increase the storage at a lower cost. The industries and businesses have used this technology in their operation, such as in automotive, healthcare, banking, and retailing. Some of the popular Cloud Service Providers (CSPs) are Amazon Web Services, Google Cloud Platform, IBM Cloud, and Microsoft Azure [2].

M. H. Miraz et al. (Eds.): iCETiC 2020, LNICST 332, pp. 3–15, 2020.
https://doi.org/10.1007/978-3-030-60036-5_1

According to Skyhigh, Cloud technologies evolve every day. The report highlights the rapid growth in the use of cloud computing by large organizations as the technology allows them to embrace the style of no-office service. However, there are risks in implementing cloud computing. The number of cybercrimes has increased over the past ten years, leading to the rise of research and development in digital forensic to help law enforcement in tackling this problem. Some of these cases involve the use of cloud computing or virtual machines such as attackers to conduct a Distributed Denial of Service (DDoS) attack to other CSPs, services, and infrastructure [3, 4]. The attacker can delete any signs of the assault after a successful attack by turning off the virtual machines that are used for the attack. In the case of crime with computer assistance, the criminals can store the sensitive and secret files in the cloud storage such as child pornography, fraud, and illegal documents. Further, they may wipe all the records in the local storage to keep them safe from law enforcement [5].

The increase of cloud computing issues has created challenges to the forensic practitioner in the investigation of cybercrime [6, 7]. Digital forensics professionals need to apply their extensive knowledge in the area and tools into cloud computing environments to help cloud companies, including both Cloud Service Provider (CSP) and cloud users, build a legal capacity to reduce the risk of cloud theft. Therefore, this paper aims to provide the potential data remnant of cloud computing usage that can be applied in the preliminary analysis for the forensic investigation. The work is based on the study in pCloud, where the information from the volatile memory is captured for analysis. It involves three scenarios in the inquiry, such as download, upload, and view the files in the cloud. The possible keyword that points to the data remnants will be retrieved as a signature or indicator on cloud usage.

This paper is divided into six sections. Section 2 will present the cloud computing architecture and the challenge in forensic. Then, an overview of pCloud is discussed in Sect. 3. Next, Sect. 4 outlines the experimental setup and methodology for the retrieval of data remnants of pCloud from the volatile memory. The discussion on the finding and the result is highlighted in Sect. 5. Finally, Sect. 6 is the conclusion of the paper.

2 Related Work

Previously, several papers conducting the forensic processes to retrieve the evidence on cloud computing from the client perspective have been presented. It is crucial to establish a procedure for different cloud service providers as they are vary and different in terms of district rules, guidelines, and requirements. The study by [8] highlights the ability to identify the potential data remnants on Microsoft SkyDrive from Windows 7 and iPhone devices. In the same year, the work in [9] was conducted in the same effort to obtain evidence regarding access, upload, and download data on Dropbox on similar devices. In both studies, the analysis of the hard disk, memory, and network was conducted to retrieve the data remnant. It was able to retrieve several data remnants that were related to the cloud platform usage such as email address, ID, password, network information, event log, and related work. As the testbed came from virtual machines (VM), both studies analyzed.vmdk and. vmem of the VM. The.vmdk of the VM can be considered as a hard disk which holds the non-volatile data in the computer. In digital forensic, normally it is undergoing offline analysis to retrieve and reconstruct the evidence. By considering that the size of the hard drive keeps increasing over the years, this process can be time-consuming. Thus, the criminal may modify or delete the data, before any action can be taken to the cloud storage.

Additionally, the .vmem file is considered a copy of the memory dump that is acquired through a hardware-based acquisition tool. Hence, it produces less modification, if not, on the contents of the memory as no additional tool (e.g. software-based acquisition) has been applied on the machine. However, it is hard to practically implement as the hardware-based acquisition must be installed on the machine before it is run in order to collect the memory. Due to these limitations, this study tries to utilize the data remnants of the cloud usage from a memory perspective which has been acquired using the software-based tool.

Apart from that, by focusing on the privacy issue, the work in [10] outlines the approach to retrieve cloud-related data from Windows, Android, and iOS platforms for pCloud. It involves the retrieval of data from hard disk, memory, and network perspectives. The study is able to obtain information regarding the activities (upload, access, and download), password, and email. However, it is unable to highlight the critical features or data structures that hold such information.

3   Cloud Computing Architecture and Challenges for Forensic Investigation

In cloud computing, there are users, Cloud Service Providers (CSPs), and three service models, such as Infrastructure as a Service (IaaS), Platform as a Service (PaaS), and Software as a Service (SaaS) layers. The users are the most powerful entity in the ecosystem of cloud computing, especially in a cloud market. They play a crucial role in the business because their demand and needs are significant in the IT industry. Therefore, it will continuously support the development of cloud services by recognizing the cloud user demand for cloud computing [11].

The IaaS is a cloud model for the user that requires a service to address infrastructure capabilities. In this model, it provides the user with necessary computing resources such as servers, storage, and networking resources. The user can control and manage the underlying infrastructure, including software, network, and operating systems. Further, the user can purchase additional computation power and storage space [12]. Examples are Amazon EC2 and Rackspace Cloud Services.

PaaS is a platform for software development or application without the need to install the tools (for development, programming, and security) on the user's devices. The CSPs provide the platform where the user can deploy and run the application as well as offer the major hardware, network, and tools [13]. Example of service is App Engine, Microsoft Azure, Engine Yard, Cloud-enabled application platform (CEAP), and Windows Azure.

SaaS gives the ability to the CSPs to provide the user with the service application installed on the cloud system. The users get the privilege to use and run the application without the need to install on their systems. They can run the application remotely from their devices through the user interface, such as a web browser [14]. The example of SaaS is the application related to file storage, social networking, and email.

In cloud architecture, several layers determine the control over the cloud computing between the user and CSPs. These layers may include the Access Control, Application, Data, Operating System, Servers, and Network [15]. The control over the layer is also crucial in the cloud forensic investigation as it will dictate the data that can be accessed and retrieved by the investigator. When considering the IaaS model, the users can access to almost every layer except for the Servers and Network Layers. The CSPs allows the users with a privilege to handle their application, and everything is under the user's responsibilities. In the PaaS model, the users only have access to the Access Control and Application Layers. Thus, in this model, the users do not have any control over the virtual machine that processes their data. As PaaS is applied for the software development, the users can handle only the application. In contrast, the development and tools, operating systems, servers, storage, and networking resources are handled by the CSPs. On the other hand, the users only have control over the Access Control layer in the SaaS. They do not have control over the hardware of the SaaS model. Therefore, SaaS is the most restricted model when compared to the other two. The CSP has an authority on the Application, Data, Operating System, Servers, and Network. When implementing the forensic acquisition, the restriction on each service model poses challenges to the forensic investigation. Numerous researches [16–19] have outlined these challenges as listed in Table 1.

Table 1. Challenges among the cloud service delivery models.

Service model	Challenges
IaaS	1. Live forensics and access to volatile data may not be possible (some vendors may not utilize persistent storage) 2. Storage is logical and focused on allocated space; acquisition images may not include data remnants or unallocated disk space 3. Unobtainable failed or obsolete hardware 4. Multi-tenant storage devices may contaminate the acquisition 5. Logging may be co-located or spread across multiple and changing devices 6. The acquisition may require large amounts of bandwidth to complete promptly 7. Data fragmentation and dispersal 8. Data ownership issues
PaaS	1. Logging relies on the CSP environment (system calls may not function in CSP) 2. Systems are more proprietary in nature
SaaS	1. The traditional acquisition is highly unlikely 2. Logging and log details depend on CSP 3. Information may be inconsistent across application programming interfaces (API) 4. Other CSPs may be involved 5. CSP applications may be complex and difficult or impossible to analyze 6. Process/application isolation 7. Systems are more proprietary in nature

4   pCloud Application

The pCloud is a private cloud computing that is purposely for file storage. It is a user-friendly application and clearly illustrates interaction easily in terms of its operation. It is available for smartphone and computer systems as it covers numbers of operating systems such as Android, iOS, macOS, Windows, and Linux. The devices create a secure virtual drive on top of the local storage space by installing the pCloud on the system (through its desktop application, pCloud Drive). The change made on the folder of pCloud in the computer, smartphone, and tablets can be seen immediately as all the devices sync and have direct access to the internet.

This application is representing the software as a Service (SaaS) architecture. Upon the launching of the application, the provider provides the cloud-based program. The underlying network is neither regulated nor operated by the users. The features of pCloud are listed as the following [20]:

- File Management: It can efficiently manage, scan, and filter the files and folders. Further, the deleted data in the archive garbage can be retrieved if it is deleted inadvertently.
- Sharing: It has a password shielded file or directory for the sharing with an option to set the expiry date to the links. Additionally, the user can create the folder upload links without a pCloud account, which can easily share or set permission.
- File Versioning: For a specified time, it will store different versions of the same files to allow the restoration process in the latest date.
- Security: It implements an AES encryption with 256-bit together with the TLS encryption for transferring the file through the network. Furthermore, it also includes an add-on feature (pCloud Crypto) that allows the user to create a virtual vault of high-level encryption with no loss of privacy.
- Synchronization and Backup.
- Accessibility: Access is available from anywhere, any system or network at any time.
- Integration: Integrate with various popular services such as Microsoft OneDrive, Dropbox, Facebook, and Instagram.

The case study in this paper will focus on retrieving the data remnant of pCloud usage from the perspective of the computer system, whereby the access of the application is through the web browser, Google Chrome.

5   Methodology

The experiment is conducted through a virtual machine with Windows OS as the testbed. The Windows 7 Ultimate (64 bits) is installed on the Oracle VM VirtualBox with Google Chrome 79.0.3945.117 as the internet browser. A dummy account for the pCloud application is created, and five files have been used for the experiment, which can be obtained from file examples [21] data collection. The username for the dummy account is rratus23@gmail.com, while the password is rempahratus2020. The description of the files is listed in Table 2. During the experiment, the process follows the procedure given in

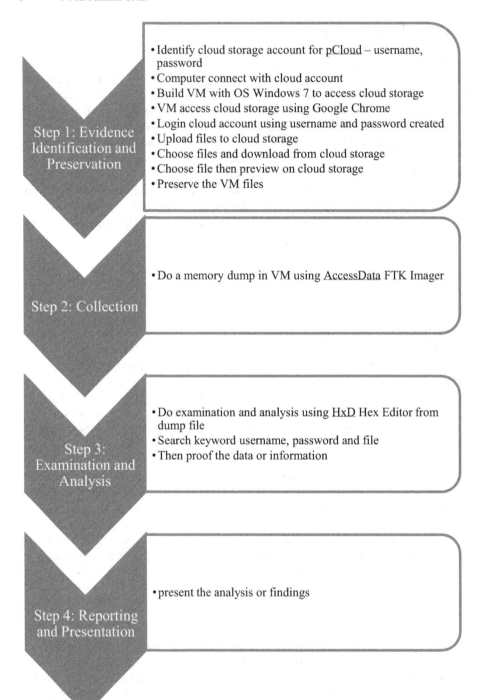

Fig. 1. The procedure of the cloud forensic investigation in the experiment.

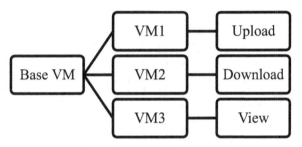

Fig. 2. Windows browser-based VMs

Table 2. Files used for the experiment.

File name	Description
fail1.pdf	A PDF file
fail2.doc	A word document
fail3.xls	An excel document
fail4.jpg	A JPEG file with extension jpg
fail5.ppt	A PowerPoint document

the study by [22]. It involves four main phases in the forensic method, such as evidence data identification and preservation, collection, analysis, and reporting. The procedure taken in this experiment is outlined in Fig. 1.

As the study focus on the volatile memory, an image of the memory is captured with the AccessData FTK Imager 3.1.4.6. The size of volatile memory is set to 2 GB. Then, each of the memory images is analyzed with the HxD Hex Editor to assess potential data remnants of the pCloud usage. Three cloned of VM are prepared, as shown in Fig. 2 to ensure each scenario (i.e., download, upload, and view) is conducted separately. The vital information that can be retrieved from the web browser is the cache and history files. Therefore, for this purpose, the data carving method is used to retrieve this information.

6   Analysis and Findings

In the experiment, access to the pCloud is through the URL: https://www.pcloud.com However, it is redirected to the page of URL: https://my.pcloud.com. Once all the five files have been applied in the scenario (i.e., scenario 1: all the files have been uploaded), then the memory image is collected. As such, there are only three memory images retrieved, that are accorded to the scenarios. Then, the forensic methods known as data carving, and keyword searches are performed to locate the data remnants for each scenario. The username, password, and name of the file are applied for the keyword.

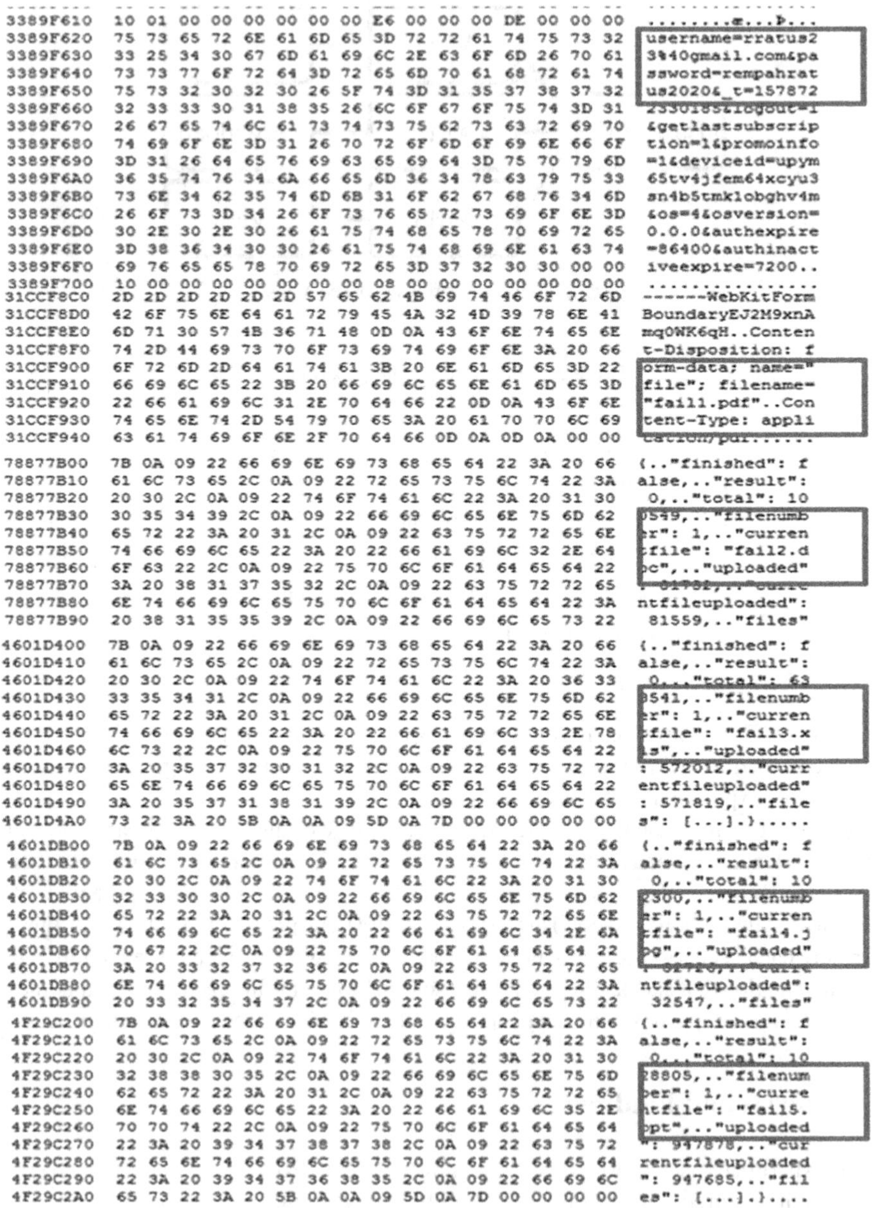

```
3389F610  10 01 00 00 00 00 00 00 E6 00 00 00 DE 00 00 00   ........æ...Þ...
3389F620  75 73 65 72 6E 61 6D 65 3D 72 72 61 74 75 73 32   username=rratus2
3389F630  33 25 34 30 67 6D 61 69 6C 2E 63 6F 6D 26 70 61   3%40gmail.com&pa
3389F640  73 73 77 6F 72 64 3D 72 65 6D 70 61 68 72 61 74   ssword=rempahrat
3389F650  75 73 32 30 32 30 26 5F 74 3D 31 35 37 38 37 32   us20206_t=157872
3389F660  32 33 33 30 31 38 35 26 6C 6F 67 6F 75 74 3D 31   2330185&logout=1
3389F670  26 67 65 74 6C 61 73 74 73 75 62 73 63 72 69 70   &getlastsubscrip
3389F680  74 69 6F 6E 3D 31 26 70 72 6F 6D 6F 69 6E 66 6F   tion=1&promoinfo
3389F690  3D 31 26 64 65 76 69 63 65 69 64 3D 75 70 79 6D   =1&deviceid=upym
3389F6A0  36 35 74 76 34 6A 66 65 6D 36 34 78 63 79 75 33   65tv4jfem64xcyu3
3389F6B0  73 6E 34 62 35 74 6D 6B 31 6F 62 67 68 76 34 6D   sn4b5tmk1obghv4m
3389F6C0  26 6F 73 3D 34 26 6F 73 76 65 72 73 69 6F 6E 3D   &os=4&osversion=
3389F6D0  30 2E 30 2E 30 26 61 75 74 68 65 78 70 69 72 65   0.0.0&authexpire
3389F6E0  3D 38 36 34 30 30 26 61 75 74 68 69 6E 61 63 74   =86400&authinact
3389F6F0  69 76 65 65 78 70 69 72 65 3D 37 32 30 30 00 00   iveexpire=7200..
3389F700  10 00 00 00 00 00 00 00 08 00 00 00 00 00 00 00   ................
31CCF8C0  2D 2D 2D 2D 2D 2D 57 65 62 4B 69 74 46 6F 72 6D   ------WebKitForm
31CCF8D0  42 6F 75 6E 64 61 72 79 45 4A 32 4D 39 78 6E 41   BoundaryEJ2M9xnA
31CCF8E0  6D 71 30 57 4B 36 71 48 0D 0A 43 6F 6E 74 65 6E   mq0WK6qH..Conten
31CCF8F0  74 2D 44 69 73 70 6F 73 69 74 69 6F 6E 3A 20 66   t-Disposition: f
31CCF900  6F 72 6D 2D 64 61 74 61 3B 20 6E 61 6D 65 3D 22   orm-data; name="
31CCF910  66 69 6C 65 22 3B 20 66 69 6C 65 6E 61 6D 65 3D   file"; filename=
31CCF920  22 66 61 69 31 69 6C 31 2E 70 64 66 22 00 0D 0A   "fail1.pdf"..Con
31CCF930  74 65 6E 74 2D 54 79 70 65 3A 20 61 70 70 6C 69   tent-Type: appli
31CCF940  63 61 74 69 6F 6E 2F 70 64 66 0D 0A 0D 0A 00 00   cation/pdf......
78877B00  7B 0A 09 22 66 69 6E 69 73 68 65 64 22 3A 20 66   {.."finished": f
78877B10  61 6C 73 65 2C 0A 09 22 72 65 73 75 6C 74 22 3A   alse,.."result":
78877B20  20 30 2C 0A 09 22 74 6F 74 61 6C 22 3A 20 31 30    0,.."total": 10
78877B30  30 35 34 39 2C 0A 09 22 66 69 6C 65 6E 75 6D 62   0549,.."filenumb
78877B40  65 72 22 3A 20 31 2C 0A 09 22 63 75 72 72 65 6E   er": 1,.."curren
78877B50  74 66 69 6C 65 22 3A 20 22 66 61 69 31 2E 64 64   tfile": "fail.dd
78877B60  6F 63 22 2C 0A 09 22 75 70 6C 6F 61 64 65 64 22   oc",.."uploaded"
78877B70  3A 20 38 31 37 35 32 2C 0A 09 22 63 75 72 72 65   : 81752,.."curre
78877B80  6E 74 66 69 6C 65 75 70 6C 6F 61 64 65 64 22 3A   ntfileuploaded":
78877B90  20 38 31 35 35 39 2C 0A 09 22 66 69 6C 65 73 22    81559,.."files"
4601D400  7B 0A 09 22 66 69 6E 69 73 68 65 64 22 3A 20 66   {.."finished": f
4601D410  61 6C 73 65 2C 0A 09 22 72 65 73 75 6C 74 22 3A   alse,.."result":
4601D420  20 30 2C 0A 09 22 74 6F 74 61 6C 22 3A 20 36 33    0,.."total": 63
4601D430  33 35 34 31 2C 0A 09 22 66 69 6C 65 6E 75 6D 62   3541,.."filenumb
4601D440  65 72 22 3A 20 31 2C 0A 09 22 63 75 72 72 65 6E   er": 1,.."curren
4601D450  74 66 69 6C 65 22 3A 20 22 66 61 69 6C 33 2E 78   tfile": "fail3.x
4601D460  6C 73 22 2C 0A 09 22 75 70 6C 6F 61 64 65 64 22   ls",.."uploaded"
4601D470  3A 20 35 37 32 30 31 32 2C 0A 09 22 63 75 72 72   : 572012,.."curr
4601D480  65 6E 74 66 69 6C 65 75 70 6C 6F 61 64 65 64 22   entfileuploaded"
4601D490  3A 20 35 37 31 38 31 39 2C 0A 09 22 66 69 6C 65   : 571819,.."file
4601D4A0  73 22 3A 20 5B 0A 0A 09 5D 0A 7D 00 00 00 00 00   s": [...].}.....
4601DB00  7B 0A 09 22 66 69 6E 69 73 68 65 64 22 3A 20 66   {.."finished": f
4601DB10  61 6C 73 65 2C 0A 09 22 72 65 73 75 6C 74 22 3A   alse,.."result":
4601DB20  20 30 2C 0A 09 22 74 6F 74 61 6C 22 3A 20 31 30    0,.."total": 10
4601DB30  32 33 30 30 2C 0A 09 22 66 69 6C 65 6E 75 6D 62   2300,.."filenumb
4601DB40  65 72 22 3A 20 31 2C 0A 09 22 63 75 72 72 65 6E   er": 1,.."curren
4601DB50  74 66 69 6C 65 22 3A 20 22 66 61 69 6C 34 2E 6A   tfile": "fail4.j
4601DB60  70 67 22 2C 0A 09 22 75 70 6C 6F 61 64 65 64 22   pg",.."uploaded"
4601DB70  3A 20 32 32 36 2C 0A 09 22 63 75 72 72 65 6E 74   : 226,.."curre
4601DB80  6E 74 66 69 6C 65 75 70 6C 6F 61 64 65 64 22 3A   ntfileuploaded":
4601DB90  20 33 32 35 34 37 2C 0A 09 22 66 69 6C 65 73 22    32547,.."files"
4F29C200  7B 0A 09 22 66 69 6E 69 73 68 65 64 22 3A 20 66   {.."finished": f
4F29C210  61 6C 73 65 2C 0A 09 22 72 65 73 75 6C 74 22 3A   alse,.."result":
4F29C220  20 30 2C 0A 09 22 74 6F 74 61 6C 22 3A 20 31 30    0,.."total": 10
4F29C230  32 38 38 30 35 2C 0A 09 22 66 69 6C 65 6E 75 6D   28805,.."filenum
4F29C240  62 65 72 22 3A 20 31 2C 0A 09 22 63 75 72 72 65   ber": 1,.."curre
4F29C250  6E 74 66 69 6C 65 22 3A 20 22 66 61 69 6C 35 2E   ntfile": "fail5.
4F29C260  70 70 74 22 2C 0A 09 22 75 70 6C 6F 61 64 65 64   ppt",.."uploaded
4F29C270  22 3A 20 39 34 37 38 37 38 2C 0A 09 22 63 75 72   ": 947878,.."cur
4F29C280  65 6E 74 66 69 6C 65 75 70 6C 6F 61 64 65 64 22   rentfileuploaded
4F29C290  22 3A 20 39 34 37 36 38 35 2C 0A 09 22 66 69 6C   ": 947685,.."fil
4F29C2A0  65 73 22 3A 20 5B 0A 0A 09 5D 0A 7D 00 00 00 00   es": [...].}....
```

Fig. 3. User credentials and uploaded files.

6.1 The User Login to Account and Upload Any File to the Platform

The overall results on uploading the files are shown in Fig. 3. It can be seen that the user credentials are consistently stored in the same arrangement for all scenarios (refer to Figs. 3, 4, and 5). The username can be identified through the "username=" while the password by "& password". It is also noted that these credentials are located under the same region in the memory image.

As for the uploading session, the information about the files is retrieved with two corresponding keywords. Firstly, it is the combination of keyword "name=" and "filename=". The keyword "name=" represents the type of file that is being uploaded, while "filename=" holds the name. In addition to that, the second combination of the keywords is the "currentfile=" and "uploaded". Similar to "filename=", the "currentfile=" holds the name of the uploaded file.

6.2 The User Login to Account and Download File to the Platform

In the context of retrieving the data remnants for the downloaded files, there is no specific keyword that can be applied which directly point to this information. However, by searching for https://my.pcloud.com, there is a possibility of obtain this information. Theoretically, the data in the volatile memory is stored in the page format. The size of one page of memory depending on the computer architecture; such it is 4096 bytes for 32-bits without Page Address Extension (PAE). Thus, by searching on the page with keyword "https://my.pcloud.com", it is possible to retrieve information about the local storage that attaches to the pCloud. In the case of the conducted experiment, the downloaded files are located in the C:\Users\<name-of-user>\ folder, as shown in Fig. 4. Additionally, the information also holds the time and date the file was created, as listed in Table 3.

Table 3. File download with date and time.

File name	Date and time
fail1.pdf	22 Aug 2016 13:37:14
fail2.doc	20 Dec 2019 11:04:16
fail3.xls	9 Jan 2020 07:35:16
fail4.jpg	20 Dec 2019 11:03:14
fail5.ppt	28 Jul 2018 18:14:18

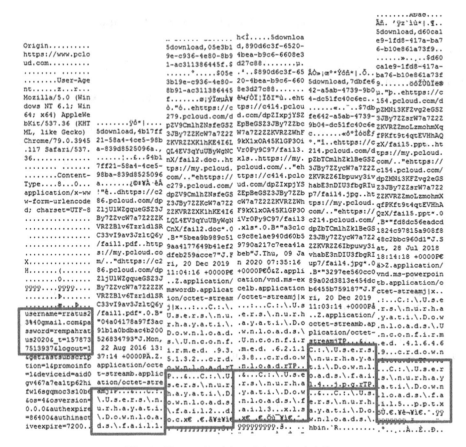

Fig. 4. User credentials and downloaded files.

6.3   The User Login to Account and Download File to the Platform

For this exercise, the pCloud account is login in another VM to preview the files that have been uploaded earlier. The preview is conducted with the Google Chrome browser, and after viewing the files, the memory image is collected. From the memory image, it is found that the information on the preview the file can be retrieved by searching "//api.pcloud.com/getpreviewlink". By applying the same assumption as in part (b), the information about the files under preview can be retrieved. This information is related to the name of the files, size, and the time the files are being viewed. The results on viewing the file are highlighted in Fig. 5 and Table 4.

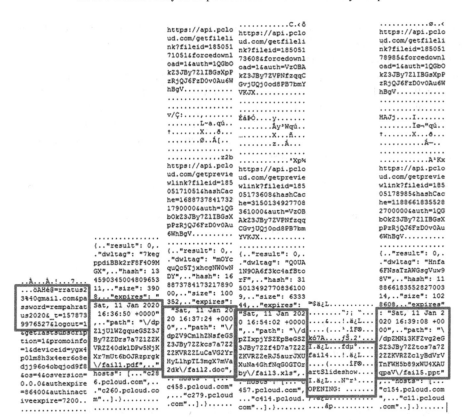

Fig. 5. User credentials and preview files

Table 4. File preview with date and time.

File name	Date and time
fail1.pdf	11 Jan 2020 16:36:50
fail2.doc	11 Jan 2020 16:37:24
fail3.xls	11 Jan 2020 16:54:02
fail4.jpg	N/A (opening on slideshow)
fail5.ppt	11 Jan 2020 16:39:08

7 Conclusion

This paper demonstrates the likelihood of reclaiming the residual information on SaaS by examining pCloud as a case study. On Windows 7, the scenarios on the pCloud are evaluated in various exercises, including upload, open, and view. It shows that all information on pCloud credentials and files used for storage could be retrieved. Though some of the credentials used in Windows 7 platforms have been plaintext, this has provided the forensic examiner with additional advantages. Furthermore, by capturing the physical memory of the pCloud service, it is also able to collect login credentials and files on the cloud, which is beneficial for the preliminary analysis in the legal process. This analysis will pave the way for forensic investigators to investigate the pCloud and other cloud storage systems. Subsequently, by analyzing the legal, privacy implications, it can therefore provide relevant solutions for cloud forensics, thereby providing additional opportunities for the use of cloud research techniques in real case scenario.

Acknowledgement. The authors would like to thank the Ministry of Education on the support given through grant FRGS/1/2018/ICT04/UKM/02/3. Additionally, we also would like to express our appreciation to Universiti Kebangsaan Malaysia and Faculty of Technology and Information Science on their support under grant GGPM-2017-026.

References

1. Freet, D., Agrawal, R., John, S., Walker, J.J.: Cloud forensics challenges from a service model standpoint: IaaS, PaaS and SaaS. In: 7th International Conference on Management of Computational and Collective Intelligence in Digital EcoSystems, pp. 148–155 (2015). https://doi.org/10.1145/2857218.2857253
2. Ahmed, A.A., Li, C.X.: Analyzing data remnant remains on user devices to determine probative artifacts in cloud environment. J. Forensic Sci. **63**(1), 112–121 (2017). https://doi.org/10.1111/1556-4029.13506
3. Majid, M.A., Ariffin, K.A.Z.: Success factors for cyber security operation center (SOC) establishment. In: INCITEST 2019 (2019). https://doi.org/10.4108/eai.18-7-2019.2287841
4. Mehmood, A., Khanan, A., Umar, M.M., Abdullah, S., Ariffin, K.A.Z., Song, H.: Secure knowledge and cluster-based instruction detection mechanism for smart wireless sensor networks. IEEE Access **6**, 5688–5694 (2018). https://doi.org/10.1109/ACCESS.2017.2770020
5. Ariffin, K.A.Z., Mahmood, A.K., Jaafar, J., Shamsuddin, S.: Tracking file's metadata from memory analysis. In: IEEE International Conference on Computer and Information Technology; Ubiquitous Computing and Communications; Dependable, Autonomic and Secure Computing, Pervasive Intelligence and Computing, pp. 975–980. IEEE (2015). https://doi.org/10.1109/cit/iucc/dasc/picom.2015.147
6. Ruan, K., Carthy, J., Kechadi, T., Crosbie, M.: Cloud forensics. In: Peterson, G., Shenoi, S. (eds.) DigitalForensics 2011. IAICT, vol. 361, pp. 35–46. Springer, Heidelberg (2011). https://doi.org/10.1007/978-3-642-24212-0_3
7. Alenezi, A., Atlam, H.F., Wills, G.B.: Expert reviews of a cloud forensic readiness framework for organizations. J. Cloud Comput. Adv. Syst. Appl. **8**, 11 (2019). https://doi.org/10.1186/s13677-019-0133-z
8. Quick, D., Choo, K.-K.R.: Digital droplets: Microsoft SkyDrive forensic data remnants. Future Gener. Comput. Syst. **29**, 1378–1394 (2013). https://doi.org/10.1016/j.future.2013.02.001
9. Quick, D., Choo, K.-K.R.: Dropbox analysis: data remnants on user machines. Digit. Invest. **10**, 3–18 (2013). https://doi.org/10.1016/j.diin.2013.02.003
10. Dargahi, T., Dehghantanha, A., Conti, M.: Investigating storage as a service cloud platform: pCloud as a case study. In: Contemporary Digital Forensic Investigation of Cloud and Mobile Applications, pp. 185–204 (2017). https://doi.org/10.1016/b978-0-12-805303-4.00012-5

11. Amanatullah, Y., Lim, C., Ipung, H.P., Juliandri, A.: Toward cloud computing reference architecture: cloud service management perspective. In: International Conference on ICT for Smart Society, pp. 1–4 (2013). https://doi.org/10.1109/ictss.2013.6588059
12. Arafat, M.Y., Mondal, B., Rani, S.: Technical challenges of cloud forensics and suggested solutions. Int. J. Sci. Eng. Res. **8**(8), 1142–1149 (2017)
13. Chaudhary, O., Siddique, A.S.: Cloud computing application: its security issues and challenges faced during cloud forensics and investigation. Int. J. Adv. Res. Comput. Sci. **8**(2), 12–16 (2017). https://doi.org/10.26483/ijarcs.v8i2.2916
14. Paul, A., Anvekar, K.M., Rishil, J., Chandra, S.K.: Cyber forensics in cloud computing. Master thesis, Department of Computer Science and Engineering, NITK, Surathkal, India (2012)
15. Zawoad, S., Hasan, R.: Cloud forensics: a meta-study of challenges, approaches, and open problems. arXiv preprint arXiv:1302.6312 (2013)
16. Neware, R., Khan, A.: Cloud computing digital forensic challenge. In: 2nd International conference of Electronics, Communication and Aerospace Technology (ICECA 2018), pp. 1090–1092 (2018). https://doi.org/10.1109/iceca.2018.8474838
17. Park, J.-H., Na, S.-H., Park, J.-Y., Huh, E.-N., Lee, C.-W., Kim, H.-C.: A study on cloud forensics and challenges in SaaS application environment. In: 18th International Conference on High-Performance Computing and Communications, pp. 734–741 (2016). https://doi.org/10.1109/hpcc-smartcity-dss.2016.0107
18. Mohtasebi, S., Dehghantanha, A., Choo, K-K R.: Cloud storage forensics: analysis of data remnants on SpiderOak, JustCloud, and pCloud. In: Contemporary Digital Forensic Investigation of Cloud and Mobile Applications, pp. 205–246 (2017). https://doi.org/10.1016/b978-0-12-805303-4.00013-7
19. O'Shaughnessy, S., Keane, A.: Impact of cloud computing on digital forensic investigations. In: Peterson, G., Shenoi, S. (eds.) DigitalForensics 2013. IFIPAICT, vol. 410, pp. 291–303. Springer, Heidelberg (2013). https://doi.org/10.1007/978-3-642-41148-9_20
20. pCloud. https://www.pcloud.com. Accessed 15 Jan 2020
21. Samples documents download. https://file-examples.com/index.php/sample-documents-download/. Accessed 15 Jan 2020
22. Easwaramoorthy, S., Thamburasa, S., Samy, G., Bhushan, S.B., Aravind, A.: Digital forensic evidence collection of cloud storage data for investigation. In: 2016 International Conference on Recent Trends in Information Technology (ICRTIT), pp. 1–6 (2016). https://doi.org/10.1109/icrtit.2016.7569516

CALIPER: A Coarse Grain Parallel Performance Estimator and Predictor

Sesha Kalyur$^{(\boxtimes)}$ and G.S Nagaraja

Department of Computer Science and Engineering, R. V. College of Engineering,
VTU, Bangalore, India
Sesha.Kalyur@Gmail.Com, nagarajags@rvce.edu.in

Abstract. Empirical studies of Program Performance, are limited by the choice and the resulting bias, from the input samples used in the experiment. Estimation and Prediction based on static analysis, are more universal, superior and widely accepted. However the higher language artifacts such as Procedures, Loops, Conditionals and Recursion which ease program development can be an hindrance to quality analysis and performance study, both in terms of time and effort spent and in some extreme cases making it impractical. However, we could transform the program, eliminate the constraints imposed by these program structures and greatly ease the process of quality analysis and performance study. This process may also reduce the errors in the estimation, and help deliver timely results, when there is still an opportunity to use them in a later analysis phase. We propose transformations prior to estimation, such as *Procedure Call Expansion*, *Loop Unrolling* and *Control Predication* collectively referred to as *Program Shape Flattening* here with the structural hindrances themselves referred to as the *Program Shape*. The outcome of this transformation, is sequential code that is easy to work with. Specifically, for parallel performance estimations, we now have code that is free from *Control Dependencies*. We use the concept of *Equivalence Classes* to group statements based on their *Data Dependence* behavior. Statements that belong to an *Equivalence Class* are mutually dependent directly or transitively. On the other hand statements that belong to separate *Equivalence Classes* are dependence free and can be run in parallel without compromising on the program correctness. With this arrangement of program statements we claim that the program run time is now equal to the run time of the class that runs the longest. While this scheme of grouping program instructions, can be viewed as a method of parallel conversion, we use this method here specifically for parallel performance estimation and prediction. After surveying the published literature, and searching for similar commercial products, we did not find a comparable technology, to assess the contributions made by Caliper, at the time of writing, and so we claim that Caliper is the only product of its kind today.

© ICST Institute for Computer Sciences, Social Informatics and Telecommunications Engineering 2020
Published by Springer Nature Switzerland AG 2020. All Rights Reserved
M. H. Miraz et al. (Eds.): iCETiC 2020, LNICST 332, pp. 16–39, 2020.
https://doi.org/10.1007/978-3-030-60036-5_2

Keywords: Analytical Model · Coarse model · Mathematical model · Maximum Available Parallelism · MAP · Parallel estimation · Parallel prediction · Performance estimation · Performance prediction · Program Shape · Program Shape Flattening · Speedup After Parallel Conversion · SAP

1 Introduction

The universal method, of estimating the performance of a program, is the wall clock method, where the time spent by the program, from start to finish, provides the measure. But when computers of different speeds are involved, a little more work is needed, in the form of converting, run times to normalized cycles, before we can compare. When we need fine grained performance, we can use specialized counters, to further our quest. However, empirical studies of program performance, are biased towards the choice of input samples used, which is an inherent limitation of this method.

As an alternative, study of program characteristics, through static analysis, is encouraged. The process seems simple, but tricky, since the cycles, are hidden in program structures, such as Procedures, Loops, Recursion and Conditions to name a few. This is even more evident, when we undertake performance study, of parallel programs and serial programs, that are scheduled for, parallel conversion. It is an unfortunate paradox that, the syntax features of an imperative language, designed to boost programmer productivity, can be a hindrance to quality analysis and performance studies. We are at the mercy of Analysis phases later on in the compilation chain to supply the information for estimation. Many of these phases also perform non trivial program transformations to assist the analysis step further, reducing the relevance of an estimation phase. If performance estimates are available early, they could be used to determine, the choice of transformations to apply. How do we get past this dichotomy? By realizing that syntactic structures are the cause, and finding a cure for it. From the perspective of a modern imperative language, this means cleaning up syntax through Procedure Expansion or Function In-lining, Loop Unrolling, Recursion to Loop Conversion, and Control Predication prior to the analysis and study phase.

Performance estimation and prediction of code, that is free of syntactic structures of high level languages are easy. Thus, converting code with these structures to sequential code, is the first step in our measurement process. We use a process called *Program Shape Flattening*, to eliminate the estimation hurdles. These syntactic structures, their number and placement which add a unique character to the program under study together, is referred to as the *Program-Shape,*

Next we use the concept of *Equivalence Class* to solve the central problem that is addressed in the paper namely, the coarse assessment of parallel performance and providing estimation and prediction to programmers. We define *Equivalence Class* as a class that holds objects that share a common property. In the current context, it holds program statements that share dependency between them. We call such a class as a *Parallel Equivalence Class*. Together, the *Parallel Equivalence Classes*, that belong to a program, hold all the statements in the given program. These *Parallel Equivalence Classes* can be run in parallel and hence the name. The number of *Parallel Equivalence Classes* and the instructions belonging to each, are good indicators, of the parallel behavior of the program. A large number of *Parallel Equivalence Classes* with less number of statements in each indicates that the given program is parallel conversion friendly.

Finally, we define ready to remember, and easy to use parallel performance indicators to aid the parallel programmer, referred to as, *Maximum Available Parallelism* which in short form is referred to as *(MAP)* and *Speedup After Parallel Conversion* which is abbreviated as (SAP). The coming sections, shall provide details, of our research activities and their outcomes.

The paper, is organized as follows: Sect. 2 which follows, examines the state of the art, in the domain of performance assessment in general, and parallel measurement in particular. Section 3 briefly looks at Asterix, our parallel compiler and transformation infrastructure. Section 4 discusses in detail, the workings of Caliper, which is an important piece, in the overall solution, provided by Asterix. Section 5 which follows, presents Caliper in action, from the concept of an example program, in a higher level, imperative language. Section 6 is dedicated to Competitive Analysis, which is a study to assess, how Caliper fares against the opposition, in academia and industry. Finally we conclude the paper, after highlighting the contributions of our work, with the research community, in perspective.

2   Previous Work

Early methods of converting, serial code to a parallel form, was a manual process, was error prone and tedious, and not very productive. Its successor, was a parallel conversion process, that involved both, the programmer and the compiler. The programmer supplied the hints and pointed out sections of code and data, that were parallel friendly, and the compiler provided a working solution.

There are many research projects that tried out the semi-manual, hints based approach. For instance the authors of [8], added parallel extensions, to a standard imperative language, to empower the language for deployment, in both shared memory by providing thread support, and in a distributed setting, through message passing and mailbox support. The authors of [30] propose a parallel conversion library, for Object Oriented Software, which supports both, Shared Memory and Cluster Paradigms. Standardization efforts, led to the design of OpenMP, which is based on the Shared Memory Tasking model, and uses clauses added to existing imperative languages [2]. This was complemented later, by the Message Passing Interface (MPI), a solution for use in the Distributed Environments, and is structured as a library [21]. OpenMP and MPI have been used in the production of, industrial strength software, especially in the scientific domain. However the fact remains that, all these approaches require programmer time and effort, to supply the hints, which translates to a loss of programmer productivity, and this prompted researchers to find better solutions.

Automated Parallel Conversion, does not involve the programmer, and the solution is entirely provided by the compiler, and has received attention of several research groups, over the years. The central aspect of this approach, is the underlying mathematical model used. Models based on Symbolic Algebra, Linear Algebra, Polyhedra and Graphs are popular [26], and the quality of the results generated, are in most cases, closely tied with the model. Polyhedra model is attractive for parallel conversion, due to its simplicity. The models has been used to extract data dependencies, and to enable transformations for shared memory multi-core targets [6]. Polyhedral models also referred to as the Polytope models, have been extensively used for loop optimizations, including Unrolling, Slicing, Sanitization, etc [34]. However the model is limited to affine expressions involving index and induction variables, and may not yield results, when dealing with irregular loop expressions, such as accesses involving sparse matrices.

Graphs are used extensively, to represent various kinds of information, including Program Dependence and Flow [23,42]. Graph models are used to detect, iteration dependencies of loops [38]. Graphs were used to generate, data dependencies and profiles of Object Oriented Programs, to solve data partitioning problem, and generate synchronization and communication [13]. Researchers have used Graph Models along with Analytical Models, to solve, Work Distribution, Communication Overheads, and Data Locality issues in Distributed Environments [16,18]. Graphs are very intuitive, widely used and the most popular of all the models, for studying program behavior. However, Graphs without a good representation, can consume large amounts of memory.

When we have a choice of models to use, for dependency analysis, how do we pick? Authors of [40] present results of an experimental evaluation, to help choose an appropriate model. How can a complete Parallel Optimization solution be structured? Authors of [11] present an Integrated Graphical Environment, based around an code editor metaphor, with support for debugging and user feedback, through code annotations.

Recent Parallel Optimization related research efforts, seem to increasingly pivot around, the data gathered at run time by profiling and sampling. Examples include, the Binary Rewrite approach to parallel conversion [32], Inter-procedural Analysis [5], Parallel conversion of Irregular Loops [4] Real World Loops with irregular structure [33]. Analysis of Object Oriented Programs through speculation [22], Combined static analysis with sampling [20], Hardware Centric Dynamic approach [10], Dynamic Feedback through sampling [7]. However all dynamic schemes, which gather behavior data, using Profile and Sampling, are biased towards the input samples used, and the resulting program coverage. Schemes that use executables as source of parallel transformations are limited by the extent of the metadata present. Speculation centric schemes are simple to implement, since they bypass extensive analysis upfront, but pay a price when hit with program dependency conflicts, which requires sufficient time and effort handling rollbacks. Schemes that focus entirely on one particular aspect of a program, such as Loops, pay a price when confronted with, programs of different genres.

When it comes to Performance Studies and Predictions how do we get the necessary information? Should we use Static Analysis Methods or resort to Dynamic Schemes? Opinions are divided across the research community. A great many researchers tread the middle ground and use both methods referred to here as Hybrid Schemes, in their research.

Authors have used Static Schemes since the beginning for Performance Estimation and Prediction. Here are some examples, Support Vector Machines (SVM) kernel techniques were used to reach Data Partitioning decisions [3], Machine Learning coupled with Performance Models were used to predict speedup [15], Static analysis was used to decide Program Distribution on Message Passing Architectures [19], Loop Distribution and Array Access Patterns were studied using static methodologies [17], Algebraic Expressions of Variables coupled with Analytical Models to collect Execution Times of different Program Sections [1], Call Graphs combined with Markov Model of Control Flow to generate Function Call Frequency estimates [44] Critical Path Analysis along with Execution Time model was used to predict run times [24], A Postmortem Analysis Tool, based on idleness and overheads to point out areas of improvement, [43]. Static Schemes are based on Code and Data Analysis, and the knowledge gained as a result of the analysis. They are more universal, since they do not use any dynamic data, collected on a target machine, by sample runs of the given program.

Other researchers have used Dynamic Schemes, for Performance Estimation and Reporting. Here are a few examples, Compile Time Models, augmented with profile data, was used for performance prediction [9], Compiler Generated Instrumentation was used to develop Performance Models [14], Parallelism Identification and Advice Tool was created using profile data [31], Instrumentation Tool was created to operate at the Program Section level using trace techniques [37], Visualization System was developed that uses Software Instrumentation and Hardware Counters [41], Deterministic Replay Debug Tool was created using Trace Driven Simulations and Models [47] A Dynamic Binary Instrumentation (DBI) framework was created, to build heavy weight tools, for analysis and profiling [39], Industrial strength Software Instrumentation Tool Set, was created for profiling, performance study, and defect fixing [35]. Information collected by Dynamic Schemes are tainted by the Sample Inputs used, and the Hardware bias of the target machine, used in the experiment. But researchers have carefully constructed input sets, and laboriously formulated data gathering scenarios to limit the sampling errors.

Hybrid Schemes have been employed by a few researchers in recent times. Here are a few examples, A Transformation Framework that uses Architecture Specific Cost Models, for estimation coupled with Dynamic Feedback as a supplement [45], Source Code Instrumentation along with Instruction Scheduling on Simulated Architectures to estimate performance [46], Performance Prediction Tool using Code Analysis and Trace Simulation [12], A toolkit for Static Analysis and Dynamic Measurements to develop Architecture Neutral Models [36]. Hybrid Schemes are attractive at a higher level, since they are supposed to provide, the benefits of both Static and Dynamic Schemes. But merging information collected through two separate sources, is always a tricky problem, exacerbated by the scenario, when the results from the two sources of collection, do not converge.

How important are the Performance Estimation and Prediction steps, in the overall Parallel Conversion process? A programmer, would like to know how much parallel potential, a program has, before he commences the conversion work. This information provided when required, can boost programmer productivity. Researchers have usually avoided this step, due to the unavailability of all the pieces of information, in the early phases of the Program Compilation process. When it is eventually available, several phases downstream, they feel that the information is outdated and useless. This has led to the wide spread belief that performance estimation is hard.

All prior research studies in the estimation and prediction domain, have relegated the performance estimation, to a later phase in the compilation process, when detailed analysis results are available, essentially ignoring the benefits of early assessment. In this research work we perform our estimation and prediction when it matters, before detailed analysis and program transformations have been carried out, and there is still an opportunity, to use the predictions for driving future transformations, including parallel conversions. This paper is entirely dedicated, to the problem of performance estimation and reporting, which is just one solution, in the tool chest of a compiler. We have reported our other research findings, elsewhere in other publications.

3   Asterix

Caliper is a parallel opportunity, prediction and estimation module. It is part of the compilation pipeline, of Asterix our compiler, optimizer and parallel converter.

We provide a high level view, of each of the Asterix modules next:

- *Paracite*
  This module is essentially, the front end of Asterix, where the lexical analysis, syntax analysis and semantics analysis occur. The input to this phase. is the program in an imperative language, and the outcome of the phase, is the equivalent program in ASIF, the Intermediate Representation (IR) in Asterix [25].
- *ASIF*
  ASIF is an acronym and stands for *Asterix Intermediate Format* the language, that mainly includes an IR instruction set invented for the Asterix compiler suite. It is based on the three address instruction format, with explicit Operand followed by the Result, And two Source operands.
- *Caliper*
  Caliper reads the code in the ASIF format, and does a coarse estimation, of the nascent parallel opportunities, that exist in the given program. This provides a starting point, for the users, to position their reference performance. The following section discusses exhaustively on the topic.

- *Graft*

  This module performs the bulk of the analysis work, on the IR code in ASIF format. The result of the analysis, is represented in the form of several tables and graphs which are consulted, for identifying code transformation opportunities, including optimizations and parallel conversions.

- *3PO*

  3PO stands for *Parallel Performance Predictor and Oracle*. This module is a fine grain, performance estimation and prediction module, which reports at the local block level, and also at the global program level and uses several mathematical models, one for each transformation category, for its operation. The various 3PO sub-models are categorized based on the nature of the transformation, or parallel conversion. Accordingly we have transformations that improve instruction counts, transformations that improve cache latency, transformations that enable other transformations including parallel conversions [29]. The main performance numbers reported are, *Inherent Parallel Potential (IPO)* and the *Expected Speedup from Parallel Conversion (ESP)* with obvious connotations for parallel conversion. For transformations, the numbers are similar but with slightly different semantics, and they are, *Inherent Speedup Potential (ISP)* and the *Expected Speedup from Transformation (EST)* using the appropriate category model.

- *Transgraph*

  This is the module in charge of, generating code transformations, that are beneficial, from a performance perspective. Some of the transformations, are solely concerned, about generating code, that is parallel friendly. The input and output for the module, is IR in ASIF code, and supplementary IR structures data such as graphs and tables.

- *Paragraph*

  This is the module, that actually generates the parallel code. The basic unit of parallel code which is conceptually a task, is called a *Prune* after morphing the phrase, *Parallel IR Unit*. Each Prune is assigned, to an independent processing element, in a virtual topology and this mapping is preserved, for the entire duration, of the application existence. The input for the module, is IR code and IR supplements, from Transgraph. Output is IR in Prune form.

- *Pigeon*

  Pigeon is a word, that originates from the phrase, *Parallel Code Generator*. It is the module that converts Prunes, to executable versions of Prunes. These executable Prunes are called *Proxies*, singular is *Proxy*. The name evolved from the phrase, *Parallel Execution Unit*, are generated and assigned, to respective execution units, in an actual physical topology in a later phase. These mappings are subject to change, during the life cycle of the application.

- *AIDE*

  AIDE stands for, *Asterix Integrated Development Environment*, is a graphical tool to display the important results, of the compilation process, starting from the source code, to the generation of Prunes and Proxies and their interdependence [27]. The various views include, Annotated Source and ASIF

IR, Caliper Predictions, 3PO Oracles, Prunes, Proxies, their distribution and orchestration
– *Concerto*
This module as the name suggests is the Distributor, Coordinator and Orchestration Manager of the Proxies in action. It chooses the mapping of Proxies to their respective processing elements, manages their remote executions and also provides synchronization primitives. In a NUMA distributed environment, it also decides on how to partition data, between the Proxies, manages mapping to processing elements and provides communication primitives for data sharing [28]. Actual mapping is handled by a sub module of *Concerto*, called the *Topology Mapper*, *TOPMAP* for short and offers a choice of, different mapping algorithms.

The Fig. 1 illustrates the different phases involved in the operation of the Asterix compiler.

The block diagram is intuitive for the most part. As seen from the figure, the higher level source program is input to the *Paracite* module and passed through a series of modules, each represented by a block in the diagram. The arrows pointed towards and away from their blocks, signify either the input(s) or the output(s) from the module respectively. The final step in the chain is the Orchestration of all the parallel run time components and combining the results in a coherent fashion, handled by the *Concerto* module. Readers may refer to the earlier descriptions of the phases of Asterix, which are synonymous with the modules here.

4   Caliper

The main objective of the Caliper module, is to provide the user, with a base expectation of parallel performance, that is inherent in the program, under consideration. This prediction can help dictate, the choice of transformations to apply on the program, including the parallel conversion decisions. The higher level syntactic structures, of an imperative program, offer impedance, to the effective computation of, performance estimates, and prediction. Each program is unique, from the perspective of the collection of the syntactic structures, constituting the program, which offer unique difficulties, for estimation and prediction. We refer to this trait of the program, as the *Shape* of the program. The transformations applied to a program, to strip the Shape of a program as the *Program-Shape-Flattening*.

Input to the Caliper module, consists of IR in ASIF format. It performs the following, Program-Shape-Flattening transformations such as, *Function-Call-Expansion*, *Loop-Unrolling* and *Control-Predication*, which are described individually later. The output from the Caliper module, is the performance estimation, in the form of *Maximum-Available-Parallelism (MAP)*, and the performance prediction, in the form of *Speedup-After-Parallel Conversion (SAP)*. These two terms, are described later.

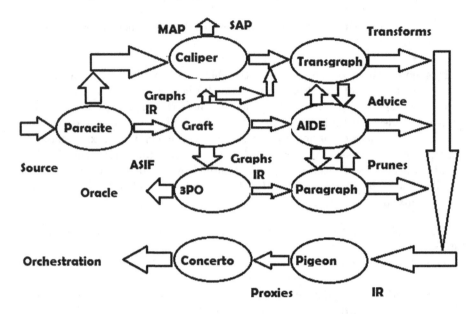

Fig. 1. Block diagram of Asterix phases and operation

The Caliper operation is characterized by the following phases:

- *Function Call Expansion*
  The purpose *Function-Call-Expansion,* is to replace, all function calls, with the code, that constitutes the function block. It should be noted that, it is a recursive process, and the process stops only, after all user defined functions, have been expanded.
  Library Functions and System Calls, are normally not considered for call expansion. They are essentially treated as any other instruction, which suffices for coarse estimates. A user program that is loaded with library calls and system calls, may skew the prediction somewhat, but it is usually not the case, with a majority of the real world programs.
- *Loop Unrolling*
  As a result of *Loop-Unrolling,* all Loops and Multi-Loops are replaced with their respective code blocks, and the instructions making up the Entry, Exit Conditions and the Loop Back Jumps removed.
- *Control Predication*
  Control Predication is a transformation, that replaces Conditional Blocks, with equivalent Predicated Blocks. The Conditional Statements, are another hindrance, to the correct estimation, of performance. However, most of the architectures, provide support for Predicated-Execution of instructions, with varying degree of support. However all of them support Conditional-Move instruction which is a powerful construct when used with predicates, to compute the condition of the move, and combined with regular instructions, com-

puting to temporary result variables, offer a powerful and compelling solution, to implement Control-Predication.

We next describe the purpose of the following performance metrics:

- *Maximum Available Parallelism*
  Maximum-Available-Parallelism, *MAP* for short, is a metric, that reports the amount of parallelism present, in a given program, as a percentage. For instance, a MAP of 33% means that, one third of the code is parallel convertible, and the other two thirds of the code, 66% is serial in nature. It should be noted, that this number, takes in to consideration, all the dependencies, that exist in the program, which includes, both the data, and the control kinds.
- *Speedup After Parallel Conversion*
  Speedup-After-Parallel Conversion, *SAP* in short form, is a metric that reports the benefits of parallel conversion. In the example discussed earlier, since 33% is subject to parallel conversion, the effective run time is determined by the 66% of the serial part, and the expected speedup, would be 1.52 and reported as a fraction.

The Fig. 2 illustrates the different steps involved, in the operation of the Caliper module. As you can see, translated IR code in ASIF format is fed to the *Inliner* module, which carries out the expansion of all function calls, and this modified IR is fed to the next module in the chain, which is the *Unroller*. This module unrolls all loops, and its output is sent to the next module in the chain, which is the *Predicator*. The purpose of this module, is to convert all conditionals in the IR to Predicated statements. The output from this module, is shape sanitized IR, that is ready for performance estimation.

4.1 Performance Estimation Equations

Performance estimation and prediction, for both serial and parallel versions, revolve around the following parameters, which are defined below, and also given are the equations for computing them.

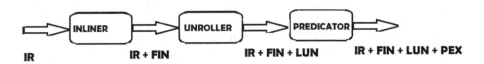

Fig. 2. Block diagram of Caliper steps and operation

1. *Serial Execution Cycles*
   Since we are measuring performance, in coarse fashion here, we are not accounting, for the individual instruction differences. Each instruction counts as one cycle, and we are also not considering, the memory hierarchy, into these computations. Fine grained estimations, are for a later pass, where

they use the *3PO* model which has an in built cycle accurate simulator, we call *Kinetics*, for accurate estimates. It includes hardware accurate models of cache, memory and storage supporting the simulator. The workings of *3PO* and *Kinetics*, are subject matter of a different paper, and we shall not discuss them any further here.

The following equation, describes the process, for measuring *Serial-Execution-Cycles*. Here C_{CYC} is the count of cycles, to run the serial version of the program, N_{INC} is the instruction count, for the given program.

$$C_{SER} = N_{INC} \tag{1}$$

2. *Parallel Execution Cycles*

Computation of the parallel execution cycles, is more involved, and requires a check, for data dependence between operands and results, belonging to different instructions. Since we have eliminated, control dependencies of all kinds, through Shape-Flattening, this is not an issue any more. A later subsection, shall describe the Shape-Flattening algorithm in more detail.

Calculating *Parallel-Execution-Cycles* involves, classifying instructions, based on their data dependence, into different equivalence classes. Instructions belonging to the same equivalence class, are data dependent with one another, and so we have to honor, their ordinal order of issue, to maintain correctness. However instructions belonging to different classes, have no data dependencies, and hence allow, concurrent execution between them. Once the equivalence classes, have been finalized, the execution time is dictated by, the longest running equivalence class. The algorithm for creating equivalent dependence classes, shall be given later in a following subsection.

The equation for computing, the parallel execution cycles, is given below. C_{PAR} is the parallel cycle count, EQC_1, EQC_2, ..., EQC_n are the total cycles needed to execute the, individual equivalence class instructions in serial fashion.

$$C_{PAR} = \max\left(EQC_1, EQC_2, \ldots, EQC_n\right) \tag{2}$$

3. *Maximum Available Parallelism*

Maximum Available Parallelism, abbreviated as *MAP* is a measure of the inherent parallelism available in a program, and is reported as a percent of the total program instructions. The following equation precisely defines the metric. C_{PAR} is the number of cycles required to run the parallel version of the program and C_{SER} is the cycle count for the serial version of the program.

$$MAP = (C_{SER} - C_{PAR}) \div C_{SER}) \times 100 \tag{3}$$

4. *Speedup After Parallel Conversion*

Speedup After Parallel Conversion, *SAP* for brevity, is an estimate of how much faster the program will run, after parallel conversion. The equation that follows, describes the metric. C_{PAR} is the number of cycles required to run the parallel version of the program and C_{SER} is the cycle count, for the serial version of the program.

$$SAP = (C_{SER} \div C_{PAR}) \tag{4}$$

4.2 Program Shape Flattening

As alluded to earlier, program syntax structures such as Functions, Loops and Conditionals, are a hindrance to effective estimation and predictions of performance. So as a first step, it is essential to flatten these high level language structures and then proceed with the estimation.

In the following paragraphs, we will give brief procedures in algorithmic form to perform these preparatory steps towards estimation. Refer to Algorithm 1 for the detailed steps.

4.3 Parallel Equivalence Classes

Parallel Equivalence Classes are a set of items, that satisfy a single property. In the context of Parallel Conversions, it means sets of instructions, that can be

---

Algorithm 1. Program Shape Flattening

1: **procedure** FLATTEN_PROGRAM
2:     INLINE_FUNCTION
3:     UNROLL_LOOP
4:     PREDICATE_CONDITION
5: **end procedure**
6: **procedure** INLINE_FUNCTION
7:     **for** Fnc ← 1, n **do**   ▷ sweep through function calls in the program
8:         GET_FUNCTION_DEFINITION(Def, Fnc)   ▷ fetch code block defined for the call
9:         REPLACE_CALL_WITH_DEFINITION(Def, Fnc)   ▷ replace call with the code block
10:     **end for**
11: **end procedure**
12: **procedure** UNROLL_LOOP
13:     **for** Glp ← 1, n **do**   ▷ sweep through loops in the program
14:         GET_LOOP_BLOCK(Blk, Glp)   ▷ fetch code block for the loop
15:         REPLACE_LOOP_WITH_PRIVATE_BLOCKS(Blk, Glp) ▷ duplicate code block for each iteration
16:     **end for**
17: **end procedure**
18: **procedure** PREDICATE_CONDITION
19:     **for** Cnd ← 1, n **do**   ▷ sweep through conditionals in the program
20:         GET_CONDITION_BLOCK(Blk, Cnd)   ▷ fetch code block for the conditional
21:         REPLACE_CONDITION_WITH_PREDICATES(Blk, Cnd)   ▷ replace condition with the predicated block
22:     **end for**
23: **end procedure**

---

executed concurrently. However it should be noted that, instructions within a particular class, are to be executed in serial, to satisfy the property of an equivalence class. When the instructions of a program, are organized in to equivalence classes, the run time of the program, is reduced from the time spent, by all instructions of the program executing serially, to the run time of the longest running equivalence class.

What follows is the algorithm to create the Equivalence Classes, also referred to as Dependence Classes here. Once created, it becomes trivial to assess the run time and predict performance. Refer to Algorithm 2 for the detailed steps.

Algorithm 2. Parallel Equivalence Classes Creation

1: **procedure** BUILD_PARALLEL_EQUIVALENCE_CLASSES
2:     BUILD_EQUIVALENCE_CLASSES
3:     MERGE_EQUIVALENCE_CLASSES
4: **end procedure**
5: **procedure** BUILD_EQUIVALENCE_CLASSES
6:     **for** Ins ← 1, n **do**   ▷ sweep through the program's instructions
7:         GET_RESULT_OPERAND(R, Ins)   ▷ fetch result operand of instruction
8:         ADD_INSTRUCTION(R, Ins)   ▷ add instruction to class R of global parallel equivalence class list
9:     **end for**
10: **end procedure**
11: **procedure** MERGE_EQUIVALENCE_CLASSES
12:     **for** Ins ← 1, n **do**   ▷ sweep through the program's instructions
13:         GET_RESULT_OPERAND(R, Ins)   ▷ fetch result operand of instruction
14:         GET_SOURCE1_OPERAND(S1, Ins)   ▷ fetch source1 operand of instruction
15:         GET_SOURCE2_OPERAND(S2, Ins)   ▷ fetch source2 operand of instruction
16:         MERGE(R, S1)   ▷ merge class S1 to class R and update global parallel equivalence class list
17:         MERGE(R, S2)   ▷ merge class S2 to class R and update global parallel equivalence class list
18:     **end for**
19: **end procedure**

---

5   Analysis

Given below is a code listing of a program, in a popular imperative language, which is used for illustrating the workings of Caliper. For listing see Listing 1.1 The program has the three structural components we alluded to earlier, which are hindrances for estimation and prediction purposes, namely a function, loop and a conditional block. See lines numbered 2, 9 and 24 for these blocks.

Listing 1.1. A program with a function, loop and condition

```
1   #include <stdio.h>
2   float cal_function() {
3      int a, b, c, d, e;
4      a = 10; b = 20;
5      c = 30; d = 40;
6      e = a + b * c / d;
7      return e;
8   }
9   float cal_loop() {
10     int i, j, k;
11     float sum[3][3][3];
12     float ssum = 0.0;
13     for (i = 0; i < 3; i++)
14        for (j = 0; j < 3; j++)
15           for (k = 0; k < 3; k++) {
16              sum[i][j][k] = i + j + k;
17           }
18     for (i = 0; i < 3; i++)
19        for (j = 0; j < 3; j++)
20           for (k = 0; k < 3; k++)
21              ssum += sum[i][j][k];
22     return ssum;
23  }
24  float cal_condition() {
25     int x = 10;
26     float y = 0.0;
27     if (x < 10) {
28        y = 2 * x;
29     }
30     else if (x == 10) {
31        y = x * x;
32     }
33     else {
34        y = x * x * x;
35     }
36     return y;
37  }
38  int main() {
39     float x, y, z;
40     x = cal_function();
41     y = cal_loop();
42     z = cal_condition();
43     printf("x = \%f\n", x);
44     printf("y = \%f\n", y);
45     printf("z = \%f\n", z);
46  }
```

The next listing consists of, the equivalent program in ASIF, with all the program structures preserved, namely the functions, loops and conditionals untouched. See Listing 1.2 for the code listing. The translated higher language code for the function, loop and conditional, can be found under the respective labels named as such. See lines 4, 18, 70 in the listing. ASIF code is easy to follow. Each block starts with a label, and so there is one for each function, loop and conditional. See lines 5, 20, 71 and 91. At the start of the block are the declarations, DCL is the opcode to define an integer and FDCL for a float. STP is the push and POP is pop. The arithmetic operators have easy to spot Mnemonics. FNC is the Call and RET is the return opcode.

Listing 1.2. ASIF Code

```
 1  ! start entry                45  for1_exit:
 2  start:                       46    MOV i, @0
 3  ! cal_function entry         47  !
 4  cal_function:                48  for4_entry:
 5    DCL a, 4                    49    MOV j, @0
 6    DCL b, 4                    50  for5_entry:
 7    DCL c, 4                    51    MOV k, @0
 8    DCL d, 4                    52  for6_entry:
 9    DCL e, 4                    53    ADR T7, &sum
10  !                            54    MUL T7, i, j
11    MUL T1, b, c               55    MUL T7, T7, k
12    DIV T2, T1, d              56    MLD T8, T7
13    ADD e, a, T2               57    ADD, ssum, ssum, T8
14  !                            58    INC k
15    STP e                      59    BLE for3_entry, k, 3
16    RET                        60  for6_exit:
17  ! cal_loop entry             61    INC j
18  cal_loop:                    62    BLE for2_entry, j, 3
19  !                            63  for5_exit:
20    DCL i, 4                   64    INC i
21    DCL j, 4                   65    BLE for1_entry, i, 3
22    DCL k, 4                   66  for4_exit:
23    FDCL sum, 4, 27            67    STP ssum
24    FDCL ssum, 4               68    RET
25    MOV i, @0                  69  ! cal_condition entry
26  for1_entry:                  70  cal_condition:
27    MOV j, @0                  71    DCL x, 4
28  for2_entry:                  72    FDCL y, 4
29    MOV k, @0                  73    JGE LB1, x, @10
30  for3_entry:                  74    NOP
31    ADR T5, &sum               75    MUL T3, @2, x
32    MUL T5, i, j               76    MOV y, T3
33    MUL T5, T5, k              77    JMP LB2
34    ADD T6, i, j               78  LB1:
35    ADD T6, T6, k              79    NEQ LB2, x, @10
36    MST T5, T6                 80    MUL T4, x, x
37    INC k                      81    MOV y, T3
38    BLE for3_entry, k, 3       82    JMP LB3
39  for3_exit:                   83  LB2:
40    INC j                      84    MUL T4, x, x
41    BLE for2_entry, j, 3       85    MOV y, T3
42  for2_exit:                   86  LB3:
43    INC i                      87    STP y
44    BLE for1_entry, i, 3       88    RET
```

```
89  | ! main entry          96  |   FNC cal_loop
90  | main:                 97  |   POP y
91  |   FDCL x              98  |   FNC cal_condition
92  |   FDCL y              99  |   POP z
93  |   FDCL z             100  | ! end entry
94  |   FNC cal_function   101  | end:
95  |   POP x
```

The next program listing consists of the ASIF code after it has passed through the structure filter which expands all functions, unrolls all loops and coverts conditionals to predicated blocks. See Listing 1.3 for reference. See line 8 for the inlined function cal_function. See lines starting from 25 for the first of the unrolled loop nests. The second unrolled loop nest starts from line 76. Each unrolled iteration is marked with a number under comment to designate the code for the corresponding iteration. At the end of each unrolled iteration is the handling (management) of index (induction) variables appropriate for the iteration. Finally the condition block starting at line 123 starts the block. PGE is a predicate which evaluates to True or False depending on the condition check and set the result variable appropriately. CMOV is the conditional move that moves the value to the result variable if the earlier predicate evaluated to true and not otherwise. There are some architectures belonging to the Very long instruction word (VLIW) class which allow predicated versions of all arithmetic operators in which case CMOV will be unnecessary. But the important thing to notice is the absence of jumps and labels which have been removed prior to estimation and prediction.

Listing 1.3. Flattened ASIF Code

```
 1   ! start entry
 2   start:
 3   ! main entry
 4   main:
 5     FDCL x
 6     FDCL y
 7     FDCL z
 8     !x = FNC cal_function
 9     DCL a, 4
10     DCL b, 4
11     DCL c, 4
12     DCL d, 4
13     DCL e, 4
14     !
15     MUL T1, b, c
16     DIV T2, T1, d
17     ADD e, a, T2
18     MOV x, e
19     !y = FNC cal_loop
20     DCL i, 4
21     DCL j, 4
22     DCL k, 4
23     FDCL sum, 4, 27
24     FDCL ssum, 4
25   ! FIN block starts, #0
26     MOV i, @0
27     MOV j, @0
28     MOV k, @0
29     ADR T5, &sum
30     MUL T5, i, j
31     MUL T5, T5, k
32     ADD T6, i, j
33     ADD T6, T6, k
34     MST T5, T6
35     INC k
36   ! #1
37     ADR T5, &sum
38     MUL T5, i, j
39     MUL T5, T5, k
40     ADD T6, i, j
41     ADD T6, T6, k
42     MST T5, T6
43     INC k
44   ! #2
45     ADR T5, &sum
46     MUL T5, i, j
47     MUL T5, T5, k
48     ADD T6, i, j
49     ADD T6, T6, k
50     MST T5, T6
51     MOV k, @0
52     INC j
53   ! #3 <#4 - #7 snipped>
54   ! #8
55     ADR T5, &sum
56     MUL T5, i, j
57     MUL T5, T5, k
58     ADD T6, i, j
59     ADD T6, T6, k
60     MST T5, T6
61     INC i
62     MOV j, @0
63     MOV k, @0
64   ! #9 <#10 - #25 snipped>
65   ! #26
66     ADR T5, &sum
67     MUL T5, i, j
68     MUL T5, T5, k
69     ADD T6, i, j
70     ADD T6, T6, k
71     MST T5, T6
72     INC i
73     MOV j, @0
74     MOV k, @0
75   ! FIN block ends
76   ! FIN block starts, #0
77     MOV i, @0
78     MOV j, @0
79     MOV k, @0
80     ADR T7, &sum
81     MUL T7, i, j
82     MUL T7, T7, k
83     ADD T8, i, j
84     ADD T8, T8, k
85     MLD T8, T7
```

```
 86 | ADD ssum, ssum, T8          113 | MUL T7, T7, k
 87 | INC k                       114 | ADD T8, i, j
 88 | ! <#1 snipped> #2           115 | ADD T8, T8, k
 89 |   ADR T7, &sum              116 | MLD T8, T7
 90 |   MUL T7, i, j              117 | ADD ssum, ssum, T8
 91 |   MUL T7, T7, k             118 | INC i
 92 |   ADD T8, i, j              119 | MOV j, @0
 93 |   ADD T8, T8, k             120 | MOV k, @0
 94 |   MLD T8, T7                121 | ! FIN block ends
 95 |   ADD ssum, ssum, T8        122 | MOV y, ssum
 96 |   MOV k, @0                 123 | !z = FNC cal_condition
 97 |   INC j                     124 | DCL x3, 4
 98 | ! #3 <#4 - #7 snipped>      125 | FDCL y3, 4
 99 | ! #8                        126 | PGE TP1, x1, @10
100 |   ADR T7, &sum              127 | MUL T3, @2, x3
101 |   MUL T7, i, j              128 | CMOV y3, T3, TP1
102 |   MUL T7, T7, k             129 | PEQ TP2, x3, @10
103 |   ADD T8, i, j              130 | MUL T4, x3, x3
104 |   ADD T8, T8, k             131 | CMOV y3, T3, TP2
105 |   MLD T8, T7                132 | AND TP3, TP1, TP2
106 |   ADD ssum, ssum, T8        133 | NOT TP3, TP3
107 |   INC i                     134 | MUL T4, x3, x3
108 |   MOV j, @0                 135 | CMOV y3, T3, TP3
109 |   MOV k, @0                 136 | MOV y, y3
110 | ! <#9 - #25 snipped>, #26   137 | !
111 |   ADR T7, &sum              138 | end:
112 |   MUL T7, i, j
```

5.1   Reporting Estimates and Prediction

For the present, Caliper reports interesting numbers in plain text in Csv format
as shown below:

```
CALIPER,,,
(Performance_Estimation_and_Prediction_Tool),,,

1., Serial Instruction Count, SIN,   472
2., Equivalence Class Count, EQC,   10
3., Mean Instruction Count, MIN,   65.8
4., Parallel Instruction Count, PIN,   249
5., Serial Execution Cycles, SEC,   472
6., Parallel Execution Cycles, PEC,   249
7., Maximum Available Parallelism, MAP,   47.25
8., Speedup After Parallel Conversion, SAP,   1.9
```

However the future version will be enhanced, to report more information in
graphical format, and will be integrated with AIDE.

Table 1. Caliper performance estimates and prediction

CALIPER (performance estimation and prediction tool)			
Sl. no.	Metric name	Code	Value
1	Serial Instruction Count	SIN	472
2	Equivalence Class Count	EQC	10
3	Mean Instruction Count	MIN	65.8
4	Parallel Instruction Count	PIN	249
5	Serial Execution Cycles	SEC	472
6	Parallel Execution Cycles	PEC	249
7	Maximum Available Parallelism	MAP	47.25
8	Speedup After Parallel Conversion	SAP	1.9

Table 1 displays the same numbers in tabular form for clarity purposes.

Serial Instruction Count is the number of instructions, detected by Caliper. Equivalence Class Count is the number of Parallel Equivalence Classes detected. Mean Instruction Count is the average count of instructions, in each class. Parallel Instruction Count is the maximum value of instruction count, among all the classes. Serial Execution Cycles is the number of execution cycles consumed, by the given program, when operating in serial mode. It should be noted that, since Caliper is designed to be a Coarse Performance Estimator and Predictor, we treat all instructions the same. Each instruction is assumed to take a cycle, for its execution and so this metric has the same value as the Serial Instruction Count. Parallel Execution Cycles is the total processor cycles, required to run the program in parallel mode, which is same as the Parallel Instruction Count. Maximum Available Parallelism as defined earlier, is a measure of the inherent parallel potential, of the given program. Speedup After Parallel Conversion is a multiple, that measures how much faster, the parallel version of the program runs, in comparison to the serial version.

The column with the heading *Code*, is the abbreviation for the metric and the column with the heading *Value* is the value reported for the corresponding metric. The program fed to Caliper, is the same program we saw earlier, and the numbers reported, are the estimates from Caliper. The two most interesting numbers are MAP which is reported as 47.25 and a SAP of 1.9. This means that, about half of the program is parallel convertible, and it will run 1.9 times faster than the serial version, after parallel conversion.

6   Competitive Analysis

We started a search of the research publications, for a solution similar to Caliper. Since the survey revealed, the absence of a comparable product in the research domain, we focused our search to the state of the art, in the industry.

We short listed the competition to the following major players in the domain, Gcc from GNU, Clang from LLVM group and Parallel Studio and Icc from Intel. We learned that none of them have a Parallel Performance, Estimation and Prediction component, that is comparable with Caliper.

However we wanted to study the results of parallel conversions, made by these compilers. We first searched for a compiler flag, that can emit diagnostics, specific to the Optimizations and Parallel Conversions, being carried out. We found a few flags we thought were relevant, such as the -openmp-report from icc. But either they were non operational, or the information required, for the comparative study was missing. Similarly, the flag to turn on the Auto Parallel conversion feature was either a place holder or missing at this point. However all of the above compilers are enabled for OpenMP and use them for parallel conversions.

We continued our quest for a parallel build enabling the openmp feature with these compilers. We used the following pragma or directive to enable the following block for possible parallel conversion.

#pragma omp parallel

We experimented by placing the pragma at various points in the source code such as the following, at Main function entry, at other Function entry points, at the start of Loops and Multi-level loops, and Control entry points, to see if it makes any difference to the LLVM assembly generated by the Clang compiler, since the -emit-llvm flag to Clang was the only viable option, to generate diagnostics. We did not see any trends in the parallel code generated, which could be used to make any useful comparison with Caliper's estimates or prediction.

The Intel Parallel Studio and its associated icc provide a flag called -openmp-report, which apparently is supposed to generate diagnostics, but we had trouble enabling after installation, so we could not get any useful data on icc also.

At this point we have to conclude the study, and claim that in comparison with the available state of the art, both in academia and industry, Caliper is the only working, Performance Estimation and Prediction Solution available, at the time of writing.

7   Conclusion

Caliper is a coarse performance estimator and predictor solution, for a given serial program, that is scheduled for parallel conversion. It operates on the IR code generated from the program, after the translation phase of compilation and provides an early indicator, about the program's expected parallel behavior, after transformation. Our solution, to the performance assessment problem, involves two phases. We perform a coarse assessment of performance, at the start of the compilation pipeline, and postpone the detailed estimation and prediction for a phase that follows the analysis phase. That way, the results of coarse prediction, are available to drive transformation, and parallel conversion decisions. The structural components of a program such as Procedures, Loops and Conditionals, their count and placement adds an unique character to the program which are referred to collectively as the *Program-Shape*. *Program-Shape* is an hindrance to effective performance estimation and prediction. So prior to the estimation phase, we perform transformations, such as *Function Call Expansion*, *Loop Unrolling* and *Control Predication* that specifically target these program structures. The transformations are referred to collectively as *Program-Shape-Flattening*. The transformation eases the process of measurement and prediction, by transforming the given program, to straight line code. After flattening transformations, we are also freed of the concerns, of Control Dependencies and they stop being a factor, in parallel performance. To collect the parallel run time estimates, we use the concept of *Equivalence-Classes*. An *Equivalence Class* collects objects, that share the class property. We use *Equivalence Classes* here to group instructions, that are mutually data dependent on each other. We refer to these classes either as *Dependence-Classes* or *Parallel-Classes*. Since instructions belonging to separate *Dependence Classes* share no dependencies, they can be safely scheduled for parallel execution. Effectively, we have converted a serial program to a set of *Dependence Classes* that can be run concurrently. Such a scenario of parallel execution of a program allows us to conclude, that the run time of the program, is now equal to, the run time of the *Dependence-Class* that runs the longest. Finally we report two numbers that we believe are of interest to a parallel programmer namely, *Maximum-Available-Parallelism* which is a measure of the inherent parallel conversion potential of the program, also referred to in short form as *MAP* and *Speedup-After-Parallel Conversion*, which predicts the expected speedup after parallel conversion, also referred to as *SAP* for the purpose of brevity. After a thorough search of published literature and comparative study of the practicing state of the art, we are convinced that there is no viable research or commercial product, that can be compared to Caliper at the time of writing.

References

1. Arapattu, D., Gannon, D.: Building analytical models into an interactive performance prediction tool. In: Proceedings of the 1989 ACM/IEEE Conference on Supercomputing, Supercomputing 1989, pp. 521–530. ACM, New York (1989). https://doi.org/10.1145/76263.76321. http://doi.acm.org/10.1145/76263.76321
2. Ayguade, E., et al.: The design of OpenMP tasks. IEEE Trans. Parallel Distrib. Syst. **20**(3), 404–418 (2009). https://doi.org/10.1109/TPDS.2008.105
3. Balasundaram, V., Fox, G., Kennedy, K., Kremer, U.: A static performance estimator to guide data partitioning decisions. SIGPLAN Not. **26**(7), 213–223 (1991). https://doi.org/10.1145/109626.109647. http://doi.acm.org/10.1145/1096 26.109647
4. Blume, B., et al.: Polaris: the next generation in parallelizing compilers. In: Proceedings of the Workshop on Languages and Compilers for Parallel Computing, p. 10-1. Springer, Heidelberg (1994)
5. Blume, W., Eigenmann, R.: An overview of symbolic analysis techniques needed for the effective parallelization of the perfect benchmarks. In: Proceedings of the 1994 International Conference on Parallel Processing - Volume 02, ICPP 1994, pp. 233–238. IEEE Computer Society, Washington, DC (1994). https://doi.org/10.1109/ICPP.1994.59

6. Bondhugula, U., et al.: Towards effective automatic parallelization for multicore systems. In: 2008 IEEE International Symposium on Parallel and Distributed Processing, IPDPS 2008, pp. 1–5 (2008). https://doi.org/10.1109/IPDPS.2008. 4536401

7. Bradel, B.J., Abdelrahman, T.S.: Automatic trace-based parallelization of Java programs. In: 2007 International Conference on Parallel Processing (ICPP 2007), p. 26 (2007). https://doi.org/10.1109/ICPP.2007.21

8. Canetti, R., et al.: The parallel C (pC) programming language. IBM J. Res. Dev. **35**(5.6), 727–741 (1991). https://doi.org/10.1147/rd.355.0727

9. Cascaval, C., DeRose, L., Padua, D.A., Reed, D.A.: Compile-time based performance prediction. In: Carter, L., Ferrante, J. (eds.) LCPC 1999. LNCS, vol. 1863, pp. 365–379. Springer, Heidelberg (2000). https://doi.org/10.1007/3-540-44905-1_23. http://dl.acm.org/citation.cfm?id=645677.663790

10. Codrescu, L., Wills, D.S.: On dynamic speculative thread partitioning and the MEM-slicing algorithm. In: Proceedings of 1999 International Conference on Parallel Architectures and Compilation Techniques, pp. 40–46 (1999). https://doi.org/10.1109/PACT.1999.807404

11. Cooper, K.D., et al.: ParaScope: a parallel programming environment. Proc. IEEE **81**(2), 244–263 (1993)

12. Cornea, B., Bourgeois, J.: A framework for efficient performance prediction of distributed applications in heterogeneous systems. J. Supercomput. **62**, 1609–1634 (2012). https://doi.org/10.1007/s11227-012-0823-5

13. Diaconescu, R., Wang, L., Mouri, Z., Chu, M.: A compiler and runtime infrastructure for automatic program distribution. In: Proceedings of the 19th IEEE International Parallel and Distributed Processing Symposium, p. 25a (2005). https://doi.org/10.1109/IPDPS.2005.7

14. Diniz, P.C.: A compiler approach to performance prediction using empirical-based modeling. In: Sloot, P.M.A., Abramson, D., Bogdanov, A.V., Gorbachev, Y.E., Dongarra, J.J., Zomaya, A.Y. (eds.) ICCS 2003, Part III. LNCS, vol. 2659, pp. 916–925. Springer, Heidelberg (2003). https://doi.org/10.1007/3-540-44863-2_90. http://dl.acm.org/citation.cfm?id=1762418.1762519

15. Dubach, C., Cavazos, J., Franke, B., Fursin, G., O'Boyle, M.F., Temam, O.: Fast compiler optimisation evaluation using code-feature based performance prediction. In: Proceedings of the 4th International Conference on Computing Frontiers, CF 2007, pp. 131–142. ACM, New York (2007). https://doi.org/10.1145/1242531. 1242553. http://doi.acm.org/10.1145/1242531.1242553

16. Fahringer, T.: Using the P3T to guide the parallelization and optimization effort under the Vienna Fortran compilation system. In: Proceedings of the Scalable High-Performance Computing Conference, pp. 437–444 (1994). https://doi.org/10.1109/SHPCC.1994.296676

17. Fahringer, T.: On estimating the useful work distribution of parallel programs under P3T: a static performance estimator. Concurr. Pract. Exp. **8**, 261–282 (1996)

18. Fahringer, T., Scholz, B.: Symbolic evaluation for parallelizing compilers. In: Proceedings of the 11th International Conference on Supercomputing, ICS 1997, pp. 261–268. ACM, New York (1997). https://doi.org/10.1145/263580.263648. http://doi.acm.org/10.1145/263580.263648

19. Fahringer, T., Zima, H.P.: A static parameter based performance prediction tool for parallel programs. In: Proceedings of the 7th International Conference on Supercomputing, ICS 1993, pp. 207–219. ACM, New York (1993). https://doi.org/10.1145/165939.165971. http://doi.acm.org/10.1145/165939.165971

20. Garcia, S., Jeon, D., Louie, C., Taylor, M.B.: The kremlin oracle for sequential code parallelization. IEEE Micro **32**(4), 42–53 (2012). https://doi.org/10.1109/MM.2012.52

21. Gropp, W., Gropp, W.D., Lusk, E., Skjellum, A., Lusk, A.D.F.E.E.: Using MPI: Portable Parallel Programming with the Message-Passing Interface, vol. 1. MIT Press, Cambridge (1999)

22. Hammacher, C., Streit, K., Hack, S., Zeller, A.: Profiling Java programs for parallelism. In: 2009 ICSE Workshop on Multicore Software Engineering, IWMSE 2009, pp. 49–55 (2009). https://doi.org/10.1109/IWMSE.2009.5071383

23. Horwitz, S., Reps, T.: The use of program dependence graphs in software engineering. In: Proceedings of the 14th International Conference on Software Engineering, pp. 392–411 (1992)

24. Jeon, D., Garcia, S., Louie, C., Taylor, M.B.: Kismet: parallel speedup estimates for serial programs. SIGPLAN Not. **46**(10), 519–536 (2011). https://doi.org/10.1145/2076021.2048108. http://doi.acm.org/10.1145/2076021.2048108

25. Kalyur, S., Nagaraja, G.S.: Paracite: auto-parallelization of a sequential program using the program dependence graph. In: 2016 International Conference on Computation System and Information Technology for Sustainable Solutions (CSITSS), pp. 7–12 (2016). https://doi.org/10.1109/CSITSS.2016.7779431

26. Kalyur, S., Nagaraja, G.S.: A survey of modeling techniques used in compiler design and implementation. In: 2016 International Conference on Computation System and Information Technology for Sustainable Solutions (CSITSS), pp. 355–358 (2016). https://doi.org/10.1109/CSITSS.2016.7779385

27. Kalyur, S., Nagaraja, G.S.: AIDE: an interactive environment for program transformation and parallelization. In: 2017 2nd International Conference on Computational Systems and Information Technology for Sustainable Solution (CSITSS), pp. 1–5 (2017). https://doi.org/10.1109/CSITSS.2017.8447848

28. Kalyur, S., Nagaraja, G.S.: Concerto: a program parallelization, orchestration and distribution infrastructure. In: 2017 2nd International Conference on Computational Systems and Information Technology for Sustainable Solution (CSITSS), pp. 1–6 (2017). https://doi.org/10.1109/CSITSS.2017.8447691

29. Kalyur, S., Nagaraja, G.S.: A taxonomy of methods and models used in program transformation and parallelization. In: Kumar, N., Venkatesha Prasad, R. (eds.) UBICNET 2019. LNICST, vol. 276, pp. 233–249. Springer, Cham (2019). https://doi.org/10.1007/978-3-030-20615-4_18

30. Kaminsky, A.: Parallel Java: a unified API for shared memory and cluster parallel programming in 100% Java. In: 2007 IEEE International Parallel and Distributed Processing Symposium, pp. 1–8 (2007). https://doi.org/10.1109/IPDPS.2007.370421

31. Kim, M., Kim, H., Luk, C.K.: Prospector: a dynamic data-dependence profiler to help parallel programming. In: HotPar 2010: Proceedings of the USENIX Workshop on Hot Topics in Parallelism (2010)

32. Kotha, A., Anand, K., Smithson, M., Yellareddy, G., Barua, R.: Automatic parallelization in a binary rewriter. In: 2010 43rd Annual IEEE/ACM International Symposium on Microarchitecture, pp. 547–557 (2010). https://doi.org/10.1109/MICRO.2010.27

33. Lazarescu, M.T., Lavagno, L.: Dynamic trace-based data dependency analysis for parallelization of C programs. In: 2012 IEEE 12th International Working Conference on Source Code Analysis and Manipulation (SCAM), pp. 126–131 (2012). https://doi.org/10.1109/SCAM.2012.15

34. Lokuciejewski, P., Cordes, D., Falk, H., Marwedel, P.: A fast and precise static loop analysis based on abstract interpretation, program slicing and polytope models. In: International Symposium on Code Generation and Optimization, CGO 2009, pp. 136–146 (2009). https://doi.org/10.1109/CGO.2009.17

35. Luk, C.K., et al.: Pin: building customized program analysis tools with dynamic instrumentation. SIGPLAN Not. **40**(6), 190–200 (2005). https://doi.org/10.1145/1064978.1065034. http://doi.acm.org/10.1145/1064978.1065034

36. Marin, G., Mellor-Crummey, J.: Cross-architecture performance predictions for scientific applications using parameterized models. In: Proceedings of the Joint International Conference on Measurement and Modeling of Computer Systems, SIGMETRICS 2004/Performance 2004, pp. 2–13. ACM, New York (2004). https://doi.org/10.1145/1005686.1005691. http://doi.acm.org/10.1145/1005686.1005691

37. Miller, B.P., et al.: The paradyn parallel performance measurement tool. Computer **28**(11), 37–46 (1995). https://doi.org/10.1109/2.471178

38. Navarro, A., Zapata, E., Padua, D.: Compiler techniques for the distribution of data and computation. IEEE Trans. Parallel Distrib. Syst. **14**(6), 545–562 (2003). https://doi.org/10.1109/TPDS.2003.1206503

39. Nethercote, N., Seward, J.: Valgrind: A framework for heavyweight dynamic binary instrumentation. SIGPLAN Not. **42**(6), 89–100 (2007). https://doi.org/10.1145/1273442.1250746. http://doi.acm.org/10.1145/1273442.1250746

40. Psarris, K., Kyriakopoulos, K.: An experimental evaluation of data dependence analysis techniques. IEEE Trans. Parallel Distrib. Syst. **15**(3), 196–213 (2004). https://doi.org/10.1109/TPDS.2004.1264806

41. de Rose, L.A., Reed, D.A.: SvPablo: a multi-language architecture-independent performance analysis system. In: Proceedings of the 1999 International Conference on Parallel Processing, ICPP 1999, pp. 311–318. IEEE Computer Society, Washington (1999). http://dl.acm.org/citation.cfm?id=850940.852859

42. Sarkar, V.: Automatic partitioning of a program dependence graph into parallel tasks. IBM J. Res. Dev. **35**(5.6), 779–804 (1991)

43. Tallent, N.R., Mellor-Crummey, J.M.: Effective performance measurement and analysis of multithreaded applications. In: Proceedings of the 14th ACM SIGPLAN Symposium on Principles and Practice of Parallel Programming, PPoPP 2009, pp. 229–240. ACM, New York (2009). https://doi.org/10.1145/1504176.1504210. http://doi.acm.org/10.1145/1504176.1504210

44. Wagner, T.A., Maverick, V., Graham, S.L., Harrison, M.A.: Accurate static estimators for program optimization. SIGPLAN Not. **29**(6), 85–96 (1994). https://doi.org/10.1145/773473.178251. http://doi.acm.org/10.1145/773473.178251

45. Wang, K.Y.: Precise compile-time performance prediction for superscalar-based computers. In: Proceedings of the ACM SIGPLAN 1994 Conference on Programming Language Design and Implementation, PLDI 1994, pp. 73–84. ACM, New York (1994). https://doi.org/10.1145/178243.178250. http://doi.acm.org/10.1145/178243.178250

46. Wang, Z., Sanchez, A., Herkersdorf, A.: SciSim: a software performance estimation framework using source code instrumentation. In: Proceedings of the 7th International Workshop on Software and Performance, WOSP 2008, pp. 33–42. ACM, New York (2008). https://doi.org/10.1145/1383559.1383565. http://doi.acm.org/10.1145/1383559.1383565

47. Zhai, J., Chen, W., Zheng, W., Li, K.: Performance prediction for large-scale parallel applications using representative replay. IEEE Trans. Comput. **65**(7), 2184–2198 (2016). https://doi.org/10.1109/TC.2015.2479630

Amazon Web Services (AWS) – An Overview of the On-Demand Cloud Computing Platform

Sadegh Hashemipour[1] and Maaruf Ali[2(✉)]

[1] Freelance Consultant, London, England, UK
`hashemipours@gmail.com`
[2] Epoka University, Rruga Tiranë-Rinas, Km 12, 1032 Vorë, Tiranë, Albania
`mali@epoka.edu.al`

Abstract. Cloud computing is increasingly becoming a norm in the global industrial landscape with web services using it as a critical backbone service provider including significant video streaming services. The purpose of this paper is to present an overview of some of the Amazon Web Service (AWS) tools and features. The paper also discusses how AWS contributes to a range of industries making them dependent on AWS's agility, scalability and deliverability of services. Implementation using information available on AWS leading portals as well as the practical experiments involving the discussed features are given. As more and more industries become dependent on Big data and AI, one can state that AWS will play a key role in the future developments across myriads of industries.

Keywords: Amazon Web Services · AWS · Internet of Things · IoT · Scalability · Parallel processing

1 Introduction

1.1 Industrial Proponents

Industry leaders such as Oracle, have coined Cloud Computing as the backbone of what is known as the fourth Industrial Revolution, or commonly called Industry 4.0 [1]. The Internet of Things (IoT), big data and analytics integrated with cloud computing are all vital components that are necessary to drive the next industrial revolution.

The name "Amazon" to most people is synonymous with two things: the Amazon River and Amazon the online mega-retailer. For the current generation, perhaps this latter is more familiar. AWS (Amazon Web Services) is perhaps the first peek into the future converged application of cloud computing. The services offered by AWS may be seen as the depiction of the real computing power of entanglement of technology with services and the large-scale deployment of scalable parallel processing. To most consumers, AWS is still a new concept first read about possibly in articles and forums. The following provides an overview of what AWS is and why it forms an essential part of global product marketing and distribution. Netflix, Dow Jones, Expedia, Philips and many other multinational corporations all employ AWS.

M. H. Miraz et al. (Eds.): iCETiC 2020, LNICST 332, pp. 40–47, 2020.
https://doi.org/10.1007/978-3-030-60036-5_3

1.2   The Amazon Global Infrastructure

Figure 1, show the Magic Quadrant for the cloud infrastructure as a service, worldwide, according to Gartner. The graph shows that the leader is still AWS.

Fig. 1. The Magic Quadrant for the cloud infrastructure as a service, worldwide [2].

The reason for the rapid uptake of cloud computing has been for the properties that is offers of security, scalability, infrastructure availability and the five nines service availability worldwide. This means that the service level agreement often has to ensure that the downtime cannot exceed six minutes in a year.

The Amazon Global Infrastructure is made of regions. Each region consists of Availability Zones, or AZs as they are known. Currently, 24 regions, with 76 available zones embedded in them serve 254 countries. This is shown in Fig. 2, below.

Fig. 2. AWS region distribution across the world [2].

The Amazon Regions operate in complete isolation from each other, giving AWS a high level of fault tolerance and stability. Low latency network links connect AZs within each region [3].

1.3 The AWS Exploitation of Cloud Services

AWS exploits the following advantages of cloud computing to provide cost-rival services globally [3]:

- "Trade capital expense for the variable cost" [3]: pay-as-you go data centres instead of investing in depreciative hardware infrastructure.
- "Benefit from massive economies of scale" [3]: since thousands of customers are paying and using the services at the same time; this reduces the overall pay-as-you-go cost.
- "Stop guessing capacity" [3]: there would be no need to estimate the network or infrastructure capacity the organisation needs continually. Using in-house systems often leads to expensive hardware installation that at some point, may no longer be needed. With AWS, one can customise and scale up or down within minutes.
- "Increase speed and agility" [3]: software-as-services, new features, new environment or platforms, are all a click away. What may take developers and IT team to set up in weeks, are available in no more than a few minutes. This feature of AWS saves time in development and cross-team corporation, hence reducing the overhead costs, as well as boosting organisational flexibility over larger projects.
- "Stop spending money running and maintaining data centres" [3]: AWS helps save time and money in maintaining data centres, allowing the organisation to harness its resources in providing better customer services.
- "Go global in minutes" [3]: configuring and deployment of a range of services and application across the world would not take more than a few minutes when using AWS.
- The whole infrastructure benefits from the uninterruptable power supply (UPS) and onsite backup generation facilities that interconnect the web of servers which take its power feed using independents grids in order to reduce the single points of failure throughout.

2 Overview of Services Provided by AWS

A comprehensive overview list of services is shown in Fig. 3 and a simpler user interface of AWS services is shown in Fig. 4. The following eight subsections summarises the main components offered by AWS. The sections covered are: Security Identity and Compliance; Compute; Storage; Database; Migration, Media Services, Machine Learning and IoT.

2.1 Security Identity and Compliance [5]

The services provided by this sub-category include the following:

- IAM – Identity Access Management, which allows granular User Access Management.
- Cognito – provides device authentication for services using Gmail and Facebook. It can allow temporary access for mobile devices, for example applications that calculate journey, sorting geographic location information.
- Secret Key Manager - use secrets manager to store, rotate, monitor and control access to secrets such as database credentials, API keys and OAuth tokens.
- GuardDuty – monitors for malicious activities on an AWS account.
- Inspector – is an agent that is installed on VPS/EC2 that check for a range of vulnerabilities over instances of EC2 and generates a severity report.
- Macie – it scans S3 buckets for Personal Identifiable Information such as Credit Card details, Tax codes. Once these items of information have been found it then alerts the user.
- Directory services – Integrating Active Directory Credentials.
- CloudHSM – Hardware Security Modules – extremely expensive bits of kits use these keys to manage the users EC2 instances.
- WAF – Web Application Firewall utilising Cross-site scripting. It provides a layer seven firewall which is useful to prevent sequel injection types of attacks.
- Shield – this provide a distributed denial of service (DDOS) attack mitigation. The "Advanced Shield" is a paid service that provides 24 h security.

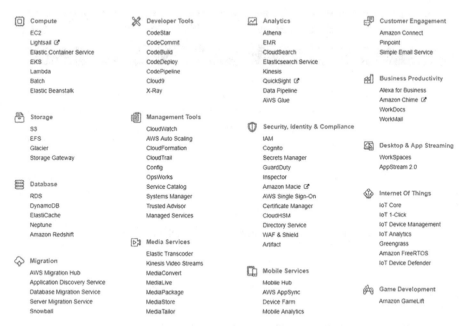

Fig. 3. Overview of AWS services [3].

2.2 Compute

The services provided by this sub-category include the following:

- EC2 – Elastic Compute Cloud – these are mainly virtual machines in AWS, however, physical machines are also available.
- Elastic beanstalk – this service is mainly for developers and code testing. The developer can deploy the web server application using PHP.
- Lambda – Code execution – this is mainly for background tasks for different types of services. For example, uploading of images and the need to overlay text can be carried out by using this Lamda function. Another example is to use Lamda to help change notes to MP3 files. For example, Lamda can be used to change the notes from text to audio. Then those files can be transferred to Alexa and Alexa can repeat those notes in audio format. Rules can be set up to send notification when a file has been upload to the user's websites.
- LightSail – dedicate VPS – fixed IP address to access server both in Windows and Linux format.
- Batch Computing – this application ranges is weather prediction to genome sequencing. This feature inherits Scalability from the Compute Service and facilitates queued processing based on priority.

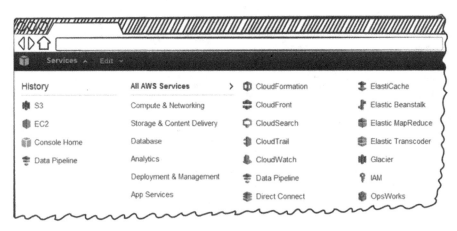

Fig. 4. Manageable control screen of AWS services [4].

2.3 Storage

The services provided by this sub-category include the following:

- Simple Storage Service S3 – this provides legacy oldest storage service. The service has buckets that can be used to upload the user generated files.

- EFS – Elastic File System – is Network Attached Storage (NAS) – where files can be mounted to multiple Virtual Machines (VMs).
- Glacier – is an archiving service for redundant or rarely used data. It provides cheap to store information that is mainly for archiving purposes of data for as little as $0.004 per gigabyte per month.
- Snowball – is concerned with servicing portable storages
- Simple, Durable, Secure, Available, Low Cost, Easy to Manage.

2.4 Database

The services provided by this sub-category include the following:

- RDS – Relational Database Service – MySQL, Microsoft Sequel Server, Arura (Amazon's own SQL), Oracle compatible.
- DynamoDB- non-relational Database.
- Elasticached – caching common queries – for example it is an online store that can store the most sold or viewed product.
- RedShift – Data Warehousing and Business Intelligence – Profit and loss analysis, and other types of product processing.

2.5 Migration

The services provided by this sub-category include the following:

- AWS Hub – tracking service that tracks applications when migrating to AWS.
- Application Discovery Service – provides an automated set of tools to achieve this. An example is the use of the SharePoint Server that has a dependency on Seroquel server or domain controller – the AS (application server) tracks these dependencies.
- Database Migration Service – for migrating the local DB to the AWS database.
- Server Migration Service – assists the user in migrating from virtual and physical servers to AWS.

2.6 Media Services

The services provided by this sub-category include the following:

- Elastic Transcoder – feed recorded videos and resize them for different devices.
- MediaConvert – create videos for broadcast and multiscreen delivery services.
- MediaLive – high-quality video streams to deliver to a range of devices, phone, setup box, etc.
- Media package protects delivery of the media.
- MediaStore provides optimised media storage for both live and on-demand video.
- MediaTailor – provides targeted advertising without losing quality.

2.7 Machine Learning

The services provided by this sub-category include the following:

- SageMaker – provides deep learning techniques based on neural networks. Deep learning is more advanced than machine learning.
- AmazonComprehend – provides product survey and data analysis of the survey.
- DeepLens AI camera – is used for surveillance by applying facial recognition at door/gate entry points.
- Lex - Powers Amazon Alexa Service – communication with clients/customers (AI-based).
- Machine Learning – entry-level machine learning; data set analysis. Providing prediction for recommending products for example.
- Polly – this application turns text to speech [6].
- Rekognition - recognises images based on AI [7].
- Amazon Translate – this is similar to Google translate.
- Transcribe – used for adding closed captions, automatic speech recognition and for converts speech to text.

2.8 IoT

The services provided by this sub-category include the protection of IoT devices from their security being compromised. The AWS service also allow the remote management, control and defense of IoT devices. An example of AWS being used to control an UAV drone is shown below in Fig. 5.

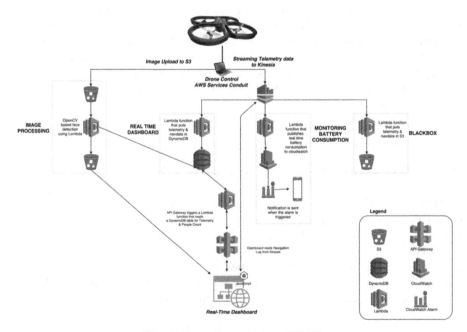

Fig. 5. Drone Control using AWS [8].

3   Conclusions

This report has given a high-level overview of the main services provided by Amazon's AWS. AWS provides a comprehensive range of services over the cloud that caters for most key infrastructure services. AWS has been adopted by the world leading multinational corporations. AWS offers its expanding services by utilising Cloud Computing technology. The services that it provides is what is required and needed by companies in terms of marketing, inventory control, data analytics and security. The possible downside of AWS is the necessity to have access to the internet. However, the benefits vastly outweigh the disadvantages.

References

1. Giraud, P., https://www.oracle.com/uk/cloud/paas/features/next-industrial-revolution.html. Accessed 13 July 2020
2. Gartner Report, Magic Quadrant for Cloud Infrastructure as a Service, Worldwide (2019). https://pages.awscloud.com/Gartner-Magic-Quadrant-for-Infrastructure-as-a-Service-Worldwide.html. Accessed 13 July 2020
3. Varia, J., Matthew, S., Overview of Amazon Web Services. https://media.amazonwebservices.com/AWS_Overview.pdf. Accessed 13 July 2020
4. Sumo Logic, AWS 101: An Overview of Amazon Web Services. https://assets.sumologic.com/resources/insight/console_snippet-1024x463.png?mtime=20190315121621&focal=none. Accessed 13 July 2020
5. https://aws.amazon.com/products/security/. Accessed 14 July 2020
6. https://eu-west-2.console.aws.amazon.com/polly/home/SynthesizeSpeech. Accessed 14 July 2020
7. https://eu-west-1.console.aws.amazon.com/rekognition/home?region=eu-west-1#/label-detection. Accessed 14 July 2020
8. Mallya, S., Simple Drone Service: From Idea to re: Invent. https://d2908q01vomqb2.cloudfront.net/cb4e5208b4cd87268b208e49452ed6e89a68e0b8/2016/10/25/SDS2-1024x663.png. Accessed 14 July 2020

Security, Wireless Sensor Networks and Internet of Things (IoT)

SIoT: Secure IoT Framework for Smart Environments

Rabie A. Ramadan[1,2](✉), Md. Haidar Sharifa[1], and Marwa. S. Salem[1,3]

[1] University of Hail, Hail, Kingdom of Saudi Arabia
rabie@rabieramadan.org
[2] Cairo University, Giza, Egypt
[3] Ain Shams University, Cairo, Egypt

Abstract. Smart environment is a new paradigm based on the IoT platforms of the Internet of Things. IoT is a new model that gives the living environment intelligence. Health and social care are critical areas where environmental knowledge can be used; where the quality of life can be enhanced and sustained without financial costs. The implementation of this modern health and social care model is largely dependent on the implemented technologies (sensors and wireless networks), the software used to make decisions, and information security, confidentiality, and reliability. IoT sensors and wearables devices collect sensitive data and have to respond to input changes in an almost real-time manner. The aim of an IoT security system is to provide the flexibility and modularization necessary to support these applications. This paper develops IoT security framework for smart environments. The framework has been developed to be integrated seamlessly with various IoT applications, separating security tasks from practical tasks and being built with separate modules for each layer (Internet, Interface and IoT device) that provide functionality relative to that layer. The framework is examined in terms of security and IoT energy consumption. The initial results show the framework satisfy the maximum security of IoT systems and it consume the minimum IoT devices energy.

Keywords: IoT · Smart environment · Security · Cloud computing

1 Introduction

Even though it is a relatively new concept, the Internet of Things (IoT) opens perspectives that can change the way we interact, not just with each other, but also with the surrounding environment. IoT is an emerging field that has gained a great deal of attention from many sectors, facilitating the advancement of automotive, infrastructure, telecommunications, or Intelligent environmental applications [1]. In addition to the enticing facilities provided by IoT systems, the technology dimensions in intelligent environments are more enlightening. In this area, IoT applications address issues of optimization, efficiency or ease of use, and devices work to support people in their day-to-day activities. IoT devices can provide a solution that enables older people or people with disabilities to live in a

M. H. Miraz et al. (Eds.): iCETiC 2020, LNICST 332, pp. 51–61, 2020.
https://doi.org/10.1007/978-3-030-60036-5_4

more independent and customized world, increase their autonomy and empower them to solve those routine procedures on their own and have a positive impact on the quality of their living standards.

At the same time, sensor data provides essential information about the current state of the environment in smart environment applications, and data must be reliable to make the right decisions. But as with any IoT device, data reliability can tend to be erratic. Because of sensors nature, hardware failures, compromised nodes, electromagnetic interference, false positives, abnormal values, or misinterpretations can occur. Furthermore, to avoid such issues, it is necessary to implement a solution capable of filtering out irregular measurements so that it is possible to distinguish between node faults and real situations requiring the immediate intervention of qualified staff.

There are intelligent environmental applications that require high-security measures due to the critical nature of sensed data, especially when considering the context of critical applications such as health care [2]. In this situation, conventional security approaches are difficult to be implemented, as an IoT system typically consists of numerous interconnected hardware (resource constrained) and multi-vendor software components which pose several concerns.

In this sense, IoT has large number of devices that need to be handled with appropriate solutions for authentication, privacy, efficient data handling. Security and privacy policies must be incorporated in smart environment applications that process sensitive data without impacting service quality. A viable security solution therefore needs to implement protective mechanisms across all layers of the IoT network, thus allowing unrestricted and consistent interaction between these layers.

An existing IoT platform such as Amazon's AWS IoT, ARM Bed from ARM and other partners, Microsoft's Azure IoT Suite, Google's Brillo/Weave, Ericsson's Calvin, Apple's HomeKit, Eclipse's Kura, or Samsung's SmartThings can be used to develop smart environment applications. Such platforms allow rapid development of applications and support a wide range of sensors and wearables. Furthermore, as discussed in [3], that framework encapsulates standard security mechanisms such as encryption, authorization, access control, and secure communication. However, these platforms do not handle important security challenges required by critical IoT applications. Data anomaly detection, remote attestation and/or packet filtering are problems that should be solved to reduce complex attacks.

In this paper, we propose a security framework that addresses these challenges, bringing improvements to applications for environmental intelligence, with emphasis on monitoring of smart environmental application. To this end, the proposed framework consists of interconnected modules that are integrated into each of the IoT system's main layers. The system is based on a custom distributed architecture that empowers middle-layer tools while providing a central management point through distributed platforms such as cloud.

In the remaining parts of the paper, the key components of the proposed platform are discussed. the related work is described in Sect. 2 while Sect. 3 discuss the proposed framework, Secure IoT Framework for Smart Environment (SIoT). Section 4 show the experimental results and discussion. Finally, the paper concludes in Sect. 5.

2 Related Work

The suggestion presented in [4] is a layered IoT system architecture and hardware and software development aspects. At the same time, many fields of implementation of the proposed model have been identified, such as smart cities. In [5], the researchers analyzed the state of the art for IoT and pointed out that when developing an IoT program, two important issues need to be considered, people's confidentiality and the protection of products and systems. To prevent these problems, it is important to develop an architecture customized to the project's intent and then implement a security system that satisfies the privacy and confidentiality requirements. For IoT frameworks, heterogenous devices are merged with other devices; therefore, collected data from such heterogenous devices as well the heterogenous devices need to be handled and analyzed properly. Data needs to be analyzed and filtered for irregularities. However, anomaly detection consumes large amount of nodes resources. Thus, a suitable anomaly detection algorithm could be implemented on different part of the system such as cloud.

Researchers suggest many ways to detect data anomalies such as machine learning, recurrent calculation, statistical calculation, decision trees [6], but if an attacker has a chance of making mistakes, or deliberately injecting malicious information, it becomes even more difficult to capture the unusual data.

Technology and technology groups have made considerable efforts to develop standard IoT frameworks such as the Internet of Things Architecture (IoT-A) [7] or the Future Internet Core Platform (FiWARE) [8] to fix the above-mentioned issues. While the second FiWARE architecture incorporates a "safety-by-design" paradigm with standard components (such as surveillance, identity and privacy protection, background security or safe storage), the first, IoT-A, introduces a model of trust which takes into account various security aspects including trust domains, trust assessment methods, behavior analysis policies, and trust federalization.

To ensure compliance with defined security rules [9], access control is based on administrative approval. The information that transits the network is vital to life in a network intended to monitor the functions of the human body and the environment. Therefore, security mechanisms need to be implemented to deter malicious attacks. Defining the principles and protocols used to improve data security is the basis for these. The IEEE 802.15.4 has seen a significant improvement and is generally discussed in [10]. Whatever the context within which an IoT system is based, the great number of embedded devices turn trust into collected information and the credibility of IoT devices into two main concepts [11]. Those two principles are also directly linked the data collected from IoT devices is tagged by a client with a different level of trust, based on the reliability of the application.

For critical applications, information can no longer be analyzed as simple environmental data without any relation to the behaviors of a person; instead, it must be categorized into different categories, based on their source and potential usage must either be processed locally or be anonymized. Therefore, trust is not only a characteristic of data read from sensors and their honesty in these types of applications, but it also becomes a requirement for the functioning of the entire IoT ecosystem (users need not only to trust the obtained information, but also to trust how the device manipulates the data before and after it is presented to them).

Returning to the relation between the first "tier" of trust and node credibility, as stated at the beginning of this section, the notion of reputation can be used to define the resulting value of the process of evaluating IoT devices based on their behavioral characteristics, such as transaction history, reliability of defined communication links or the performance of sent information. Trustworthiness of an IoT system directly affects communications with other devices where data published by a company with a poor credibility rating has a low likelihood of consumption. Therefore, its actions will detect a malicious node inserted in the IoT network, regardless of when an attack is launched. Given this ability, several models have been proposed for evaluating a node's credibility rate, based on various mathematics, physics or other aspects such as Bayesian [12], subjective logic [13], entropy [14, 15] or biological elements [16, 17].

Although the concept of a reputation evaluation model may be for a variety of domains, authors in [18, 19] highlighted five essential stages that need to be integrated into a reputation-based architecture which are: data collection, nodes selection, transaction execution, scoring and reputation rate assessment, updating the reputation level of a node, and, users' scoring in nodes.

The authors in [20] propose the implementation of a trustworthy data assessment solution for devices in a participatory sensing setting, by expanding the usual applications contained in an IoT framework. The adaptiveness of a reputational assessment system, despite the dynamic nature of this sensing environment, is another benefit and a desired feature.

While these reputational security mechanisms may provide improvements to the overall safety of an IoT System, they are not protected from traditional attack methods which can be adapted to operate in an architecture that evaluates reputation. Regular security protocols such as Transport Layer Protection (TLS)/Datagram Transport Layer Security (DTLS) communications, encryption and Access Control Lists (ACL) must be implemented in the IoT architecture to combat these potential problems. The overhead in power consumption is another problem with reputation-based security mechanisms, given the additional computations required to determine the reputation for each node.

3 Secure IoT Framework for Smart Environment (SIoT)

In this section, we introduce SIoT as a secure IoT framework for smart environment. Considering that IoT networks are widely adopted today, developing a security system for smart environments should be based on a modular architecture that enables scalability.

In the beginning, homes were a traditional for smart environments, extending over time to offices, public spaces, and hospital environments. The system proposed has a multi-level layout that includes one role at each level for independent surveillance and activity. The framework presented in the following subsections introduces distributed architecture where distributed processing and storage could be possibly involved. However, a Controller is introduced to manage the communications among the nodes as well as between the nodes and processing and storage elements.

An important feature to be provided in smart environment applications by an IoT security framework is a secure infrastructure that allows data to be transmitted from endpoint sensors to the distributed services such as cloud. An IoT protection platform must also offer additional services to the network, such as sensor anomaly detection, which is important in the context of smart environments. Our proposed architecture provides support for running a controller side anomaly detection algorithm to detect sensor data anomalies in real time, thereby meeting the needs of smart environment applications. In addition, the controller element in our system processes requests including normal and critical data. However, due to the importance of the controller, it is protected by Denial of Service (DoS) to mitigate any attack on the system.

The approach suggested combines different security elements at all levels of the IoT network, as shown in Fig. 1. A trust relationship based on the authentication mechanism is established to ensure the interaction of different security modules. The IoT security system allows such trust relationships to be formed using X.509 electronic certificates, asymmetric keys or symmetric keys, depending on the device's constraints. In addition, the solution provides an anomaly detection module that detects and quantifies node activity at the gateway level to create a more secure process.

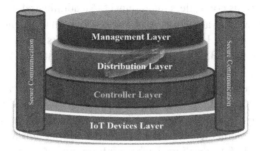

Fig. 1. Proposed Secure IoT Platform for Smart Environments

The figure shows four layers including management, distributions, controller, and IoT devices layers. At the same time, the secure communication is applied at all layers in both directions. The following subsections briefly explain the main functionalities of the framework layers.

- **Management Layer**

The management layer is the top layer of the proposed framework where it involves some of the management tools as well as it offers comfortable interface for user security configuration. It also contains traffic monitoring tools and easy setup to the monitoring parameters where the administer is able to configure the security level based on the type of used application. It includes other modules such as logging and Denial of Services (DoS) attack detection and prevention.

- **Distribution Layer**

This layer represents the services and their execution side. The distribution layer could be any type of Internet based facility or data center. Cloud could be the most suitable layer for the smart environment services. However, to verify the security of the data and the services, we added an sublayer over the cloud authentication layer, Cloud Based Security (CBS). The first feature introduced by the CBS is the aspect of oversight and implementation of specific security rules and policies, intended to prevent the influx of malicious data due to a rogue Controller. In addition to filtering traffic flows, the CBS also serves as a controller and application layer network discovery module by aggregating services available on various CBSs. As a note, the services that the CBS aggregates are resources that can be connected to by the IoT system administrators and the underlying devices. Data collected within the IoT framework is available to other IoT systems by maintaining this service.

Still, these connections are monitored and secured by the CBS, enforcing the access control rules defined when connecting to these "exterior" services. As a policy enforcement point, the CBS only allows the flow of traffic from endpoint IoT devices to secure upper layer services (legitimate CBS entities).

The CBS has mechanisms to ensure secure communication between the Controller layer and itself, or between users and the services it is designed to provide, by being a central hub where various controllers interconnect. An administrator manually provides the security tokens needed to authenticate and authorize both users and controllers in the CBS management interface. In addition to these active tasks using the CBS in various IoT system scenarios, the CBS is mostly a passive component. This is because the main idea behind our CBS is to act as a repository where it includes a secure repository management tool where data is stored in encrypted format. Here the standard encryption mechanisms could be applied without any of the previous concerns due to the efficiency of the cloud resources. Anomaly detection is also implemented in this layer. Special secure database is implemented for the controllers' information and controllers may select the best trusted link to reach its database information. Again, the communication between the controllers and the cloud layer is encrypted as well, secure channels.

At this point, the CBS is only allowed to store the above-mentioned data types and ensure safe access to them without having the means to manipulate them. Furthermore, if a certain degree of trust is maintained from the time the IoT environment is developed and configured, the CBS could be expanded to enable software integration and upgrade methods, resulting in a consistent map of anomalies being observed throughout the IoT.

- **Controller Layer**

While different IoT network models exist, controller-centric is one of the most widely used applications for smart environments. One of the main advantages of the controller-centric design is that it consists of a core computer that applies IoT sensor communication logic. From the cost perspective, providing a controller-centered network allows a fleet of sensors with limited capabilities to be deployed, provided that the controller can be used to offload protection and data processing functions.

The controller is the component that connects the endpoint network segment to the upstream network components, performs translation from lightweight to classic communication protocols, or performs various security tasks such as authentication, authorization, access control, or packet filtering. The controller may also function as a network access server on different layers. By the use of the extensible authentication Protocol

(EAP), or the CoAP payloaded user/password authentication protocol, the controller can authenticate the Messages Queuing Telemetry Transport (MQTT).

IoT controller do not have the same technical limitations as IoT endpoint devices, making them ideal for offloading certain resource-intensive tasks from low-end devices, such as security operations. Using a controller -centered model often provides a number of benefits in the overall economy of the IoT network, reducing the latency required to process IoT transmitted information (real-time applications) and the traffic between the sensors and the cloud backend. As a central element of the IoT network, the controller needs adequate mechanisms of defense against sophisticated DoS attacks to provide network reliability and meet real-time constraints.

Different architectures turn IoT device into software hypervisor, benefiting from the IoT controller capabilities. For example, the controller may run an MQTT broker application or a multi-sensor CoAP client that aggregates data.

The controller is central to two main tasks in our IoT security system: the integration of the anomaly sensor detection unit, and an advanced filtering mechanism for the network packet. The tasks of the IoT controller listed above highlight the need for a security check plane, enabling the transmission of commands and data on the sensor anomaly status and packet filtration by the IoT endpoint devices.

The Cloud platform plays the role of a sensor data repository in this protection scheme, storing the data published by IoT. The controller measurement of anomaly status is carried out locally, and the cloud component is a passive item, which does not require information to be altered following reported events. The proposed IoT security system uses an algorithm of sensor anomaly detection with a well-defined interface. Therefore, the protection framework abstracts the actual implementing of anomaly algorithms and provides only a plug-in module to run any form of algorithm for anomaly detection. The protection system serves as a computer repository for applying the input data from the cloud platform in a personalized anomaly detection algorithm. The IoT Security Architecture addresses the particular requirements of each implementation scenario by implementing a generic sensor anomaly detection algorithm. Even if the IoT controller is not a system with major resource constraints, it is important to take the power consumption into account if the sensor detection algorithm is run. To deal with this problem, we propose a controller power consumption model, named time Active Time Series for Anomaly Detection (ATS).

Our approach consists of two main components, the component of Data Conversion and the component of Learning. Several general features are extracted from the raw data set Tl to integrate temporal property of time series information and form the function dataset Fl. In order for the initial detection model to learn, feature-based and instance-based learning methods are then applied to Fl. The unlabeled time series Tu follows the same method of extraction of features and forms the Fu function dataset.

A small number of insightful samples from Fu are recommended by the learning element for labeling via strategy for Uncertainty and Context Diversity (UCD). The marked information will then be used to retrain the template of base detection. We get the final anomaly detector after T rounds of learning. Figure 2 shows the architecture of the proposed ATS model.

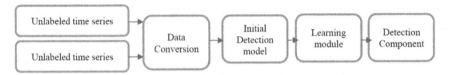

Fig. 2. ATS modle for anamoly detection

- **IoT Devices Layer**

This layer includes all of the IoT devices that are used in smart environment application. There are some authentications protocol are installed on the devices beforehand for total security. Also, we assume that in some of the powerful devices, light anomaly detection and basic encryption techniques are enabled for better security. We propose an attestation system that implements a safe message protocol and relies on an external module for measuring integrity (e.g., TPM, protocol, and relies on an external module for measuring integrity. Whenever a node's integrity is verified by the Controller, it sends an IMA node). It sends a Node Examination Request (NER) message to the IoT system whenever the gateway wants to check the validity of a node. The NER request is a nonce and an IoT application Request (NER) message. The NER message consists of a nonce and a Hash-based Hash-based Message Authentication Code (HMAC) signature, measured over the nonce value. A pre-shared key between the endpoint device and the controller is used to identify the Signature message authentication code (HMAC) while the endpoint device is exchanged with the controller by means of the user key.

4   Experimental Result

In this section, the framework components are implemented and simulated for initial results. A proof-of-concept is executed where we incorporated a Zuul proxy solution to enforce the monitoring and access control functionality of the cloud framework in order to manage connections and enforce security rules. With the Zuul proxy acting as a network aggregator, the packet filtering mechanisms and the service find mechanisms were used. The Cloud module's passive component, namely the database of the smart world, needs to store information in a graph-like structure. In view of this, we opted to use a Not Only Structured Query Language (NoSQL) approach to implement the database and selected MongoDB for this purpose, due to its maturity and the availability of drivers for several programming languages. We used the standard Java Jetty HyperText Transfer Protocol (HTTP) client for the cloud communication to access REST resources that the cloud module exposes: sensing data publishing, sensing data recovery. With a Zuul proxy serving as a network aggregator, the packet filtering systems and the service discovery method can be used.

Packet filtering is a complex task that resource-restricted endpoint IoT devices cannot perform. In order to reduce the safety allocated resources (CPU cycles, memory), this process requires continuous improvements even on the controller side. Since IoT network applications require low latency communications, a DoS attack could be performed even if the controller allocates resources to drop malicious packets and is therefore unable to transmit the legitimate packets in the required time frame. We evaluated a scenario in which an attacker performs a DoS using the MQTT-SN protocol to evaluate the packet filtering module for our controller side IoT system. Typically, IoT controller are low-cost devices mounted at the network edge. Such systems are not equipped with specialized hardware-based filters such as Application-Specific Integrated Circuits (ASIC), Field Programable Gates Arrays (FPGA) or SmartNIC.

Two packet filters are also implemented, one on the controller side, XDP packet filter, and the other one is userspace packet filter. When using a kernel XDP packet filter [https://www.iovisor.org/technology/xdp] compared to a userspace packet filter, we observed the drop rate of MQTT-SN per second follows the same pattern, shown in Fig. 3. However, it seems that XDP on the controller side has higher drop rate than the one on the userspace by, on average, 70 k packets as a result of sending 150 million MQTT-SN packets.

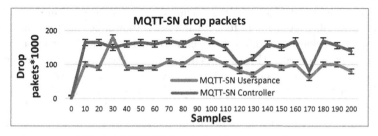

Fig. 3. MQTT-SN dropped packets comparison

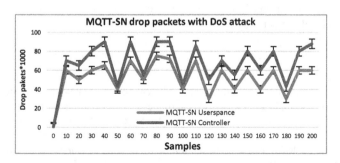

Fig. 4. MQTT-SN dropped packets comparison with DoS atatck

Figure 4, the results of a second test case are presented, where in a case of DoS attack, we analyze the rate of packets per second. The DoS attack scenario is a malicious system sending 150 million MQTT-SN packets with a QoS value of 1 and a legitimate device sending the same number of packets with a QoS value of 0. As can be observed, when using the method of filtering the XDP kernel, the controller can process 15 k more valid packets than when using the alternative userspace.

The experimental results of the DoS attack show that our proposed method dramatically improves the fall rate without the need for any hardware. This solution off - the-shelf permits the installation of low-cost gates which can handle the IoT network safety and network functionality. The choice of hardware to be mounted on the IoT network edge therefore offers versatility. In addition to this, the energy consumption on the controller side is significantly decreased by eliminating the need for specialized equipment to process the packet (e.g. ASICs). In software, the implementation of security filtering functions also provides flexibility in software updates, taking into account the constantly changing techniques of IoT attack. In comparison, while the ASIC filtering mechanism will improve the performance of falling packets, the transition to hardware generation results in increased costs and delays, which could not be appropriate to the flexibility of IoT markets.

5 Conclusion

The proposed security architecture was developed to be implemented for the development of an IoT security system on a low-cost commodity IoT hardware. The proposed security architecture is designed to be implemented on low-cost commodity IoT. The experimental results examine both functional aspects (power consumption model) and offload, trying to achieve a trade-off between performance and cost, as outlined in the experimental security aspects (DoS attacks mitigation mechanism) to confirm one of the main outcomes of the framework characteristics. As far as security threats are concerned, we may infer that our framework is immune to DoS attacks and power exhaustion attacks based on experimental results. The simulated DoS attack consists of one or more infected IoT devices that send malicious network packets to the controller, handling this attack on the controller side by manipulating packets while serving regular requests. The power consumption model also manages the energy exhaustion attack on the gateway side, which delays the execution of the anomaly detection algorithm in a stochastic manner when the battery of the gateway is small.

References

1. Liu, J.: Design and implementation of an intelligent environmental-control system: perception, network, and application with fused data collected from multiple sensors in a greenhouse at Jiangsu, China. Int. J. Distrib. Sens. Netw. **12**, 5056460 (2016). https://doi.org/10.1177/155014775056460
2. Gubbi, J., Buyya, R., Marusic, S., Palaniswami, M.: Internet of Things (IoT): a vision, architectural elements, and future directions. Fut. Gener. Comput. Syst. **29**(7), 1645–1660 (2013). https://doi.org/10.1016/j.future.2013.01.010
3. Ammar, M., Russello, G., Crispo, B.: Internet of Things: asurvey on the security of IoT frameworks. J. Inf. Secur. Appl. **38**, 8–27 (2018)
4. Gordana, G., Mladen, V., Nebojsa, M., Dragan, V.: The IoT architectural framework, design issues and application domains. Wirel. Personal Commun. **92**, 127–148 (2017)
5. Bandyopadhyay, D., Sen, J.: Internet of Things: applications and challenges in technology and standardization. Wirel. Personal Commun. **58**, 49–69 (2011)
6. Haque, S.A., Rahman, M., Aziz, S.M.: Sensor anomaly detection in wireless sensor networks for healthcare. Sensors. **15**, 8764–8786 (2015)
7. Bauer, M., et al. Internet of things—architecture IOT-A deliverable D1.5—final architectural reference model for the IoT v3.0 (2019). https://iotforum.org/wp-content/uploads/2014/10/D1.5.pdf

8. Saleem, S., Ullah, S., Kwak, K.S.: A study of IEEE 802.15.4 security framework for wireless body area networks. Sensors **11**, 1383–1395 (2011)

9. Eder, T., Nachtmann, D., Schreckling, D.: Trust and reputation in the Internet of Things; Technical report, Universitat Passau, Passau, Germany (2013)

10. Zimmerman, T.G.: Personal area networks: near-field intrabody communication. IBM Syst. J. **35**, 609–617 (1996)

11. Ibrahim, A., Ahmed, A., Ha, S., Hamid, A., Gani, A., Khurram, M.: Trust and reputation for Internet of Things: fundamentals, taxonomy, and open research challenges. J. Network and Comput. Appl. **145** (2019). https://doi.org/10.1016/j.jnca.2019.102409

12. Nielsen, M., Krukow, K., Sassone, V.: A: bayesian model for event-based trust. Electron. Notes Theory Comput. Sci. **172**, 499–521 (2007)

13. Yaun, J., Zhou, H., Chen, H.: SLAD: subjective logic anomaly detection framework in wireless sensor networks. Int. J. Distrib. Sensor Networks **8**, 1–21 (2011)

14. Honjun, D., Zhiping, J., Xiaona, D.: An entropy-based trust modeling and evaluation for wireless sensor networks. In: Proceedings of the International Conference on Embedded Software and Systems, Sichuan, China, 29–31, pp. 27–34 (2008)

15. Hong, L., Jiaming, T., Yan, S.: Entropy-based trust management for data collection in wireless sensor networks. In: Proceedings of the 5th International Conference on Wireless Communications, Networking and Mobile Computing, Beijing, China, 24–26 September, pp. 1–4 (2009)

16. Mármol, F.G., Pérez, G.M.: Providing trust in wireless sensor networks using a bio-inspired technique. Telecommun. Syst. **46**, 163–180 (2011)

17. Marzi, H., Li, M.: An enhanced bio-inspired trust and reputation model for wireless sensor network. Procidia Comput. Sci. **19**, 1159–1166 (2013)

18. Marti, S., Garcia-Molina, H.: Taxonomy of trust: categorizing P2P reputation systems. Comput. Netw. **50**, 472–484 (2006)

19. Mármol, F.G., Pérez, G.M.: Towards pre-standardization of trust and reputation models for distributed and heterogeneous systems. Comput. Stand. Interfaces **32**, 185–196 (2010)

20. Alswailim, M.A., Hassanein, H.S., Zulkernine, M.: A reputation system to evaluate participants for participatory sensing. In Proceedings of the 2016 IEEE Global Communications Conference (GLOBECOM), Washington, DC, USA, pp. 1–6 (2016)

21. Bassam, W., Mohamed, M., Rabie, A., Ayman, E.: Evaluation of lightweight block ciphers based on General Feistel Structure (GFS). WAS Sci. Nat. J. **2**(1) (2020)

22. Bassam, W., Mohamed, M., Rabie, A., Ayman, E., Fatma, H.: Enhanced version of GOST cryptosystem for lightweight applications. WAS Sci. Nat. J. **2**(1) (2020)

Review of Hybrid Control Designs
for Underactuated Quadrotor with Unmodelled
Dynamic Factors

Ghulam E. Mustafa Abro[1]($\boxtimes$), Vijanth Sagayan Asirvadam[1], Saiful Azrin B. Zulkifli[1], and Syed Aqeel Raza[2]

[1] Department of Electrical and Electronic Engineering,
Universiti Teknologi PETRONAS, Seri Iskandar 32610, Malaysia
Mustafa.abro@ieee.org
[2] Global Data, London EC4Y 0BS, UK

Abstract. This review paper presents the study related to three main challenges such as underactuation, hybrid control designs for the stabilization purpose and an effect of unmodelled dynamic factors. In addition to this, manuscript addresses different approaches to acquire dynamic model for quadrotor with less assumptions such as system identification and Newton Euler formulation techniques. The paper details the short comings related to hybrid control designs proposed for the stabilization of quadrotor in multiple flight modes. Moreover, one may find the discussion related to the constraints while tackling the ground effect and coping up with rotor's efficiency loss.

Keywords: Underactuated · Unmodelled dynamics · Quadrotor · Hybrid control and fault recovery designs

1 Introduction

Quadrotor is one of the systems, having degree of freedom (DOF) greater than the number of actuators deployed on to it, are known as underactuated systems. These systems are very difficult to control but very significant because of less power consumption, reduced cost and flexible to exhibit the natural dynamic motion. Researchers considered either the simple dynamic model or a model with few assumptions to propose hybrid control designs for tasks i.e. robust trajectory tracking, set point regulation and hovering. Unfortunately, these unmodelled dynamic factors and uncertainties are continuously changing and therefore the control design proposed for trajectory tracking may not provide better results all the time. This is one of the reasons that quadrotor like unmanned aerial vehicles have been a concerning area of research for control engineering experts. Thus, one may find several control strategies for the stabilization of such an underactuated quadrotor unmanned aerial vehicle that comprises of four control inputs but six degrees of freedom (DOF). The major purpose to write this review paper, is to address the limitations in the same area. It has been seen that control designs are directly implemented

M. H. Miraz et al. (Eds.): iCETiC 2020, LNICST 332, pp. 62–85, 2020.
https://doi.org/10.1007/978-3-030-60036-5_5

for fully actuated systems but are never proposed directly for underactuated systems like quadrotor craft. This results in an additional step for performing linearization of the dynamic model [1].

1.1 Fully Actuated Versus Underactuated Systems

Before going into the differences in between fully and underactuated systems [2]; one may first review some of the fundamentals such that the equation of motions can be derived using either Lagrangian formulation method illustrated as:

$$\frac{d}{dt}\left(\frac{\partial L}{\partial \dot{q}}\right) - \frac{\partial L}{\partial q} = F(q)u \tag{1}$$

$$L = T - V \tag{2}$$

In the provided Eq. 2, T and V are potential and kinetic energies of the system respectively whereas $q \in \Re^n$ the configuration vector, $u \in \Re^m$ the actuator input vector hence $F(q) \in \Re^{n \times m}$ will be a non-square matrix and mathematically this can be re-written as:

$$D(q)q + C(q, \dot{q})\dot{q} + G(q) = F(q)u \tag{3}$$

Equation 3 is the general equation that can be used for both fully and underactuated systems where $D(q) \in \Re^{n \times n}$ is the inertia matrix, $C(q, \dot{q}) \in \Re^n$ illustrates centrifugal terms and last but not the least $G(q)$ denotes the gravity. Discussing the fully actuated system, is a system in terms of the configuration of $(q, \dot{q}, t)$ if and only if it has the ability to command an instant change in acceleration of body which is in arbitrary direction or in motion which means mathematically:

$$rank((F(q)) = \dim(q) \tag{4}$$

Whereas an under-actuated system can be defined in same way, but it has no ability to command an instant change in acceleration of body in arbitrary direction which means:

$$rank((F(q)) < \dim(q) \tag{5}$$

In simple words one may conclude that a system can be said as an under-actuated system if its external forces are not able to exert an acceleration to its states in all directions. One can say that the input matrix $F(q)$ as shown in Eq. 3 and thus it results an underactuation depending directly on the system states. One can know the complexity of underactuated system through Eq. 6; mathematically this can be illustrated as:

$$\dim(q) - rank(F(q)) = Degree \ of \ underactuation \tag{6}$$

Originally the classical control theories were developed for the fully actuated system and they were all adequate for both linear and nonlinear systems including and for this the feedback linearization is given as:

$$\bar{u} = F(q)^{-1}[C(q, \dot{q})\dot{q} + G(q) + D(q)v] \tag{7}$$

In above Eq. 7, (v) is basically a control input signal and the input matrix as shown $F(q)$ must be invertible for the law but this not the same case for underactuated systems. Genuinely this is the problem that motivates the researchers to take initiative for the problem of underactuation and it has been seen that Partial feedback linearization method had been introduced for the same issue which is now widely used for such underactuated vehicles [3, 4].

1.2 Categories of an Underactuation

An underactuation has been divided into several categories [5, 6] and can be explained in four ways in which first category is the by-default underactuated systems. These are the systems which are limited by design such that two wheeled mobile robots [7], underactuated hovercraft [8] and tri-rotor unmanned aerial vehicles [9]. The second category is underactuation due to modification in their design, this modification occurs due to several reasons such as increasing the maximum efficiency, getting less energy consumption and cost. The most common examples for this category can be two thrust satellite. The third category is ideal underactuated systems, these systems have no practical application, but they are available just to explore the best control design study i.e. ball-and-beam system. Last category inducts with the systems that were fully actuated before but due to failure in the number of actuators they turned into underactuated system for instance robotic arm. The stabilization and tracking tasks had been very concern topic for an underactuated quadrotor craft and this can be further sub-divided into three common problems namely set point regulation which deals in designing a control strategy that leads the states of your underactuated system to equilibrium condition i.e. hovering. Second problem is trajectory planning, it deals with the control scheme that involves the finding of an appropriate trajectory. In other words, this will lead your system to go from zero configuration q_{io} to a desired configuration q_d whereas the last technical problem for underactuated system is to propose control scheme that will minimizes the tracking error. In case of leader following method, such control problem is known as trajectory tracking.

1.3 Model of Quadrotor Unmanned Aerial Vehicle

This paper reviews the quadrotor type of unmanned aerial vehicle; it has 04 actuators with 06 degree of freedom (DOF) that makes it highly unstable control system. On other part, it also contains some of the significant features i.e. low cost, low maintenance and vertical take-off and landing capability. Discussing its mechanism, it is modelled in a cross setup with arms in geometrical symmetry along with 04 propellers having fixed-pitched blades. As far as its airflow is concerned then its direction is downwards to create lift. In order to keep its balance while at fly and to remove the tail rotor it is a must condition that adjacent propellers must rotate counter wise to each other. The system state variables are basically controlled by varying the number of revolutions per minute (RPM) of four motors which no doubt bring a change in attitude angles and these are directly dependent on the velocities of every propellers. It is studied that if quadrotor is controlled with proper control design then it can attend the certain altitude and attitude subsequently [10]. Before understanding of quadrotor model, it is to study that there are two frames of references namely body frame of reference and earth frame of reference. This study is compulsory as during modelling one would map states from one frame type to another [11]. It is studied that the equations of motion, aerodynamic forces and input turning effect (torque) are obtained through body frame of reference which is non-inertial frame too whereas the other one is earth frame of reference or known as inertial frame of reference. These two frames are used to define the motion of underactuated quadrotor UAV. The earth inertial frame of reference is denoted by (E-frame) and symbolized by (O_E, x_E, y_E, z_E) where O_E is defined as axis of origin and (x_E, y_E, z_E) are defined as North West and structure with respect to earth. By using this E-frame one can see the linear positions of gravity as denoted by ξ and the ZYX Euler angles Θ are illustrated in Fig. 1.

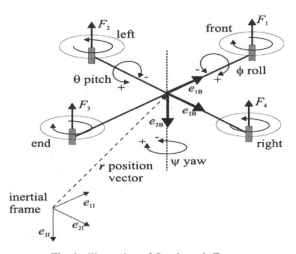

Fig. 1. Illustration of Quadrotor's Frame

Moreover, the top reference frame in Fig. 1 is the B-frame attached to the quadrotor body that it is denoted as $(e_{1B}, e_{2B}, e_{3B}, z_B)$ where the center point of this frame is defined as axis of origin and coincides with the center of cross structure of quadrotor. The directions in this frame are denoted as x_B, y_B, z_B towards front, left and up respectively. The B-Frame defines the linear velocity V, the angular velocity ω and the torque as τ. The linear positions can be determined using a simple vector in between E-Frame and B-Frame as illustrated in the Fig. 1. The Euler angles $(\Theta = [\phi \, \theta \, \psi]^T)$ representing the attitude [Roll, Pitch and Yaw] respectively which are defined by B-Frame with reference to E-Frame. This can further help in developing the rotation matrix to map the orientation such that in [12]; given as:

$$D = \begin{bmatrix} c_\theta c_\psi & -c_\theta c_\psi + c_\psi s_\phi s_\theta & s_\phi s_\psi + c_\phi c_\psi s_\theta \\ c_\theta c_\psi & c_\phi c_\psi + s_\phi s_\theta s_\psi & -c_\psi s_\phi + c_\phi s_\theta s_\psi \\ -s_\theta & c_\phi c_\theta & c_\phi c_\theta \end{bmatrix} \tag{8}$$

Where $s_x = \sin(x)$ and $c_x = \cos(x)$ in provided rotational matrix as shown above in Eq. 8. One may use this transfer matrix in order to build a relationship in between the E-frame and B-Frame [12].

$$\dot{\Theta} = T\omega, T = \begin{bmatrix} 1 & s_\phi t_\theta & c_\phi t_\theta \\ 0 & c_\phi & -s_\phi \\ 0 & \frac{s_\phi}{c_\theta} & \frac{c_\phi}{c_\theta} \end{bmatrix} \qquad (9)$$

Where $t_x = \tan(x)$, it is further observed that any UAV either quadrotor usually controlled at their nearest equilibrium state because this is the state where they have all Euler angles such that roll, pitch and yaw are less than 15° and therefore the Eq. 9 can be further simplified as $\dot{\Theta} = \omega, T = I_{3\times 3}$.

2 Literature Review

2.1 Modelling Approaches for Quadrotor Craft

This review paper addresses all previously contributed works along with their short comings under three domains i.e. Multiple flight modes, rotor effectiveness loss and ground effects. For proposing control design for any system, the dynamic model must be acquired by considering all uncertainties. These models of quadrotor and their equations of motion are derived by keeping some assumptions and thus every model differs from one to another. Thus, the precise and practical dynamic model of quadrotor is very hard and critical to control because it is dominated by the effects of unmodelled dynamic factors [13]. Researchers often ignore these factors and propose several assumptions and approximations. Thus, it has been admitted that the existing techniques for deriving mathematical model and proposing control approach are inappropriate [14] for trajectory tacking at fast forward, heave flight actions and take-off and landing vertically with ground effects. Furthermore, an alternative solution for modeling quadrotor, people suggested system identification technique as most significant tool to derive the dynamic model for quadrotor via using various data of test flights in order to overcome the difficulty such that hardly obtained parameters of quadrotor but yet there are very few research contributions towards system identification [15]. In these hardly obtained parameters following have been obtained by a conventional identification method [16–18]. These parameters comprise of type of rotors and specifications of blade, masses and displacements, rotational inertia [19] and motor constants [20, 21] etc. In [22] first time Levenberg-Marquardt optimization and quadratic optimization techniques were proposed to derive these rotor parameters. This systematic approach even performed both the comparative analysis in between the real system to estimated model and got to some extent the estimated model closer to real one but the error rate was 58% and it was suggested in future recommendations that this error can be minimized further by any other optimization technique. For system identification there are basic steps to follow as illustrated in below:

a. Sensor Input signals
b. Acquisition of data and Parameters

c. Selecting model morphology
d. Selecting Identification Strategy
e. Optimization till best outcome is achieved

One may opt for the system identification depending over the dynamics and application of proposed system [23] as illustrated in Fig. 2 which is not yet to be filled by several contributors hence this area again attracts the researchers.

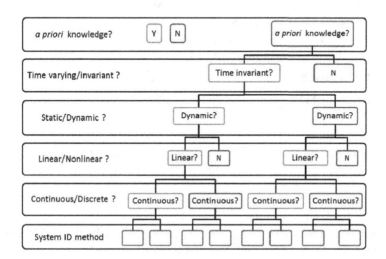

Fig. 2. System identification tree [15]

It is studied that system identification is one of the significant and valuable method for determining system dynamics and can be considered on multi-rotorcrafts such as quadrotor by using already proposed techniques [15]. It is because, these models for system identification can be used as first principle models for optimizing the quadrotor UAV. These techniques are studied and tabulated in Table 1. These are the techniques related to identify any sort of physical system and it is used in the field of unmanned aerial vehicles but so far at this stage, very few techniques had been compensated for multi-rotor crafts such as quadrotor craft [1].

2.2 Study of Control Schemes for Quadrotor UAV

Once the dynamic model of underactuated quadrotor is achieved, the next big challenge is to design the control algorithm. Since the dynamics of quadrotor changes instantaneously while performing the flight i.e. nearer to ground; it is because of the ground effect and this effect adds again a bit more challenge to control design. Researchers went through the sophisticated algorithm in which they have divided system into other subsystems with the deployment of either artificial algorithm or machine learning algorithms. These subsystems are divided into multiple feedback loops as illustrated in order to tackle such unmodelled disturbances as shown in Fig. 3. Since this technique of dividing the systems

Table 1. Summary of UAV Identification methods

No.	Data Source	Model type
1.	Inertial measurement Unit, GPS and Magnetic Compass [24]	State Space
2.	Inertial measurement Unit, GPS and Magnetic Compass [25]	State Space
3.	IMU [26]	Nonlinear SS
4.	Inertial measurement unit, Ultrasonic sensor, & Positioning transducer [27]	Transfer function & State Space both were used.
5.	Hardware in loop simulations HILs [28]	Multilayered Perception MLP
6.	INS & GPS [29]	State space
7.	IMU & GPS [30]	State space
8.	IMU & GPS [31]	State space
9.	IMU [32]	State space
10.	IMU & GPS [33]	Fifth& first- order Auto-regressive exogenous ARAX

into multi-feedback subsystems helped researchers to get the desired trajectory globally yet there are some of the internal parameters that may raise instability [35–37]. In the list of control designs, the usage of Back Stepping control design (BSC) for Lagrange form of dynamics [38] and using with barrier Lyapunov function [39] is used to resolve the series dynamics via step by step recursive process. Moreover, BSC is among the most common techniques to stabilize the quadrotor as per review yet it can be problematic too in case of explosion in terms (the change in uncertain parameters with a nonlinear time delays) [39].

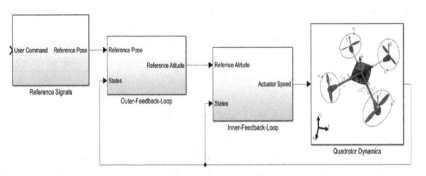

Fig. 3. Multiple feedback loops for quadrotor [34]

During the survey of literature, the hybrid techniques for underactuated quadrotor such as Fuzzy logic based Proportional Integral derivative F-PID control scheme [40] is used for flight stability under the influence of unknown condition. The proposed fuzzy model is Mamdani fuzzification model that leads to discontinuous output and for the case of quadrotor the continuous feedback output for the stability in flight control is required. Merging the same F-PID algorithm with Dijkstra's path planning algorithm demonstrates somehow the effectiveness but again the model for quadrotor taken into consideration was highly depending on the exact plant parameters which means they neglected the plant aerodynamics and gyroscopic effects [40]. Later researchers propose Deep Neural Network (DNN) for hand drawn trajectory that not only enhanced the maneuvering ability of UAV but also approximated the nonlinear functions. However, it needs an extensive training via using the data acquisition of pre-flight which is not possible to gather or transfer before every take-off and landing vertically [41].

For tackling the problems of quadrotor like tracking error minimization and stabilization; researchers proposed discontinuous solutions [41, 42]. These discontinuous solutions had been introduced lately yet may excite some unmodeled dynamics of quadrotor. In addition to this, switching output feedback control [43] for UAVs is proposed to model them as linear time varying system and it guarantees the stability, but it specified to deal with the time depending delays rather than providing a generic strategy. Another switch-mode control approach [44] that is used to achieve the tracking of cartesian space motion and to tackle the pitch angle of proposed quadrotor craft is based on Lyapunov functions dully arranged in collateral form [44]. This technique basically divided the system into further three individual subsystems in roll ϕ, pitch θ and yaw ψ domains. Furthermore, the local sub-feedback systems were designed using Partial Feedback Linearization (PFL) and Model Reference Adaptive Control (MRAC). This solution [44] provided a better way for handling the underactuation in quadrotor but the control signals suffer from the chattering effect (switching of control signals at x-axis with high frequency and with non-zero magnitude). The technique has been illustrated in Fig. 4.

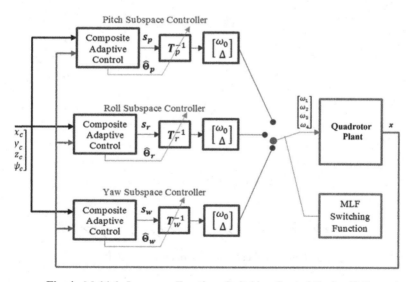

Fig. 4. Multiple Lyapunov Functions Switching Control Design [34]

On same technique another attempt was made considering the model for attitude error and compensating uncertainties [45]. In this case the strategy was proposed for maneuvering the quadrotor at large angle rotation and attitude stabilization. The technique suggests the switching in between two control designs as per the attitude error value. The switching depends over the tracking error, hence if it is large one then in order to drive the system into region of attraction second controller scheme is switched whereas in case of smaller error a more complex control scheme is used to get high accuracy while tracking. Although several practical implementations had been performed but the overall system stability had been remained unproven.

Discussing ground effect, which is one the major faults in quadrotor while VTOL as illustrated in Fig. 5. This problem led researchers to propose intelligent control strategies specifically for near ground maneuvering. In the research [46] a hybrid control technique has been suggested for the stated ground effect problem, but the proposed algorithm has been applied to a dynamic system model without considering the uncertainties and assumed to be a perfect standard model. This ground effect problem can be resolved to some extent with hybrid automation approach [47]. This approach allows for capturing the different maneuvers even nearer to ground. In this proposed work, it suggests dividing the landing problem into 03 maneuvers [47]. This technique moreover presents the experimental results too but had needed to acquire some of the assumptions again i.e. angle of landing pad. Major drawback of this technique was the landing like sliding on slope which is an unconventional maneuver. Foremost importantly, it requires the current mode of operation also to be known and thus it has need to be deployed with additional number of sensors too.

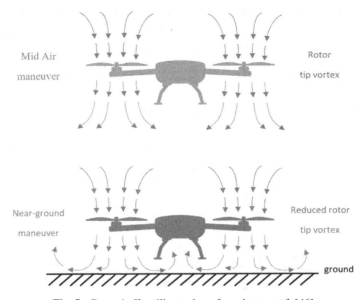

Fig. 5. Ground effect illustration of quadrotor craft [46]

Some of the researchers also suggested Unscented Kalman Filter (UKF) [48] for resolving the ground effect during VTOL; this was an estimation algorithm which surpass extended Kalman filter and estimates aerodynamic disturbances generated during flight for highly non-linear system. To some extent this technique produces fine results, but still high performance is achieved by tuning the parameters manually which will be a tough assignment for non-experts. It did not take consideration for system uncertainty and this utilizes perfect knowledge of the plant parameters. Table 2 presents all pros and cons of proposed control designs in order to address the underactuation and ground effect of quadrotor craft.

2.3 Studying Fault Tolerant Control Designs

The main part of any autonomous system is either the sensor or actuator and if any of them may have a change in their performance then the such type phenomena may bring up an imbroglio to proposed control system and such thing is known as failure. In quadrotor craft such failure may happen and hence there are two ways for resolving such issue [49]; one is to make physical redundancy in the specific components which no doubt will increase the cost and will surely increase the complexity. Secondly is to design a reliable control design which will sure the acceptable performance instead of being failure such technique is known as fault tolerance control design.

Furthermore, it is to discuss some of the fault tolerant techniques for quadrotor UAV along with their pros and cons. Fault tolerant control is a system comprises of two major components such that an integrated health detection circuit based on an active sensorization and secondly control system. One may find several techniques for fault identification or diagnosis [50] and implementation of necessary actions as per the situation [51]. Among all schemes, one of the frequent schemes is to introduce the actuator redundancy which basically introduces separate modules that may have an ability to fly your UAV alone [52]. In this scheme various modules were connected to each other and various topologies can be transformed in case of failure. In addition to this, the scheme consists of modules and feedback controller. The first will identify the directions or rotor having malfunction in order to select the topology and second one is responsible for the overall system stabilization. The proposed technique has been gone through various simulation results but limited to only for one configuration for experimental validation [35]. The same work for differently connected modules had been validated [53] through cascaded feedback but due to complex topology structure only one condition for hovering had been implemented and tested. One may face biggest challenge in this technique is to design the control design using either approximation or estimation techniques for a system consisting of at least ten or maximum hundred modular changes. The example of introducing the system redundancy in modular UAVs is illustrated in Fig. 6.

Such system redundancy as illustrated can be simply added by just adding number of extra actuators [54] with modification in a hexagon type of shape and adding further number of rotors, making the number of actuators to six. This system then turns out to be much controllable even in the case of failure of one rotor, yet its hardware software validation was questionable. Similar case is presented in [55] for coaxial octocopter that provides detection, isolation and recovery of fault errors quickly. The proposed

Table 2. Control Designs for Quadrotor flight mode

Approaches	Pros	Cons
Cascaded Feedback Control Design [34]	Used inner and outer feedback loop strategy and linearize the model through PFL method	Assumed some internal dynamics hence in practical scenario the instability may be raised
Back Stepping Control with Lagrange form [38] [39]	Overcome the cascaded dynamics via step by step recursive process	It may create problem of explosion in terms [39]
Fuzzy based PID [40]	Provides Stability during flight control [40] even in case of unknown conditions	It provides discontinuous output because of Mamdani fuzzification model
F-PID based Dijkstra's algorithm [40]	Demonstrates somehow the effectiveness in path planning	Considers exact plant parameters & neglected the aero dynamics effects
Discontinuous Switching output feedback control [43]	It guarantees the stability for proposed UAV type	Specified just to time dependent delays rather than providing generic solution
Discontinuous switching control based on (MLF) [44]	Proposed to achieve the tracking motion & pitch angle of quadrotor	Control signals have chattering effect & experimental results were unproven
Hybrid control technique [46]	It has been suggested for the stated ground effect problem	The proposed algorithm has been applied to a dynamic system model without considering the uncertainties and assumed to be a perfect standard model
Hybrid Automation Approach [47]	It divides landing problem into 03 maneuvers. This presents the experimental results too	It acquires assumptions i.e. angle of landing pad Drawback was unconventional maneuver Deployed with additional number of sensors too
Unscented Kalman Filter (UKF) based Control Design [48]	Resolves ground effect during VTOL It used an estimation algorithm that surpass extended Kalman filter and estimates aerodynamic disturbances	Manually Parameter tuning for high performance and It does not consider uncertainties

technique was also tested by various flights by adding artificial fault to system's motor. This technique was much focused on altitude but ignored completely the x-y plane. After complying the hardware redundancy, one can also use software-based approach purely to

Fig. 6. Modular UAVs with different configurations [53]

propose the fault tolerant system such that Thau Observer (TO) [56]. This software-based approach basically detects the malfunction in any sensor or actuator of any sort of UAV. This technique was just limited to fault diagnosis only and not comprises of neither fault isolation nor estimation and applicable on simple dynamic control systems. In addition to this, this technique does not consider the model uncertainties. The advanced TO algorithm then introduced [57] entitled as adaptive Thau observer for quadrotor and several experiments related to flight has been performed however, the adaptive TO did not consider the effect of external disturbances and uncertainty anymore thus the fault error was inaccurate. Next to this advancement took place and researchers work over fault error minimization including the uncertain parameters and external noises and disturbances as well [58]. This technique was proposed on the bases on optimization and its performance was tested on a testbed of quadrotor by inducting 30% effectiveness loss in one of their motors. Researchers use the simple Kalman, extended, unscented Kalman filter [59] and Taylor series expansion for reviewing the statistics of nonlinear systems. A new addition of dual unscented Kalman filter was proposed [60] in order to estimate the states of systems along with uncertain parameters simultaneously but fault diagnosis results were failed to be robust. The major reservations were that the results were only based on simulations.

After studying these techniques, it is understood that the fault control design should be efficient in all means because no one knows what type of fault may appear in one's quadrotor system. It may be the losing the thrust effectiveness of one or may be more than one rotor which is the most critical issue so far studied. In such cases when one or more than one rotor loss the effectiveness one may find the adaptive feedback control design [61] that illustrate the simulation results when single rotor losses effectiveness by 50% for more than 10 s and in second case when two rotors losses the effectiveness together by 20 to 30% for 5 s. The simulations were produced on an assumption that the hovercraft is at hovering state. Discussing another estimation approach for detection the effectiveness loss in quadrotors of proposed craft that rely on immersion and invariance observer method; this technique was merged with sliding mode control (SMC). In contrast with the previous technique of adaptive feedback this only stabilizes attitude angles but does not work for position control with even 20% loss in effectivity. All results were computed based on nonlinear model, but they were computed in hardware in loop testbed [62]. Above all the major fault in quadrotor is the failure in rotor's working and in such case researchers have proposed techniques [63] by which the quadrotor crafts try to maintain a slow speed and still follow the planned path but this technique is totally based on simulation whereas the dynamic model considered was also simple and linear hence the further validation is required still. Furthermore, it has been seen that there are several techniques which proposes the rotating of UAV around a fixed and defined axis freely and can be controlled by just a variation in the thrust [64] but this technique is again proposed for the failure of one or more than one rotor in quadrotor craft. Technique [64] has been validated experimentally as well as in simulations but there is less focus on controlling the heading angle of quadrotor for especially large aerial vehicles. Some of them also proposed the emergency landing of UAV in case of rotor failure [65]. They incorporated the conventional PID and backstepping control [66] but it is suggested for sever fault when it happens. The list of all reviewed works is mentioned in Table 3.

2.4 Control Designs for Unmodeled Uncertainties

During the model derivation it is very compulsory for identifying and considering the uncertainties. These uncertainties are classified into two types mainly parametric and non-parametric uncertainties. The unknown changes like time varying parameters i.e. quadrotor carrying the unknown payloads hence such parameters are known as parametric certainties [67, 68]. Whereas non-parametric uncertainties deal with the unmodeled nonlinearities either or unwanted disturbances such that effect of wind. From few times it has been seen that either robust, adaptive or robust adaptive control schemes have been proposed for both parametric changes [68]. Generally, adaptive control scheme is one of the strategies that perform by adapting the condition whereas robust technique tries to perform consistent even if any external disturbance may arrive in the system.

Mainly, it is studied that in past recent decade people have been working on the minimization of above-mentioned uncertainties via using Robust, Adaptive, Artificial Intelligence or amalgamating all these algorithms together. One of the adaptive algorithm techniques [69] proposed was based on Backstepping (BS) feedback linearization that presents very fine convergence for tracking error comparatively to other traditional and conventional controllers i.e. PID. BS based feedback linearization utilizes expensive tools and sensors to acquire the all parametric uncertainties. It was one of the good techniques but only focused on tracking error. Discussing further, one may find the adaptive backstepping control technique with the inclusion of passivity technique that was proposed for two major reasons. The BS control technique was included to resolve the coupling issue in proposed model along with underactuation problem where adaptive scheme was responsible to consider parametric uncertainties but only parametric quantity this technique was focusing on was the compensation for mass [70]. Considering the importance of such autonomous aerial vehicles such that quadrotor people presented various applications of quadrotor [71] but unfortunately the control law, researchers proposed was majorly focused only one uncertainty parameter that is mass only and ignored other parametric and nonparametric uncertainties. Some of researchers proposed

Table 3. Research Contributions for Fault recovery

Approach	Pros.	Cons.
Modular Physical Redundancy [52]	An actuator redundancy technique that introduces separate modules that may have an ability to fly your UAV alone [52]	The proposed technique has been gone through various simulation results, but experiment validation was not provided in all means [52]
Modular Physical Redundancy based on different configurations [53]	Similar case is presented in [55] for coaxial octocopter that provides detection, isolation and recovery of system	This technique was much focused on altitude but ignored completely the x-y plane
Thau Observer (TO) Algorithm [56]	This software-based approach basically detects the malfunction in any sensor or actuator of any sort of UAV This technique was just limited to fault diagnosis only	Comprises of neither fault isolation nor estimation and applicable on simple dynamic control systems. This does not consider the model uncertainties
Adaptive Thau Observer ATO Algorithm [57]	Experimental validation has been done related to flight	Does not consider external disturbances thus provide max error
Adaptive TO algorithm with UKF technique [60]	It works on fault error minimization including the uncertain parameters and external noises [58]	Fault diagnosis results were not robust. The major reservations were that the results were only based on simulations
Adaptive feedback control design [61]	It presents the simulation results when single rotor losses effectiveness by 50% for more than 10 s and in second case when two rotors losses the effectiveness together by 20 to 30% for 5 s	This technique provides only simulated results, and all were produced on an assumption that the hovercraft is at hovering state
Immersion and invariance observer-based SMC Control [62]	Providing good results with 20% effectiveness loss in rotors	They were computed in hardware in loop testbed (Simulation) [62]
Maintaining Constant Speed [63]	Proposes to maintain a slow but constant speed to follow planned path	Totally based on simulation whereas the dynamic model considered was also simple and linear
Tilting the rotating axis & varying thrust [64]	It is controlled by tilting variation in thrust	Here less focus was set on controlling the heading angle of big quadrotor

(continued)

Table 3. (*continued*)

Approach	Pros.	Cons.
Fault Control Using PID [65] & BSC [66]	Suggested for emergency landing	Only considered for emergency landing

an adaptive command filtered BS control design [72] which considered all uncertainties like mass, inertia and effectiveness of rotor etc. This seems to be focused to follow the tracking in simulations only. In [73] again an adaptive integral BS control technique has been proposed that presented good rejection to external disturbances but once again ignored the parametric variables.

This same technique has been modified by using integral separated scheme in order to avoid the integration wind up on large tracking error [74]. In addition to this, proposed technique [74] had been regarded as good but hard switching conditions which later distract the role of integral control scheme if the trajectory error computed is greater than a certain threshold value. This technique provided experimental results too. The same technique was modified and provided only results for altitude control whereas there had been high noise rate for attitude results [75]. Model Reference Adaptive Control (MRAC) is also one of the emerging control strategies which is mainly proposed for decentralization. This strategy has been proposed for quadrotor [76] to overcome the uncertainty in model but it could not overcome the uncertainty that appears in either control input or in external noises. Some researchers introduced model identification (MI) based MRAC which is proposed mainly for the attitude stabilization and self-tuning [77]. Mainly the aim of this MI-MRAC technique was to resolve time dependent parameters by incorporating repeated least square estimation including exponentially forgetting principle. This provided the good results in terms of simulation, but no experimental results were presented. Researchers further advanced the MRAC and proposed direct and indirect MRAC technique which claimed to be the robust for parametric uncertainties even for the loss of effectiveness in any one of the rotors of quadrotor. It uses small angle approximation for linearization hence it raises the question for practical implementation [78].

In most of the uncertainties like air wind and gust robust controllers are also proposed with the addition of any nominal controller. The nominal controller is added to take care of trajectory tracking whereas the robust control is introduced to cope up with problems like nonlinear dynamics and coupling etc. Following the same trend, researchers have proposed the linear time invariant control system comprises of Proportional-Derivative with simple compensator [79]. Another advancement had been demonstrated by combining the compensator of 1st order along with quaternion in order to avoid the singularity [80]. The technique was very popular for addressing against all types of disturbances and extended also for 6 degree of freedom (DOF) motion tracking. However, experimental results presented; were limited to tracking a specific trajectory and less focus on stabilizing positions. For disturbances, one may find lots of research contributions related to sliding mode control (SMC). This control technique basically exhibits robustness against any type of disturbances under matching conditions that can be linear combination of positions and velocity errors of the systems. In result of implementing this technique [81] the desired error of state variables is defined by a linear hyperplane hence it provides convergence of such errors towards zero infinity time rate but for bounded disturbances. There are several researchers who proposed SMC for tracking control and attitude even in the presence of system uncertainty such that in [82]. Their research contribution was better comparatively in terms of simulation results only but if one sees their experimental results; there is a huge difference in validation because of the influence of actuator's limited bandwidth and noises [83]. SMC has various benefits but the most common problem with this control design is chattering in its control signals which can be minimized to some extent but not completely [84]. People tried for using second order SMC based analysis for selecting the co-efficient of sliding manifold to tackle highly nonlinear relationship, but this provided not enough asymptotic convergence for aggressive systems like quadrotor where stabilization time is our main concern [85]. In addition to the research of SMC, researchers proposed Terminal Sliding mode control T-SMC design for minimizing nonlinear tracking error [86]. This results the derivation of state variables to sliding plane in short span of time and converge the error dynamics to zero within finite time, yet the chattering problem remained unresolved. The use of block control technique with super twisting SMC is also proposed [88] in which the block control is used to improve the robustness and reducing the chattering problem but did not consider the unmodeled uncertainties of quadrotor like co-efficient of aerodynamics. These results are fine yet chattering appears on overall performance of tracking for real experiments. In order to remove this chattering phenomenon researcher proposed the use of Backstepping Control with Integral SMC [90] this demonstrates for 25% uncertainty and disturbances along with good tracking errors. This tracking error rapidly converges to zero as well hence this approach found to be chattering free approach. Just after the advent of artificial intelligence, researchers are also utilizing the benefits of intelligent algorithm in order to propose intelligent control algorithm. These algorithms basically provide a learning model for tackling the parametric and non-parametric uncertainties too through Robust Adaptive Techniques. Since an adaptive technique is better with approach with modeled and structured uncertainties but poor with unmodeled and non-parametric uncertainties hence adaptive is merged with robust technique. In number of approaches, one may find the technique entitled as robust nonlinear composite adaptive control [92] proposed just for predefined path, but it does not consider the measurement noise and other parametric factors i.e. unknown mass, system inertia, thrust and drag co-efficient etc. Another approach in which one may need no training and may achieve good results under external disturbances and actuator saturation is Adaptive Neural Network (ANN) [92] scheme but this scheme has ignored the measurement of noises in a system.

Since radial form of neural network known as RBFNN; has been used as nonlinear function approximator before hence one may use cerebellar model arithmetic compiler instead of radial neural network [92] in order to get stabilization of quadrotor at hovering state even after the manipulation in payloads. The experimental results were produced on a test bed and due to high weights chattering phenomenon has been generated. For disturbance rejection and to compensate the parametric changes one may use robust integral approach with inner and outer loops with an inclusion of immersion and invariance

(I&I). Reading one of such research works [91] where it contracts the classical adaptive method and does not need linear parameterization. Results generated through this technique were studied to be good however, the use of estimated parameter in feedback control remain limited. The Table 4 summarizes all reviewed works on the uncertainty's problems.

Table 4. Research contributions for Uncertainty Problem

Approach	Method	Uncertainties	Disturbance	Demonstration
Adaptive Strategies	Backstepping Control BSC [69]	–	–	Experimental
	Adaptive BSC [69]	Mass	–	Simulation
	Passivity based Adaptive BSC [70]	Mass	–	Simulation
	Command Filtered BSC [72]	Mass, Inertia & Motor Co-efficients	–	Simulation
	Adaptive Integral BSC [73]	Unmodeled	External	Simulation
	Adaptive BSC + Integral separated Scheme [74]	Mass	External	Simulation & Experimental
	Model Reference Adaptive Control MRAC [76]	–	External	Experimental
	Composite MRAC [77]	Mass and Inertia	–	Simulation
	Composite MRAC [78]	Mass, Inertia & Motor Co-efficients	–	Simulation
Robust Strategies	PD + Robust Compensator [80]	Unmodeled	External	Experimental
	Discrete time SMC [82, 83, 84]	–	External	Simulation
	Second order SMC [85]	–	External	Simulation
	Terminal SMC [86]	–	External	Simulation
	Dynamic TSMC [87]	–	External	Simulation

(*continued*)

Table 4. (*continued*)

Approach	Method	Uncertainties	Disturbance	Demonstration
	Super twisting SMC [88]	–	External	Simulation & Experimental
	SMC + Disturbance Observer [89]	Mass, Inertia & aerodynamics	External	Simulation
	BC + SMC [90]	Mass, Inertia, & aerodynamics	External	Simulation
	BC + SMC + RBFNN [92]	Inertia	External	Simulation
	Learning based Robust Control [90]	Unmodeled	External	Experimental
	Lyapunov Adaptive + Robust Control [90]	Mass & Motor Co-efficients	External	Experimental
	Robust Composite Adaptive Control [92]	Mass & Motor Co-efficients	–	Simulation
	MRAC + RBFNN [92]	Motor Co-efficients	External	Simulation
Robust + Adaptive Strategies	Robust + CMAC [92]	Unmodeled	External	Experimental
	Robust + I&I adaptive control [91]	Unmodeled	External	Experimental

BSC Backstepping Control
MRAC Model Reference Adaptive Control
PD Proportional Derivative
SMC Sliding Mode Control
RBFNN *Radial Basis Function Neural Network*
I & I *Immersion and Inversion*

3   Challenges and Constraints

One of the biggest challenges with respect to dynamic model of quadrotor craft is to acquire its dynamic model considering all unmodeled uncertainties so that the dynamic model can be portrayed like a real-world model for proposed quadrotor craft. Researchers have proposed dynamic model with exact standard uncertainties either or with few changes into consideration. The complete dynamic model can be obtained [89] by considering mass, inertia, motor co-efficients and aerodynamic effect [89] too. Thus, the simulation results for the fixed values can be obtained easily but during the flight mode a quadrotor craft experiences various changes hence these values are continuously changing. Discussing further, the case of ground effect [48], rotor failure [52, 53, 56, 63] and loss of rotor's effectiveness [61, 62] or all of them [63] the dynamic model of proposed quadrotor is also varying with time.

Moreover, taking an example of package drop off case where a quadrotor is dedicated to pick a package and drop it somewhere hence by the change in the mass of package, the dynamics will be surely changed. One can neither sense these values again and again because all the time it will not be possible to collect the data for individual flight. Moreover, after the detailed study it has been observed that there are special control designs for each individual flight mode hence a single generic control design is needed to operate quadrotor into multiple flight modes. After reading the literature, such control algorithms do exist that can tackle multiple flight modes but due to switching scheme as per the behavior all the time it produces high oscillations known as chattering or Zeno phenomenon.

4   Conclusion

Simply there is a serious need of a control scheme that detects the behavior and react accordingly for all of three cases namely variable flight modes, fault tolerance and specially unmodelled uncertainties that may occur instantly in the system during flight. This review concludes the three main problems such that acquiring the exact dynamic model with less assumptions, hybrid control design for multiple flight modes and lastly tackling unmodeled uncertainties. The implementation is suggested for further modification of either manipulating Model Predictive Control MPC [44], adaptive Sliding mode control technique or both using multiple Lyapunov functions MLFs. The proposed hybrid technique can be used with filter design for disturbance rejection capability, measured noise suppression and chattering phenomenon. Furthermore, one may use the estimators and observer techniques to overcome these unmodelled dynamic factors.

Acknowledgement. The author would like to acknowledge Center for Graduate Studies Universiti Teknologi PETRONAS, Malaysia for providing an opportunity of Graduate Assistantship at Department of Electrical and Electronic Engineering. Moreover, the author also acknowledges the support of Global Data, London for sponsoring this publication.

References

1. Emran, B.J., Najjaran, H.: A review of quadrotor: an underactuated mechanical system. Ann. Rev. Control (2018)
2. Jiang, Z.-P.: Controlling underactuated mechanical systems: a review and open problems. Advances in the Theory of Control, Signals and Systems with Physical Modeling, pp. 77–88 (2011)
3. Spong, M.W.: Partial feedback linearization of underactuated mechanical systems. In Proceedings of IEEE/RSJ International Conference on Intelligent Robots and Systems (IROS 1994), vol. 1, pp. 314–321. IEEE (1994)
4. Spong, M.W., Praly, L.: Control of underactuated mechanical systems using switching and saturation. In: Stephen, M.A. (ed.) Control Using Logic-Based Switching. Lecture Notes in Control and Information Sciences, vol. 222, pp. 162–172. Springer, Heidelberg (1997). https://doi.org/10.1007/BFb0036093

5. Liu, Y., Hongnian, Yu.: A survey of underactuated mechanical systems. IET Control Theory Appl. **7**(7), 921–935 (2013)
6. Xin, X., Liu, Y.: Control design and analysis for underactuated robotic systems. Springer, Heidelberg (2014). https://doi.org/10.1007/978-1-4471-6251-3
7. Asif, M., Memon, A.Y., Khan, M.J.: Output feedback control for trajectory tracking of wheeled mobile robot. Intell. Autom. Soft Comput. **22**(1), 75–87 (2016)
8. Mustafa Abro, G.E., Jabeen, B., Manan, A.: Stabilization of non-holonomic 03 DOF hovercraft using robust RST control design. Sukkur IBA J. Emer. Technol. **2**(1), 45–50 (2019)
9. Ali, Z.A., Wang, D., Masroor, S., Loya, M.S.: Attitude and altitude control of trirotor UAV by using adaptive hybrid controller. J. Control Sci. Eng. (2016)
10. Hoffmann, G., Huang, H., Waslander, S., Tomlin, C.: Quadrotor helicopter flight dynamics and control: theory and experiment. In: AIAA Guidance, Navigation and Control Conference and Exhibit, p. 6461 (2007)
11. Puri, A.: A survey of unmanned aerial vehicles (UAV) for traffic surveillance. Department of computer science and engineering, University of South Florida, pp. 1–29 (2005)
12. Gentle, J.E.: Matrix Algebra: Theory. Computations, and Applications in Statistics (2007)
13. Zhang, X., Li, X., Wang, K., Lu, Y.: A survey of modelling and identification of quadrotor robot. In: Abstract and Applied Analysis, vol. 2014. Hindawi (2014)
14. Huang, H., Hoffmann, G.M., Waslander, S.L., Tomlin, C.J.: Aerodynamics and control of autonomous quadrotor helicopters in aggressive maneuvering. In: 2009 IEEE International Conference on Robotics and Automation, pp. 3277–3282. IEEE (2009)
15. Hoffer, N.V., Coopmans, C., Jensen, A.M., Chen, Y.: A survey of small low-cost unmanned aerial vehicle system identification. J. Intell. Rob. Syst. **74**(1–2), 129–145 (2014)
16. Sonntag, D.: A study of quadrotor modeling [M.S.dissertation], Linkopings Universitet, Link¨oping, Sweden (2011)
17. Derafa, L., Madani, T., Benallegue, A.: Dynamic modelling of four rotors helicopter parameters. In: 2006 IEEE International Conference on Industrial Technology, pp. 1834–1839. IEEE (2006)
18. Pounds, P., Mahony, R., Corke, P.: System identification and control of an aerobot drive system. In: Proceedings of the Information, Decision and Control Conference (IDC 2007), pp. 154–159, Adelaide, Australia, February 2007
19. Amir, M.Y., Abbass, V.: Modeling of quadrotor helicopter dynamics. In: 2008 International Conference on Smart Manufacturing Application, pp. 100–105. IEEE (2008)
20. Derafa, L., Madani, T., Benallegue, A.: Dynamic modelling and experimental identification of four rotors helicopter parameters. In: 2006 IEEE International Conference on Industrial Technology, pp. 1834–1839. IEEE (2006)
21. McColl, C., Iyyer, N.: A template for successful development and implementation of an aircraft life tracking program. In: Proceedings of 11th Joint NASA/FAA/DOD Conference on Aging Aircraft (2008)
22. Mettler, B., Tischler, M.B., Kanade, T.: System identification of unmanned helicopter dynamics. In: Annual Forum Proceedings- American Helicopter Society, vol. 2, pp. 1706–1717 (1999)
23. Yuan, W., Katupitiya, J.: A time-domain grey-box system identification procedure for scale model helicopters. In: Proceedings of the 2011 Australasian Conference on Robotics and Automation (2011)
24. Bottasso, C.L., Leonello, D., Maffezzoli, A., Riccardi, F.: A procedure for the identification of the inertial properties of small-size UAVs. In: XX AIDAA Congress, vol. 3 (2009)
25. Bhandari, S., Colgren, R., Lederbogen, P., Kowalchuk, S.: Six-dof dynamic modeling and flight testing of a UAV helicopter. In: AIAA Modeling and Simulation Technologies Conference and Exhibit, p. 6422 (2005)

26. Putro, I.E., Budiyono, A., Yoon, K.-J., Kim, D.H.: Modeling of unmanned small scale rotor-craft based on neural network identification. In: 2008 IEEE International Conference on Robotics and Biomimetics, pp. 1938–1943. IEEE (2009)

27. Garratt, M., Ahmed, B., Pota, H.R.: Platform enhancements and system identification for control of an unmanned helicopter. In: 2006 9th International Conference on Control, Automation, Robotics and Vision, pp. 1–6. IEEE (2006)

28. Lei, X., Yuhu, D.: A linear domain system identification for small unmanned aerial rotorcraft based on adaptive genetic algorithm. J. Bionic Eng. **7**(2), 142–149 (2010)

29. Chowdhary, G., Jategaonkar, R.: Aerodynamic parameter estimation from flight data applying extended and unscented Kalman filter. Aerosp. Sci. Technol. **14**(2), 106–117 (2010)

30. Luo, Y., Chao, H., Di, L., Chen, Y.Q.: Lateral directional fractional order (PI) α control of a small fixed-wing unmanned aerial vehicles: controller designs and flight tests. IET Control Theory Appl. **5**(18), 2156–2167 (2011)

31. Roza, A., Maggiore, M.: A class of position controllers for underactuated VTOL vehicles. IEEE Trans. Autom. Control **59**(9), 2580–2585 (2014)

32. Naldi, R., Furci, M., Sanfelice, R.G., Marconi, L.: Global trajectory tracking for underactuated vtol aerial vehicles using a cascade control paradigm. In: 52nd IEEE Conference on Decision and Control, pp. 4212–4217. IEEE (2013)

33. Naldi, R., Furci, M., Sanfelice, R.G., Marconi, L.: Robust global trajectory tracking for underactuated VTOL aerial vehicles using inner-outer loop control paradigms. IEEE Trans. Autom. Control **62**(1), 97–112 (2016)

34. Naldi, R., Forte, F., Serrani, A., Marconi, L.: Modeling and control of a class of modular aerial robots combining under actuated and fully actuated behavior. IEEE Trans. Control Syst. Technol. **23**(5), 1869–1885 (2015)

35. Das, A., Lewis, F., Subbarao, K.: Backstepping approach for controlling a quadrotor using lagrange form dynamics. J. Intell. Rob. Syst. **56**(1–2), 127–151 (2009)

36. Wei, Y., Li, C., Sun, Y., Ma, G.: Backstepping approach for controlling a quadrotor using Barrier Lyapunov Functions. In: 2017 36th Chinese Control Conference (CCC), pp. 6235–6239. IEEE (2017)

37. Gautam, D., Ha, C.: Control of a quadrotor using a smart self-tuning fuzzy PID controller. Int. J. Adv. Rob. Syst. **10**(11), 380 (2013)

38. Li, Q., Qian, J., Zhu, Z., Bao, X., Helwa, M.K., Schoellig, A.P.: Deep neural networks for improved, impromptu trajectory tracking of quadrotors. In: 2017 IEEE International Conference on Robotics and Automation (ICRA), pp. 5183–5189. IEEE (2017)

39. DeCarlo, R.A., Branicky, M.S., Pettersson, S., Lennartson, B.: Perspectives and results on the stability and stabilizability of hybrid systems. Proc. IEEE **88**(7), 1069–1082 (2000)

40. Branicky, M.S.: Multiple Lyapunov functions and other analysis tools for switched and hybrid systems. IEEE Trans. Autom. Control **43**(4), 475–482 (1998)

41. Nikolakopoulos, G., Alexis, K.: Switching networked attitude control of an unmanned quadrotor. Int. J. Control Autom. Syst. **11**(2), 389–397 (2013)

42. Emran, B.J., Najjaran, H.: Switching control of quadrotor with adaptation mechanism. In: 2016 IEEE International Conference on Systems, Man, and Cybernetics (SMC), pp. 004872–004877. IEEE (2016)

43. Voos, H., Bou-Ammar, H.: Nonlinear tracking and landing controller for quadrotor aerial robots. In: 2010 IEEE International Conference on Control Applications, pp. 2136–2141. IEEE (2010)

44. Cabecinhas, D., Naldi, R., Silvestre, C., Cunha, R., Marconi, L.: Robust landing and sliding maneuver hybrid controller for a quadrotor vehicle. IEEE Trans. Control Syst. Technol. **24**(2), 400–412 (2015)

45. McKinnon, C.D., Schoellig, A.P.: Unscented external force and torque estimation for quadrotors. In: 2016 IEEE/RSJ International Conference on Intelligent Robots and Systems (IROS), pp. 5651–5657. IEEE (2016)
46. Blanke, M., Kinnaert, M., Lunze, J., Staroswiecki, M., Schröder, J.: Diagnosis and Fault-Tolerant Control, vol. 2. Springer, Berlin (2006). https://doi.org/10.1007/978-3-540-35653-0
47. Sobhani-Tehrani, E., Khorasani, K.: Fault Diagnosis of Nonlinear Systems Using a Hybrid Approach, vol. 383. Springer, Cham (2009). https://doi.org/10.1007/978-0-387-92907-1
48. Rabbath, C.A.: Safety and reliability in cooperating unmanned aerial systems. World Scientific (2010)
49. Forte, F., Naldi, R., Serrani, A., Marconi, L.: Control of modular aerial robots: combining under-and fully-actuated behaviors. In: 2012 IEEE 51st IEEE Conference on Decision and Control (CDC), pp. 1160–1165. IEEE (2012)
50. Oung, R., D'Andrea, R.: The distributed flight array: Design, implementation, and analysis of a modular vertical take-off and landing vehicle. Int. J. Robot. Res. 33(3), 375–400 (2014)
51. Giribet, J.I., Sanchez-Pena, R.S., Ghersin, A.S.: Analysis and design of a tilted rotor hexacopter for fault tolerance. IEEE Trans. Aerosp. Electron. Syst. 52(4), 1555–1567 (2016)
52. Saied, M., Lussier, B., Fantoni, I., Francis, C., Shraim, H., Sanahuja, G.: Fault diagnosis and fault-tolerant control strategy for rotor failure in an octorotor. In: 2015 IEEE International Conference on Robotics and Automation (ICRA), pp. 5266–5271. IEEE (2015)
53. Freddi, A., Longhi, S., Monteriù, A.: A diagnostic TO for a class of unmanned vehicles. J. Intell. Rob. Syst. 67(1), 61–73 (2012)
54. Zhaohui, C., Noura, H., Susilo, T.B., Younes, Y.A.: Engineering implementation on fault diagnosis for quadrotors based on nonlinear observer. In: 2013 25th Chinese Control and Decision Conference (CCDC), pp. 2971–2975. IEEE (2013)
55. Cen, Z., Noura, H., Susilo, T.B., Younes, Y.A.: Robust fault diagnosis for quadrotor UAVs using adaptive Thau observer. J. Intell. Robot. Syst. 73(1–4), 573–588 (2014)
56. Ma, L., Zhang, Y.: DUKF-based GTM UAV fault detection and diagnosis with nonlinear and LPV models. In: Proceedings of 2010 IEEE/ASME International Conference on Mechatronic and Embedded Systems and Applications, pp. 375–380. IEEE (2010)
57. Amoozgar, M.H., Chamseddine, A., Zhang, Y.: Experimental test of a two-stage Kalman filter for actuator fault detection and diagnosis of an unmanned quadrotor helicopter. J. Intell. Robot. Syst. 70(1–4), 107–117 (2013)
58. Ranjbaran, M., Khorasani, K.: Fault recovery of an under-actuated quadrotor aerial vehicle. In: 49th IEEE Conference on Decision and Control (CDC), pp. 4385–4392. IEEE (2010)
59. Hao, W., Xian, B.: Nonlinear adaptive fault-tolerant control for a quadrotor UAV based on immersion and invariance methodology. Nonlinear Dyn. 90(4), 2813–2826 (2017)
60. Akhtar, A., Waslander, S.L., Nielsen, C.: Fault tolerant path following for a quadrotor. In: 52nd IEEE Conference on Decision and Control, pp. 847–852. IEEE (2013)
61. Mueller, M.W., D'Andrea, R.: Relaxed hover solutions for multicopters: application to algorithmic redundancy and novel vehicles. Int. J. Robot. Res. 35(8), 873–889 (2016)
62. Lippiello, V., Ruggiero, F., Serra, D.: Emergency landing for a quadrotor in case of a propeller failure: a pid based approach. In: 2014 IEEE International Symposium on Safety, Security, and Rescue Robotics (2014), pp. 1–7. IEEE (2014)
63. Lippiello, V., Ruggiero, F., Serra, D.: Emergency landing for a quadrotor in case of a propeller failure: a backstepping approach. In: 2014 IEEE/RSJ International Conference on Intelligent Robots and Systems, pp. 4782–4788. IEEE (2014)
64. Emran, B.J., Dias, J., Seneviratne, L., Cai, G.: Robust adaptive control design for quadcopter payload add and drop applications. In: 2015 34th Chinese Control Conference (CCC), pp. 3252–3257. IEEE (2015)

65. Min, B.-C., Hong, J.-H., Matson: Adaptive robust control (ARC) for an altitude control of a quadrotor type UAV carrying an unknown payload. In: 2011 11th International Conference on Control, Automation and Systems, pp. 1147–1151. IEEE (2011)

66. Choi, Y.-C., Ahn, H.-S.: Nonlinear control of quadrotor for point tracking: actual implementation and experimental tests. IEEE/ASME Trans. Mechatron. **20**(3), 1179–1192 (2014)

67. Huang, M., Xian, B., Diao, C., Yang, K., Feng, Y.: Adaptive tracking control of underactuated quadrotor unmanned aerial vehicles via backstepping. In: Proceedings of the 2010 American Control Conference, pp. 2076–2081. IEEE (2010)

68. Ha, C.S., Zuo, Z., Choi, F.B., Lee, D.: Passivity-based adaptive backstepping control of quadrotor-type UAVs. Robot. Auton. Syst. **62**(9), 1305–1315 (2014)

69. Choi, I.-H., Bang, H.-C.: Adaptive command filtered backstepping tracking controller design for quadrotor unmanned aerial vehicle. Proc. Inst. Mech. Eng. Part G: J. Aerospace Eng. **226**(5), 483–497 (2012)

70. Younes, Y.A., Drak, A., Noura, H., Rabhi, A., Hajjaji, A.E.: Quadrotor position Control using cascaded adaptive integral backstepping controllers. In: Applied Mechanics and Materials, vol. 565, pp. 98–106. Trans Tech Publications Ltd. (2014)

71. Fang, Zheng, and Weinan Gao. "Adaptive integral backstepping control of a micro-quadrotor." In 2011 2nd International Conference on Intelligent Control and Information Processing, vol. 2, pp. 910–915. IEEE, 2011

72. Fang, Z., Gao, W.: Adaptive backstepping control of an indoor micro-quadrotor. Res. J. Appl. Sci. Eng. Technol. **4**(21), 4216–4226 (2012)

73. Mohammadi, M., Shahri, A.M.: Adaptive nonlinear stabilization control for a quadrotor UAV: theory, simulation and experimentation. J. Intell. Robot. Syst. **72**(1), 105–122 (2013)

74. Schreier, M.: Modeling and adaptive control of a quadrotor. In: 2012 IEEE International Conference on Mechatronics and Automation, pp. 383–390. IEEE (2012)

75. Dydek, Z.T., Annaswamy, A.M., Lavretsky, E.: Adaptive control of quadrotor UAVs: a design trade study with flight evaluations. IEEE Trans. Control Syst. Technol. **21**(4), 1400–1406 (2012)

76. Liu, H., Bai, Y., Geng, L., Zhong, Y.: Robust attitude control of uncertain quadrotors. IET Control Theory Appl. **7**(11), 1583–1589 (2013)

77. Liu, H., Xi, J., Zhong, Y.: Robust motion control of quadrotors. J. Franklin Inst. **351**(12), 5494–5510 (2014)

78. Shtessel, Y., Edwards, C., Fridman, L., Levant, A.: Sliding Mode Control and Observation. Springer, New York (2014). https://doi.org/10.1007/978-0-8176-4893-0

79. Lee, D., Jin Kim, H., Sastry, S., Feedback linearization vs. adaptive sliding mode control for a quadrotor helicopter. Int. J. Control Autom. Syst. **7**(3), 419–428 (2009)

80. Xiong, J.-J., Zhang, G.: Discrete-time sliding mode control for a quadrotor UAV. Optik **127**(8), 3718–3722 (2016)

81. Bartolini, G., Ferrara, A., Usai, E.: Chattering avoidance by second-order sliding mode control. IEEE Trans. Autom. Control **43**(2), 241–246 (1998)

82. Zheng, E.-H., Xiong, J.-J., Luo, J.-L.: Second order sliding mode control for a quadrotor UAV. ISA Trans. **53**(4), 1350–1356 (2014)

83. Xiong, J.-J., Zheng, E.-H.: Position and attitude tracking control for a quadrotor UAV. ISA Trans. **53**(3), 725–731 (2014)

84. Xiong, J.-J., Zhang, G.-B.: Global fast dynamic terminal sliding mode control for a quadrotor UAV. ISA Trans. **66**, 233–240 (2017)

85. Luque-Vega, L., Castillo-Toledo, B., Loukianov, A.G.: Robust block second order sliding mode control for a quadrotor. J. Franklin Institute **349**(2), 719–739 (2012)

86. Besnard, L., Shtessel, Y.B., Landrum, B.: Quadrotor vehicle control via sliding mode controller driven by sliding mode disturbance observer. J. Franklin Inst. **349**(2), 658–684 (2012)

87. Ramirez-Rodriguez, H., Parra-Vega, V., Sanchez-Orta, A., Garcia-Salazar, O.: Robust back-stepping control based on integral sliding modes for tracking of quadrotors. J. Intell. Rob. Syst. **73**(1–4), 51–66 (2014)
88. Peng, C., Bai, Y., Gong, X., Gao, Q., Zhao, C., Tian, Y.: Modeling and robust backstepping sliding mode control with Adaptive RBFNN for a novel coaxial eight-rotor UAV. IEEE/CAA J. Autom. Sin. **2**(1), 56–64 (2015)
89. Berkenkamp, F., Schoellig, A.P.: Safe and robust learning control with Gaussian processes. In: 2015 European Control Conference (ECC), pp. 2496–2501. IEEE (2015)
90. Lee, T.: robust adaptive attitude tracking on formula not shown with an application to a quadrotor UAV. IEEE Trans. Control Syst. Technol. **21**(5), 1924–1930 (2013)
91. Emran, B.J., Yesildirek, A.: Robust nonlinear composite adaptive control of quadrotor. Int. J. Dig. Inf. Wirel. Commun. **4**(2), 213–225 (2014)
92. Zhao, B., Xian, B., Zhang, Y., Zhang, X.: Nonlinear robust sliding mode control of a quadrotor unmanned aerial vehicle based on immersion and invariance method. Int. J. Robust Nonlinear Control **25**(18), 3714–3731 (2015)

A Review of Underwater Acoustic, Electromagnetic and Optical Communications

Maaruf Ali[1](✉) ⓘ and Mahdi H. Miraz[2] ⓘ

[1] Epoka University, Rruga Tiranë-Rinas, Km 12, 1032 Vorë, Tiranë, Albania
mali@epoka.edu.al
[2] The Chinese University of Hong Kong, Shatin, NT, Hong Kong SAR
m.miraz@ieee.org

Abstract. This is a review paper that covers the various technologies used for underwater communications. Research in this domain was initially restricted and in the defence sector but is now gaining much civilian exposure and applications. Communication was mainly with submarines using extremely low and very low electromagnetic frequencies. The review covers communication using acoustic waves, electromagnetic waves, combining acoustic and radio transmission and finally optical transmission. The benefits of various technologies are summarized, including hybrid techniques. For short distance communications, for example between Scuba divers and the ship, optical frequencies are feasible. For long distance undersea communications, very low electromagnetic frequencies are still the most established way to maintain contact, whilst the vessel remain submerged.

Keywords: Underwater communication · Acoustic communication · Extremely low frequency · ELF · Very low frequency · VLF · Optical communications

1 Underwater Communications

1.1 Introduction

As human exploration moved across the land and then into space, it may come as a surprise that the least explored domain is underwater and the subsea land. The need to communicate across this challenging medium presents many problems that need to be addressed. The main factor being the propagation characteristics of water with its very high attenuation per kilometre (km), whatever mode of transmission is used, be it light, sound or electromagnetic waves. This paper presents a brief survey of the techniques utilised to overcome these challenges of reliably conveying information as efficiently as possible with the least amount of distortion and energy expended.

The paper is structured as follows: Sect. 2 covers the propagation characteristics in water for acoustic, electromagnetic and light as the carrier for the information to be transmitted. Section 3 looks at Acoustic Transmission systems. Section 4 covers EM wave underwater transmission systems. Section 5 discusses the more modern underwater optical communication systems. Section 6 is a discussion covering all the techniques, followed by Sect. 7 being the concluding section.

© ICST Institute for Computer Sciences, Social Informatics and Telecommunications Engineering 2020
Published by Springer Nature Switzerland AG 2020. All Rights Reserved
M. H. Miraz et al. (Eds.): iCETiC 2020, LNICST 332, pp. 86–97, 2020.
https://doi.org/10.1007/978-3-030-60036-5_6

2   Propagation Characteristics of Water

Section Two introduces the propagation transfer characteristics of acoustic waves, EM Waves and Optical Waves.

2.1   Sound (Acoustic) Wave Propagation Transfer Characteristics Curves

An extensive study on the frequency of sound (acoustic) waves related to frequency in different oceans were extensively carried out by Ainslie and McColm in 1998 [1]. The results of their investigation are given in Fig. 1, below.

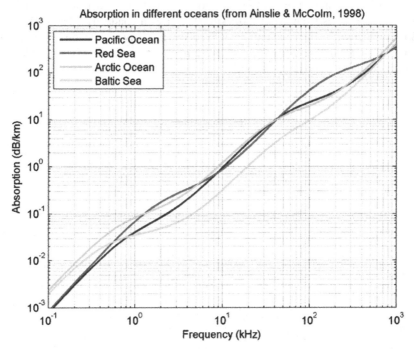

Fig. 1. Sound absorption versus audio frequency in different oceans (http://resource.npl.co.uk/ acoustics/techguides/seaabsorption/ainslie_ocean.gif, last accessed 2020/7/19.), adapted from [1].

Figure 1, clearly shows the limited feasible frequency range that can be practically utilised for acoustic wave underwater propagation. Any frequency over 1 kHz will experience attenuation of the order of >1,000 dB/km. The plot also shows that infra-sound from 10 Hz and below suffer attenuation of 1 dB/km and less with decreasing frequency. Three problems exist here: the first being the generation of the these frequencies with sufficient amplitude (energy); secondly the transducer to generate such low acoustic frequencies; thirdly the extremely narrow bandwidth of using such low frequencies mean the bitrate will be very low, of the order of bits per second. The attenuation is so severe, that it is worse than what is encountered with terrestrial mobile communications, satellite communications links and in fact deep space interplanetary links. A frequency of 100 Hz can be utilized if sufficient power is used to overcome the attenuation in order to cover the required range. The plot also shows that the attenuation is dependent on the geographic ocean area. For the Baltic Ocean, using an acoustic wave with a frequency of 100 Hz will experience an attenuation of 100 dB over a distance of only 10 km.

2.2 EM Wave Propagation Transfer Characteristics Curve

Electromagnetic waves suffer from a very high rate of attenuation when travelling through water. As can be seen in Fig. 2, below, for an EM frequency of 100 Hz, the attenuation rate varies from about 2 dB/km (0.0001 S/m conductivity) to 600 dB/km (10 S/m conductivity). The conductivity of the ocean lies between the top two lines. The plot thus indicates that submarines must utilise frequencies of tens of Hertz or less for long distance undersea communication.

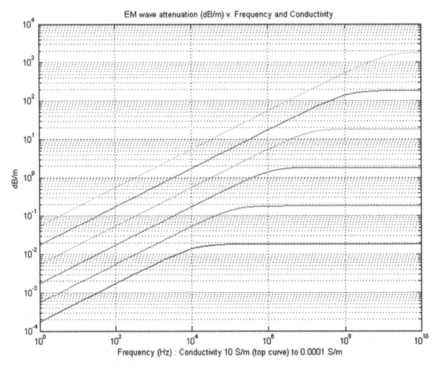

Fig. 2. EM wave attenuation versus EM frequency and conductivity [2]

Figure 3, below shows the plot of attenuation in dB/m against the frequency in Hertz from 10 kHz to 1 GHz. Note the logarithmic scale for both axes and that the attenuation is expressed per metre and not kilometre. As an example, at a frequency of 5 MHz in seawater, an attenuation rate of over 100 dB/m is experienced. Figure 3 also shows the severe attenuation of 8 dB per metre in freshwater.

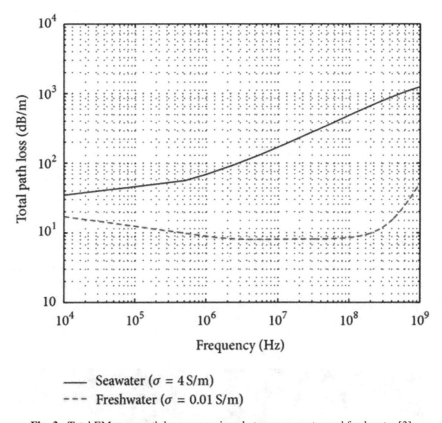

— Seawater ($\sigma = 4$ S/m)
- - - Freshwater ($\sigma = 0.01$ S/m)

Fig. 3. Total EM wave path loss comparison between seawater and freshwater [3].

The problem of attenuation of underwater radio waves also increases with the depth of the water. This is shown in Fig. 4, below. For a frequency of 10 MHz, going from a depth of 0.5 m to 5 m underwater results in a path loss increase of 700 dB/m. It should be noted that submarines often operate at depths of 200 m or more.

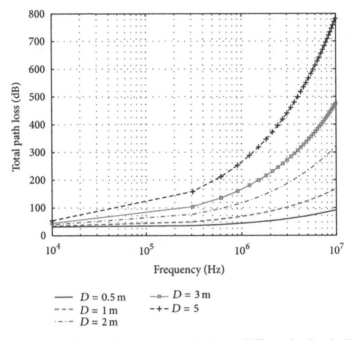

Fig. 4. Total Path Loss with Frequency Variations at Different Sea Depths [3].

The increase in attenuation of EM waves in water is also positively related to the increase in salinity and conductivity of the ocean. As the level of salinity increases, so does the level of EM wave attenuation. Figure 5 shows the level of salinity of the world's oceans.

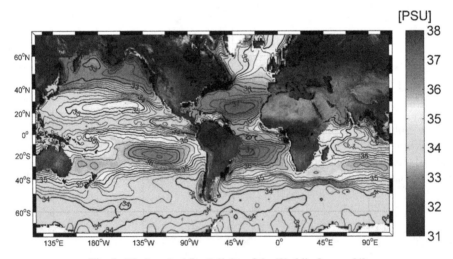

Fig. 5. The Level of Sea Salinity of the World's Oceans [4].

Similarly, as the level of conductivity increases, so does the level of EM wave attenuation. Figure 6 shows the conductivity variation of the world's oceans.

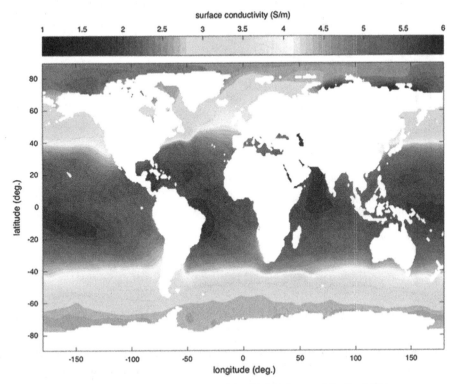

Fig. 6. Electrical Conductivity of the Global Ocean of the Earth [5].

As can be seen from Figs. 5 and 6, the Baltic Ocean has one of the lowest salinity and conductivity and hence it also has one of the lowest levels of EM wave attenuation. The salinity and conductivity are not static and varies throughout the seasons, temperature, depth and other parameters. Knowing these seasonal fluctuations may help better plan the technologies to be employed and deployed for underwater communications. These will include the power level to be used for transmission and the calculated range achievable considering ocean noise due to shipping, the migration of whales and other sea life.

2.3 Light (Optical) Wave Transfer Characteristics Curve

Light absorbance in water also suffers from extreme attenuation when compared to propagation through air. From the results, neither choosing ultraviolet spectral frequencies nor infrared optical frequencies offer any advantage in penetrating through water. Blue and violet light suffers from the least absorption, penetrating to a sea depth of 300 m as shown in Fig. 7, below.

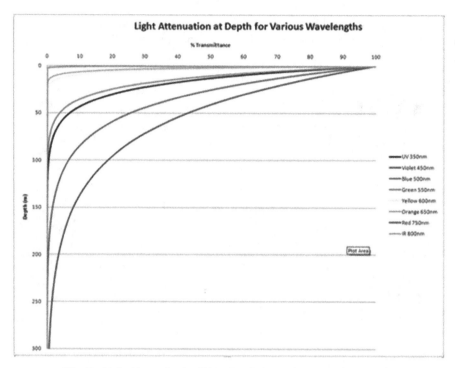

Fig. 7. Light Absorption by Water Depth for Various Wavelengths [6].

Water also presents significant short-range scattering that makes using laser point-to-point links very limited [7]. However, a data rate of 1 gigabit per second has been reported for a laser link of 15 m [7] underwater.

3 Acoustic Transmission

Acoustic transmission uses hydrophones to detect underwater soundwaves. Hydrophones specifically designed may also be used to generate the soundwaves. Sound travels faster in water than in the air. Sound waves also exert greater pressure upon the transducer. Due to the noisy and severe multipath inducing environment underwater [7], orthogonal frequency division multiplexing (OFDM) is preferred [8] over the other traditional modulation schemes for conveying soundwaves underwater. An array of hydrophones may also be set-up as an underwater array to help combat multi-path effects and obtain a greater signal-to-noise ratio over a longer range. "JANUS" [8, 9], is the NATO protocol for acoustic underwater transmission that was approved in 2017. This scheme uses 900 Hz and 60 kHz to communicate up 28 km away [8]. The JANUS protocol may also be utilised with various IoT (Internet of Things) [10] devices to enable IoT M2M (machine-to-machine) [11] communication at the fastest possible data rate.

4 Electromagnetic Wave Underwater Transmission

ELF and SLF transmissions use long pseudo-random sequences with error correcting codes for relaying information to the submarine to often change to a different mode of communications frequency. VLF transmissions also operate in a similar manner but achieving a higher bitrate of transmission. They all employ a trailing wire from the submarine to receive the radio signal transmitted by the base. ELF, SLF and VLF are all receive only mode by the submarine. The submarine needs to rise to a shallower depth to use higher frequencies. They may even employ an antenna to poke through the sea surface for communicating at higher frequencies, higher bitrates and for establishing satellite links. Table 1 summarizes the EM bands used for submarine communications.

Table 1. EM Bands used in submarine communications.

Band	Frequency	Penetration	Bitrate (/s)
ELF (Extremely Low Frequency	3 Hz–30 Hz	100 s of m	A few characters
SLF (Super Low Frequency)	30 Hz–300 Hz	100 s of m	A few characters
VLF (Very Low Frequency)	3 kHz–30 kHz	10–20 m	300 bits

Hybrid Systems – Combining Acoustic and EM Waves (Radio)

Combining different technologies may be employed to continue the communication chain from the submarine through the water to the air and into space. One such technique is to use acoustic waves emitted by the submarine to vibrate the surface of the sea and then use high resolution surface scanning radar from an airborne vehicle or drone to convert these vibrations into a modulated radio frequency. This technique is, however, prone to catastrophic failure in turbulent and choppy sea conditions.

5 Optical Underwater Communication

The range offered by laser based optical communications is often not beyond ten metres in the sea [12]. Thus they are only useful for communicating for surface skimming submarines needing to communicate with surface buoys to be used as a relay link [13]. Scuba divers may also use optical links if they are not diving beyond ten metres from the surface. Using blue-green laser to implement a 100–150 Mbit/s optical link in water achieved these distances as shown in Table 2 [14], below. [15] reported a distance of 20 m at a bitrate of 100 Mbps.

Table 2. Transmission distances in four types of simulated seawater [14].

Water type	Extreme distance (m)	Bit Error Rates (BERs)
Tap Water	16	2.2×10^{-4}
Clear Seawater	4.8	2.2×10^{-4}
Coastal Seawater	3.2	1.7×10^{-5}
Turbid Seawater	1.6	0.0×10^{-12}

6 Discussion

The properties of four different underwater transmission media are shown in Table 3 below. The choice depends on the intended range of operation primarily. For long distance communications and if the submarine has to remain submerged, then acoustic transmission must be used. For short distance communication then EM waves may be employed. For very short-range communication of 50 m or less and for high data rates then optical communication may be used. However, recent research suggests that magneto-inductive coupling offers a range of 100 m at a bit rate of megabits per second with low latency [17].

Table 3. A comparison between different underwater transmission media [3, 16–18].

Parameters	Magneto Inductive (MI) coupling [17]	EM waves	Acoustic waves	Optical waves
Frequency band	500 Hz and 2.5 kHz	30 Hz–300 Hz	10 Hz–15 kHz	10^{12} Hz–10^{15} Hz
Required transmitted power (W)	Few W	Few mW to 100 s of W	Tens of W	Few W
Antenna size [18]	~0.2 m	~0.5 m	0.1 m	0.1 m
Attenuation [18]	7 dB/m (500 Hz) 10 dB/m (2.5 kHz)	3.5–5 dB/m	0.1-4 dB/m	0.39 dB/m (ocean) 11 dB/m (turbid)
Propagation Speed (m/s)	Unreported assume same as EM	High ~2.255×10^8	Very Slow ~ 1,500	Very high ~2.255×10^8
Delay	Moderate	Moderate	High	Low

(continued)

Table 3. (*continued*)

Parameters	Magneto Inductive (MI) coupling [17]	EM waves	Acoustic waves	Optical waves
Line of sight (LOS)	LOS and non-LOS	LOS and non-LOS	LOS and non-LOS	LOS only
Environmental impact	Minimal	Minimal	High	High
Achievable data rates	High (~Mbps)	High (~Mbps)	Very Low (~ Kbps)	Very high (~Gbps)
Network coverage	Short range – 10–100 m	Short range - 10 m	Very Long Range - kms	Typically very short range – 10–100 m
Impact on marine life	Not known	Not known	Negative	Not Known
Performance parameter	Conductivity as a dependency	Conductivity and permittivity	Temperature, Salinity and Pressure	Absorption, scattering, turbidity and organic matter

The impact of the environment in Table 3, includes the sea ambient noise, turbidity, temperature changes, salinity, pressure, depth and the environment geometry. More specifically for [17]: MI (conductivity); EM (conductivity, multipath); Optical (light scattering, ambient light noise); Acoustic (Doppler, multipath, ambient sound, salinity, temperature and pressure).

An extensive survey of optical hybrid systems covering terrestrial indoor, outdoor and underwater scenarios is given in [18].

7   Conclusions

Acoustic transmission is still the preferred mode for long distance communications for undersea vehicles despite the low bitrate. If the submarine can rise to a shallower depth than a link may be established to a surface repeater to convey the submarine signal via terrestrial radio or satellite communications. Underwater communications is still being researched being limited by the physical properties of wave propagation in water, whether acoustic, optical or electromagnetic. A promising technology after acoustic transmission is magneto-inductive coupling offering a range of 100 m with a bitrate of megabits per second and low latency.

References

1. Ainslie, M.A., McColm, J.G.: A simplified formula for viscous and chemical absorption in sea water. J. Acoust. Soc. Ame. **103**(3), 1671–1672 (1998). https://doi.org/10.1121/1.421258, https://asa.scitation.org/doi/10.1121/1.421258
2. https://qph.fs.quoracdn.net/main-qimg-0d37099e3e0534fd4b516e3f2bede31a. Accessed 09 Aug 2020
3. Hattab, G., El-Tarhuni, M., Al-Ali, M., Joudeh, T., Qaddoumi, N.: An underwater wireless sensor network with realistic radio frequency path loss model. Int. J. Distrib. Sens. Netw. **9**(3), 1–9 (2013). https://doi.org/10.1155/2013/508708
4. http://www.salinityremotesensing.ifremer.fr/_/rsrc/1467884561066/sea-surface-salinity/salinity-distribution-at-the-ocean-surface/annual_clim.jpg?height=1641&width=3015. Accessed 09 Aug 2020
5. https://media.springernature.com/lw785/springer-static/image/art%3A10.1186%2Fs40623-017-0739-7/MediaObjects/40623_2017_739_Figa_HTML.gif. Accessed 09 Aug 2020
6. https://4.bp.blogspot.com/_klNpOBDR6nI/TL8BUHf5meI/AAAAAAAAAAk/RrV0Ch4kbQ0/s1600/Light+attenuation+cw+pic.bmp. Accessed 09 Aug 2020
7. Mullen, L.: Optical propagation in the underwater environment. In: Proceedings of the SPIE 7324, Atmospheric Propagation VI, 732409, 2 May 2009. https://doi.org/10.1117/12.820205
8. Wikipedia. Underwater acoustic communication. https://en.wikipedia.org/wiki/Underwater_acoustic_communication. Accessed 11 Aug 2020
9. Mitchell, R.: Nato Adopts New Protocol Standard for Underwater Communications. July 18 2017. https://www.allaboutcircuits.com/news/janus-nato-new-protocol-standard-underwater-communications/. Accessed 11 Aug 2020
10. Miraz, M.H., Ali, M., Excell, P.S., Picking, R.: Internet of nano-things, things and everything: future growth trends. Fut. Internet **10**, 68 (2018). https://www.mdpi.com/1999-5903/10/8/68. Accessed 11 Aug 2020
11. Benattia, A., Ali, M.: Convergence of technologies in the M2M space. In: IEEE Applied Electronics 2008 International Conference, The Department of Applied Electronics and Telecommunications, University of West Bohemia, Pilsen, Czech Republic, 10–11 September 2008, pp. 9–12. ISBN 987-80-7043-654-7
12. Shaw, A., Al-Shamma'a, A. I., Wylie, S. R., Toal, D.: Experimental investigations of electromagnetic wave propagation in seawater. In: Proceedings of the 36th European Microwave Conference, Manchester, UK, pp. 572–575 (2006). https://doi.org/10.1109/eumc.2006.281456
13. Scholz, T.: Laser based underwater communication experiments in the Baltic Sea. In: 2018 Fourth Underwater Communications and Networking Conference (UComms), Lerici, 2018, pp. 1–3 (2018). https://doi.org/10.1109/ucomms.2018.8493174
14. Li, Y., Yin, H., Ji, X., Wu, B.: Design and implementation of underwater wireless optical communication system with high-speed and full-duplex using blue/green light. In: 2018 10th International Conference on Communication Software and Networks (ICCSN), Chengdu, pp. 99–103 (2018). https://doi.org/10.1109/iccsn.2018.8488232
15. Zhou, Z., Yin, H., Yao, Y.: Wireless optical communication performance simulation and full-duplex communication experimental system with different seawater environment. In: 2019 IEEE International Conference on Signal Processing, Communications and Computing (ICSPCC), Dalian, China, pp. 1–4 (2019). https://doi.org/10.1109/icspcc46631.2019.8960905
16. Aravind, J.V., Kumar, S., Prince, S.: Mathematical modelling of underwater wireless optical channel. In: 2018 International Conference on Communication and Signal Processing (ICCSP), Chennai, pp. 0776–0780 (2018). https://doi.org/10.1109/iccsp.2018.8524194

17. Jouhari, M., Ibrahimi, K., Tembine, H., Ben-Othman, J.: Underwater wireless sensor networks: a survey on enabling technologies, localization protocols, and internet of underwater things. IEEE Access **7**, 96879–96899 (2019). https://doi.org/10.1109/access.2019.2928876
18. Chowdhury, M.Z., Hasan, M.K., Shahjalal, M., Hossan, M. T., Jang, Y.M.: Optical wireless hybrid networks: trends, opportunities, challenges, and research directions. IEEE Commun. Surv. Tutor. **22**(2), 930–966. Secondquarter 2020. https://doi.org/10.1109/comst.2020.2966855

Optically Inspired Cryptography and Cryptanalysis: A Survey and Research Directions

Jinfeng Li[1,2]([⊠]) (iD)

[1] University of Southampton, Southampton SO17 1BJ, UK
jinfeng.li@soton.ac.uk
[2] Imperial College London, London SW7 2AZ, UK
jinfeng.li@imperial.ac.uk

Abstract. Keeping images safe and secure in data transmission or storage by optical cryptography has emerged as a revolutionary technology to meet the challenge posed by the evolving cyber threat landscape. This paper reviews the states-of-the-arts optical cryptography and cryptanalysis techniques with a special focus on different optical encryption technologies and their limitations. Specifically, security gaps in the classic Double Random Phase Encoding approach and its variants are identified. Case studies into vulnerable attacking scenarios are conducted for cryptanalysis purposes. Perspectives on the future directions of optically inspired cryptology research are given accordingly.

Keywords: Cryptanalysis · Cryptography · Double Random Phase Encoding · Optical cryptanalysis · Optical cryptography · Optical encryption

1 Evolution of Optical Cryptographic Techniques

There are two closely related research branches in cryptology, i.e. cryptography and cryptanalysis. Cryptography is tasked with creating secure cryptosystems by converting plaintext (e.g. original image in this work) into the ciphertext (i.e. encrypted image in this work), and then reversing the process by recovering the plaintext from the ciphertext through decryption. On the contrary, cryptanalysis aims to attack such cryptosystems by spotting the systems' vulnerabilities [1]. For instance, the goal of a cryptanalyst is to discover powerful methods for obtaining the original image or the key function. A Yin-Yang cosmological concept [2] as illustrated in Fig. 1 can be used to characterise the interrelationship between cryptography and cryptanalysis, i.e. they are inseparable and contradictory opposites. Like two sides of the same coin, they are mutually supported and complementary, i.e. given the cryptanalysis breaches a cryptosystem, cryptographers will be motivated to rebuild a more secure cryptosystem. Historically from the Kerckhoffs' Principle [3], the security of the encryption should rely purely on the key, instead of any secret encryption algorithms. Following this, diverse technologies on manipulating the keys have emerged, allowing the authentic parties to exchange information without breaching the data integrity, confidentiality, and authenticity.

© ICST Institute for Computer Sciences, Social Informatics and Telecommunications Engineering 2020
Published by Springer Nature Switzerland AG 2020. All Rights Reserved
M. H. Miraz et al. (Eds.): iCETiC 2020, LNICST 332, pp. 98–110, 2020.
https://doi.org/10.1007/978-3-030-60036-5_7

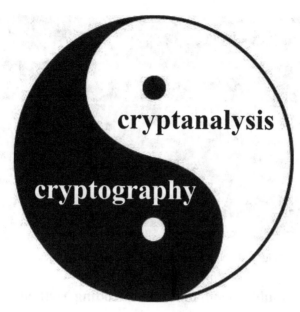

Fig. 1. The analogy of cryptography and cryptanalysis to the Yin-Yang cosmological concept.

In particular, optical properties can be harnessed to encrypt and decrypt image information, hence unlocking a myriad of game-changing applications targeting the mitigation of unauthorised use of image data. Optical encryption is characterised with many degrees of freedom due to the higher dimensional data, including amplitude, phase, wavelength, and polarisation. The optical encryption encompasses non-linear transformations, which are naturally parallel processes with high bandwidths. The decryption key size can be increased without affecting the decode speed.

A high-level timeline of various optical cryptographic techniques is depicted in Fig. 2 below. Since the pioneering development of Double Random Phase Encoding (DRPE) [4], tremendous research and development interest in the DRPE-related variations and optimisations have emerged over the last two decades. Specifically, DRPE, multifactor optical encryption and authentication (MOEA), and asymmetric encryption are surveyed in this work, with their main weaknesses explored by cryptoanalysis that informs the future research direction of the optical cryptography.

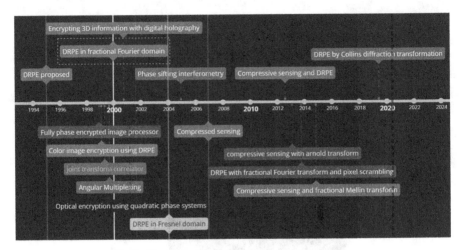

Fig. 2. Evolution of optical cryptographic methods.

2 Review of Double Random Phase Encoding Method

Double Random Phase Encoding (DRPE) represents a hardware approach to encrypt images optically, with an advantage of encrypting the image before converting it into digital data, which is arguably more secure than digitally capturing the image followed by encryption, as the original plaintext data is never recorded [4]. Two random phase masks (statistically independent) are used, with the second one of them serving as the key (as explained in the following subsections).

2.1 DRPE Encryption

Assuming the originally unencrypted image prior to encryption is denoted as $o(x, y)$, and the image encrypted is represented by $e(x, y)$, the process of the encryption can be described mathematically in Eq. (1) by 2D fast Fourier transform ($\mathcal{F}$) and 2D inverse Fourier transform ($\mathcal{F}^{-1}$), respectively. Accordingly, Fig. 3 below depicts the two random phase-only masks (keys), with the left one (in light blue) positioned in the input image plane (unencrypted), and the right one (in navy blue) arranged in the Fourier domain.

$$e(x, y) = \mathcal{F}^{-1}\left(\mathcal{F}\left(o(x, y)e^{i2\pi \phi(x,y)}\right)\right)e^{i2\pi \varphi(u,v)} \tag{1}$$

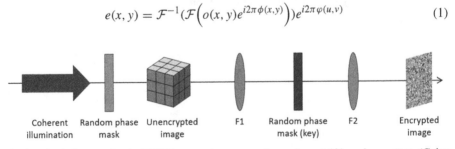

Fig. 3. Block diagram for the DRPE encryption process in a coherent 4f imaging system. (Color figure online)

The first random phase mask (light blue in Fig. 3) is not the key for encryption, but for spreading the image in the frequency domain. In another word, the first random phase mask makes the second random phase key (navy blue in Fig. 3) more effective. The second mask functions as the key for encryption in this setup. The optical transforms in this system are linear in nature, which can be numerically simulated by fast Fourier transforms. With the image encoded by the random phase, the resulting image is encrypted into a stationary white noise with a complex amplitude.

2.2 DRPE Decryption

As opposite to the encryption mentioned above, decryption is a process recovering of the original image $o(x, y)$ from the encrypted image $e(x, y)$, which can be mathematically expressed by Eq. (2) below.

$$o(x, y) = \mathcal{F}^{-1}\left(\mathcal{F}\left(e(x, y)e^{-i2\pi\varphi(u,v)}\right)\right)e^{-i2\pi\phi(u,v)} \tag{2}$$

The mechanism can be represented graphically by Fig. 4 below, where the random phase mask (key) alters the phase information for the conjugate of the encrypted image, and the Fourier transform recreates the original image's amplitude. Parameters of the hardware (such as the focal lengths and distances) should be adjusted accordingly.

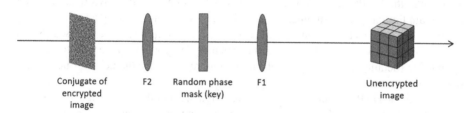

Fig. 4. Block diagram for the DRPE decryption process in a coherent 4f imaging system.

Based on this, an experimental demonstration of the image encryption and decryption by the DRPE is shown in Fig. 5 below for a picture of Quick Response (QR) code [5]. The original binary data picture (left) exhibits 32×32 pixels. With two diffusers serving as random phase masks, the encrypted image (middle) noise-like is obtained. The reconstructed image (right) is recovered using the same key.

Fig. 5. Demonstrating the encryption and decryption for a Quick Response (QR) code picture.

Apart from this, a wider range of other forward-thinking applications can be envisaged, including secure sensing as well as biometric security [6], such as encoding the retina and face information. Accordingly, it can also be used to verify the sensing device as well as the biometric data, e.g. for verification in the retinal scanning, facial recognition, and fingerprint verification systems [7].

2.3 Limitations on Linearity and Speckles

Security of the DRPE inspired optical cryptography is under active investigations. The three main limitations are summarised, i.e. linearity, coherence, and speckles.

First, the intrinsically linear optical processes are susceptible to be reversed [8], as well as the phase retrieval [9] attacks. Attackers may decrypt any image with some prior knowledge (detailed in the cryptoanalysis section later), hence the need for non-linear optical hash transforms.

Second, the DRPE system requires coherent lights. Modelling as an algebraic system may allow incoherent light. Third, one of the major technical hurdles for the current optical encoding is the speckle [10] (a common issue inherently exists in the coherent techniques). The DRPE system with a coherent light is vulnerable to speckles in the reconstructed image. To reduce the residual speckle noise in the optical encryption, metadata is required in addition to the encoded image. [8] proposed a data container approach by encoding the image as QR code. This speckle-resistant approach enables dynamic content to be packaged in a single container to be encrypted.

3 Review of DRPE Extensions

As shown from the aforementioned timeline (Fig. 2) that in addition to the classic Fourier domain, alternative transforms are possible in diverse processing domains, such as Fresnel [11] and Fractional Fourier [12], etc., with new security keys added to enhance the overall security level. Furthermore, integral imaging [13] allows encryption of 3D information, while compressive imaging [14] with post-decryption image processing introduces geometrical recovery errors. Illumination-based implementations by photon counting [15] reduce the illumination brightness to make the unencrypted image less legible, thus enhancing the defense-in-depth concept.

Digital holographic DRPE captures the phase and amplitude of a DRPE encrypted image using holography and a charge-coupled device (CCD) camera, converting phase and amplitude data to digital information. This method is limited by the pixel size and number. The sequential phase shift changes the random phase mask to eliminate conjugate images and DC components. For a single recording phase shift, a reference wave is spatially multiplexed with a phase shift as shown in Fig. 6 below. The future of the phase-shifting [16–22] digital holographic DRPE is arguably limited by the pixel size and the sensor resolution (the sensor with each pixel is capable of sensing the amplitude, phase, polarisation, and wavelength).

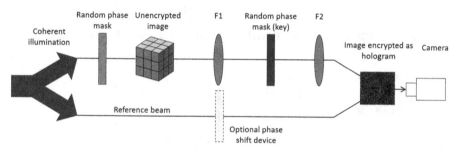

Fig. 6. Block diagram of digital holographic DRPE.

4 Review of Multifactor Optical Encryption and Authentication

As distinct from the sequential encryption methods discussed above, the multifactor optical encryption and authentication (MOEA) originated in 2016 [8] is able to simultaneously authenticate up to four factors, which are optically combined and encrypted into a single ID code, with an optical correlator employed to match the factors to the ID tag. This can be applied to a parcels delivery case as shown in Fig. 7 below using a single ID code to enable the simultaneous verification of a matrix of information. The block diagram for an optical processor for MOEA is illustrated in Fig. 8 below.

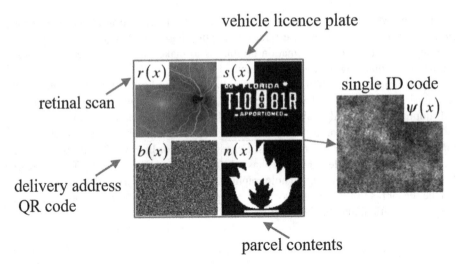

Fig. 7. MOEA with a single ID code produced applied to parcels delivery [8].

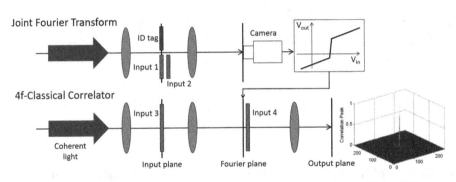

Fig. 8. MOEA optical processor setup (left) and auto-correlation peak (right) [23].

Four methods are being envisaged to improve the MOEA implementations. The first strategy lies in the non-linear step in correlator with more robust alignment, yet it poses the greatest challenge for practical applications [24–26]. Second, photon counting can reduce the number of pixels with relevant information, and enables sparse ID arrays. Third, limiting the ID code to binary or 2-bit values could still maintain sufficient authentication. Last but not least, encrypting in the Fresnel domain can reduce the quantities of lenses.

5   Review of Asymmetric Encryption

The DRPE is a symmetric encryption in nature, i.e. the encoding key is identical to the decoding key. This inherently suffers from key distribution security problems. In response to this, the attack-free asymmetric encryption (where the encoding key differs from the decoding key) is proposed based on the twice phase truncated Fourier transform. The mechanism and setups are shown in Fig. 9 for the encryption, and Fig. 10 for the decryption.

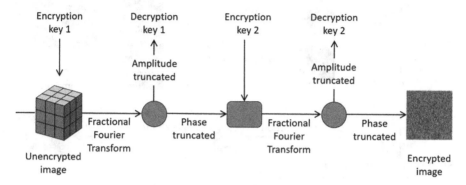

Fig. 9. Amplitude and phase truncation encryption procedure.

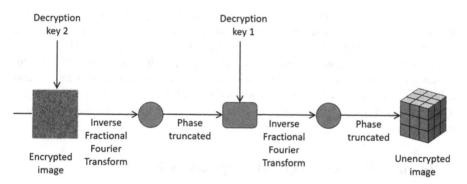

Fig. 10. Amplitude and phase truncation decryption procedure.

Note that in Fig. 10 above, the decryption keys might be dependent on the original plaintext image. Stronger encryption calls for the plaintext independent decryption keys. Colour encryption [8] is another possibility to realise the asymmetric encryption. A three-channel colour case and a single channel colour scheme are sketched in Fig. 11 below.

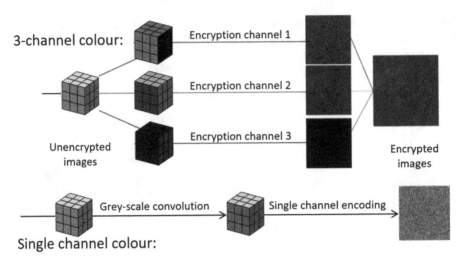

Fig. 11. Block diagram showing the principle of colour encryptions.

Nevertheless, the asymmetric encryption is vulnerable to specific attacks targeting the random phase keys. In response to this, polarisation encoding [27] can be used to improve the security. Other methods using different optical transforms, such as the Fresnel and gyrator transforms [28], and the wavelet transform [29] could be incorporated. Last but not least, the multispectral fusion [8] countermeasure is promising, i.e. with low and high-frequency spectral components combined into a single image. In these ways, the asymmetric encryption brings down the risk and therefore the cost of the information security system.

6   Recent Advances in Optical Cryptoanalysis

Prior parts have been concerned about optical cryptosystems with a focus on DRPE. This section will introduce the science of attacking such cryptosystems, i.e. cryptanalysis. We have understood that from an optics point of view for the DRPE, there is linearity between the encoded image and the original image even though the encrypted image has become a stationary white noise. Due to this linearity, the vulnerabilities of DRPE to certain cryptanalysis attacks targeting the random phase keys and the plaintext image are reviewed in this chapter.

6.1   Brute Force Attack on DRPE

Based on no prior knowledge of the encryption system, brute force attack attempts every phase mask possibility until the correct one is found. The vulnerability of this attack depends on the key space. By way of illustrations in an amplitude-only DRPE system with an amplitude-only map in the input image, the second phase mask serves as the security key, while the phase-only first mask does not need to be considered as a key during decryption. In another words, the size of the key-space is only dependent on the second phase mask (pixel number and levels of quantization in phase).

By ways of illustration for a 100×100 pixels phase key and 256 phase levels, an attacker needs to attempt $256^{\wedge}10000$ key combinations for exact decryption. Nevertheless, approximate decryption is possible at the cost of a compromised image quality post decryption, as evidenced in a two-phase levels key-search attack. The second simplification is partial windowing, which alleviates the key search's burden due to a reduced number of pixels included. For instance, the attacker can search for keys with reduced pixels to 30 by 30. The third simplification is a combination of the above methods. Although there is a slump in the attempting numbers compared to the original attempts, this number remains huge and computationally intractable, hence allowing the DRPE to be generally resistant against brute force attacks even for approximate decryptions. However, due to the linearity between plaintext and cyphertext, DRPE is more vulnerable to cryptanalysis attacks [8, 30], e.g. chosen-plaintext attacks (users guided by attackers to input specific images) and known-plaintext attacks (few original-ciphered images pairs are known to the attackers).

6.2 Chosen and Known-Plaintext Attacks

Two simple yet highly effective chosen-plaintext (ciphertext) attack scenarios are reviewed. First, the attacker can analyse the encrypted image of an impulse (δ) input (a single bright pixel surrounded by black space), hence deriving the key in the following two cases. If the single bright pixel is centred, the second phase mask key is exactly the encrypted image (times a constant phase factor). In a non-centred situation, the second phase mask key is also the encrypted image but times a linearly varying phase that is known. For both cases, the key can be recovered with ease, and the security is breached.

Another way to implement the impulse attack is by obtaining and subtracting the ciphered images corresponding to an impulse (δ) input image, e.g. using two original images that are different in only one pixel that is an impulse. This attack is possible as enabled by the linear encryption process.

In a known-plaintext attack, the unencrypted original images are free from the aforementioned attacking requirements and assumptions, while the keys can still be cracked through the solution of a linear sets of equations based on two unencrypted-encrypted images pairs (known). Albeit computationally intensive, it is demonstrated feasible, e.g. by using a Gaussian elimination approach with back substitutions.

It is worth noting that the optical encryption methods discussed in this work are applying for both image data at rest and image data in transit without a specific performance difference, as the vulnerability to the aforementioned attacking scenarios are identical for both cases. This is distinct from most of the other encryption techniques that exhibit a performance difference between protecting stored data and safeguarding data being transmitted.

7 Future Research Directions

The status of optically encoding an image by DRPE and its variants are reviewed. To address the linearity-induced vulnerabilities and to further tackle the challenges of non-traditional attack methods that continue to evolve, new generations of nonlinear encryption systems are required for both DRPE and MOEA, as evidenced firstly by the recent advances in nonlinear techniques based on joint-transformation correlator architectures and the Collins Diffraction Transformation [31]. Secondly, encryption in phase-space [8] is immune to impulse response and attacks related to phase retrieval. The plaintext image input is processed as a phase-space distribution using an ambiguity function, creating 4D encrypted distribution for a 2D image. Both phase masks serve as keys, i.e. a significant increase in the key space for enhanced security. Thirdly, a true nonlinear propagation by placing photorefractive crystals [8] is reported.

In addition to the need for expanding the optically inspired cryptography into different technological domains and applications [32–37], conducting a more systematic cryptanalysis by leveraging machine learning [38], deep learning [39], and building a rigorously unified optical information security framework with improvements in efficiency, reliability, and money savings are of fundamental importance to enable the optical cryptographic technology to remain competitive against the counterpart of quantum cryptography [40].

References

1. Li, J.F.: Vulnerabilities mapping based on OWASP-SANS: a survey for static application security testing (SAST). Ann. Emerg. Technol. Comput. **4**(3), 1–8 (2020)
2. Wang, R.R.: Yinyang: the way of heaven and earth in Chinese thought and culture. J. Chin. Philos. **42**, 256–259 (2015)
3. Petitcolas, F.A.P.: Kerckhoffs' principle. In: van Tilborg, H.C.A., Jajodia, S. (eds.) Encyclopedia of Cryptography and Security. Springer, Boston (2011). https://doi.org/10.1007/978-1-4419-5906-5
4. Refregier, P., Javidi, B.: Optical image encryption based on input plane and Fourier plane random encoding. Opt. Lett. **20**, 767–769 (1995)
5. Matoba, O., Nomura, T., Cabré, E.P., Millán, M.S., Javidi, B.: Optical techniques for information security. In: Proceedings IEEE 97, 1128–1148 (2009)
6. Suzuki, H., Takeda, M., Obi, T., Yamaguchi, M., Ohyama, N., Nakano, K.: Encrypted sensing for enhancing security of biometric authentication. In: 2014 13th Workshop on Information Optics (WIO), pp. 1–3. Neuchatel (2014)
7. Suzuki, H., Yamaguchi, M., Yachida, M., Ohyama, N., Tashima, H., Obi, T.: Experimental evaluation of fingerprint verification system based on double-random-phase encoding. Opt. Express **14**, 1755–1766 (2006)
8. Javidi, B., et al.: Roadmap on optical security. J. Opt. **18**, 083001 (2016)
9. Nakano, K., Takeda, M., Suzuki, H., Yamaguchi, M.: Security analysis of phase-only DRPE based on known-plaintext attack using multiple known plaintext–ciphertext pairs. Appl. Opt. **53**, 6435–6443 (2014)
10. Deng, Y.B., Chu, D.P.: Coherence properties of different light sources and their effect on the image sharpness and speckle of holographic displays. Sci. Rep. **7**, 5893 (2017)
11. Situ, G.H., Zhang, J.J.: Double random-phase encoding in the Fresnel domain. Opt. Lett. **29**, 1584–1586 (2004)
12. Unnikrishnan, G., Joseph, J., Singh, K.: Optical encryption by double-random phase encoding in the fractional Fourier domain. Opt. Lett. **25**, 887–889 (2000)
13. Markman, A., Wang, J.G., Javidi, B.: Three-dimensional integral imaging displays using a quick-response encoded elemental image array. Optica **1**, 332–335 (2014)

14. Li, J., Li, J.S., Pan, Y.Y., Li, R.: Compressive optical image encryption. Sci. Rep. **5**, 10374 (2015)

15. Cabré, E.P., Cho, M., Javidi, B.: Information authentication using photon-counting double random-phase encrypted images. Opt. Lett. **36**, 22–24 (2011)

16. Yontem, A.O., Li, J.F., Chu, D.P.: Imaging through a projection screen using bi-stable switchable diffusive photon sieves. Opt. Express **26**, 10162–10170 (2018)

17. Li, J.F., Chu, D.P.: Liquid crystal-based enclosed coplanar waveguide phase shifter for 54–66 GHz applications. Crystals **9**(12), 650 (2019)

18. Cai, L.Z., Xu, H., Li, J.F., Chu, D.P.: High FoM liquid crystal based microstrip phase shifter for phased array antennas. In: 2016 International Symposium on Antennas and Propagation (ISAP), pp. 402–403. IEEE, Okinawa (2016)

19. Li, J.F., Xu, H., Chu, D.P.: Design of liquid crystal based coplanar waveguide tunable phase shifter with no floating electrodes for 60–90 GHz applications. In: 2016 46th European Microwave Conference (EuMC), pp. 1047–1050. IEEE, London (2016)

20. Cai, L.Z., Xu, H., Li, J.F., Chu, D.P.: High figure-of-merit compact phase shifters based on liquid crystal material for 1–10 GHz applications. Jpn. J. Appl. Phys. **56**, 011701 (2017)

21. Li, J.F.: Structure and optimisation of liquid crystal based phase shifter for millimetre-wave applications. Apollo, University of Cambridge Repository, doctoral thesis (2019)

22. Li, J.F.: Low-loss tunable dielectrics for millimeter-wave phase shifter: from material modelling to device prototyping. IOP Conf. Ser. Mater. Sci. Eng. (2020)

23. Rajput, S.K., Nishchal, N.K.: An optical encryption and authentication scheme using asymmetric keys. J. Opt. Soc. Am. A **31**, 1233–1238 (2014)

24. Li, J.F., Guo, X.Y.: Global deployment mappings and challenges of contact-tracing apps for COVID-19. SSRN Electronic Journal (2020)

25. Guo, X.Y., Li, J.F.: A novel twitter sentiment analysis model with baseline correlation for financial market prediction with improved efficiency. In: Sixth International Conference on Social Networks Analysis, Management and Security, pp. 472–477. IEEE, Granada (2019)

26. Li, J.F., Guo, X.Y.: COVID-19 contact-tracing apps: a survey on the global deployment and challenges. arXiv preprint arXiv:2005.03599 (2020)

27. Javidi, B., Nomura, T.: Polarization encoding for optical security systems. Opt. Eng. **39**(9), 602–652 (2000)

28. Khurana, M., Singh, H.: Asymmetric optical image triple masking encryption based on gyrator and fresnel transforms to remove silhouette problem. 3D Res. 9, 38 (2018)

29. Mehra, I., Nishchal, N.K.: Optical asymmetric image encryption using gyrator wavelet transform. Optics Commun. **354**, 344–352 (2015)

30. Frauel, Y., Castro, A., Naughton, T., Javidi, B.: Resistance of the double-random-phase encryption against various attacks. Opt. Express **15**, 10253–10265 (2007)

31. Vilardy, J.M., Perez, R.A., Torres, C.O.: Optical image encryption using a nonlinear joint transform correlator and the Collins diffraction transform. Photonics **6**, 115 (2019)

32. Li, J.F.: Fault-event trees based probabilistic safety analysis of a boiling water nuclear reactor's core meltdown and minor damage frequencies. Safety **6**(2), 28 (2020)

33. Li, J.F.: Numerical solution of one-speed one-dimensional diffusion equation based on finite difference and source iteration. SSRN Electronic Journal (2020)

34. Li, J.F.: 60 GHz optimised nickel-free gold-plated enclosed coplanar waveguide liquid crystal phase shifter. In: International Microwave Workshop Series on Advanced Materials and Processes for RF and THz Applications. IEEE, Suzhou (2020)

35. Li, J.F.: Public perceptions of nuclear energy in the post-Fukushima world. SSRN Electronic Journal (2020)

36. Li, J.F.: Modelling nuclear fuel assembly with thermal-hydraulic feedback and burnup using WIMS-PANTHER-Serpent. J. Phys. Conf. Ser. (2020)

37. Li, J.F.: Design of a four-stage pipelined reduced instruction set computing microprocessor. SSRN Electronic Journal (2020)
38. Zhou, L.N., Xiao, Y., Chen, W.: Machine-learning attacks on interference-based optical encryption: experimental demonstration. Opt. Express **27**, 26143–26154 (2019)
39. Hai, H., Pan, S.X., Liao, M.H., Lu, D.J., He, W.Q., Peng, X.: Cryptanalysis of random-phase-encoding-based optical cryptosystem via deep learning. Opt. Express **27**, 21204–21213 (2019)
40. Fehr, S.: Quantum cryptography. Found. Phys. **40**, 494–531 (2010)

AI, Big Data and Data Analytics

Sentiment Analysis of Turkish Twitter Data Using Polarity Lexicon and Artificial Intelligence

Harisu Abdullahi Shehu[1], Md. Haidar Sharif[2(✉)], Sahin Uyaver[3], Sezai Tokat[4], and Rabie A. Ramadan[2,5]

[1] Victoria University of Wellington, Wellington, New Zealand
[2] University of Hail, Hail, Kingdom of Saudi Arabia
md.sharif@uoh.edu.sa
[3] Turkish-German University, Istanbul, Turkey
[4] Pamukkale University, Denizli, Turkey
[5] Cairo University, Cairo, Egypt

Abstract. Sentiment analysis is a process of computationally detecting and classifying opinions written in a piece of writer's text. It determines the writer's impression as achromatic or negative or positive. Sentiment analysis became unsophisticated due to the invention of Internet-based societal media. At present, usually people express their opinions by dint of Twitter. Henceforth, Twitter is a fascinating medium for researchers to perform data analysis. In this paper, we address a handful of methods to prognosticate the sentiment on Turkish tweets by taking up polarity lexicon as well as artificial intelligence. The polarity lexicon method uses a dictionary of words and accords with the words among the harvested tweets. The tweets are then grouped into either positive tweets or negative tweets or neutral tweets. The methods of artificial intelligence use either individually or combined classifiers e.g., support vector machine (SVM), random forest (RF), maximum entropy (ME), and decision tree (DT) for categorizing positive tweets, negative tweets, and neutral tweets. To analyze sentiment, a total of 13000 Turkish tweets are collected from Twitter with the help of Twitter's application programming interface (API). Experimental results show that the mean performance of our proposed methods is greater than 72%.

Keywords: Artificial intelligence · Entropy · Sentiment · SVM · Turkish · Twitter

1 Introduction

Sentiment analysis is extremely advantageous in social media monitoring as it permits us to reach a general summary of a wider public opinion behind some topics. Communication helps to comprehend the meaning of information conveyed from senders to receivers. Magazines, newspapers, radio, television, and the Internet are treated as the primary means of communication. Social media aids to bring options to communicate with thousands of people. The number of people is increasingly growing to use the social

© ICST Institute for Computer Sciences, Social Informatics and Telecommunications Engineering 2020
Published by Springer Nature Switzerland AG 2020. All Rights Reserved
M. H. Miraz et al. (Eds.): iCETiC 2020, LNICST 332, pp. 113–125, 2020.
https://doi.org/10.1007/978-3-030-60036-5_8

media day by day. Users of social media can post their views and thoughts on them freely. Multi-purpose applications of social media allow users to facilitate more than one task e.g., messaging, audio call and video chatting, photo and video sharing, sharing and reading news from online, and so on. Hence, social media became an important part of modern life. Social media helps to analyze sentiment by a considerable margin. Sentiment analysis computes and identifies the view of a person from a specified piece of text. It usually determines the general inclusive concept of a person towards a given product, topic, or thing. Sentiment has been represented through social media using images and written text information [1]. Twitter, LinkedIn, Flickr, and Facebook permit their users to post their opinions without secrecy. Currently, Twitter is used extensively rather than others [2]. Especially, many people use Twitter because of football matches and political events for supporting their favorite groups [3]. Thus, Twitter provides billions of data for the data scientist to mine people's opinions. There is a minimum of at least 35 Turkic languages which are spoken by the Turkic people. There are about 15 million and about 65 million of the Turkic native speakers in Southeast Europe and Western Asia respectively [4]. The Turkish language is the frequently spoken language among the Turkic languages. There are many text-based studies found in the literature on sentiment or opinion analysis in English language [5]. But a handful of written text-based studies are found for Turkish [6–10]. This because of its inherent complexity [11]. Besides, sentiment analysis is extremely difficult on Turkish texts over English texts [12]. The hidden suffix of Turkish makes a word negative within words or a negative word might have dissimilar message in a sentence (e.g., Tables 1, 2, 3 and 4). Therefore negations should be handled with care.

In reference to English, only few studies have been carried out on sentiment analysis in Turkish written texts. For examples, Kaya et al. [13] analyzed the sentiment of Turkish political news. They used dataset which was collected from miscellaneous news sites using a machine learning-based approach. They claimed that maximum entropy and N-Grams language model outperformed SVM and Naive Bayes within the maximum accuracy between 65% and 77%. Nevertheless, their study was domain-specific because the used data consists of political news only. However, they performed another research [6] where they determined the sentiment classification of Turkish sentiment columns. They applied transfer-learning from an untagged Twitter data to tagged political data for finding positive and negative information. They got somewhat improvement accuracy by using maximum entropy, SVM, and Naive Bayes. Shehu et al. [9, 10] proposed an approach to analyze sentiment from written Turkish texts harvested from Twitter. Tweets were classified into small and large classes. The small class contained 3000 tweets, whereas the large class contained 10500 tweets. Machine learning classifiers RF and SVM were used hierarchically to classify tweets. They claimed that their experimental results outperformed other existing methods by achieving a maximum accuracy of 86.4% and 82.8% on the small and large datasets, respectively. Coban et al. [7] analyzed a particular transportation company to get information about the customer satisfaction of the company based on what their customers tweet on Twitter. They tried to determine the tweet is either positive or negative. They started with data that consists of 20000 sentences but ends up with 14777 after the accomplishment of pre-processing. Naive Bayes classifier, multinomial Naive Bayes classifier, SVM, and KNN (K-Nearest Neighbor) algorithm were used to determine the performance. Multinomial Naive Bayes classifier showed the best accurate result having 66.06%. Ogul et al. [8] performed another domain-specific study based on Turkish hotel reviews. The AUC (area under the curve) of a ROC (receiver operating characteristics) had been applied for evaluating the performance of their study. The best result was obtained using the Random Forest classifier with an AUC value of 0.89 (out of 1 scale) on both positive and negative comments. Guven et al. [14] applied different stages of "gizli" (latent) Dirichlet allocation (GDA) to classify Turkish tweets having an average accuracy of 69%. Coban et al. [15] applied SVM and extreme learning machine (ELM) to analyze Twitter sentiment with an average accuracy of 72%. Anastasia et al. [16] worked on sentiment analysis of online Twitter data for transportation management support by applying SVM, Naive Bayes, and DT with an average accuracy of 69%.

In this paper, we have addressed a handful of methods founded on polarity lexicon (PL) and artificial intelligence (AI) classifiers of SVM (support vector machine), random forest (RF), maximum entropy (ME), and decision tree (DT) to predict the sentiment or opinion from Turkish written texts of tweeter data. We have applied Zemberek [17] library for operating the Turkish written texts of tweeter data. The Zemberek [17] library helped to achieve good precision and accuracy [18]. To deal with negation, we applied Zemberek [17] library for determining every feasible stem as well as edit the stem of everything in the tweet at least twice when a word seems to be multiple. The operation of data includes free from impurities, tokenization, putting on stemming, and taking away stopwords. About 13000 tweets have been accumulated from Turkish Twitter by applying Twitter's application programming interface (API). The method of polarity lexicon uses a total of 6800 English words. But those words are used for a long time of interval [19]. They are manually translated into Turkish using online translators. Pre-processing operations delete links, unwanted numbers, punctuation, and unnecessary characters from the obtained data. After pre-processing, we can get useful data. For example, we have used 10500 from 13000 downloaded tweets as our cardinal dataset. The stopword dataset and stemmed dataset are derived from our cardinal dataset. On the basis of contents, data are grouped as negative or positive or neutral. A fraction of 3000 and 10500 of the raw, stopword, and stemmed data having the same dispersion from every group are deemed as the first dataset and the second dataset to be applied in conducting experiments before and after any change are performed on the data. The method of PL deploys equal dispersion of complete dataset from every group for various testing. The method of AI with the help of SVM, RF, ME, and DT utilizes 750 out of 1000 tweets from every group of the small dataset for training. But the leftover 1000 $-750 = 250$ data are applied for testing. Analogously, the large dataset applies 2500 out of 3500 tweets from every group for training and the residual 3500 $-2500 = 1000$ tweets for testing. The results of the experiment demonstrate that SVM does better on stemmed data having about 76% accuracy, but RF does better on raw data having about 88% accuracy. The accuracy of ME is more or less 83%, whereas DT exhibits the lowest performance. The accuracy of PL starts augmenting from 45% to 57% when the data are being transformed from the raw data towards the stemmed data. The rest of this paper explains our implementation steps, cardinal experimental results, and conclusion.

Table 1. Hidden negation examples in Turkish.

Words	Suffixes	Meaning in English
Uçtu	Uç-tu	Flew
Uçmadı	Uç-ma-dı	Did not fly

Table 2. Meaning changing negative words.

Sentences	Meaning in English
Saç kurut**ma** makinesi kullanarak saçınızı kurutabilirsiniz	You can dry your hair using a hair dryer
Yürü**me** yolunu takip ederek ilerleyelim	Let's proceed by following the walking path

Table 3. Example of how Turkish base words are stretched out to generate new meaning.

Word	Suffixes	English Meaning
Gitmek	Git-mek	To go
Gitmemek	Git-me-mek	Not to go
İçiyorum	İ-çi-yo-rum	I am drinking (sth)
İçmiyorum	İç-mi-yo-rum	I am not drinking (sth)
Görebilirim	Gö-re-bi-li-rim	I can see
Görebilirdim	Gö-re-bi-lir-dim	I could have seen

Table 4. Example of changing the polarity of a root word.

Word	Suffixes	English Meaning	Semantic polarity
Becerikli	Becerik-li	Skilled	Positive polarity
Beceriksiz	Becerik-siz	Incompetent	Negative polarity

2 Implementation Steps

In this section, we are going to explain the implementation steps of our methods for predicting the sentiments from Turkish tweets. Basically, the techniques of PL as well as AI have been applied. AI methods are divided into SVM, RF, ME, and DT. Figure 1 demonstrates the flowcharts of our methods.

2.1 Processing Methods

Not only cleaning but also some pre-processing techniques (e.g., tokenization, deleting stopwords, and using stemming to the tweets) are involved by the dint of Zemberek [17] library with an aim of getting a better accuracy. Two examples of tweets harvested in their raw form without any pre-processing method are given below.

- "mehmetakifcakir: Su hayvan kadar olamayanlarimiz var #merhamet https://t.co/3Ws dilbanh".
- "CetinGurbulak: Sevgi ve umut gönlünüzde sevdikleriniz yaninizda olsun…Mutlu bir aksam dilerim….\n#sendeyaz".

Tokenization allows making a character sequence into many pieces usually called tokens which simultaneously delete some punctuation and so on. Here, we refer to the resulting word after the application of the tokenization operation and the removal of stopword to as stopword data. The following two examples show how the raw tweets are transformed after tokenization is being applied and stopwords are removed from them.

- ["mehmetakifcakir:, su, hayvan, olamayanlarimiz, #merhamet, https://t.co/3wsdil banh"]
- ["cetingurbulak:, sevgi, umut, gönlünüzde, sevdikleriniz, yaninizda, olsun…mutlu, aksam, dilerim….\n#sendeyaz"]

Stemming helps in determining the root of a word by chopping its end. The stemming technique edits words at least once based on how the words are applied in a given context. Below is an example of how tokenize tweets and stopwords free words are transformed after stemming have been applied to them.

- su hayvan merhamet
- sevgi umut gönlü sev sev ol mutlu aksam ak dil dil dil dil

2.2 Method of Polarity Lexicon (PL)

The PL method brings up a dictionary of words as well as corresponds to those words in the yielded tweets. Based on the matching information every tweet is grouped to be either positive, negative or neutral tweet. Figure 1 (a) shows the proposed system flowchart of this method. The dictionary of words accommodates more than a combination of 6800 negative and positive English words [19]. The bag of words in the dictionary are translated into Turkish manually. Upon passing all tweets through preprocessing, tokenization, as well as stemming stages, a tweet associated with each token is to be recognized within a word of the dictionary. The sentiment polarity of any tweet is calculated on finding the exact word within the words of the dictionary. If a word got a match in the list of negative words, then that word will be treated as negative and vice-versa. All tweets are analyzed for their polarities to fall into the groups of positive tweet or negative tweet or neutral tweet. A tweet falls into the group of positive tweets if the number of positive words in it are greater than those of negative words in it. A tweet falls into the group of negative tweets if the number of negative words in it are greater than those of positive words. A tweet falls into the group of neutral tweets if positive and negative numbers are the same or there is no match found.

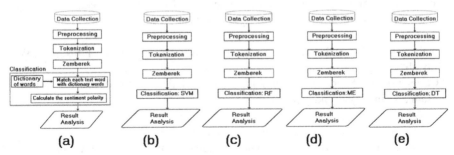

Fig. 1. (a) Polarity Lexicon; (b) SVM; (c) Random Forest; (b) Maximum Entropy; (b) Decision Tree.

2.3 Processing Methods of Artificial Intelligence

Machine learning classifiers including SVM, RF, ME, and DT are applied for grouping the tweets into positive, negative or neutral tweet. Processing methods using flowcharts are explained in Fig. 1 (b), (c), (d), and (e) for SVM, RF, ME, and DT, respectively.

Support Vector Machine (SVM)
The SVM is a supervised machine learning algorithm. It can be used for a wide range of applications even laser scanned data points [20–22] to solve classification or regression problems. It is a discriminative classifier formally explained with a separating hyperplane. In 2 dimensional spaces, the hyperplane is a straight line separating a plane in two components wherein every group lay on either side [23]. The key idea of SVM is to find line separators in the search space for separating various groups.

Random Forest (RF)
Another very important supervised learning algorithm is RF algorithm. It does create random forests using some specific technique [24]. In practice, RF would be the best-known supervised learning algorithm due to its precision and accuracy. If there exists a larger number of trees in the forest, then it provides a more accurate result.

Maximum Entropy (ME)
Entropy is a degree of disorder in a system [25]. The idea of ME hints that the probability distribution that best represents the current level of knowledge is the one with the largest entropy [26]. Entropy and the probability have an inverse relationship, a higher probability means a lower entropy and vice-versa.

Decision Tree (DT)

The method of DT states successive disintegration levels of training data space and the data are divided by using a predicament on the feature value [27]. The predicate or condition is the presence of one or more words. The division is performed recursively as far as the leaf nodes restrain inescapable lowest numbers of reports which are applied for grouping.

3   Results and Discussion

This section illustrates the data collection technique followed by our obtained experimental results along with discussion and comparisons with other alternative existing methods.

3.1   Data Collection

The dataset (both training and testing tweets) are gathered together from Twitter with the help of Twitter's API found in R version 3.4.3. In the end, Turkish tweets are harvested. The tweets are harvested in two forms. The Search API is an uncomplete index of any tweet. Yet it is an index of the latest tweet. Currently, the index involves 6 to 9 days of tweets as shown below. The first parameter indicates a tweet topic in which any user can harvest, second parameter hints tweet's number, and finally, the third parameter addresses for language option for the user.

```
tweets <- searchTwitter(search.string, n=no.of.tweets, lang="tr")
```

Modification can be done to retrieve tweets from any date up to a specific period of time as:

```
tweets <- searchTwitter(search.string, n=no.of.tweets, lang = "tr",
                        since = '2018-1-12', until = "2018-1-13")
```

The above lines of code, *since* and *until* are annexed for the API in a specific way such that users can harvest tweets that are tweeted not only within 6 to 9 days of tweeting them but also from a specified period of time that we wish to harvest them from.

3.2   Calculation of Sentiment Polarity

The word dictionary holds a total of 6800 negative as well as positive English words that were compiled over many years. Upon all tweets passing through necessary stages, every token in a tweet corresponds to a word of the dictionary. The sentiment polarity of any tweet is calculated upon finding the exact match in the dictionary. If a word exactly matches the group of positive words, then it should be considered as positive, and so on. To identify any tweet as a positive tweet or negative tweet or neutral tweet, the tweet's polarity will be analysed at the end.

3.3   Result Analysis

The word cloud in Fig. 2 represents the most occurrence words (about 200 times) in the positive, negative, and the neutral tweet in the first and second datasets. Figures 3 and 4 illustrate the obtained performance for PL, SVM, RF, ME, and DT to classify positive tweets, negative tweets, and neutral tweets by taking into consideration of first dataset and second dataset. Their F1-Scores have been estimated. F1 score conveys the balance between precision and recall.

Fig. 2. First row indicates the word cloud of (a) positive, (b) negative, and (c) neutral words in the first dataset. Second row demonstrates the word cloud of (d) positive, (e) negative, and (f) neutral words in the second dataset.

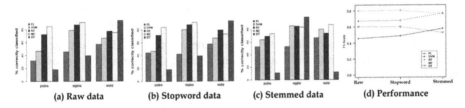

(a) Raw data   (b) Stopword data   (c) Stemmed data   (d) Performance

Fig. 3. Performance evaluation for PL, SVM, RF, ME, and DT deeming first dataset.

On applying the first dataset the performance evaluation as indicated by the bar chart in Fig. 3 (a), it is noticeable that the method of ME performed the best. It achieved a higher performance in the overall case with an accuracy of 83.6% followed by Random Forests with 79.1%, SVM with 64% and, then DT with 50.3%. The polarity lexicon showed the minimum performance with an accuracy of 44.8%. Similarly, taking into account the first dataset, the performance bar chart of Fig. 3 (b), it is noticeable that Maximum Entropy achieved the best performance. It achieved a higher performance in the overall case with an accuracy of 82.9% followed by Random Forest with 79.7%, SVM with 64.9%,

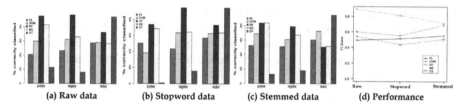

Fig. 4. Performance evaluation for PL, SVM, RF, ME, and DT using second dataset.

DT with 50.3%, and then polarity lexicon with 48.2%. Assuming the first dataset, the performance bar chart of Fig. 3 (c) gives that Maximum Entropy performed the best. It achieved a higher performance in the overall case with an accuracy of 81.3% followed by SVM with 76.4%, Random Forest with 75.9%, polarity lexicon with 57%, and then DT with 40.7%. The ME algorithm outperformed all other algorithms by classifying positive data, SVM performed better on negative and neutral data in contrast to how it performed on positive data, at the same time outperform PL and RF by grouping negative tweets and neutral tweets from stemmed data. ME did not only achieve the best accuracy of 83.6% on raw data of the first dataset but also outperform all other algorithms in classifying the tweets in 2 of the 3 classes on each kind of dataset. The performance of PL increased continuously across the way with the manipulation of raw data to stopword data and then stemmed data. DT algorithm started with its best accuracy of 50.3% on raw data, it went ahead to maintain the same accuracy on stopword data but then decreased to 40.7% on stemmed data. RF achieved maximum accuracy of 79.7% using stopword data, both PL and SVM achieved maximum accuracy of 57% and 76.4% using stemmed data, respectively.

Using the second dataset the performance bar chart of Fig. 4 (a), it is noticeable that Random Forest showed the best performance. It achieved a higher performance in the overall case with an accuracy of 88.5% followed by Maximum Entropy with 68.7%, SVM with 60%, polarity lexicon with 48.3%, and then DT with 44.5%. Similarly, considering the second dataset the performance bar chart of Fig. 4 (b), it is noticeable that Random Forest demonstrated the best performance. It achieved a higher performance in the overall case with an accuracy of 80.9% followed by Maximum Entropy with 67.8, SVM with 55%, polarity lexicon with 50.4% and then DT with 37.5% Again, deeming the second dataset the performance bar chart of Fig. 4 (c), it is noticeable that Random Forest showed the best performance. It achieved a higher performance in the overall case with an accuracy of 71.2% followed by Maximum Entropy with 67.8%, SVM with 67.6%, polarity lexicon with 54.7%, and then DT with 41.9%. The PL exhibited the same behaviour as in the first dataset due to the fact that its performance continued to augment as the data were being manipulated from raw data to stopword data and finally stemmed data. SVM did better to classify neutral data from stemmed data. RF and ME outperformed the other two methods by classifying positive tweets and negative tweets by taking into consideration of the second dataset. DT algorithm started with its best accuracy of 44.5%, decreased the accuracy to as low as 37.5% on stopword data, and then increased to 41.93% on stemmed data. PL and SVM performed worse on the second to the first dataset and achieved their best accuracy of 54.7% and 67.6%, respectively when the data were stemmed. On the other hand, RF performed better on the second dataset and achieved its best accuracy of 88.5% on raw data. Like PL and SVM, ME also performed worse on the second dataset and then went ahead to achieve an accuracy of 68.8% on the raw data of the second dataset which was better than PL and SVM.

3.4 Comparative Study

In this subsection, we have compared our obtained results with various existing similar methods. From Table 5, it is noticeable that solely the work of Anastasia et al. [16] applied a greater number of datasets as compared to ours. At the same time, in all the other studies that used the same algorithm to that of ours to classify the tweets. Only the work of Shehu et al. [9] used the combination of both RF and SVM with accuracy 86.4%. But we have achieved an accuracy of 88.5% using RF alone. Shehu et al. [10] obtained the average performance of 73.9% using three methods, whereas our mean performance was 72.2% from five methods. The average performance of our methods is greater than that of Guven et al. [14], Coban et al. [15], and Anastasia et al. [16]. Usually, no individual approach outperformed the outcomes of tweets grouping using identical datasets as we have obtained.

Table 5. Comparison of our results with other existing results.

References	Techniques	Dataset	Dataset size	Maximum Accuracy	Average Accuracy
Our Results	PL SVM RF ME DT	Twitter	3000 and 10500	57.0% 76.4% 88.5% 83.6% 45.5%	72.2%
Shehu et al. [9]	RF + SVM	Twitter	3000 and 10500	86.4%	–
Shehu et al. [10]	PL SVM RF	Twitter	3000 and 10500	57.0% 76.4% 88.5%	73.9%
Guven et al. [14]	GDA stage1 GDA stage2 GDA stage3	Twitter	4000	60.4% 70.5% 76.4%	69.1%
Coban et al. [15]	SVM ELM	Twitter	10000	74% 70%	72.0%
Anastasia et al. [16]	SVM NB DT	Twitter	126405	72.97% 61.25% 72.97%	69.0%

3.5 Future Work

For future studies, acronyms dictionary can be used to correct every used abbreviation. Words expressed in a painting style specifying to a specific tweet would be transferred into words instead of obtaining its link. Additional words would be introduced into the record of the dictionary. More words will lead to the achievement of better accuracy results. A hybrid method that will involve the use of all the multiple algorithms to classify the tweets at a time would also be developed to ensure the achievement of better accuracy. A complete statistical analysis [28] along with computational complexity [29] deeming various computer hardware implementations [30–32] would be studied in the future to make a good comparison of the performance of diverse approaches more effectively.

4 Conclusion

We addressed a few methods founded on PL and AI classifiers to predict the sentiment on Turkish tweets. RF performed the best to classify positive tweets. In the case of stemmed data, SVM performed better than others to classify negative tweets and neutral tweets. RF showed a maximum accuracy of about 80% using stopword data and about 89% on raw data from first and second datasets, respectively. SVM showed a maximum accuracy of approximately 76% and 68% using stemmed data of first and second datasets, respectively. The maximum performance of ME was about 84%. The performance of DT was not overlooked. Future investigation would involve an initialism dictionary that improves every abbreviation. Words inscribed in a picture related to a specific tweet would be translated into words instead of using its link. New words would be inserted into the word dictionary.

References

1. Anjaria, M., Guddeti, R.M.: Influence factor based opinion mining of Twitter data using supervised learning. In: Proceedings of the 6th International Conference on Communication Systems and Networks (COMSNETS), pp. 1–8 (2014)
2. Karabulut, Y.E., Kucuksille, E.U.: Twitter profesyonel izleme ve analiz araci. J. Techn. Sci. **8**, 17–24 (2018)
3. Jurgens, P., Jungheer, A., Shoen, H.: Small worlds with a difference: new Gatekeepers & the filtering of political information on Twitter, Association for Computing Machinery Web Science (2011)
4. Kornfilt, J.: Turkish and the Turkic languages. In The world's major languages. 2nd edition In: Comrie, B. (eds.) Oxford, UK: Routledge (2017)
5. Pang, B., Lee, L.: Opinion mining and sentiment analysis. Found. Trends in Inf. Retrieval **2**, 1–135 (2008)
6. Kaya, M., Fidan, G., Toroslu, I.H.: Transfer Learning using Twitter Data for Improving Sentiment Classification of Turkish Political News, pp. 139–148. Springer, Switzerland (2013). https://doi.org/10.1007/978-3-319-01604-7_14
7. Coban, O., Ozyer, B., Ozyer, G.T.: Sentiment analysis for Turkish Twitter feeds. In: 23th Signal Processing and Com. Applications Conference (2015)
8. Ogul, B.B., Ercan, G.: Sentiment classification on Turkish hotel reviews. In: 24th Signal Processing and Com. Applications Conference (2016)

9. Shehu, H.A., Tokat, S.: A hybrid approach for the sentiment analysis of Turkish twitter data. In: Hemanth, D., Kose U. (eds.) Artificial Intelligence and Applied Mathematics in Engineering Problems. ICAIAME 2019. LNDECT, vol. 43. Springer, Cham (2020). https://doi.org/10.1007/978-3-030-36178-5_15

10. Shehu, H.A., Tokat, S., Sharif, M.H., Uyaver, S.: Sentiment analysis of Turkish Twitter data. In: AIP Conference Proceedings, vol. 2183, issue 1, pp. 080004 (2019)

11. Saglam, F., Sever, H., Genc, B.: Developing Turkish sentiment lexicon for sentiment analysis using online news media. In: IEEE/ACS 13th International Conference of Computer Systems and Applications (2016)

12. Vural, A.G., Cambazoglu, B.B., Senkul, P., Tokgoz, Z.O.: A framework for sentiment analysis in Turkish: application to polarity detection of movie reviews in Turkish. In: Computer and Information Sciences III (Gelenbe E., Lent R. eds), Springer London, pp. 437–445 (2013). https://doi.org/10.1007/978-1-4471-4594-3_45

13. Kaya, M., Fidan, G., Toroslu, I.H.: Sentiment analysis of Turkish political news. In: International Joint Conferences on Web Intelligence and Intelligent Agent Technology, vol. 01, Institute of Electrical and Electronics Engineers Computer Society, pp. 174–180 (2012)

14. Guven, Z.A., Diri, B., Cakaloglu, T.: Classification of Turkish Tivit by n-Stage Latent Dirichlet Allocation. Electric Electronics, Computer Science, Biomedical Engineerings' Meeting (2018)

15. Coban, O., Ozyildirim, B.M., Ozel, S.A.: An empirical study of the extreme learning machine for Twitter sentiment analysis. Int. J. Intell. Syst. Appl. Eng. 6(3), 15 (2018)

16. Anastasia, S., Budi, I.: Twitter sentiment analysis of online transportation service provider. In: Proceedings of the International Conference on Advanced Computer Science and Information Systems (ICACSIS), pp. 359–365 (2016)

17. Akin, A.A., Akin, M.D.: Zemberek, an open source NLP framework for Turkic languages. https://github.com/ahmetaa/zemberek-nlp. Accessed 1 Mar 2019

18. Sharif, M.H.: An eigenvalue approach to detect flows and events in crowd videos. J. Circ. Syst. Comput. 26(7), 1–50 (2017)

19. Hu, L.: Sentiment analysis. https://www.cs.uic.edu/liub/fbs/sentiment-analysis.html#datasets. KDD, 2004 (2004)

20. Galip, F., Sharif, M.H., Caputcu, M., Uyaver, S.: Recognition of objects from laser scanned data points using SVM. In: First International Conference on Multimedia and Image Processing (ICMIP), pp. 28–35 (2016)

21. Sharif, M.H., Shehu, H.A., Galip, F., Ince, I.F., Kusetogullari, H.: Object tracking from laser scanned dataset. Int. J. Comput. Sci. Eng. Techn. 3(6), 19–27 (2019)

22. Sharif, M.H.: Particle Filter for Trajectories of Movers from Laser Scanned Dataset, Mediterranean Conference on Pattern Recognition and Artificial Intelligence (MedPRAI), pp. 133–148 (2019)

23. Patel S.: SVM (Support Vector Machine) – Theory, (3th May). https://medium.com/machine-learning-101/chapter-2-svm-support-vector-machine-theory-f0812effc72. (2017)

24. Kubat, M.: An Introduction to Machine learning. Springer, Switzerland, pp. 85 (2015)

25. Sharif, M.H., Djeraba, C.: An entropy approach for abnormal activities detection in video streams. Pattern Recogn. 45(7), 2543–2561 (2012)

26. De Martino, A., De Martino, D.: An introduction to the maximum entropy approach and its application to inference problems in biology. Heliyon 4(4), 1–33 (2018)

27. Quinlan, J.R.: Induction of decision trees. Mach. Learn. 1(1), 81–106 (1986)

28. Kusetogullari, H., Sharif, M.H., Leeson, M.S., Celik, T.: A reduced uncertainty-based hybrid evolutionary algorithm for solving dynamic shortest path routing problem. J. Circ. Syst. Comput. 24(5), 1550067 (2015)

29. Sharif, M.H.: A numerical approach for tracking unknown number of individual targets in videos. Dig. Signal Process. 57, 106–127 (2016)

30. Sharif, M.H.: High-performance mathematical functions for single-core architectures. J. Circ. Syst. Comput. **23**(4), 1450051 (2014)
31. Hennessy, J.L., Patterson, D.A.: Computer Architecture: A Quantitative Approach, The Morgan Kaufmann Series in Computer Architecture and Design, 6th Edition (2017)
32. Solihin, Y.: Fundamentals of Parallel Multicore Architecture, Chapman & Hall/CRC Computational Science, 1st Edition. (2015)

Big Data Analytics in Healthcare: A Review of Opportunities and Challenges

Marjan Mansourvar$^{(\boxtimes)}$, Uffe Kock Wiil, and Christian Nøhr

Centre of Health Informatics and Technology, The Maersk Mc-Kinney Moller Institute,
University of Southern Denmark, Odense M, Denmark
{marm,ukwiil,cn}@mmmi.sdu.dk

Abstract. Big data analytics is a rapidly expanding issue in computer engineering, and health informatics is one of the most challenging topics. Big data investigation in healthcare could certainly make improvements to medical study as well as the quality of treatment offered to patients. Machine Learning (ML) algorithms due to powerful and efficient handling of data analytics could gain knowledge from data to discover patterns and trends in the database to make predictive models. Our study aims to review the most recent scholarly publications about big data analytics and its applications which include predictive models in healthcare. A systematic search of articles in the three most significant scientific databases: ScienceDirect, PubMed, and IEEE Xplore was carried out following the PRISMA methodology. This study shows how machine learning algorithms are evolving into a promising field for supporting intelligent decisions by analyzing large data sets and thereby improving treatments while reducing costs. However, there remain challenges to overcome and there is still room for improvement to develop methods and applications. Finally, we outline the unsolved issue and the future perspectives for health sciences in the big data era.

Keywords: Big data analytics · Machine learning · Predictive model · Healthcare · Data science

1   Introduction and Motivation

Currently, big data is one of the rapid growing fields in computer engineering, and health informatics (HI) is one of the most challenging domains [1, 2]. The health domain is suffering from unsure, undiscovered, incompetent, heterogeneous, noisy, soiled, unwanted, and missing data that complicates the modeling of artifacts [3]. This makes it very difficult to design automated applications for this area. Although, data that are normally invisible and not accessible to the human, however, could be urgently required for stronger final decision assistance [4, 5]. An additional problem is the fact that the majority of the data in HI are non-standardized and non-structured [6, 7]. The use of big data analytics (BDA) techniques, such as forecasting, and optimization are important to recognize meaningful patterns and present insights to decision makers. Machine learning (ML) algorithms are introduced as one of the most powerful techniques for big data processing in healthcare.

© ICST Institute for Computer Sciences, Social Informatics and Telecommunications Engineering 2020
Published by Springer Nature Switzerland AG 2020. All Rights Reserved
M. H. Miraz et al. (Eds.): iCETiC 2020, LNICST 332, pp. 126–141, 2020.
https://doi.org/10.1007/978-3-030-60036-5_9

ML presents the techniques and technologies to modify mounds of data into helpful information and facts for making decisions [8]. The adoption of data intensive ML algorithms appear in most of the applications [9] in various areas of informatics research such as pattern discovery, making predictive models and visualization to understand data [10, 11]. ML is a non-trivial extraction of implicit previously unidentified and eventually valuable information from data. An ML solution offers a user-oriented strategy to new and the hidden patterns in the data [12, 13]. The observed information could be used by the medical administrators to increase the value of service methods which are both sensible and helpful to the data owner [14–16]. This conceptualization of ML implies that the aim of ML would be to acquire new and in-depth thinking and unparalleled knowledge extraction about big datasets that could then be applied to help to make decisions [17, 18]. ML is a specific technique of data analytics which automates building models and use particular algorithms that can uncover hidden insights from data [19, 20].

Possibly the most popular and significant application in ML algorithms is predictive modeling (PM). ML could be referred to as the procedure of discovering earlier unknown behaviors and trends of the data source and employing that knowledge to create predictive models [16, 21]. For example, the data management can be effective in disease prevention. Predictive models apply technical and statistical approaches to go through big amounts of data, evaluating it to predict results for individual patients [22, 23] (see Fig. 1).

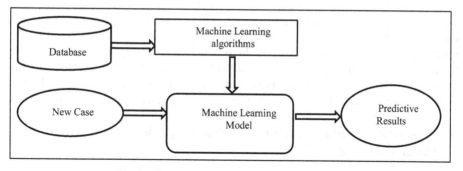

Fig. 1. The processes to build a predictive model

The promising value of predictive models in healthcare has made a high interest in industry and academic researchers [24]. Hence, the published papers in the era of big data analytics in the healthcare area has quickly raised in recent years [25]. Nevertheless, there have been only a few literature reviews which shows an all-encompassing impact and related challenges of predictive models and BDA in healthcare. The literature is still largely fragmented [5].

Our study aims to overcome this gap in the literature. We survey four use cases of PM in healthcare - that is, key examples - where some of the most obvious opportunity exists to improve the quality of treatment and at the same time reducing costs by using BDA, they are: readmissions of patients with heart failure, patients in high-risk for adverse drug events, fall events among elderly people, and high risk patient in hospital admition. It attains to answer the question of the research on: How "Machine learning algorithms" fits in healthcare domain to improve care delivery? Decision making in medicine has become complicated, however, patients and physicians like simple solutions. Every patient has become a "big data" issue, with large quantities of various data on past trajectories and pre-sent situations. Patients can be informed earlier of potential health risks because of warnings from their symptom's evaluation, achieved from predictive algorithms relayed by the doctors [26, 27]. This study explores the challenges that arise from PM use, the potential value that can be reaped, and the future directions of BDA in healthcare.

2 Methodology

The principle analysis for the framework of the study is provided by the information achieved from the current literature. To conduct the study, we followed the key origins of systematic reviews (PRISMA). The process of methodology is shown in Fig. 2. A review is carried out to capture most new related published literature on three significant online databases: Web of Science, PubMed, and IEEE Xplore. We reviewed only the publications in English between 2007 and 2019. The search for articles on electronic databases including the keywords "big data analytics" or "machine learning", "healthcare", and "predictive model".

The initial search revealed 844 articles. After a title examination, a total of 43 articles were elected as per the criteria of paper selection. The keywords and abstract of the papers have scrutinized and 31 related publications were selected for further review. The full text of 31 papers has read. Publications with discussing technical perspectives of machine learning and predictive models in healthcare were beyond the scope of this study and have excluded. Of the 31 papers screened, a total of 22 articles were considered in this review. The final publications involved the papers testing the capabilities of proposed big data techniques for healthcare data analysis; papers that refer to predictive models in healthcare data; benefits, and the big data application in healthcare and its challenges in health domain. The following section summarizes the research results in this study.

3 Research Results - Machine Learning Applications in Building Predictive Models

3.1 Predictive Models in Health Care Organizations

In healthcare, big data technology employs predictive algorithms to discover and control very practical use cases, for example instances in which sample is likely to be accomplished [28]. ML algorithms can distinguish patients who are more prone to recurring illnesses and identify diagnose of the patients. Furthermore, around 90 percent of emergency admissions are preventable [29]. ML algorithms are used to help diagnose and provide patients with proper care delivery all while reducing expense by keeping patients out of heavy treatment [20]. This part of the paper reviews the use of four famous cases of predictive models (PMs). The four cases are reducing readmissions for heart failure, identifying high-risk inpatients for ad-verse drug events, predictive falls among elderly, and predictive risks to individual patients. They are some of the most significant opportunities that exist to improve the quality of treatment using ML algorithms. We discuss the features, advantages, and challenges that will need to consider improving the usability of models.

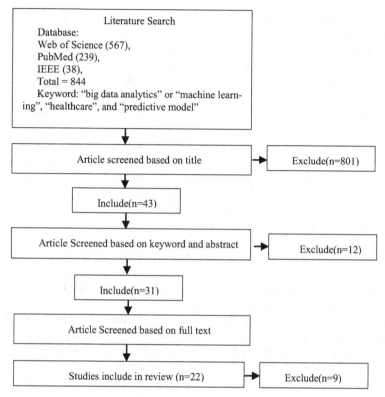

Fig. 2. Methodology process

3.1.1 Reducing Readmissions for Heart Failure (HF)

High rates of readmissions within one month of discharge revealed at several hospitals come with emphasized research for applying of predictive algorithms to determine patients at the maximum risk for re-hospitalization and also possibility of utilizing the inferred likelihoods to direct medical decisions [30]. In a study reported to the US Congress in 2007, the Medicare Payment Advisory Commission stated that around 12Bill. US$ is paid each year by Medicare to likely preventable readmissions within one month of patient discharge [31]. The Center for Medicare and Medicaid Services (CMS) is encouraged associations to decrease readmissions rates. Up to one-third of HF readmissions are being posited to be avoided, consequently, exposing big potential for enhancing treatment delivery [32]. Medical care institutions need to apply a model to predict who is more likely to be re-hospitalized. Accurate Heart Failure prediction algorithms could be helpful to both patients and doctors. Accurate HF prediction algorithms assist medical scientists in planning health care studies by focusing on high risk individuals with heterogeneous features for disease adjusting medical interventions [33]. Several studies of readmissions rates have been carried out and tested within the last twenty years [34–37]. These studies have investigated decreasing in readmission rates by studying post-discharge treatment control, patient education and self-management guidance, scheduled outpatient visits, and also telemedicine. Post-discharge treatment studies reported in the literature usually stated greater reduction of readmission rates with the intervention being examined. Registered reductions in levels of re-hospitalization differs between a few percentage points to 50% or more [38]. Although an intensive post-discharge plan has appeared efficient in avoiding readmissions, it could be prohibitively costly to offer this treatment to a diverse group of individuals. Several re-hospitalization reduction systems have been developed as patient-specific, with involvement of individuals into the prevention plan based on risk rating [39, 40].

Numerous Heart Failure prediction systems are designed and also tested in several groups and are applied in routine medical care to control HF patients within different levels of success and adoption. Though, two main constraints barring the scale of adoption of these prediction systems for HF: (1) These HF systems were comprised of medical trial data from sources that express a group of individuals with limited generalizability. (2) These models are not ideal for providing precise prediction in the real world of health community [41].

These types of clinical trial systems do not involve known comorbid elements found in the real population which could be accurately based on heart failure. Therefore, with raising heart failure information which allows monitoring of real-world patient criteria, it is crucial to build and determine a prediction system for HF prognosis of individuals used in cycle medical process rather than those derived from clinical trial data sources. Nevertheless, there are some problems, from a modeling perspective, in developing predictive models. For example, models have to be highly precise with few false positive instances; models are required to be highly interpretable, as clinical suppliers could use them to determine clinically prognostic markers that help them to make knowledgeable medical judgments [42], and finally the systems should cut down overfitting so they are flexible enough to make accurate predictions on new patients.

3.1.2 Predictive Algorithm to Predict High-Risk Patients for Adverse Drug Events (ADE)

Adverse drug events, as a frequent medical problem [62], are another field where analytics tends to be useful in healthcare. Although adverse events are very expensive and lead to significant morbidity and mortality, some are preventable [43]. Applying a predictive algorithm to detect patients at risk for ADE and to prevent or reduce ADE can be one desirable approach. However, until now attempts to predict which individuals are in risk of ADE have not been very effective [28, 44]. Nevertheless, analytics have the potential capability to forecast with high precision that an individual would face an ADE and to recognize patients in the beginning of such an event by examining genetic and genomic data, laboratory information, details on vital signals, and other data. Sakuma et al. have designed a clinical predictive method that helps physicians to identify individuals who are at high risk for ADE in Japan [45]. They presented a first-prediction model that enables doctors and physicians to have a rapid evaluation of which patients have an increased probability of experiencing and ADE. The rule had utilized the target of high-risk individuals for interventions and can also be applied to discover ADE in earlier times, to reduce the affect they produce. Their method has a potential capability to help health professionals to predict patients at risk. Their research must be interpreted with caution due to several restrictions inherent to the research design.

First, a number of ADEs have not been observed in the graphs and may hence go unnoticed. However, their method to identify ADE used current standard rules and other sturdy options to calculate ADE have not yet been confirmed. Second, they have misclassified potential factors as not found, when in fact they were not analyzed. Moreover, the possible factors could be subjective as records were limited and because of the decisions of personal physicians. They assign the thresholds of at risk people on the basis of the moderate possibility of ADE in the entire cohort and used them as proof, as plainly as possible, for practicing physicians to recognize and utilize quickly; however, thresholds may seem arbitrary. In other words, the usability of the thresholds must be proven in future studies. In summary, as their research was carried out at city tertiary care clinics in Japan, the obtained effectiveness may not transfer to other countries.

3.1.3 Predictive Model for Falls Among Elderly People

Almost one third of individuals aged sixty-five years and older and living in their home encounter at least one falls each year [46]. Fall is a main reason in non-fatal damage [47]. According to the information from the year 2000, the overall rate for nonfatal fall-related accidents is calculated at nineteen billion US dollars a year, and the entire annual expense of fall-related deaths across all medical controls is about 170 million dollars in the United States. Studies of the literature determine that a large portion of the individuals hospitalized to clinics because of falls are subsequently admitted to nursing homes, and experience considerable constraint in their routine lifestyle [48]. It is crucial to determine individuals at higher chance for falling to ensure that these people could be consistently checked and examined for main disorders and medical treatments. Several studies have been dedicated to finding risk features for falls in the aged group, however an instant comparison of existing research is challenging because of low certain-ty and reliability in definitions, methodological problems, different populations, and variability in the du-rations of follow-up [49]. In addition, there will be a complicated causal relationship between risk features and fall event. However, study outcomes have discovered aged era, gender, conceptual impairment, history of injury, and balance problems as the primary risk features in falls [50]. Based on the current researches, medicines like psychotropic and anti-arrhythmic drugs, digoxin, and sedatives can considerably improve the falling risk, by opioids have the most significant effect on elderly [51, 52]. Several studies on fall risks depend on healthcare data; however, although this sort of information is comprehensive and precise, it is also unavailable before an individual is admitted to an emergency department. Models included patient-level items like healthcare co-morbidities, demographic information and social features, with factors from medical examination ratings received in routine check-ups being more suitable, as they are utilized a predictive rule before a fall appears.

Hosseinzadeh et al. [53], presented a predictive model for falls depending on public health administrative information. They looked at the co-morbidities and medicines with known Central Nervous Systems side-effects. They have used data about the yearly prescribed quantity of these medications, as this was well-known to be a potentially crucial risk feature for falls. Their primary outcomes were encouraging, as the predictive results was similar or much better than some available studies [54]. Nevertheless, conflicting outcomes with some earlier advised theories in some drugs sets point to the need for a more comprehensive experiment regarding the initial drugs employed and perhaps the time model of the prescriptions. Essentially, their method must also offer fall possibilities and include a predictable time when these events may occur.

3.1.4 Predictive Rules for Risks to Individual Patient

It is very important to identify the patient's individual risk. Various systems were designed applying numerous factors and criteria, as different systems may fit particular subgroups of patients [55, 56]. For instance, several graphs and calculators utilized the Framingham technique to assess cardiovascular disease (CVD) risk. Some systems are effective, while they have ignored the CVD risk in individuals with diabetes [57, 58]. To be able to achieve a patient-specific guidance at the point of care, it is vital that doctors understand the information from the perspective of that individual [59, 60]. Those situations are associated with customized medication, which highlights the personalization of healthcare.

Jiang [61] presented a model for online selection driven by the confidence intervals (CI) of predictions; therefore, hospitals could select the tool with the aim of supporting their patients. His method automated the procedure and displays proper discrimination and calibration, since it was calculated by the operating characteristic curve (AUC) and the Hosmer–Lemeshow (HL) evaluation in the risk's prediction for the patient. Thereby it has selected the strategy as one of the best for the patient at hand supplied the available data. Another benefit of the algorithm was that the method was able to analyze models trained in a different way. A possible strategy to choosing the right method for an individual is to examine the patient with individuals in the study group utilized to design the system. Nevertheless, it was non-trivial to gather data from every published research. The limitations are partly associated with the regulations and laws on security or confidentiality [28, 62]. Hence, the objective of an effective pattern is designing a tool to decide the more effective predictive method for an individual patient from an applicant pool of systems without the need of the accessibility to training datasets. However, the majority of the previous models identifying real-world physical algorithms are not qualified in healthcare decision support as they are depending on the physical regulations which aren't relevant to the health decision making [63–65]. Although several researches have presented good predictive precision for cohort studies, they could not mention which system is the most suitable for the individual patient. Because of the real-world concerns relevant to security and privacy, it is hard to access the raw information which were useful to develop these predictive systems. In addition, there is no pattern to focus on prevention in hospital admission based on primary care services [66]. This type of inconsistency and problems offers another reason for planning to improve effective predictive method.

The above-mentioned predictive models discussed are summarized chronologically in Table 1. The problems and challenges will be discussed in the next section.

Table 1. Summary of Predictive Models (PMs) in health care

	Models	Advantages	Imitations
1	Reducing Readmissions for Heart Failure	- Validated in multiple cohorts and have used in routine medcal care to manage HF patients with varying level of success and adoption	- Derived from clinical trials databases that demonstrate a population of patients with limited generalizability - Not always include multiple co-morbid factors found in a real-world population
2	Predictive algorithm to detect high-risk patients for adverse drug event (ADE)	- Prevent some adverse drug event in earlier times - savning cost and medicine	- Not very effective - Limited with small papulation
3	Predictive model for falls in elderly people	- Prevent morbidity and cost reduction	- Unavailable before the patient's individual present to an emergency division by the damages - Low accuracy and reliability
4	Predictive rules for risks to individual patient	- Good accuracy for cohort studies	- Didn't clear which algorithm will be most appropriate for the individual - No pattern to focus on prevention in hospital admission based on primary care services

4 Discussion and Challenges

This survey presented the application of big data analytics in health data. Healthcare is one of the domains which could significantly benefit of the growing of data and its availability [7]. Previously, physicians have been treating patients by looking symptoms; however, physicians are beginning to diagnose patients within a concept known as evidence-based treating. This includes considering huge amounts of data aggregated from medical trials and some other treatment pathways on the large scale and applying decisions according to the best information available. Human is able to create one or two good models in a week whereas machine learning (ML) algorithms could make thousands of models a week [67]. ML is a technique for analysis data that automates model building, as it relates to the model's development. ML algorithms can find insights that are not immediately observable from data [68]. Machine learning is becoming popular in the biomedical and health domains as a result of its predictive power [69]. Physicians are able to predict medical insurance fraud, clinical cost, disease analysis, disease diagnosis, and the length of stay in a medical center by applying ML techniques [11]. Furthermore, predictive models (PM) are able to achieve frequent patterns from healthcare dataset, for example associations between health conditions with a specific disease, relationships among medical problems, or relationships among medicines [70]. We have discussed four practical cases for using ML in developing predictive models for medical organizations in which they will be highly beneficial to medical professionals to improve rational decision making. The evidence of advantage varies widely across the use cases, but the improvement of care and treatment quality for the patients in each case seems to be significant. Prediction of patient outcome has become evident and visible in health informatics and is a popular research area, which has established a basis for future innovations [28]. Accordingly, with growing accessibility to health data that enables monitoring of real-world patients features and results, it is important to create and validate predictive models [71]. Furthermore, PM is used for diagnosing and direct patients to an appropriate treatment all while retaining costs by keeping patients out of expensive, time intensive emergency care centers [20].

Designing computational prediction models to predict future situations or gravity of the illness can assist to improve the quality of healthcare. Main benefits involve helping medical professionals to control their patients efficiently by offering a proper treatment plan; preventing hospitalization, a significant driver of expenses; and helping health scientists to design clinical trials by focusing on high risk individuals with heterogeneous features for disease-modifying health interventions [72]. The healthcare domain is growing quickly, with an expanding range of treatments and diagnostics fueled by developments in immunology, genetics, and biology features. Patients are older, have more coexisting diseases and use more drugs. They visit physicians more often and go through more diagnostic examination, which causes exponential collection of electronic health records (EHR) data. Each patient considers a "big data analytics" problem, with various of data on past trajectories or existing details. All of this data challenges our collective power to think. Decision making in Healthcare is becoming maddeningly complicated, and at the same time patients are looking for simple treatments and diagnosis [73, 74]. The initial step to a solution is admitting the deep mismatch between the human mind's capabilities and medicine's complexity.

In spite of this, there are some challenges in developing prediction models from a modeling point of view. Some of the problems include: models must have high accuracy with few false positive conditions; models are required to be highly interpretable before medical organizations will use them to recognize clinically relevant prognostic markers that help them to make smart medical decisions, and the models have to reduce overfitting so they are generalizable tending to gain accurate predictions on the new patients. Although many prediction models have been created and verified on information of cohort researches, little attention has been paid to guarantee the reliability of a forecast for an individual, which is crucial for point of care judgments. Since the objective of prediction models is to forecast results in new individuals, a significant problem in prognostic investigation would be to determine what facts beyond validation are required before physicians can confidently use a model on their patient [75, 76]. There are several main different arguments in applying ML in the biomedical and other fields. First, in most cases, the quality of data in the biomedical sectors is poor compared to that present in other areas as a result of various factors. For example, medical data unavoidably contains missing values [77]. This occurs as even individual patients with similar disease might not always experience equal checkups and laboratory tests (because of different ages, signs, and family backgrounds) which leads to different data sources being produced. Furthermore, health data generally includes time-series features, hence scientists should manage such data with specific evaluations of the time features [78].

Furthermore, since medical information systems or clinical data source are mostly created for financial goals and not for medical reasons, it could be particularly challenging to receive high quality information for medical data analysis [79, 80]. The majority of the historical patient data are paper based or in scanned digital form, therefore this information could not be useful for data analysis without major data preprocessing [78]. For example, plain transcription mistake or data entry errors may be identified through the data preparation or evaluation phrases. These errors could lead to the detection of suspicious models in healthcare fields [81]. Furthermore, while digital health data are becoming an extremely useful source for building prediction models for enhancing patient control, analysis of health data unavoidably is included in safety and legal challenges. Therefore, ML in the healthcare domains is significantly different to what is done in other domains [82].

In the United States, for example, this is a significant consideration where malpractice regulations are strict, and people are litigious [83]. Scientists in the healthcare area should ensure patient privacy and man-age the data in accordance with the rules and regulation [84]. Successful confidentiality preserving methods involve the deidentification of individual data analyses which are expected to comply with regulations concerning human subject study [85]. In medical care, however, it is equally crucial when applying ML to assure patient privacy and sustain confidentially of sensitive data since it is for scientists to make data sources accessible for other scientists [86]. Typically, this continues to be a sensitive balance as data quality and accessibility are affected by the requirement to preserve patient privacy [87]. The probability of increased legal responsibility can clarify why medical care suppliers hesitate to present even de-identified or private health information for data analysis applications.

5   Conclusion, Open Issues, and the Future of Health Sciences

This study reviewed the emerging landscape of big data analytics in healthcare application. Specifically, this study assessed the best current literature in the concept of big data, machine learning algorithms, application of big data analytics in healthcare, causes for applying predictive models in healthcare and strategies to use them.

Big data analytics provide innovation in areas ranging from engineering to healthcare informatics. Healthcare informatic is updating rapidly, with verity of diagnosis and treatment. People needs accurate treatment, and it is becoming more and more expensive. Big data techniques and machine learning algorithms can assist us with critical challenges [45]. Machine learning algorithms increasingly add the value to healthcare by improving the care quality and outcomes and presenting cost-effective care. The predictive model aspect of big data analytics enables the shift from experience-based medicine to evidence-based medicine. The main benefit is warning diseases in the earlier levels when they could treat more effectively and easily; managing specific individual and population health and detecting health care fraud more quickly and efficiently [90]. McKinsey estimates that big data analytics can enable more than $300 billion in savings per year in

U.S. healthcare, two thirds of that through reductions of approximately 8% in national healthcare expenditures [68]. Therefore, it is certainly important to critically review the exploration of the information provided from big data analytics (i.e. what information, from which resources and for what purpose, what is the opportunities, what are the challenges, what should be explored, what is the future direction). However, the literature lacks detailed description of these characteristics especially with regards to healthcare.

This review aims to highlight the impact of big data analytics on the quality and reliability of healthcare data and presents the problems, challenges, and opportunities of using machine learning (ML) in building prediction models. This review presents a significant starting point in the application of machine learning in the future of health research. We critically survey state of the art ML techniques and categorize them into four use cases of reducing readmissions for heart failure, identify high-risk patients for adverse drug event, predictive falls in older adults, and predictive rules for risks to the individual patient. Mapping the existing literature provide health-related foundations and the society to identify at first the impact from big data analytics and also revalue strategies, mitigate risks, and draw upon new opportunities for further development. However, we also discussed the restrictions and requirements for improved techniques and tools in regard to the specialists and researchers. Predictive models use machine learning algorithms to gain knowledge from historical information and predict based on the new information. This presents a great opportunity for data discovery and making decision. ML has many challenges that limit its medical application by scientific researchers. There is a lot of information available within the medical systems; however, there is an absence of effective analysis methods to discover hidden interactions or trends in the dataset. Big data analytics is faced with many challenges, but this research field is still in initial phase. Machine learning models need user parameters because each ML algorithm features its own theoretical assumptions. End users do not tender sufficient details about the parameter or their selection. To make the challenge worse, prediction outcomes are often extremely sensitive to specific parameters. Furthermore, the precision of the predictive system is not sufficient to be utilized in clinics or hospitals. In addition, there is a lack of full ML package for data discovery. A proper predictive model needs to sup-port intelligent data analysis that automatically chooses and removes data for ML goals and utilize do-main knowledge for different data analysis, and also fully automates the data discovery process so it ap-plies the existing information to predict for better knowledge discovery.

ML algorithms learn from the human knowledge, they also learn human mistakes, like overdiagnosis, over testing, failing to realize patients who need to care, and mirroring ethnicity or gender biases. Ignoring these contents will result in automating and even magnifying challenges in the healthcare system. Knowing all these challenges demands a deep knowledge with the medical decisions and the data they generate, a reality that emphasizes the significance of viewing machine learning algorithms as thinking partners, rather than replacements, for doctors. While all these challenges will be solved, it is being highly claimed that big data analytics and machine learning algorithms can become a key technique needed by the healthcare.

References

1. Holzinger, A.: Interactive machine learning for health informatics: when do we need the human-in-the-loop? Brain Inform. **3**(2), 119–131 (2016)
2. Herland, M., Khoshgoftaar, T.M., Wald, R.: A review of data mining using big data in health informatics. J. Big Data **1**(1), 2 (2014)
3. Ola, O., Sedig, K.: The challenge of big data in public health: an opportunity for visual analytics. Online J. Public Health Inform. **5**(3), 223 (2014)
4. Kaisler, S., Armour, F., Espinosa, J.A., Money, W.: Big data: issues and challenges moving forward. In: System Sciences (HICSS), 2013 46th Hawaii International Conference on, 2013, pp. 995–1004. IEEE (2013)
5. Mehta, N., Pandit, A.: Concurrence of big data analytics and healthcare: a systematic review. Int. J. Med. Inform. **114**, 57–65 (2018)
6. Holzinger, A., Dehmer, M., Jurisica, I.: Knowledge discovery and interactive data mining in bioinformatics-state-of-the-art, future challenges and research directions. BMC Bioinform. **15**(6), I1 (2014)
7. Holzinger, A., Jurisica, I.: Knowledge discovery and data mining in biomedical informatics: the future is in integrative, interactive machine learning solutions. In: Holzinger, A., Jurisica, I. (eds.) Interactive Knowledge Discovery and Data Mining in Biomedical Informatics. LNCS, vol. 8401, pp. 1–18. Springer, Heidelberg (2014). https://doi.org/10.1007/978-3-662-43968-5_1
8. Kumar, V., Velide, L.: A Data Mining Approach For Prediction And Treatment Ofdiabetes Disease (2014)
9. Kaur, B., Singh, W.: Review on heart disease prediction system using data mining techniques. Int. J. Recent Innov. Trends Comput. Commun. **2**(10), 3003–3008 (2014)
10. Elgendy, N., Elragal, A.: Big data analytics: a literature review paper. In: Perner, P. (ed.) ICDM 2014. LNCS (LNAI), vol. 8557, pp. 214–227. Springer, Cham (2014). https://doi.org/10.1007/978-3-319-08976-8_16
11. Witten, I.H., Frank, E., Hall, M.A., Pal, C.J.: Data Mining: Practical Machine Learning Tools and Techniques. Morgan Kaufmann (2016)
12. Mittal, S., Hasija, Y.: Applications of deep learning in healthcare and biomedicine. In: Dash, S., Acharya, B.R., Mittal, M., Abraham, A., Kelemen, A. (eds.) Deep Learning Techniques for Biomedical and Health Informatics. SBD, vol. 68, pp. 57–77. Springer, Cham (2020). https://doi.org/10.1007/978-3-030-33966-1_4
13. Balakrishna, S., Thirumaran, M., Solanki, V.K.: IoT sensor data integration in healthcare using semantics and machine learning approaches. In: Balas, V.E., Solanki, V.K., Kumar, R., Ahad, Md.A.R. (eds.) A Handbook of Internet of Things in Biomedical and Cyber Physical System. ISRL, vol. 165, pp. 275–300. Springer, Cham (2020). https://doi.org/10.1007/978-3-030-23983-1_11
14. Larose, D.T.: Discovering Knowledge in Data: An Introduction to Data Mining, Wiley (2014)
15. Sun, J., Reddy, C.K.: Big data analytics for healthcare. In: Proceedings of the 19th ACM SIGKDD international conference on Knowledge discovery and data mining, 2013, pp. 1525–1525. ACM (2013)
16. Shukla, D., Patel, S.B., Sen, A.K.: A literature review in health informatics using data mining techniques. Int. J. Softw. Hardw. Res. Eng. **2**(2), 123–129 (2014)
17. Mansourvar, M., Shamshirband, S., Raj, R.G., Gunalan, R., Mazinani, I.: An automated system for skeletal maturity assessment by extreme learning machines. PLoS ONE **10**(9), e0138493 (2015)
18. Mansourvar, M., et al.: Automated web-based system for bone age assessment using histogram technique. Malaysian J. Comput. Sci. **25**(3), 107–121 (2012)

19. Tomar, D., Agarwal, S.: A survey on Data Mining approaches for Healthcare. Int. J. Biosci. Bio-Technol. **5**(5), 241–266 (2013)
20. Chaurasia, V., Pal, S.: Data mining approach to detect heart diseases (2014)
21. Gupta, G.: Introduction to data mining with case studies. PHI Learning Pvt. Ltd. (2014)
22. Obermeyer, Z., Lee, T.H.: lost in thought—the limits of the human mind and the future of medicine. N. Engl. J. Med. **377**(13), 1209–1211 (2017)
23. Galetsi, P., Katsaliaki, K., Kumar, S.: Values, challenges and future directions of big data analytics in healthcare: a systematic review, Soc. Sci. Med. **125**, 112533 (2019)
24. Swain, A.K.: Mining big data to support decision making in healthcare. J. Inf. Technol. Case Appl. Res. **18**(3), 141–154 (2016)
25. Forkan, A.R.M., Khalil, I., Atiquzzaman, M.: ViSiBiD: a learning model for early discovery and real-time prediction of severe clinical events using vital signs as big data. Comput. Netw. **113**, 244–257 (2017)
26. Bates, D.W., Saria, S., Ohno-Machado, L., Shah, A., Escobar, G.: Big data in health care: using analytics to identify and manage high-risk and high-cost patients. Health Aff. **33**(7), 1123–1131 (2014)
27. Ingber, M.J., et al.: Initiative to reduce avoidable hospitalizations among nursing facility residents shows promising results. Health Aff. **36**(3), 441–450 (2017)
28. Jencks, S.F., Williams, M.V., Coleman, E.A.: Rehospitalizations among patients in the Medicare fee-for-service program. N. Engl. J. Med. **360**(14), 1418–1428 (2009)
29. Zuckerman, R.B., Sheingold, S.H., Orav, E.J., Ruhter, J., Epstein, A.M.: Readmissions, observation, and the hospital readmissions reduction program. N. Engl. J. Med. **374**(16), 1543–1551 (2016)
30. Kocher, R.P., Adashi, E.Y.: Hospital readmissions and the Affordable Care Act: paying for coordinated quality care. JAMA **306**(16), 1794–1795 (2011)
31. Harjola, V.P., et al.: Contemporary management of acute right ventricular failure: a statement from the heart failure association and the working group on pulmonary circulation and right ventricular function of the european society of cardiology. Eur. J. Heart Fail. **18**(3), 226–241 (2016)
32. Ong, M.K., et al.: Effectiveness of remote patient monitoring after discharge of hospitalized patients with heart failure: the better effectiveness after transition–heart failure (BEAT-HF) randomized clinical trial. JAMA Internal Med. **176**(3), 310–318 (2016)
33. Pocock, S.J., et al.: Predicting survival in heart failure: a risk score based on 39 372 patients from 30 studies. Eur. Heart J. **34**(19), 1404–1413 (2012)
34. Murtaugh, C.M., et al.: Reducing Readmissions among Heart Failure Patients Discharged to Home Health Care: Effectiveness of Early and Intensive Nursing Services and Early Physician Follow-Up. Health Serv. Res. **52**(4), 1445–1472 (2017)
35. Hu, X., Huang, W., Su, Y., Qu, M., Peng, X.: Depressive symptoms in Chinese family caregivers of patients with heart failure: a cross-sectional study, Medicine, **96**, 13 (2017)
36. Avati, A., Jung, K., Harman, S., Downing, L., Ng, A., Shah, N.H.: Improving palliative care with deep learning. BMC Med. Inform. Decis. Mak. **18**(4), 122 (2018)
37. van Walraven, C., et al.: Derivation and validation of an index to predict early death or unplanned readmission after discharge from hospital to the community. Can. Med. Assoc. J. **182**(6), 551–557 (2010)
38. Amarasingham, R., et al.: An automated model to identify heart failure patients at risk for 30-day readmission or death using electronic medical record data. Med. Care **48**(11), 981–988 (2010)
39. Califf, R.M., Pencina, M.J.: Predictive Models in Heart Failure, ed: Am Heart Assoc (2013)
40. Letham, B., Rudin, C., McCormick, T.H., Madigan, D.: An Interpretable Stroke Prediction Model using Rules and Bayesian Analysis. 2013, ed (2013)

41. Jha, A.K., Chan, D.C., Ridgway, A.B., Franz, C., Bates, D.W.: Improving safety and eliminating redundant tests: cutting costs in US hospitals. Health Aff. **28**(5), 1475–1484 (2009)
42. Falconer, N., Barras, M., Cottrell, N.: Systematic review of predictive risk models for adverse drug events in hospitalized patients. Br. J. Clin. Pharmacol. **84**(5), 846–864 (2018)
43. Sakuma, M., Bates, D.W., Morimoto, T.: Clinical prediction rule to identify high-risk inpatients for adverse drug events: the JADE Study. Pharmacoepidemiol. Drug Saf. **21**(11), 1221–1226 (2012)
44. Scheffer, A.C., Schuurmans, M.J., Van Dijk, N., Van Der Hooft, T., De Rooij, S.E.: Fear of falling: measurement strategy, prevalence, risk factors and consequences among older persons. Age Ageing **37**(1), 19–24 (2008)
45. Alptekin, F., Uskun, E., Kisioglu, A.N., Ozturk, M.: Unintentional non-fatal home-related injuries in Central Anatolia, Turkey: frequencies, characteristics, and outcomes. Injury **39**(5), 535–546 (2008)
46. Deandrea, S., et al.: Risk factors for falls in community-dwelling older people: a systematic review and meta-analysis, Epidemiology, **48**, 658–668 (2010)
47. Howcroft, J., Kofman, J., Lemaire, E.D.: Review of fall risk assessment in geriatric populations using inertial sensors. J. Neuroeng. Rehabilit. **10**(1), 91 (2013)
48. Kerr, G.K., Worringham, C.J., Cole, M.H., Lacherez, P.F., Wood, J.M., Silburn, P.: Predictors of future falls in Parkinson disease. Neurology **75**(2), 116–124 (2010)
49. Ensrud, K.E., et al.: Comparison of 2 frailty indexes for prediction of falls, disability, fractures, and death in older women. Arch. Intern. Med. **168**(4), 382–389 (2008)
50. Muir, S.W., Berg, K., Chesworth, B., Speechley, M.: Use of the Berg Balance Scale for predicting multiple falls in community-dwelling elderly people: a prospective study. Phys. Ther. **88**(4), 449–459 (2008)
51. Hosseinzadeh, A., Izadi, M., Precup, D., Buckeridge, D.: Mining administrative data to predict falls in the elderly population, Adv. Artif. Intell. **205**, 305–311 (2012)
52. Buckeridge, D., et al.: Risk of injury associated with opioid use in older adults. J. Am. Geriatr. Soc. **58**(9), 1664–1670 (2010)
53. Wei, W., Visweswaran, S., Cooper, G.F.: The application of naive Bayes model averaging to predict Alzheimer's disease from genome-wide data. J. Am. Med. Inform. Assoc. **18**(4), 370–375 (2011)
54. Jiang, X., Osl, M., Kim, J., Ohno-Machado, L.: Calibrating predictive model estimates to support personalized medicine. J. Am. Med. Inform. Assoc. **19**(2), 263–274 (2011)
55. Steyerberg, E.W., et al.: Predicting outcome after traumatic brain injury: development and international validation of prognostic scores based on admission characteristics, PLoS Med. **5**, 8 (2008)
56. Steyerberg, E.W.: Clinical prediction models. SBH. Springer, Cham (2019). https://doi.org/10.1007/978-3-030-16399-0
57. Soni, J., Ansari, U., Sharma, D., Soni, S.: Predictive data mining for medical diagnosis: An overview of heart disease prediction. Int. J. Comput. Appl. **17**(8), 43–48 (2011)
58. Jiang, X., Boxwala, A.A., El-Kareh, R., Kim, J., Ohno-Machado, L.: A patient-driven adaptive prediction technique to improve personalized risk estimation for clinical decision support. J. Am. Med. Inform. Assoc. **19**(e1), e137–e144 (2012)
59. Farhan, W., Wang, Z., Huang, Y., Wang, S., Wang, F., Jiang, X.: A predictive model for medical events based on contextual embedding of temporal sequences. JMIR Med. Inform. **4**, 4 (2016)
60. Wu, X., Zhu, X., Wu, G.-Q., Ding, W.: Data mining with big data. IEEE Trans. Knowl. Data Eng. **26**(1), 97–107 (2014)
61. Mai, J.-E.: Looking for Information: A Survey of Research on Information Seeking, Needs, and Behavior. Emerald Group Publishing (2016)

62. Chen, M., Mao, S., Liu, Y.: Big data: a survey. Mob. Netw. Appl. **19**(2), 171–209 (2014)

63. Fournaise, A., Espensen, N., Jakobsen, S., Andersen-Ranberg, K.: Increasing primary health-care services are associated with acute short-term hospitalization of Danes aged 70 years and older, European Geriatric Medicine (2017)

64. Simard, P.Y., et al.: Machine teaching: A new paradigm for building machine learning systems," arXiv preprint arXiv:1707.06742 (2017)

65. Groves, P., Kayyali, B., Knott, D., Kuiken, S.V.: The'big data'revolution in healthcare: Accelerating value and innovation (2016)

66. Kim, N.-H., An, D., Choi, J.-H.: Introduction. In: Prognostics and Health Management of Engineering Systems, pp. 1–24. Springer, Switzerland (2017). https://doi.org/10.1007/978-3-319-44742-1

67. Krumholz, H.M.: Big data and new knowledge in medicine: the thinking, training, and tools needed for a learning health system. Health Aff. **33**(7), 1163–1170 (2014)

68. Klein, A., et al.: The ACTA PORT-score for predicting perioperative risk of blood transfusion for adult cardiac surgery, BJA: British J. Anaesthesia, **119**(3), 394–401 (2017)

69. Mazinani, I., Ismail, Z.B., Shamshirband, S., Hashim, A.M., Mansourvar, M., Zalnezhad, E.: Estimation of Tsunami bore forces on a coastal bridge using an extreme learning machine. Entropy **18**(5), 167 (2016)

70. Henney, A.M.: Editorial to "Computational models of liver disease 2016"," ed: Elsevier (2017)

71. Wang, Y., Kung, L., Byrd, T.A.: Big data analytics: Understanding its capabilities and potential benefits for healthcare organizations. Technol. Forecast. Soc. Chang. **126**, 3–13 (2018)

72. Traeger, A.C., O'Hagan, E.T., Cashin, A., McAuley, J.H.: Reassurance for patients with non-specific conditions–a user's guide. Brazilian Journal of Physical Therapy (2017)

73. DeCou, J., Johnson, K.: An introduction to predictive modelling of drug concentration in anaesthesia monitors. Anaesthesia **72**(S1), 58–69 (2017)

74. Lee, C.H., Yoon, H.-J.: Medical big data: promise and challenges. Kidney research and clinical practice **36**(1), 3 (2017)

75. Capobianco, E.: Systems and precision medicine approaches to diabetes heterogeneity: a big data perspective. Clin. Trans. Med. **6**(1), 23 (2017)

76. Wu, J., Li, H., Cheng, S., Lin, Z.: The promising future of healthcare services: when big data analytics meets wearable technology. Inf. Manag. **53**(8), 1020–1033 (2016)

77. Ebrahimi, A., Nielsen, A.S., Will, U.K., Mansourvar, M., 2019, June. The prediction of alcohol use disorder: a scoping review. In: 2019 IEEE Symposium on Computers and Communications (ISCC), pp. 1062–1067. IEEE (2019)

78. Wang, Y., Hajli, N.: Exploring the path to big data analytics success in healthcare. J. Bus. Res. **70**, 287–299 (2017)

79. Chen, M., Hao, Y., Hwang, K., Wang, L., Wang, L.: Disease prediction by machine learning over big data from healthcare communities. IEEE Access **5**, 8869–8879 (2017)

80. Obermeyer, Z., Emanuel, E.J.: Predicting the future—big data, machine learning, and clinical medicine. New England J. Med. **375**(13), 1216 (2016)

81. Malin, B.A., Emam, K.E., O'keefe, C.M.: Biomedical data privacy: problems, perspectives, and recent advances, ed: BMJ Publishing Group (2013)

82. Mooney, S.J., Pejaver, V.: Big data in public health: terminology, machine learning, and privacy. Annu. Rev. Public Health **39**, 95–112 (2018)

83. Rostow, T.: What happens when an acquaintance buys your data: a new privacy harm in the age of data brokers. Yale J. Reg. **34**, 667 (2017)

84. López-Martínez, F., Schwarcz, A., Núñez-Valdez, E.R., Garcia-Diaz, V.: Machine learning classification analysis for a hypertensive population as a function of several risk factors. Expert Syst. Appl. **110**, 206–215 (2018)

85. Mansourvar, M., Andersen-Ranberg, K., Nøhr, C., Wiil, U. K.: A Predictive model for acute admission in aged population. In: MIE, pp. 96–100 (2018)

86. Eisenberg, R.S., Price, W.N.: Promoting healthcare innovation on the demand side. J. Law Biosci. **4**(1), 3–49 (2017)
87. Pedersen, D.H., Mansourvar, M., Sortsø, C., Schmidt, T.: Predicting dropouts from an electronic health platform for lifestyle interventions: analysis of methods and predictors. J. Med. Internet Res. **21**(9), e13617 (2019)

A Multi-level Consensus Clustering Framework for Customer Choice Modelling in Travel Industry

Sujoy Chatterjee[1,2] and Nicolas Pasquier[1](✉)

[1] CNRS, I3S, Université Côte d'Azur, Sophia Antipolis, France
pasquier@i3s.unice.fr
[2] Ulsan National Institute of Science and Technology, Ulsan, Republic of Korea
sujoy@unist.ac.kr

Abstract. In the travel industry context, customer segmentation, that is the clustering of travelers to distinguish segments of customers with similar needs and desires, is a major issue for improving the personalization of recommendations in flight search queries. Indeed, when booking travel itineraries, different customers purchase tickets according to different criteria, like price, duration of flight, layover time, etc. However, clustering algorithm application is a challenging task because of two central issues inherent to the unsupervised nature of the grouping of instances: The choice of the clustering algorithm and parameterization and the evaluation of the resulting clusters of instances. Essentially, each clustering algorithm and evaluation measure relies on an assumption of the distribution model of the instances in the data space. The relevance of the resulting clustering mainly depends to which extent they are adapted to the analyzed data space properties. We present a Multi-level Consensus Clustering framework that combines the results of several clustering algorithmic configurations to generate a multi-level consensus clustering solution in which each cluster represents an agreement between the different clustering results. Relevant agreements are identified using a closed sets-based approach and represented in a hierarchical representation providing the end-user a representation of the consensus cluster construction process and their inclusion relationships. We show how this framework developed for Customer Choice Modeling in travel context can provide a better segmentation and refine the customer segments by identifying relevant sub-segments represented as sub-clusters in the hierarchical representation, and we present the technical and scientific challenges posed by the approach.

Keywords: Consensus clustering · Ensemble clustering · Multi-level clustering · Closed sets · Travel search queries · Customer Choice Modelling

1 Introduction

In travel industry, the Customer Choice Modelling (CCM) application aims to model the decision process of a traveler, or a category of travelers, the analysis and the prediction

© ICST Institute for Computer Sciences, Social Informatics and Telecommunications Engineering 2020
Published by Springer Nature Switzerland AG 2020. All Rights Reserved
M. H. Miraz et al. (Eds.): iCETiC 2020, LNICST 332, pp. 142–157, 2020.
https://doi.org/10.1007/978-3-030-60036-5_10

of his preferences and the choices he makes in different contexts. Since the needs and wishes of travelers vary according to different features, like the number of children they have, the trip duration or the price of the tickets for example, a better understanding of travelers behaviors, through the segmentation of travelers according to their distinct characteristics, is necessary for improving travel search query recommendations.

The use of clustering techniques in Customer Choice Modeling aims to discriminate the *segments of customers*, or *business classes*, according to their properties in the data space as outlined in Fig. 1. Customer segments are identified as clusters, i.e. groups with similar properties, of customers in the data space of travel search queries. This data space is defined by the traveler search query parameters and their results, such as the booking of a proposed travel or service.

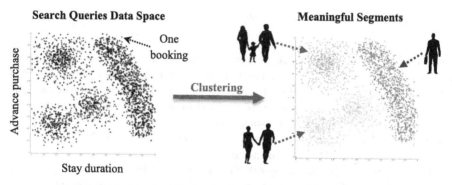

Fig. 1. Clustering of search queries for customer segment identification.

The characterization of the resulting clusters aims to identify the different segments of customers, each segment corresponding to a category of travelers with different needs and requirements as outlined in Fig. 2. During this step, the specific features of each cluster and their weight in the booking result probabilities are extracted by a comparative analysis of the clusters. Finally, for each segment, personalized booking options can be defined according to this characterization of clusters. New search queries recommendations can then be adapted according to the segment they correspond to.

While many clustering algorithms have been proposed in the literature, it is widely agreed that none of them can generate a relevant clustering result in all contexts. Indeed, each clustering algorithm is based on a different assumption about the subjacent model of the distribution of instances in the data space, e.g., density-based or centroid-based. The parameterization of the algorithm defines a way to put this model into practice on the dataset. See [7, 16, 23] for comprehensive reviews about clustering algorithms. Choosing an adequate algorithmic configuration, that is choosing an algorithm and setting its parameters, for clustering a dataset is a challenging central issue since the relevance of the resulting clustering relies on how well it is suitable for the characteristics of the data space being analyzed [12, 24].

The resulting clusterings of a dataset are usually evaluated using unsupervised evaluation measures. These measures are called *internal validation measures* as they are

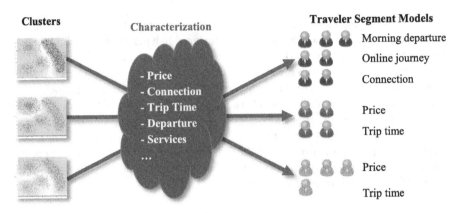

Fig. 2. Characterization of search query clusters for traveler segment modelling.

based solely on the properties of clusters in the data space and do not use other information, making them unsupervised by nature. Each internal validation measure evaluates how much the clusters match a specific underlying model of the distribution of instances in the data space. Hence, different measures can provide different results for the same clustering and overrate clustering results from algorithms that are based on the same assumption about the data distribution as the measure. See [6, 11, 21] for extensive studies about clustering validation measures.

To overcome the issue of the algorithmic configuration choice, different algorithmic configurations providing different clustering solutions for the same dataset, *consensus clustering* approaches were proposed. These approaches combine clusters extracted by diverse clustering algorithmic configurations, called *base clusterings*, to generate consensus clusters corresponding to agreements between *base clusters* for improving clustering robustness. The set of base clusterings is also called the *ensemble* and the consensus clustering approach called *ensemble clustering* in the literature. See [4, 9, 20] for comprehensive reviews and studies on ensemble clustering algorithmic approaches. The evaluation of the relevance of a consensus clustering is performed by the analytical comparison between clusters in the clustering solution and clusters in the base clusterings. The most frequently used measures are the Adjusted Rand Index (ARI) and the Normalized Mutual Information (NMI) that evaluates the relevance of the consensus clustering as its average similarity with all base clusterings in the ensemble [14, 18, 19]. Such consensus clustering validation measures provide an efficient solution to identify and rank the best agreements among all the base clusterings regarding the possible different data distribution models, e.g., density-based or centroid-based, in sub-spaces of the data space corresponding to clusters.

In order to characterize the behavior of customers, appropriate segmentation of customers is highly needed. On the other hand, most of the clustering algorithms assume some specific dataspace distribution over the dataset while producing the clusters. Therefore, the different clustering algorithms applied even on the same dataset may generate the different diverse clustering solutions. Moreover, from the perspective of customer search data in the travel context, it is very difficult to know the prior information regarding the number of clusters over the customers. There is limited research that address the issues of customers segmentation resulting from different clustering algorithms. Note that, each clustering algorithm seeks to provide the actual number of clusters when applied to the dataset. Therefore, motivated by these shortcomings, consensus clustering can act as a major role in order to find better clustering over the dataset. In this proposed conceptual model, the effort is made to find the better segmentation of customers without specifying the actual number of clustering from the individual base clustering having number of clusters in a certain range.

The article is organized as follows. Section 2 presents the proposed framework, Sect. 3 describes the technical and the scientific challenges addressed, and Sect. 4 concludes the article.

2   Multiple Consensus Clustering Framework

The proposed framework was developed on the basis of the Multiple Consensus Clustering approach introduced with the *MultiCons* algorithm [2]. This approach is a *multi-level clustering* approach providing as a result a hierarchical decomposition of the consensus clusters generated. In this hierarchy, named *ConsTree* for tree of consensuses, the levels depict consensus clusterings of the dataset, each level corresponding to a different number of agreements between the base clusterings. In multi-level clustering, a cluster at a level in the produced hierarchy can be decomposed into several smaller clusters in the sub-levels of the hierarchy. This hierarchy can then be presented to the end-user as tree-like graphical representation where nodes are clusters and edges represent inclusion relationships between clusters of successive levels. The proposed framework can be adapted to other multi-level clustering approaches.

The benefit of multi-level clustering in Customer Choice Modelling is to provide a data representation context that can both discriminate the business classes, i.e., segments of customers, according to their properties in the data space and refine them by distinguishing different sub-classes of a class, representing *sub-segments of customers*, according to the different modeling properties of each sub-cluster in the data space [8].

2.1   Multiple Consensus Clustering Approach

Multi-level clustering provides a relevant framework for the simultaneous identification of business classes and sub-classes as illustrated in Fig. 3. In this example, we assume the original dimensions of the dataset representing travel characteristics are summarized through a two-dimensional reduction, such as obtained by a component reduction approach for example, and the generated clusters in this two-dimensional data space, representing customer segments, are characterized by their distinctive features regarding dimensions in the initial data space. In this schematic example, the customer segment C-2 is specialized into two customer sub-segments, namely C-2-1 and C-2-2, corresponding to two sub-clusters. These sub-clusters can be identified as two subspaces corresponding to significant variations in density in the data space of segment C-2 represented as a green area.

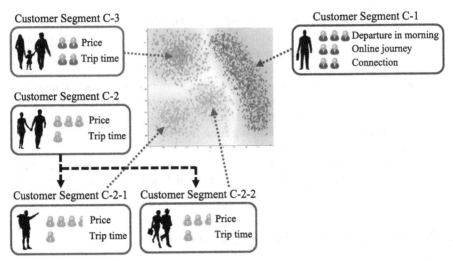

Fig. 3. Business segment specialization by multi-level consensus cluster analysis. (Color figure online)

The objective of multiple consensus clustering is to identify such a specialization of business classes in the generated hierarchy of consensus clusters. We can observe in the example two-dimensional data space in Fig. 3 that the variations in the density of data points in the sub-spaces corresponding to clusters C-1, C-2 and C-3 can enable their identification using a density-based clustering algorithm by choosing appropriate values for the size and density of neighborhood algorithm parameters. Furthermore, the sub-spaces corresponding to clusters C-2-1 and C-2-2 can be distinguished in the sub-space of cluster C-2 by choosing different adequate values for these parameters. Then, in the resulting hierarchy of consensus clusters such as represented in the tree of consensuses shown in Fig. 4, a level of the hierarchy will correspond to clusters C-1, C-2 and C-3 and a lower level in the hierarchy will contain the four clusters C-1, C-2-1, C-2-2 and C-3. The second of the above-mentioned levels will be a sub-level of the first that corresponds to a higher rate of agreements among the base clusterings. Note that in the tree of consensuses representation, the size of nodes is proportional to the number of instances the corresponding cluster contains.

2.2 Traveler Choice Modelling Problem Decomposition

The proposed multiple consensus clustering framework can be viewed as a semi-supervised algorithmic process in the sense that it combines unsupervised internal validation of multi-level consensus clusters and supervised business metric based *external validation* of multi-level consensus clusters. Interested readers can refer to [1, 10, 15] for definitions and studies related to semi-supervised clustering concepts. It relies on the decomposition of the problem of traveler choice modelling into the three following tasks:

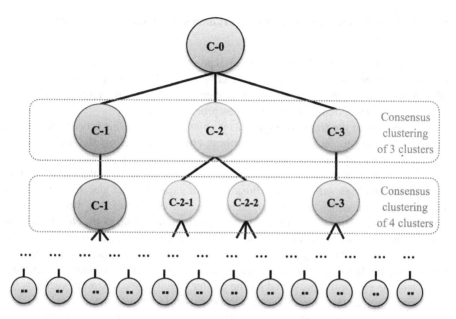

Fig. 4. Example representation of business segment specialization in the multiple consensus clustering tree-like hierarchy.

1. **Identify traveler segments: How can search queries be grouped by similarity?**
   The first task is to identify segments of travelers, each segment corresponding to a category of travelers with different needs and requirements. A segment can be refined and represented as several clusters in the data space corresponding to slightly different features, i.e., sub-segments.
2. **Understand traveler choice patterns: What is the likelihood of a search offer to be booked?**
   The second task consists to learn a predictive model for assessing the probability of a travel search query to lead to a booking or not through the analysis of the features of successful and unsuccessful search queries.
3. **Optimize bookings for each segment: What really matters and to which extent it does?**
   The third task is to connect clusters with traveler classes so that each cluster is representative of a segment, or a sub-segment, of travelers, and to identify discriminative feature of clusters, i.e. search queries feature values that distinguish the segments.

This decomposition of the problem of Customer Choice Modeling relies on the capability of multi-level consensus clustering to distinguish sub-segments of the predefined customer segments when each sub-segment corresponds to slightly different properties regarding its instance modeling in the data space compared to other sub-segments.

2.3   Multi-level Consensus Clustering Framework for Customer Choice Modelling

The proposed framework relies on a sequential process that integrates successively unsupervised, semi-supervised and supervised techniques to identify customer segments and sub-segments, according to the similarity of their searching and booking activities, that are as significant as possible from a business process viewpoint.

An overview of the framework process is shown in Fig. 5. This process first builds multi-level consensus clusters, evaluates these clusters and selects the most relevant ones considering both internal and external validations. Then, an interactive analysis of the hierarchical relationships between clusters depicted in the tree-like representation provides the end-user with a visual illustration for exploring and identifying the most relevant clusters and the business segments they correspond to. The most important criteria (ranges of values for variables price, trip duration, connections, etc.) for delimiting each customer segment are then identified according to prior expertise and the automatic characterization of the clusters they correspond to. This distinctive characterization of segments will then allow to predict the segment of a new customer by assigning him/her to the segment represented by the cluster which characterization vector is the most similar to the customer, that is the closest cluster in the data space.

This interactive process starts with the preprocessing of the dataset according to end-users choices, arising from dataset exploration, in order to ensure the applicability of clustering algorithmic configurations used to generate the base clusterings. These algorithmic configurations are defined to ensure that two central properties of the clustering ensemble are satisfied. The first is the required diversity of the search space for consensus

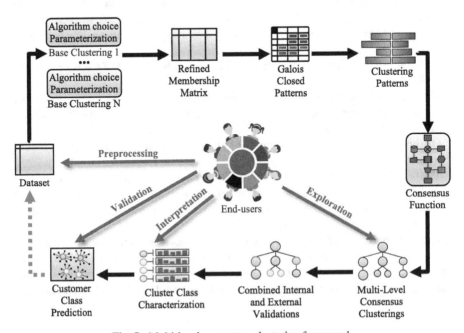

Fig. 5. Multi-level consensus clustering framework.

clusters, that is the ensemble of base clusterings should cover a sufficiently wide range of clustering approaches and parameterizations. The second is to ensure the robustness of the final solution by centering this search space on the number of clusters corresponding to optimal internal and external validation measures according to the number of base clustering connected components. Then, the clustering ensemble is represented as a refined membership matrix depicting assignments to base clusters for each instance. Galois closed patterns are extracted from the matrix to identify all existing agreements to cluster instances together between the base clusterings. These closed patterns correspond each to a maximal, regarding inclusion relation, set of instances clustered together and its associated maximal, regarding inclusion relation, set of base clusters containing these instances. They are then iteratively processed in increasing order of their number of base clusters for generating clustering patterns, each one representing an agreements for clustering a (maximal) set of instances. A consensus function is then applied to the clustering patterns as a merge/split process, considering their properties regarding the number of agreements and disagreements between base clusterings on grouping the sets of instances they correspond to, for generating consensus clusters. This closed patterns-based process can treat datasets with very large number of instances N since, contrarily to most other consensus clustering approaches, it does not require the processing of a co-association matrix of size N^2 but only of a membership matrix which size is N.M, where M is the number of base clusters, with $M \ll N$, and regarding the demonstrated scalability properties of Galois closed sets extraction algorithms [3, 17, 25].

Generated consensus clusters and their hierarchical relationships, regarding inclusion relation, are graphically represented in the tree of consensuses. Each level of this graphical representation depicts a consensus clustering, i.e., a partitioning of all instances in the dataset, and each node of a level represents a consensus cluster, that is a maximal grouping of instances agreed among base clusterings. The edges between nodes of two successive levels represent cluster regroupings leading to a new consensus cluster of instances. Depicting the consensuses creation process, this visualization allows the end-users to choose the most relevant result among the different consensus clustering solutions, i.e., between different levels of agreements among the base clusterings. The clustering solution having the best overall similarity with the clustering ensemble is recommended in the graphical representation as the final consensus clustering solution. This MultiCons approach visualization is extended in this framework to facilitate and precise the interpretation of the consensus cluster creation process and their properties, and to allow the end-users to choose the most relevant consensus multi-level clusters that can originate from different consensus clusterings, i.e., different levels of the hierarchy. Algorithmic and statistical methods developed for this extension consider the properties of the structure of the hierarchy, e.g., the stability of consensus clusters and not only the stability of consensus clusterings, and the relationships between clusters in the data space, e.g., overlapping sets between sets of instances and sets of base clusters that define the clustering patterns and weighting of base clusterings according to their number of clusters. The stability of a consensus cluster refers to the individual recurrence of a group of instances among successive levels of the hierarchy while the stability of a consensus clustering refers to the recurrence of a partitioning of all instances, i.e., a set of clusters, among successive levels of the hierarchy.

This automatic, or semi-automatic depending on end-user preferences, processing of the hierarchical tree of consensuses structure allows to generate new internal and external validation measurements for each cluster, based on closed pattern properties in the data space, that are significant to characterize each selected consensus cluster and distinguish it from others selected consensus clusters. From these characterizations, a vector that is representative and distinctive of each cluster is generated. Then, the business segment of new instances, regarding business metrics, is predicted using a mapping function that assigns new instances to their closest cluster in the data space identified as the most similar cluster characterization vector. Preliminary experimental results on the comparison of this closed patterns-based multiple consensus clustering approach and other state-of-the-art consensus clustering approaches were conducted in collaboration with Amadeus IT Group. They showed the relevance of the resulting consensus clusters regarding Amadeus business metrics used for flight search recommendations.

The most relevant and significant results of the validation by the end-users of the predictions of the assigned segment to instances can be integrated in subsequent iterations of the process. These results can be represented as cannot-link and must-link constraints in order to use semi-supervised clustering algorithms among the base clusterings for example.

3 Technical and Scientific Challenges

This section details the central scientific and technological challenges addressed during the development and implementation of the framework, and its experimental application in the context of the Amadeus flight search recommendation engine, with central results and findings, and future extensions of the realizations.

3.1 Data Space Exploration and Description Regarding Base Clustering Algorithm Parameterizations

To conduct experimental and comparative studies an initial dataset was constructed by extracting search queries of flight bookings for flights departing from the U.S.A. during one week of January 2018. This dataset contains the 9 most relevant variables identified according to Amadeus business expertise and metrics: Distance between the airports, geography, number of passengers, number of children, advance purchase, stay duration, day of the week of the departure, day of the week of the return, and day of the week of search. The Geography variable values are encoded as categorical ordinal values: 0 for domestic flights with departure and arrival airports in the same country, 1 for continental flights with departure and arrival airports on the same continent and 2 for intercontinental flights. This dataset contains a very large number of instances representing customers, in the order of millions.

The exploratory analysis of the dataset space showed that an important proportion of the instances have very similar variable values, and the populations are divided into several strata based on similar characteristics. For the purpose of rapid prototyping and testing of the developed and compared algorithmic approaches, and to enable the application of algorithms that have limitations regarding the number of instances processed, a sampling was performed on the sub-populations to generate a stratified sampling of the whole dataset while preserving the distribution properties of the original dataset. For experimental evaluations, three stratified samples containing respectively 500, 1000 and 1500 instances were created. The effect of the stratified sampling for the 'distance between airports' variable can be observed in Fig. 6 showing the histograms of the distribution of the variable values in the original dataset and in the two largest stratified samples created.

3.2 Definition of Base Clustering Algorithmic Configurations

Consensus clustering results depend to a significant extent on the relevance of the set of base clusterings used to generate the clustering ensemble, which constitutes the search space for the consensus function. A major concern for generating a relevant set of base clusterings is to define an interval of values for the number of clusters generated by base clusterings that ensures diversity in both the solutions and the levels of resolution of clusters. This parameter, usually denoted as the K parameter, is required by most classical clustering algorithms.

This work showed the important impact of the clustering ensemble properties regarding both a sufficient diversity in the search space, i.e., the potential consensus clusters explored, and a centering of this search space on the most stable number of connected components, for defining an interval of K values for K-parameter based algorithms. Ensuring these properties are satisfied through the generation of an enhanced search space, in the refined clustering ensemble and membership matrix, is a major step for obtaining relevant consensus clusters.

3.3 Definition of Clustering Patterns by Analysis of Agreements Between Base Clusterings

Closed patterns extracted from the refined membership matrix consist each of a set of instances and a set of base clusters that agreed to cluster together these instances. They constitute the initial clustering patterns of the algorithmic process that generates new clustering patterns by combination of existing ones in an incremental manner. This process was enhanced during this work to extend the comparative analysis of the final clustering patterns and thus optimize the generation of consensus clusters.

A new measure for evaluating the relevance of each clustering pattern, that is a set of instances and the corresponding set of base clusters, was developed to compare, select and combine them using the maximum information at our disposal. This measure considers at the same time:

- The number of agreements and disagreements between base clusterings on grouping the set of instances of the clustering pattern.
- The inclusion relationships between sets of instances and sets of base clusters of compared clustering patterns.
- The sizes of the sets of instances of the closed patterns extracted from base clusterings.
- The number of clusters in the base clusterings that affects the probability of co-occurrence of instances in a cluster.

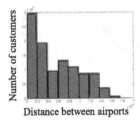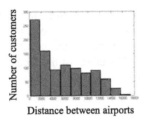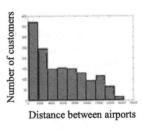

Fig. 6. Distribution of values for the 'distance between airports' variable in the original dataset (left), the stratified sample of size 1000 (middle) and the stratified sample of size 1500 (right).

This new measure was shown to be able, contrarily to the initial measure, to provide distinct values for clustering patterns with different properties regarding the base clusterings they correspond to.

3.4 Comparative Analysis of Multi-level Clusters by Internal and External Validation Criteria

The problem of the evaluation of the quality of both consensus clusterings and consensus clusters is a central issue to generate a relevant solution. The state-of-the-art and comparative study of validation measures of clusterings and clustering ensembles shows that, basically, two types of performance evaluation are used:

- Internal validation in which the evaluation is done with the dataset itself only. This evaluation is based on the analysis of relationships between instances in clusters regarding their distribution in the data space and their common properties. For this, many indices are defined in literature, like Silhouette index, Entropy, R-Squared (RS), Root-Mean-Square Standard Deviation (RMSSTD), Semi-Partial R-squared (SPR), Distance between two clusters (CD), Partition Coefficient (PC), Classification Entropy (CE), Partition Index (PC), Separation Index (S), Xie and Beni's index (XB), Inter-Cluster Density (ID), Davies-Bouldin (DB) index, Dunn's Index (DI), Alternative Dunn Index (ADI), etc.
- External validation in which existing prior knowledge about the dataset is involved. This prior knowledge is represented either as class labels for the dataset instances, when each instance can be assigned a business segment, or as another clustering result in which assigned clusters are considered as instance segment labels and the evaluated clustering is then compared to this existing clustering result. The most commonly used indices for this are the Average Rand Index (ARI) and the Normalized Mutual Information (NMI), although several other indices were proposed in the literature such as Accuracy, Cohesion, Entropy, F-measure, Purity, etc.

The new measures developed for internal and external validation aim to extend the information classically used for internal and external validations, that is the list of co-occurrences of pairs of instances in the clusters, by integrating in the calculation the information provided by the clustering patterns, e.g., the new clustering pattern relevance measure developed, and their hierarchical relationships such as depicted in the tree of consensuses.

The new measures developed are based on the closed sets-based framework of Formal Concept Analysis. The main motivation relies on the fact that the ARI and NMI popular metrics basically compare the similarities among pairs of clustering solutions (external evaluation concept). However, in a specific clustering solution the quality of individual clusters (internal evaluation concept) is not considered and all clusterings are treated the same way which is not realistic in the considered type of scenarios. Frequent closed sets-based measures become an interesting solution in this context being more effective when little or no information is available regarding the number of actual clusters in the dataset, as well as when only base clustering solutions are available instead of the initial dataset.

3.5 Automatic Analysis of Consensus Cluster Generation Process for Identifying Strong Clusters and Outlier Instances

Using the proposed new measures for comparing clusters in the tree of consensuses, based on clustering patterns, and an analysis of the hierarchical relationships in the tree, both outlier instances and multi-level strong groups of instances can be identified if present. Outlier instances are identified through their unstable behavior from the viewpoint of the clustering process: They are successively associated and separated with the same instances in different levels of the tree. Strong groups are identified through their stability over different successive levels of the tree of consensuses, such as the C-1 and C-3 cluster in Fig. 4, that thus represent strong clusters, with maximal agreement, regarding the base clusterings.

Results of initial experimentations of the proposed approach were able to identify such a structure of clusters, where a significant cluster from the viewpoint of the customer segment representation is divided into three sub-segments with significant distinctive features regarding the new measures results. These initial results were evaluated using Amadeus specific business metrics that validated the relevance of the three sub-segments identified regarding the prediction of query search result booking.

3.6 Definition of the Class Prediction Process Based on Similarity Analysis of New Instance Features and Discriminative Characterizations of Clusters

Once the selected multi-level consensus clusters have been validated regarding both internal and external validations, and business metric, each cluster is associated to the business segment or sub-segment of customers it corresponds to. The clusters are then characterized in the data space to identify the criteria that discriminate them, that is the features that distinguish the instances in a cluster from the instances in other clusters. These criteria are combined to generate a classifier, that is an algorithmic process for predicting the class of new instances, i.e., the business segment or sub-segment of each new customer.

Different approaches for defining the class prediction model were tested, considering both the relevance of the generated predictions and the computational efficiency and scalability of the process. These approaches consist to determine which cluster is the nearest to the new instance in the data space considering the assessed distance (minimal, maximal, average, etc.) between the new instance and each cluster. The best results were obtained when a representative vector consisting of variable value domains is computed for each cluster and the distance is evaluated between the new instance and each representative vector.

Once the new instance class prediction process is validated, the next step consists to evaluate the capability of the approach to efficiently distinguish and predict significant business segments and sub-segments according to business objective classes defined by the Customer Choice Modelling application context.

4   Conclusion

During the development of the proposed multi-level consensus clustering framework, several consensus clustering algorithms, internal and external clustering validation measures and integrations of supervised, semi-supervised and unsupervised techniques were studied, with the objective to obtain a better aggregation of individual clustering solutions. From the results, a conceptual framework for implementing an improved customer segmentation and choice modelling solution in travel context was designed.

The techniques developed during this project first aim to solve central issues for the Customer Choice Modeling data clustering steps by providing a multi-level consensus clustering based solution that:

- Does not require the user to define the number of clusters to generate as a parameter of the clustering solution, but automatically determine the number of clusters according to base clustering properties.
- Generates multiples consensus clustering solutions corresponding to different levels of agreements between the base clusterings. This property allows to choose the most relevant consensus solution considering both internal and external validation criteria.
- Generates a robust clustering solution that does not rely solely on a particular modeling assumption of clusters, i.e., a unique category of algorithms and a unique parameterization.
- Provides a hierarchy of consensus clusters, allowing the end-users to select clusters at different levels of precision regarding the business segments. In this hierarchy, a segment can be refined as several sub-segments, each corresponding to the same business class of instances but with slight variations regarding their distinctive features or the business objectives.
- Automatically identifies strong clusters, i.e., groups of instances agreed by a maximal number of base clusterings, and outlier instances, i.e., instances with features that do not hold the general properties of similar instances or the instances in the same clusters. This identification relies on the analytical comparison of consensus clusters and their hierarchical relationships.
- Generates a graphical representation of hierarchical relationships of consensus clusters, depicting their generation process, to help the end-users in the interpretation of the resulting consensus clusters.

- Can automatically identify the best multi-level consensus clusters obtained according to internal validation criteria and their ranking based on their structural properties and hierarchical relationships.

The second category of techniques developed aim to connect, from a business viewpoint, the unsupervised results of clustering and the classes of instances, that is the customer segments and sub-segments. These techniques aim to:

- Combine the results of internal and external validations for identifying the most relevant multi-level consensus clusters from a business objective perspective. These clusters should represent significant groups of instances from both the viewpoints of their distinct features in the data space and the business class each one corresponds to.
- Provide a statistical and analytical exploration solution for the business-related evaluation of the generated multi-level consensus clusters regarding internal (data space based) and external (business metric based) cluster validations, and of the obtained consensus clustering solution.
- Identify the discriminative features of clusters, that are required to distinguish instances assigned to different clusters, regarding distribution model properties of the cluster data sub-spaces.
- Generate an instance class prediction model by the comparative analysis of discriminative features of the selected clusters.
- Provide support to the end-users for the semi-automatic tasks of the process, such as the evaluation and validation of classes of clusters regarding business related objectives, predefined business classes and external metrics.

The techniques developed meet the central needs identified for Customer Choice Modelling in travel industry. The first is the capability to identify relevant business segments and sub-segments by the grouping of search queries according to their similarity. The second is the understanding of customer choice patterns, in order to predict the likelihood of a search query recommendation to be booked. The third is the optimization of the rate of bookings of search query recommendations for each business segment by the identification of search query features that really matters and the quantification of how much they matter for each segment. Importantly, since the proposed framework relies, among other things, on semi-supervised techniques, it has the capacity to be adapted to situations in which preferences of customers can switch in response to contextual changes as might happen in situations where travel business might be influenced by unusual circumstances such as a pandemic like the Coronavirus pandemic [12].

We have described the technical and scientific challenges encountered during the development and implementation of the proposed framework in collaboration with Amadeus IT Group. The experimental evaluations carried out on Amadeus data about search queries of flight bookings have shown the feasibility and relevance of the proposed approach for Customer Choice Modelling in travel industry [5]. The tests conducted have shown a significant increase in the probabilities of flight search queries booking using the recommendations generated from the prediction of the segments and sub-segments of travelers extracted by the multi-level consensus clustering process.

Acknowledgments. This work has been supported by the French government, through the UCA^{JEDI} Investments in the Future project managed by the National Research Agency (ANR) with the reference number ANR-15-IDEX-01.

References

1. Agovic, A., Banerjee, A.: Semi-Supervised Clustering. Data Clustering: Algorithms and Applications, Chapter 20. Chapman & Hall, pp. 505–534 (2013)
2. Al-Najdi, A., Pasquier, N., Precioso, F.: Using frequent closed itemsets to solve the consensus clustering problem. Int. J. Softw. Eng. Knowl. Eng. **26**(10), 1379–1397 (2016)
3. Bertet, K., Demko, C., Viaud, J.F., Guérin, C.: Lattices, closures systems and implication bases: a survey of structural aspects and algorithms. Theor. Comput. Sci. **743**, 93–109 (2018)
4. Boongoen, T., Iam-On, N.: Cluster ensembles: a survey of approaches with recent extensions and applications. Comput. Sci. Rev. **28**, 1–25 (2018)
5. Chatterjee, S., Pasquier, N., Nanty, S., Zuluaga, M.A.: Multi-objective consensus clustering framework for flight search recommendation, 17 p. Cornell University (2020). https://arxiv.org/abs/2002.10241
6. Dalton, L., Ballarin, V., Brun, M.: Clustering algorithms: on learning, validation, performance, and applications to genomics. Curr. Genomics **10**(6), 430–445 (2009)
7. Fahad, A., et al.: A survey of clustering algorithms for big data: taxonomy and empirical analysis. IEEE Trans. Emerg. Top. Comput. **2**(3), 267–279 (2014)
8. Färber, I., et al.: On using class-labels in evaluation of clusterings. In: KDD MultiClust International Workshop on Discovering, Summarizing and Using Multiple Clusterings. ACM, Washington DC (2010)
9. Ghosh, J., Acharya, A.: A Survey of Consensus Clustering. Handbook of Cluster Analysis, Chapter 22. Chapman & Hall, pp. 497–518 (2016)
10. Grira, I., Crucianu, M., Boujemaa, N.: Unsupervised and semi-supervised clustering: a brief survey. Rev. Mach. Learn. Tech. Process. Multimed. Content **1**, 9–16 (2005)
11. Halkidi, M., Batistakis, Y., Vazirgiannis, M.: On clustering validation techniques. J. Intell. Inf. Syst. **17**, 107–145 (2001)
12. Hamid, O.H., Braun, J.: Reinforcement learning and attractor neural network models of associative learning. In: Sabourin, C., Merelo, J.J., Madani, K., Warwick, K. (eds.) IJCCI 2017. SCI, vol. 829, pp. 327–349. Springer, Cham (2019). https://doi.org/10.1007/978-3-030-16469-0_17
13. Hennig, C.: Clustering Strategy and Method Selection. Handbook of Cluster Analysis, Chapter 31. Chapman & Hall, pp. 703–730 (2016)
14. Hubert, L., Arabie, P.: Comparing partitions. J. Classif. **2**(1), 193–218 (1985)
15. Jain, A., Jin, R., Chitta, R.: Semi-Supervised Clustering. Handbook of Cluster Analysis, Chapter 20. Chapman & Hall, pp. 443–468 (2016)
16. Kriegel, H.-P., Kröger, P., Zimek, A.: Clustering high-dimensional data: a survey on subspace clustering, pattern-based clustering, and correlation clustering. ACM Trans. Knowl. Discov. Data **3**(1), 1–58 (2009). Article 1
17. Mondal, K.C., Pasquier, N., Mukhopadhyay, A., Maulik, U., Bandhopadyay, S.: A new approach for association rule mining and bi-clustering using formal concept analysis. In: Perner, P. (ed.) MLDM 2012. LNCS (LNAI), vol. 7376, pp. 86–101. Springer, Heidelberg (2012). https://doi.org/10.1007/978-3-642-31537-4_8
18. Van der Hoef, H., Warrens, M.J.: Understanding information theoretic measures for comparing clusterings. Behaviormetrika **46**, 353–370 (2019)

19. Vinh, N.X., Epps, J., Bailey, J.: Information theoretic measures for clusterings comparison: variants, properties, normalization and correction for chance. J. Mach. Learn. Res. **11**, 2837–2854 (2010)
20. Vega-Pons, S., Ruiz-Shulcloper, J.: A survey of clustering ensemble algorithms. Int. J. Pattern Recognit Artif Intell. **25**(3), 337–372 (2011)
21. Rendón, E., Abundez, I., Arizmendi, A., Quiroz, E.M.: Internal versus external cluster validation indexes. Int. J. Comput. Commun. **5**(1), 27–34 (2011)
22. Xiong, H., Li, Z.: Clustering Validation Measures. Data Clustering Algorithms and Applications, Chapter 23. CRC Press, pp. 571–605 (2014)
23. Xu, D., Tian, Y.: A comprehensive survey of clustering algorithms. Ann. Data Sci. **2**(2), 165–193 (2015)
24. Xu, R., Wunsch, D.: Survey of clustering algorithms. IEEE Trans. Neural Netw. **16**(3), 645–678 (2005)
25. Yahia, S.B., Hamrouni, T., Nguifo, E.M.: Frequent closed itemset based algorithms: a thorough structural and analytical survey. ACM SIGKDD Explor. Newsl. **8**(1), 93–104 (2006)

Bangla Speech Recognition Using 1D-CNN and LSTM with Different Dimension Reduction Techniques

Md. Nazmus Sabab[1], Mohammad Abidur Rahman Chowdhury[1],
S. M. Mahsanul Islam Nirjhor[1], and Jia Uddin[2(✉)]

[1] Brac University, 66 Mohakhali, Dhaka 1212, Bangladesh
sababnazmus@gmail.com, rahmanbidkafoo@gmail.com,
mahsanulnirjhor@gmail.com
[2] Technology Studies, Endicott College, Woosong University, Daejeon, Korea
jia.uddin@wsu.ac.kr

Abstract. This paper presents a model of Bangla speech recognition using machine learning algorithms. Mel-frequency Cepstral Coefficient (MFCC) and Mel Spectrogram are extracted from a Bangla dataset. Commonly used dimension reduction techniques, Principal Component Analysis (PCA), Kernel-PCA (k-PCA), and T-distributed Stochastic Neighbor Embedding (t-SNE) are applied to the extracted features as a dimension reduction technique. At the end, as a classification tool, 1-dimensional Convolutional Neural Network (1D-CNN) and Long-Short Term Memory (LSTM) are utilized. Experimental results demonstrate that among the dimension reduction techniques, PCA demonstrates comparatively higher accuracy than the other state-of-art models by exhibiting 94.58% and 83.12% accuracy for 1D CNN and LSTM, respectively. In addition, it has been observed that dimension reduction techniques have no positive impact on 1D-CNN and LSTM. Without any dimension reduction technique, MFCC with 1D-CNN has demonstrated better accuracy compared to MFCC with LSTM by showing 97.26% and 93.83% of accuracy, respectively.

Keywords: Speech recognition · Neural network · MFCC · LSTM · CNN · PCA · K-PCA · T-SNE · Bangla speech recognition · Bengali speech recognition

1 Introduction

With total of 265 million speakers, Bangla language ranks the 7th most spoken language in the world [1]. But it is a matter of regret that research of Bangla language detection is very insufficient compare to other languages [2]. For Bangla speech recognition, one of the most difficult tasks is to collect a standard large dataset due to the scarcity of publicly available Bangla speech dataset. Since the last decade, speech recognition systems have been developed successfully by using different feature extraction methods and neural network models [3]. Nahid et al. (2017) developed a Bangla speech recognition system

© ICST Institute for Computer Sciences, Social Informatics and Telecommunications Engineering 2020
Published by Springer Nature Switzerland AG 2020. All Rights Reserved
M. H. Miraz et al. (Eds.): iCETiC 2020, LNICST 332, pp. 158–169, 2020.
https://doi.org/10.1007/978-3-030-60036-5_11

using MFCC (Mel Frequency Cepstral Coefficient) as a feature extraction method and trained the features using a deep LSTM model. Their system achieved 13.2% of the word detection error rate [4]. Rahman et al. (2018) proposed a system for Bangla speech recognition with Dynamic time warping (DTW) and Support vector machine (SVM) [21], which achieved 86.08% accuracy [5]. Among different feature extraction methods, MFCC is mostly used because it can provide greater accuracy for speech recognition [6, 7]. For feature extraction, Davis et al. conducted research by comparing parametric representations for recognizing words from continuously spoken sentences. Mel Frequency Cepstrum, Linear Frequency Cepstrum, Linear Prediction Cepstrum were used in this research. They concluded that MFCC gives better accuracy than the other methods [8]. In speech recognition, dealing with high dimensions of acoustic features and high training complexity due to redundant data are often considered as the main practical difficulties or "Curse of dimensionality" [9, 10]. Moreover, large sets of features require very high memory and computing power [11] which makes the training unfit for few machines, and as a solution dimension reduction techniques are becoming the inevitable tools [10].

For Bangla speech recognition, existing methods never implemented the dimension reduction technique. By removing multi-collinearity, dimension reduction techniques increase the computational performance of the neural network model and assist some algorithms to deal with large dimensions [12].

In this paper, we have experimented with different dimension reduction techniques such as PCA (principal component analysis), kernel PCA, and t-SNE (t-distributed stochastic neighbor embedding) on MFCC and Mel spectrogram features in order to observe the impact of it on CNN and LSTM classifier. The use of the dimension reduction technique is a novel approach for Bangla speech recognition.

The rest of the paper is organized as follows. Section 2 explains the methodology used for this research. The descriptions of the dataset, network structure for each CNN and LSTM model, experimental results are discussed in Sect. 3. The comparative analysis of the experimental results from different classifiers and dimensionality reduction techniques is discussed in Sect. 4. Finally, Sect. 5 concludes the paper.

2   Methodology

Most of the early research done on Bangla language focused on building a recognizer with the number of features that could be obtained through the feature extraction techniques of the audio dataset. However, in this model, we have considered using dimension reduction techniques on extracted features to remove redundant features for less computation and run-time, as well as to examine how different algorithms work with different dimension reduction techniques. These techniques are widely used to improve the computational performance of the learning process [12, 13]. Different techniques perform differently for which we provided a comparative analysis and also compared results against the results without any feature reduction.

First, Bangla audio data have been gathered from different native speakers and converted to WAV format. MFCC and Mel spectrogram have been used for extracting the features from audio data. Then, for dimension reduction-PCA, kernel PCA, and t-SNE have been utilized. The advantages of dimension reduction are that it reduces space required as the data is more compressed and also reduces the time complexity of the learning of the neural network as it has to learn from fewer features. If there are any redundant features originally, the transformation process can reduce to eliminate their influence. After feature reduction, the data have been trained on 1D CNN and LSTM separately.

The extracted MFCC features are also trained directly without feature reduction on 1D CNN and LSTM to compare and observe the impact of dimension reduction techniques. A detailed description of the structure of each network model has been discussed in Sect. 3.

3   Results and Discussion

The dataset, network structure of 1D CNN and LSTM of each experiment without and with dimension reduction techniques and detailed results obtained from each the recognition model are presented in this section.

3.1   Dataset

Although Bangla is one of the most spoken languages, the resources for speech recognition are not publicly available. Due to the scarcity of datasets, we had to make our data for this research purpose. First, audio voice recordings from some random Bangla speakers have been collected. Later on, those audio samples have been trimmed eliminating silent and other noisy parts with the Audacity software. Then, those files have been converted to WAV format. Multiple speakers have been introduced in the dataset.

For the dataset, 11 Bangla words have been chosen which are 11 digits (0–10) of Bangla language. Total 4152 voice samples of single utterance have been prepared. A single speaker uttering the same word for example ' 'সাত" (seven) on two different occasions may sound different which is illustrated in Fig. 1.

Figure 2 illustrates the difference between the utterances of the same word by different speakers. The examples below were given for ' 'তিন' (three).

The approaches used to extract features are MFCC and Mel spectrogram and the extracted features were optimized by using the PCA, k-PCA, and t-SNE dimension reduction techniques. The following subsections present model description and experimental results for 1D CNN and LSTM without and with dimension reduction.

3.2   MFCC with 1D CNN

In this model, 128 MFCC coefficients are fed directly into a 1D convolutional layer with 64 neurons with a kernel size of 3. The output is entered into another 1D convolutional layer also comprising of 64 neurons. Both of these layers have a kernel size of three. The layer follows is a max-pooling layer of size 3 which is followed by a 1D global average pooling. The output is fed into a dropout layer and final layer is a dense layer with the activation function set to sigmoid. The loss function of the overall model is binary cross-entropy and optimizing function is rmsprop. This model obtained an accuracy of 97.26% in 50 runs which is illustrated in Fig. 3.

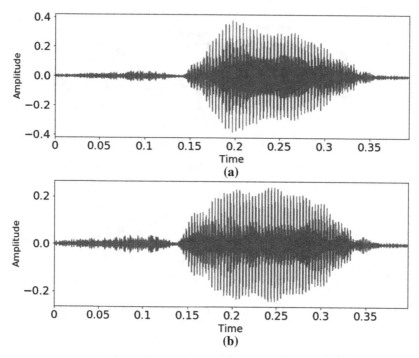

Fig. 1. (a) ' 'সাত' ' for speaker 1, (b) another ' 'সাত' ' for speaker 1.

3.3 MFCC with LSTM

The recurrent LSTM used in this system has two LSTM layers with 128 neurons. Each LSTM layer of 64 neurons is followed by a dropout layer and a recurrent dropout layer. For regularizer function, we have used kernel, recurrent and bias regularizers with various values. The final layer is a dense layer configured with the activation function of softmax. For categorical cross-entropy and optimizing algorithm, we used the loss function-adamax. This model obtained an accuracy of 93.83% for 50 epochs. Figure 4 represents the accuracy and loss graph, respectively.

3.4 PCA with 1D CNN

Here, PCA is used as a dimensionality reduction technique. PCA is an unsupervised dimensionality reduction technique that reduces the complexity of data by projecting the data from a higher dimension to a new smaller or equal dimension subspace sustaining the correlation and variance in new subspace [14, 15]. In this model, MFCC features are fed into the PCA technique and reduced the component number from 128 to just 6. Then the PCA reduced features are fed into 1D CNN. For our Neural Network model, the first layer is a 1D convolutional layer with 64 neurons followed by another 1D convolutional layer also comprising of 64 neurons. Both of these layers have a kernel size of three. The output from each layer has to go through an activation layer of the function of relu (Rectified Linear Unit). This particular activation learns much faster than the tanh

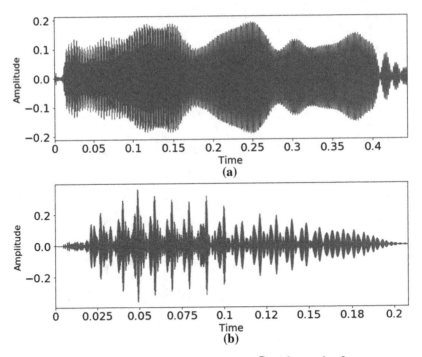

Fig. 2. (a) ' তিন ' for speaker 1, (b) ' তিন ' for speaker 2.

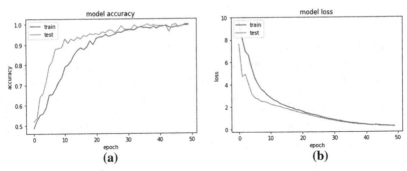

Fig. 3. (a) Accuracy of 1D CNN using MFCC, (b) loss of 1D CNN using MFCC.

or sigmoid functions. Next, we added a 1D Max pooling layer with a kernel size of 3 followed by a 1D Global Average pooling layer. Both of these layers do not have any learnable parameters and their function is merely to reduce the output significantly. The output from Global Average Pooling is fed into the Dropout layer. The purpose of these layers is to switch off certain nodes at random to reduce the complexity of the network and thus improve the network's validation accuracy. The final layer is the dense layer, which is a fully connected layer. Fully connected means each neuron in the dense layer receives input provided by the previous layer. The output of this layer is the general output that we are looking for. The loss function that is used by this model is binary

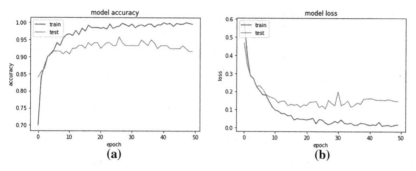

Fig. 4. (a) Accuracy of LSTM using MFCC, (b) loss of LSTM using MFCC.

cross-entropy and the optimizing algorithm we used is rmsprop. This model obtained an accuracy of 94.58% for the dataset after 50 runs, which is depicted in Fig. 5.

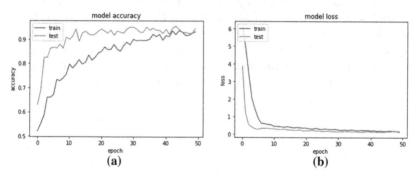

Fig. 5. (a) Accuracy of 1D CNN using PCA, (b) loss of 1D CNN using PCA.

3.5 PCA with LSTM

This recurrent LSTM has two LSTM layers with 32 neurons for each layer. The successive output from these layers goes through a dropout layer followed by a recurrent dropout layer. For regularizer function, kernel, recurrent and bias regularizers are used with various values. The final layer is a dense layer configured with the activation function of softmax. The loss function here for this model is the categorical cross-entropy and the optimizing algorithm we used is adamax. This model obtained an accuracy of 83.12% after 50 epochs as illustrated in Fig. 6.

3.6 t-SNE with 1D CNN

The t-SNE used for reducing MFCC features gave a very poor 1-dimensional convolutional neural network with an accuracy of 49% only. Here we have experimented with building network models of various depths. However, an ideal network structure was

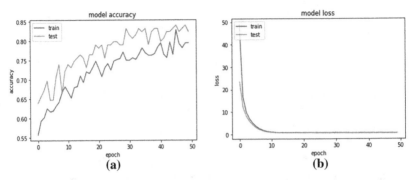

Fig. 6. (a) Accuracy of LSTM using PCA, (b) loss of LSTM using PCA.

never seemed to be found. We have utilized both shallow and deep network model but the accuracy remained at around 49%–50% with high loss. Thus we have concluded that the features provided by t-SNE contain very poor information in classification.

The shallow network we attempted was a 4-layer CNN with neuron numbers 64, 64, 128, and 256, respectively. There is a 1D max-pooling layer after the second layer and each of the CNN layers is followed by an activation layer of the function relu. Next is a global average pooling layer followed by a dropout layer. Finally, a dense layer gives the output. The accuracy function and loss function are shown in Fig. 7.

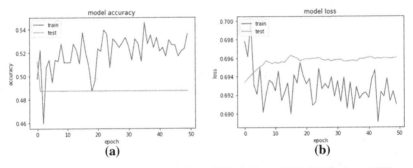

Fig. 7. (a) Accuracy of 1D CNN using t-SNE, (b) loss of 1D CNN using t-SNE.

3.7 t-SNE with LSTM

Like the CNN model, LSTM model also performed poorly when we used the t-SNE. This is the model we settled with after deeper models not giving any better accuracy. We have 2 LSTM layers of 64 and 32 units successively. We have used dropout and recurrent dropout layers for each model. The final layer is a dense layer. The model provided 51% accuracy and no significant improvement has been observed when increasing epoch. This system also had a very high loss. Figure 8 illustrates the accuracy and loss, respectively.

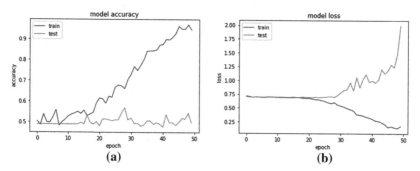

Fig. 8. (a) Accuracy of LSTM using t-SNE, (b) loss of LSTM using t-SNE.

3.8   Kernel-PCA with 1D CNN

Here, K-PCA is used as a Dimensionality Reduction Technique. The main difference between PCA and K-PCA is PCA works with linear data while K-PCA works with non-linear data. To deal with non-linear problems, K-PCA implements kernel function to represent PCA in higher dimensional space [16]. Although this method seems to provide good performance in speech recognition [17], due to high computational complexity [18, 19] K-PCA does not assist in improving real-time performance [20] of the speech recognition system.

In this experiment, Mel spectrogram features are fed into the K-PCA technique and reduced the component number from 128 to 6. The reason we used Mel-spectrogram over MFCC here because the matrix of the MFCC produces negative eigenvalues and when the square root is computed produces nun values. For the neural network model, the first layer is a 1D convolutional layer with 64 neurons with an activation layer following configured to relu. This is followed by another 1D convolutional layer comprising of 64 neurons also followed by an activation layer configured to relu. Both of these convolutional layers have a kernel size of three. After this, there is a 1D max-pooling layer followed by 1D global average pooling layer. The output from the Global Average Pooling is fed into the Dropout layer. The purpose of these layers is to switch off certain nodes at random to reduce the complexity of the network and thus improve the network's validation accuracy. The final layer is a fully connected dense layer.

The loss function that is used by this model is- binary cross-entropy and the optimizing algorithm we used is- rmsprop. This model obtained an accuracy of 72.13% for the test dataset after 50 runs as illustrated in Fig. 9.

3.9   Kernel-PCA with LSTM

This LSTM has two LSTM layers with 64 neurons in the first, and 32 neurons in the second layer. The output from these layers goes through a dropout out layer and the successive output is passed through the recurrent dropout layer. For regularizer function kernel, recurrent and bias regularizers are used with various values. The final layer is a dense layer configured with the activation function of softmax. The loss function here for this model is the categorical cross-entropy and the optimizing algorithm we used is

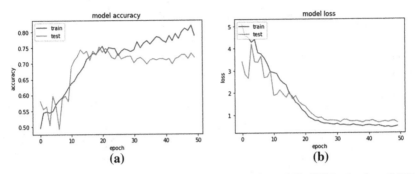

Fig. 9. (a) Accuracy of 1D CNN using kernel-PCA, (b) loss of 1D CNN using kernel-PCA.

adamax. Our model obtained an accuracy of 73.98% for the test dataset after 50 runs as shown in Fig. 10.

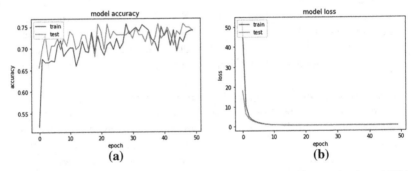

Fig. 10. (a) Accuracy of LSTM using kernel-PCA, (b) loss of LSTM using kernel PCA.

4   Comparative Analysis

We have compiled our results based on the accuracy of the model versus the number of features used. The CNN model using MFCC as features gave a very high accuracy for all number of features as illustrated in Fig. 11(a).

For the LSTM model, Mel Spectrogram features provided average higher accuracy for any number of features as illustrated in Fig. 11(b).

After applying the feature reduction algorithm and training it on the 1D-CNN model, it has been observed that PCA coefficients exhibit very high accuracy among all the other techniques. T-SNE transformation demonstrates the accuracy around 49–50%; whereas the k-PCA shows a moderate accuracy around 72%–75% for the features as illustrated in Fig. 12(a).

After applying feature reduction algorithm and training it on the LSTM model, it has been observed that PCA coefficients hold a better accuracy than all the other techniques which changes slightly when changing the number of features being transformed. PCA

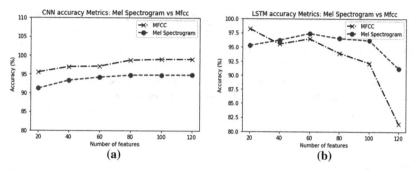

Fig. 11. (a) CNN accuracy for Mel spectrogram vs MFCC, (b) LSTM accuracy for Mel spectrogram vs MFCC.

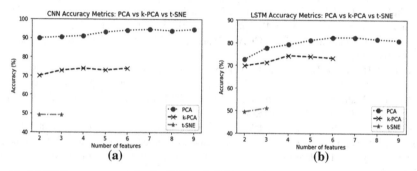

Fig. 12. (a) CNN accuracy metrics for PCA vs k-PCA vs t-SNE, (b) LSTM accuracy metrics for PCA vs k-PCA vs t-SNE.

features give their peak accuracy with the LSTM model when transformed to 5 features per window. T-SNE transformation again gave the least accuracy of around 49%–51%. And k-PCA gave peak accuracy when transformed to 4 features per window as illustrated in Fig. 12(b).

5 Conclusion

The paper shows a comparative analysis of different dimension reduction techniques for 1D CNN and LSTM classifiers. Moreover, in the beginning, MFCC features are directly used on 1D CNN and LSTM without dimension reduction so that impact of dimension reduction can be observed. Through the experimental evaluation, it is concluded that among the dimension reduction techniques, PCA outperforms the other state-of-art models by exhibiting better accuracy. After 50 epochs, the model has exhibited 94.58% of accuracy for 1D CNN and 83.12% for LSTM, respectively. Whereas, K-PCA has shown only 72.13% accuracy for 1D CNN and 73.98% for LSTM. Among the dimension reduction techniques, t-SNE has shown the worst results by experiencing approximately 49%–51% accuracy with a high loss for both classifiers.

However, it is concluded that dimensionality reduction techniques have not shown any positive impact on accuracy. MFCC without dimension reduction has demonstrated better results which are 97.26% and 93.83% accuracy for 1D CNN and LSTM respectively. In this case, 1D CNN outperforms LSTM.

For future research, dimension reduction techniques can be used to experiment on time series data instead of MFCC coefficient or mel-spectrogram. Also, further implementation of dimension reduction techniques can be done on a very large scale Bangla dataset that may provide different results.

References

1. Eberhard, D.M., Simons, G.F., Fennig, C.D. (eds.): Ethnologue: Languages of the World. Twenty-Third edn. SIL International, Dallas (2020). http://www.ethnologue.com
2. Nahid, M.M.H., Islam, M.A., Islam, M.S.: A noble approach for recognizing Bangla real number automatically using CMU Sphinx4. In: 2016 5th International Conference on Informatics, Electronics and Vision (ICIEV), Dhaka, pp. 844–849. IEEE (2016). https://doi.org/10.1109/iciev.2016.7760121
3. Nasib, A.U., Kabir, H., Ahmed, R., Uddin, J.: A real time speech to text conversion technique for Bengali language. In: 2018 International Conference on Computer, Communication, Chemical, Material and Electronic Engineering (IC4ME2), Rajshahi, pp. 1–4 (2018). https://doi.org/10.1109/ic4me2.2018.8465680
4. Nahid, M.M.H., Purkaystha, B., Islam, M.S.: Bengali speech recognition: a double layered LSTM-RNN approach. In: 2017 20th International Conference of Computer and Information Technology (ICCIT), Dhaka, pp. 1–6. IEEE (2017). https://doi.org/10.1109/iccitechn.2017.8281848
5. Rahman, M.M., Roy Dipta, D., Hasan, M.M.: Dynamic time warping assisted SVM classifier for Bangla speech recognition. In: 2018 International Conference on Computer, Communication, Chemical, Material and Electronic Engineering (IC4ME2), pp. 1–6. IEEE (2018). https://doi.org/10.1109/ic4me2.2018.8465640
6. Wang, Y., Lawlor, B.: Speaker recognition based on MFCC and BP neural networks. In: 2017 28th Irish Signals and Systems Conference (ISSC), pp. 1–4. IEEE (2017). https://doi.org/10.1109/issc.2017.7983644
7. Bhattarai, K., Prasad, P.W.C., Alsadoon, A., Pham, L., Elchouemi, A.: Experiments on the MFCC application in speaker recognition using Matlab. In: 2017 Seventh International Conference on Information Science and Technology (ICIST), pp. 32–37. IEEE (2017). https://doi.org/10.1109/icist.2017.7926796
8. Davis, S.B., Mermelstein, P.: Comparison of parametric representations for monosyllabic word recognition in continuously spoken sentences. In: Readings in Speech Recognition, pp. 65–74. Elsevier (1990). https://doi.org/10.1016/b978-0-08-051584-7.50010-3
9. Zahorian, S., Hu, H.: Nonlinear dimensionality reduction methods for use with automatic speech recognition. In: Speech Technologies. InTech (2011). https://doi.org/10.5772/16863
10. Fewzee, P., Karray, F.: Dimensionality reduction for emotional speech recognition. In: 2012 International Conference on Privacy, Security, Risk and Trust and 2012 International Conference on Social Computing, Amsterdam, pp. 532–537. IEEE (2012). https://doi.org/10.1109/socialcom-passat.2012.83
11. Sharma, S., Kumar, M., Das, P.K.: A technique for dimension reduction of MFCC spectral features for speech recognition. In: 2015 International Conference on Industrial Instrumentation and Control (ICIC), Pune, pp. 99–104. IEEE (2015). https://doi.org/10.1109/iic.2015.7150719

12. Velliangiri, S., Alagumuthukrishnan, S., Thankumar Joseph, S.I.: A review of dimensionality reduction techniques for efficient computation. Procedia Comput. Sci. **165**, 104–111 (2019). https://doi.org/10.1016/j.procs.2020.01.079
13. Kavilkrue, M., Boonma, P.: Dimensionality reduction algorithms for improving efficiency of PromoRank: a comparison study. In: Unger, H., Meesad, P., Boonkrong, S. (eds.) Recent Advances in Information and Communication Technology 2015. AISC, vol. 361, pp. 19–29. Springer, Cham (2015). https://doi.org/10.1007/978-3-319-19024-2_3
14. Mahapatra, K., Chaudhuri, N.R., Kavasseri, R.: Online bad data outlier detection in PMU measurements using PCA feature-driven ANN classifier. In: 2017 IEEE Power and Energy Society General Meeting, Chicago, IL, pp. 1–5. IEEE (2017). https://doi.org/10.1109/pesgm.2017.8273997
15. Momo, N., Abdullah, U.J.: Speech recognition using feed forward neural network and principle component analysis. In: Thampi, S., Krishnan, S., Corchado Rodriguez, J., Das, S., Wozniak, M., Al-Jumeily, D. (eds.) Advances in Signal Processing and Intelligent Recognition Systems, SIRS 2017. Advances in Intelligent Systems and Computing, vol. 678. Springer, Cham (2018). https://doi.org/10.1007/978-3-319-67934-1_20
16. Schölkopf, B., Smola, A., Müller, K.-R.: Kernel principal component analysis. In: Gerstner, W., Germond, A., Hasler, M., Nicoud, J.-D. (eds.) ICANN 1997. LNCS, vol. 1327, pp. 583–588. Springer, Heidelberg (1997). https://doi.org/10.1007/BFb0020217
17. Lima, A., Zen, H., Nankaku, Y., Tokuda, K., Kitamura, T., Resende, F.G.: Sparse KPCA for feature extraction in speech recognition. In: Proceedings of IEEE International Conference on Acoustics, Speech, and Signal Processing (ICASSP 2005), pp. I/353–I/356. IEEE (2005). https://doi.org/10.1109/icassp.2005.1415123
18. Lima, A., Zen, H., Nankaku, Y., Tokuda, K., Kitamura, T.: On the use of kernel PCA for feature extraction in speech recognition. IEICE Trans. Inf. Syst. **E87-D**(12), 2802–2811 (2004)
19. Kim, M.-S., Yang, I.-H., Yu, H.-J.: Robust speaker identification using greedy kernel PCA. In: 2008 20th IEEE International Conference on Tools with Artificial Intelligence, pp. 143–146. IEEE (2008). https://doi.org/10.1109/ictai.2008.105
20. Kim, K.I., Jung, K., Park, S.H., Kim, H.J.: Texture classification with kernel principal component analysis. Electron. Lett. **36**, 1021 (2000). https://doi.org/10.1049/el:20000780
21. Islam, R., Uddin, J., Kim, J.M.: An acoustic emission sensor based fault diagnosis of induction motors using Gabor filter and multiclass SVM. J. Ad-hoc Sens. Wirel. Netw. **34**, 273–287 (2016)

Comparative Analysis of Dimension Reduction Techniques Over Classification Algorithms for Speech Emotion Recognition

Aditi Biswas[1]([⊠]), Sovon Chakraborty[2], Abu Nuraiya Mahfuza Yesmin Rifat[3], Nadia Farhin Chowdhury[1], and Jia Uddin[4]

[1] Brac University, Dhaka, Bangladesh
{aditi.biswas,nadia.farhin.chowdhury}@g.bracu.ac.bd
[2] Ahsanullah University of Science and Technology, Dhaka, Bangladesh
sovonchakraborty2014@gmail.com
[3] University of Dundee, Dundee, Scotland, UK
2397931@dundee.ac.uk
[4] Technology Studies, Endicott College, Woosong University, Daejeon, Korea
jia.uddin@wsu.ac.kr

Abstract. The research work aimed to present a comparative study of increasing the performance of classifier algorithms by using dimension reduction algorithms. The dataset had been collected from Ryerson Audio-Visual Database (RAVDESS). The research had been conducted to detect five emotional speech (happy, sad, angry, fearful, neutral) accurately. At first Mel Frequency Cepstrum Coefficients (MFCC) were extracted where seven dominant features had been extracted. Two other features were directly extracted from the dataset. Then different classifier algorithms (Random Forest, Gradient Boosting and Support Vector Machine) had been applied to the dataset. This initial study showed that Random Forest had the highest accuracy level of 61.26%. After that, dimension reduction techniques namely Recursive Feature Elimination, Principal Component Analysis and P-value Calculation had been applied to the dataset. Then classifier algorithms were used for accuracy again. Later this study showed that a progress in terms of accuracy (63.12%) had resulted from Gradient Boosting.

Keywords: Mel Frequency Cepstrum Coefficients · Random Forest · Gradient Boosting · Support Vector Machine · Recursive Feature Elimination · Principal Component Analysis

1 Introduction

Machine learning has played a crucial part in the research of computational learning theory. It became an integral part of artificial intelligence to construct algorithms based on data patterns and historical data relationships. It is so far the most successful technique to be utilized in the field of information examination to by conceiving a model and its

M. H. Miraz et al. (Eds.): iCETiC 2020, LNICST 332, pp. 170–184, 2020.
https://doi.org/10.1007/978-3-030-60036-5_12

calculations [1]. Hence, it helps in discovering previously unknown patterns or features through historical learnings and trends in data. Speech Emotion Recognition (SER) has been being studied for over two decades [2] and is getting popular in the field of Human Computer Interaction. Mel-Frequency Cepstrum Coefficient is the most used representation of spectral property of voice signals. It is the best for speech recognition as it takes human perception sensitivity and frequencies into consideration [3]. Emotion recognition has a vital role in the conversational analysis as it can be a performance parameter for identifying unsatisfied customers [4].

For the experimental evaluation of this study, features were extracted using the Mel-frequency Cepstral Coefficients features (MFCC) [3]. The dataset in this experiment comprised of audio files of human speech. MFCC derived from human speech samples played a vital role in the field of speech signal processing. They are widely used in applications including speaker verification, speaker recognition, emotion detection, etc. The Mel-frequency scale is a quasi-logarithmic spacing roughly resembling the resolution of the human auditory system. This makes the MFCC features "biologically inspired." Therefore, MFCC or MFCC based features can effectively detect the emotions of humans from speech [5].

In the previous studies, scientists have integrated MFCC to identify the paralinguistic material in the feature vector. The vector feature was the first 19 coefficients with a total of 63 from the MFCC [6]. The available raw signal did not comprise of enough information to train and test. Therefore, the speech signals were synthesized in a way so that the signal becomes strong enough for both training and testing. Methods of MFCC using cepstral-based sub-band parameters increased the effectiveness of classification [7]. The emotion misclassification efficiency can be reduced by using Synthetic enlargement of MFCCs [8]. Chen et al. have categorized seven emotions and directed at enhancing speech recognition in an autonomous speaker by using the three-level techniques of emotional voice recognition [9]. This technique classified distinct feelings starting from coarse to fine and selects an appropriate function using the Fisher rate.

However, most of these features were not correlated and were redundant. When the features were high in number, it became more difficult to model and function on the training set. This was where the dimension reduction algorithms came into play to reduce the number of random variables[1]. These algorithms are useful as they decrease the computational complexities, exclude the noise or irrelevant features, and reduce the space and infrastructure demand [10]. Thus, the model in this study used several dimension reduction methods to create a comparison between them to demonstrate the enhancement of outcomes of machine learning classifiers.

This study presents a comparative analysis of different dimension reduction techniques, namely - Recursive Feature Elimination (RFE), P-value Calculation and Principle Component Analysis (PCA) for speech emotion dataset using machine learning algorithms.

The rest of the paper is organized as follows. Section 2 presents detailed architecture of the proposed model. Experimental results analysis is in Sect. 3. Finally conclude the paper is in Sect. 4.

---

[1] GeeksforGeeks, http://www.geeksforgeeks.org/dimensionality-reduction.

2   Proposed Model

A detailed framework of the system is depicted in Fig. 1. From the audio dataset features were extracted by using MFCC. After that, feature reduction algorithms were applied to find the best features. Lastly, machine learning algorithms were applied in finding accuracy of emotion recognition.

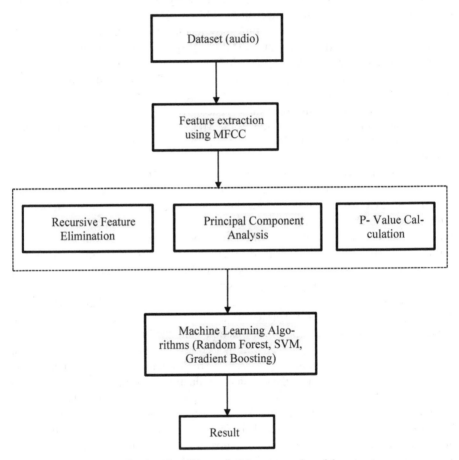

Fig. 1. Block diagram of the proposed model.

The following sub-sections of this paper will discuss the different blocks associated with the model (Fig. 1).

2.1   Dataset Description

The dataset used in this study is named as Ryerson Audio-Visual Database of Emotional Speech and Song (RAVDESS) [11]. The multimodal dataset of emotional speech and song was created in 2018 where 24 professional actors performed in North American accent [11]. Although there were seven types of emotion (calm, happy, sad, angry, fearful, neutral, and disgust) in the dataset, only 920 speech trails were utilized in the experimental evaluation, as depicted in Table 1. The justification to use 920 trails was because audio emotional files of 'neutral' and 'calm' did not have any distinction in terms of expression between them. The same reason was applicable in case of 'fearful' and 'disgust' emotions files.

Table 1. Emotions with trail number

	Happy	Sad	Angry	Fearful	Neutral
Male	96	96	96	96	96
Female	88	88	88	88	88
Total trails	920				

2.2 Methods

For this research purpose Random Forest (RF) [20], Gradient Boosting (GB) and Support Vector Machine (SVM) [19] algorithms were applied. These classifiers were selected considering the following advantageous points that can help to acquire better accuracy. They were:

- All of them were ensemble method[2] [13].
- All of these methods reduce variance, bias, and noise. In particular, all three classifiers reduced noise while RF and GB decreases variance, and GB eliminates bias [12].
- SVM does not work well with large data set, however RF and GB can be used efficiently while working with large dataset [12].
- The research work was focused on both boosting (GB) and bagging (RF) in order to achieve more accurate result [12].
- The advantage of applying GB is the predictive accuracy, flexibility and no need for data pre-processing [13].

2.3 MFCC and Feature Extraction

MFCC. The Mel scale compares the perceived frequency or pitch of a mere sound to its actual measured frequency. Incorporating this scale made our features more closely aligned with human speech recognition[3]. The formula of restoration from the frequency to the Mel scale is as follows-

$$M(f) = 1125\ln(1 + f/700) \tag{1}$$

---

[2] blog.statsbot.co, https://blog.statsbot.co/ensemble-learning-d1dcd548e936.

[3] practicalcryptography.com, http://practicalcryptography.com/miscellaneous/machinelearning/guide-mel-frequencycepstral-coefficients-mfccs.

In case of emotion detection from audio, MFCC is very effective [5]. It plays an important role in speech signal processing. MFCC features are identified as "biologically inspired" as the Mel-frequency scale roughly resemble the resolution of the human auditory system which in turn played a vital role to select the MFCC based features for this research study [5].

Feature Extraction. With a trial of 2.15 s and frequency of 512 Hz, 14 coefficients were derived from MFCC. Eventually, for each trial a 14 × 215 dimension matrix was generated. The first row was considered only for each trial. Finally seven features were considered from MFCC. Mean, Median, Standard Deviation, Variance, Mode, Kurtosis and Skewness. All these seven features are statistical features. Amplitude and Pitch were another two features which were extracted directly from dataset.

Among the selected nine features, the majority of them were statistical because of their significance in recognition study. In the research area of recognition for example human emotions classification [14], speaker identification [15], early stage internet traffic identification [16], gene expression classification [17] and many other statistical features are widely used. Skewness, Kurtosis and Standard Deviation are statistical distribution properties of MFCCs. In speaker identification study, the effectiveness of these features was proved by enhancing the training speed of the proposed model [15].

2.4 Dimension Reduction Techniques

Recursive Feature Elimination (RFE). RFE aims to remove dependencies and collinearity by the means of significant attributes of features and by recursively extracting a small number from the min each loop which is expected to exist in the model. RFE required a specified number of features to be retained. However, often it is not known beforehand that how many features are valid. RFE worked on the feature ranking system. The first model had been fitted on the linear regression based on all variables. Then it calculated the variable coefficients and their importance. After that, it ranked the variable on the basis of linear regression fit and removed the low-ranking variable in each of the iteration [18]. The significance of applying RFE in the experiment was due to the fact that it made the machine learning algorithms more efficient. Moreover, reduction of complexity and over-fitting, and accuracy improvement were some of the key reasons for applying RFE in this research[4].

Principal Component Analysis (PCA). Principal Component Analysis (PCA) is a dimension reduction technique applied to determine the principal component of the dataset. In matrix notation it can be expressed as-

$$Y_1 = aT_1X \tag{2}$$

here, X represents features.

---

[4] analyticsvidhya.com, https://www.analyticsvidhya.com/blog/2016/12/introduction-to-feature-selection-methods-with-an-example-or-how-to-select-the-right-variables.

PCA was chosen as a dimension reduction technique in this study for its usefulness[5] in removal of correlated features, reduction of overfitting, improvement of algorithm performance and visualization, etc.

Adding too many features after a certain point will decrease the performance. This is referred to as "The Curse of Dimensionality". With the growth of dimensionality, the sample density decreases exponentially and causes overfitting. PCA plays an important role in case of dimension reduction and reduces the probability of overfitting.

PCA filters out which features are important. It mathematically measures how the variables are associated with a covariance matrix. It finds out the direction of dispersed data using an eigenvector along with the relative importance of these directions. PCA helps to drop the eigenvectors not having a high significance[6].

P-Value Calculation. P-value has significance in statistics as is defined as the probability of obtaining results as extreme as the observed result. P-value helps to calculate the significant outcomes while running a hypothesis test in statistics. In this case, all hypothesis tests must eventually use a P-value to measure the strength of the evidence. The P-value ranges from 0 to 1 and is interpreted[7] as Table 2-

Table 2. Interpretation of P-Value

P-Value	Interpretation
Less than or equal to 0.05	Strong evidence against null hypothesis
Greater than 0.05	Weak evidence against the null hypothesis
Very close to the cut-off (0.05)	Considered to be marginal

For this experiment, P-Value with ≤0.05 had been considered. There are various ways to calculate P-Value such as t-test, ANOVA test etc. Here we considered one sample t-test for the calculation of P-Value. The one sample t-test formula was derived as-

$$t = \frac{\bar{x} - \mu}{\sqrt{s^2/n}} \tag{3}$$

Here, $\bar{x}$, s^2, n and μ are sample mean, sample variance, sample size and specified population mean, respectively[8].

Easy calculation and interpretation, robustness and generalization were the reasons behind choosing t-test among all other methods of P-Value calculation[9].

---

[5] i2tutorials.com, https://www.i2tutorials.com/what-are-the-pros-and-cons-of-the-pca/.

[6] hackernoon.com, https://hackernoon.com/dimensionality-reduction-using-pca-a-comprehensive-hands-on-primer-ph8436lj.

[7] dummies.com, www.dummies.com/education/math/statistics/what-a-P-Value-tells-you-about-statistical-data/.

[8] statsdirect.com, www.statsdirect.com/help/parametric_methods/single_sample_t.htm.

[9] prosancons.com, https://www.prosancons.com/education/pros-and-cons-of-t-test/.

3   Experimental Setup and Result Analysis

In the experimental evaluation, we extracted the features from the dataset using five different types of emotions- happy, angry, sad, fearful and neutral for both male and female by following the machine-learning algorithms: Random Forest, Gradient Boosting, and Support Vector Machine. Finally, the extracted features of different emotion signals after applying the dimension reduction techniques were used in machine learning algorithms to generate an improved result and to establish the three different dimension reduction classifier result analysis.

P-Value was calculated using MATLAB and other calculations were carried out using Python. Python class Scikit-learn and Keras were applied for classification and performance analysis.

After extracting features, RF, SVM and GB were used for classification. For random forest, the accuracy for happy, angry, sad, neutral and fearful expressions were 61.24%, 60.46%, 61.26%, 60.05% and 59.47%, respectively. In the same way 60.12% (happy), 59.65% (angry), 60.36% (sad), 60.25% (neutral) and 58.80% (fearful) accuracies were achieved for Gradient Boosting and 58.43% (happy), 60.36% (sad), 59.47% (angry), 59.50% (neutral) and 55.80% (fearful) for SVM. Table 3 describes the overall accuracies for each algorithm.

Table 3. Accuracy comparison of different classifiers

SVM	Gradient Boosting	Random Forest
60.36%	60.36%	61.26%

RFE for Random Forest. Table 4 represents the rank of the rank of the features that RFE determined for Random Forest algorithm.

Table 4. RFE ranks feature for Random Forest

Name of features	Rank
Mean	1
Standard Deviation	4
Median	3
Amplitude	7
Pitch	9
Variance	5
Mode	6
Kurtosis	8
Skewness	2

After acquiring this result, dimension reduction techniques (RFE, P-Value, PCA) were applied to observe any further improvement of result accuracy. For dimension reduction RFE ranked the features according their importance. The results of applying all selected dimension reduction techniques are given in Table 4.

The accuracy result with various features combination areas is depicted in Fig. 2.

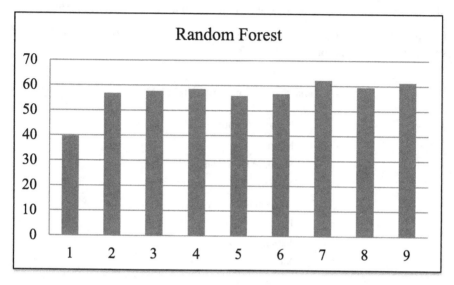

Fig. 2. Random Forest accuracies using RFE in bar chart form

Table 5 shows the accuracy data of Random Forest after applying RFE.

Table 5. Random Forest accuracies using RFE

Features	Result (%)
1	39.634
2	56.75
3	57.65
4	58.55
5	55.85
6	56.75
7	62.16
8	59.46
9	61.26

The best accuracy was 62.16% which was achieved by using 7 features according to rank.

RFE aimed to eliminate weak features but after applying it on RF, it decreased the significance of variables that were correlated along with the importance of causal variable. In case of RF, RFE was able to perform better to scale low dimensional data compared to high dimensional data. Besides, RF was unable to reduce bias and the use of decision trees. So in case of this research, it had an accuracy level of 62.16%.

RFE on SVM. There was no significance on SVM after using RFE as applying RFE results in the same rank for all features (Table 6).

Table 6. RFE ranks feature for SVM

Name of features	Rank
Mean	1
Standard Deviation	1
Median	1
Amplitude	1
Pitch	1
Variance	1
Mode	1
Kurtosis	1
Skewness	1

As RFE gave same importance to all features in this case, the accuracy for SVM remained the same as before (60.36%).

RFE on Gradient Boosting. Table 7 represents the rank of the rank of the features that RFE determined for Gradient Boosting algorithm.

Table 7. RFE ranked features for Gradient Boosting

Name of features	Rank
Mean	4
Standard Deviation	3
Median	2
Amplitude	8
Pitch	9
Variance	5
Mode	7
Kurtosis	6
Skewness	1

The accuracy result with various features is shown in Fig. 3.

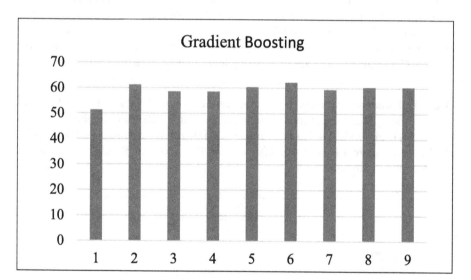

Fig. 3. Gradient Boosting accuracies using RFE in bar chart form

Table 8 shows the accuracy data of Gradient Boosting after applying RFE.

Table 8. Gradient Boosting accuracies using RFE

Features	Result (%)
1	51.35
2	61.26
3	58.55
4	58.55
5	60.36
6	63.12
7	59.45
8	60.36
9	60.36

The best accuracy was 63.12% using 6 features according to rank.

GB increased the accuracy mainly by reducing bias where RF was unable to reduce. As GB applied boosting, in terms of variance it depended upon the parameters which included the number of trees, depth of trees and learning rate. Also, GB focused step by step with the dataset here. It solved the objective function stepwise and the learning rate was good. Consequently, GB has an accuracy level after 63.16% after applying RFE on it.

P-Value Calculation. As stated before, the features where P-Value is higher than 0.05 were discarded. In this experiment Amplitude and Pitch had values higher than 0.05 (0.389255041 and 0.862034339 respectively) and therefore were removed these from consideration. Figure 4 clearly demonstrates that Pitch and Amplitude have higher p-Value than other features.

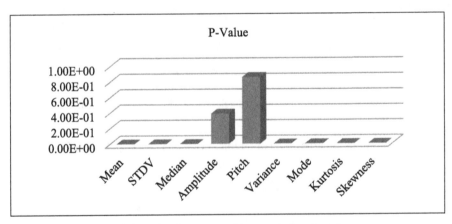

Fig. 4. P-Value from t-test of features in bar chart form

Table 9 represents the P-Value of the features that was calculated from t-test.

Table 9. All features P-Value from t-test

Name of features	Rank
Mean	1.05E−131
Standard Deviation	1.06E−155
Median	7.11E−169
Amplitude	0.389255041
Pitch	0.862034339
Variance	9.71E−113
Mode	2.87E−45
Kurtosis	4.19E−10
Skewness	4.56E−167

After eliminating amplitude and pitch, SVM shows an improvement in accuracy (Fig. 5). However, RF and GB- accuracies decreased to 57.65% and 59.46% from 61.26% and 60.36% respectively. As P value calculation worked on random error rather than systemic error, so it was unable to show any improvement on GB and RF.

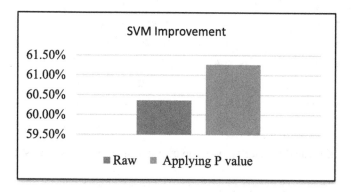

Fig. 5. Improvement of SVM in bar chart form

PCA. Since the variables in the dataset used in that study are not correlated, PCA cannot be used to improve result accuracy. The result is being demonstrated in Fig. 6 and Table 10.

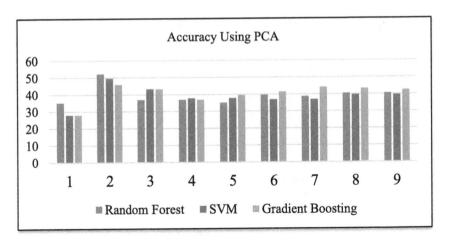

Fig. 6. All three classifiers accuracies after using PCA in bar chart form

Table 10. All three classifiers accuracies after using PCA

PCA features	Random Forest	SVM	Gradient Boosting
1	35.13%	27.92%	27.92%
2	52.25%	49.54%	45.94%
3	36.93%	43.24%	43.24%
4	36.93%	37.83%	36.93%
5	35.13%	37.83%	39.63%
6	39.64%	36.93%	41.44%
7	38.74%	36.94%	44.14%
8	40.54%	39.64%	43.24%
9	40.54%	39.63%	42.34%

Table 11 illustrated the summary of the overall of the result research study.

Table 11. Each classifier's comparison of accuracies

	Random Forest	SVM	Gradient Boosting
Without dimension reduction	61.26%	60.36%	60.36%
With RFE	62.16%	60.36%	66.16%
With P-Value	57.65%	61.26%	59.46%
With PCA	52.25%	49.54%	45.94%
Highest accuracy	62.16%	61.26%	63.12%

4   Conclusion and Future Work

This study had conducted a comparative analysis of the dimension reduction techniques for identifying the methods which can give more accurate results on the task of emotion detection using the content of RAVDESS dataset. We had used the features- mode, kurtosis, and skewness in performance evaluation. Experimental results showed that the PCA worked better for the supervised classifiers with two dimensions by exhibiting 52.25%, 49.54%, and 45.94% of accuracy for RF, GB and SVM respectively. The P-Value showed 57.65%, 61.26%, and 59.46% of accuracy for the Random Forest, Gradient Boosting and SVM respectively after the elimination of two features - Pitch and Amplitude. 62.16%, 60.36% and 63.12% are the best accuracies for RF, SVM and GB respectively after applying RFE. At last, the comparative study concluded that GB shows 63.12% accuracy in six dimensions having applied RFE, which was the highest accuracy of all.

For future study we will be focusing on other datasets like Toronto Emotional Speech Set (TESS)[10]. Earlier studies have shown that there are no further major improvements except that result. Although, Convolutional Neural Network (CNN) has a great significance on dimension reduction, for this research only the effects of the dimension reduction techniques over machine learning algorithms were compared.

References

1. Angra, S., Ahuja, S.: Machine learning and its applications: a review. In: International Conference on Big Data Analytics and Computational Intelligence (ICBDAC), Chirala, India, p. 1 (2017). https://doi.org/10.1109/icbdaci.2017.8070809
2. Akçay, M.B., Oğuz, K.: Speech emotion recognition: emotional models, databases, features, preprocessing methods, supporting modalities and classifiers. Speech Commun. **116**, 56–76 (2020). https://doi.org/10.1016/j.specom.2019.12.001
3. Kerkeni, L., Serrestou, Y.: Speech emotion recognition: methods and cases study. In: 10th International Conference on Agents and Artificial Intelligence, Funchal, Madeira, Portugal (January 2018). https://doi.org/10.5220/0006611601750182
4. Lugovic, S., Dunder, I., Horvat, M.: Techniques and applications of emotion recognition in speech. In: 39th International Convention on Information and Communication Technology, Electronics and Microelectronics (MIPRO), Opatija, Croatia, pp. 1278–1283 (2016). https://doi.org/10.1109/mipro.2016.7522336
5. Sato, N., Obuchi, Y.: Emotion recognition using mel-frequency cepstral coefficients. Inf. Media Technol. **2**(3), 835–848 (2007). https://doi.org/10.11185/imt.2.835
6. Shah, F.A., Krishnan, V.R., Sukumar, R.A., Jayakumar, A., Anto, B.P.: Speaker independent automatic emotion recognition from speech: a comparison of MFCCs and discrete wavelet transforms. In: International Conference on Advances in Recent Technologies in Communication and Computing, Kottayam, Kerala, India, pp. 528–531 (2009). https://doi.org/10.1109/artcom.2009.231
7. Krishna, K.V., Satish, P.K.: Emotion recognition in speech using MFCC and wavelet features. In: 3rd IEEE International Advance Computing Conference, Ghaziabad, India (2013). https://doi.org/10.1109/iadcc.2013.6514336

---

[10] University of Toronto, https://tspace.library.utoronto.ca/handle/1807/24487.

8. Momo, N., Abdullah, Uddin, J.: Speech recognition using feed forward neural network and principle component analysis. In: Advances in Signal Processing and Intelligent Recognition Systems, SIRS 2017. Advances in Intelligent Systems and Computing, vol. 678. Springer, Cham (2018). https://doi.org/10.1007/978-3-319-67934-1_20

9. Mohino, P.R.G., Diaz, S.A., Zureral, M.R.: MFCC based enlargement of the training set for emotion recognition in speech. Signal Image Process.: Int. J. (SIPIJ) 5(1), 29 (2014). https://doi.org/10.5121/sipij.2014.5103

10. Chen, L., Mao, X., Xue, Y., Cheng, L.L.: Speech emotion recognition: features and classification models. Digit. Signal Process 22(6), 1154–1160 (2012). https://doi.org/10.1016/j.dsp.2012.05.007

11. George, F.P., Shaikat, I.M., Hossain, P.S.F., Parvez, M.Z., Uddin, J.: Recognition of emotional states using EEG signals on the basis of time-frequency analysis and SVM classifier. Int. J. Electr. Comput. Eng. (IJECE) 9(3), 1012–1020 (2019). https://doi.org/10.11591/ijece.v9i2.pp1012-1020

12. Dawood, H., Guo, P.: Comparison of linear dimensionality reduction methods in image annotation. In: Seventh International Conference on Advanced Computational Intelligence (ICACI), Wuyi, China, p. 1 (March 2015). https://doi.org/10.1109/icaci.2015.7184729

13. Steven, R., Livingstone, F., Russo, A.: The Ryerson Audio-Visual Database of Emotional Speech and Song (RAVDESS): a dynamic, multimodal set of facial and vocal expressions in North American English. PLoS ONE 4(2), 1 (2018). https://doi.org/10.1371/journal.pone.0196391

14. Ali, R.F., Khan, R., Ahmad, N., Maqsood, I.: Random forests and decision trees. Int. J. Comput. Sci. Issues 09(05), 272 (2012)

15. Natekin, A., Knoll, A.: Gradient boosting machines, a tutorial. Front Neurorobotics 7, 1–21 (2013). https://doi.org/10.3389/fnbot.2013.00021

16. Cha, Y.T., San, W.: Effectiveness of statistical features for human emotions classification using EEG biosensors. Res. J. Appl. Sci. Eng. Technol. 5(21), 5083–5089 (2013). https://doi.org/10.19026/rjaset.5.4401

17. Molla, K.I., Hirose, K.: On the effectiveness of MFCC and their statistical distribution properties in speaker identification. In: IEEE Symposium on Virtual Environments, Human-Computer Interfaces and Measurement Systems (VCIMS), Boston, MA, USA (2004). https://doi.org/10.1109/vecims.2004.1397204

18. Peng, L., Yang, B.: Effectiveness of statistical features for early stage internet traffic identification. Int. J. Parallel Program. 44(1), 181–197 (2016). https://doi.org/10.1007/s10766-014-0337-2

19. Uddin, J., Nguyen, D., Kim, J.M.: A reliable fault detection and classification model of induction motors using texture features and multi-class support vector machines. J. Math. Problems Eng. 2014, 1–9 (2014). https://doi.org/10.1155/2014/814593

20. Wei, G., Zhao, J., Yu, Z., Feng, Y., Li, G., Sun, X.: An effective gas sensor array optimization method based on random forest. In: IEEE SENSORS, New Delhi, India, pp. 1–4 (2018). https://doi.org/10.1109/icsens.2018.8589580

Investigations on Performances of Pre-trained U-Net Models for 2D Ultrasound Kidney Image Segmentation

Deepthy Mary Alex$^{(\boxtimes)}$ (ID) and D. Abraham Chandy (ID)

Department of Electronics and Communication Engineering, Karunya Institute of Technology and Sciences, Karunya Nagar, Coimbatore 6411114, India
deepthymalex@gmail.com

Abstract. The importance of segmentation in medical applications is inevitable and hence its performance and accuracy is a priority. The semi-automated and automated segmentation of kidneys from 2D ultrasound images is quite challenging due to the intensity distribution differences within the kidney and also due to the intensity similarity with the nearby organs. Deep learning have paved its way into outperforming traditional techniques in various fields of applications efficiently, but the amount of data used is imperious. The relevance of deep learning in biomedical application is also inevitable as it makes the application completely automatic and precise. This paper investigates the performances of pre-trained U-Net model using various backbones for segmentation of kidneys from 2D ultrasound images. Experimentation results obtained shows that U-Net model with VGG-16 backbone outperformed with a promising accuracy of 0.89, thus demonstrating that segmentation can be done even with limited count of images within the dataset.

Keywords: Kidney segmentation · Ultrasound · Deep learning · U-Net · Data augmentation · Transfer learning

1 Introduction

In medical field, the two main cognitive and challenging tasks faced by diagnostic experts are the analysis and interpretation of the acquired image from any medical imaging modality. Over the years, researchers have come up with various semi-automated and automated techniques and technologies to provide solutions for the same. Most recent techniques presented by researchers involves deep learning for these applications. The most competent wheels within wheels machine learning category that as paved its way in various applications such as biometrics, speech recognition, object detection etc. [1] is Deep Learning. The results obtained for deep learning techniques is promising yet it faces few challenges [2]. One of the many challenges is the need for a large dataset to obtain computational efficiency. When considering biomedical field, especially medical image analysis, the procurement of a large dataset is quite demanding [3].

© ICST Institute for Computer Sciences, Social Informatics and Telecommunications Engineering 2020
Published by Springer Nature Switzerland AG 2020. All Rights Reserved
M. H. Miraz et al. (Eds.): iCETiC 2020, LNICST 332, pp. 185–195, 2020.
https://doi.org/10.1007/978-3-030-60036-5_13

Inorder to overcome this problem, the researches presented data augmentation [4] has a pre-processing technique. Data augmentation is described as a method used to escalate the dataset content by applying various techniques such as cropping, padding, flipping etc. on the images present in the dataset [5]. Another way of applying deep learning on small dataset is by using transfer learning technique [6]. Transfer learning method uses a model pre-trained for some purpose on a tremendously huge number of image data to be reused for a new task [7]. In this paper we have considered data augmentation and transfer learning for kidney segmentation from 2D Ultrasound (US) images. Segmentation of kidney from 2D US images was favored due to its advantages such as low cost, non-invasive, radiation free, portability and real time possibility over other imaging modalities in the field of medicine namely Computed Tomography (CT) and Magnetic Resonance Imaging (MRI).

Segmentation is an art of separating an image into multiple segments such that the boundaries and objects within an image can be identified or detected [8]. The role played by segmentation in medical imaging applications is vital since it enables the experts in exploring the anatomical structure of the organs, identifying the area of interest such as lesion etc., radiation therapy treatment planning and evaluate the tissue measures etc. [9]. Several research have been carried out to segment kidney both using semi-automated and automated techniques. Automation of kidney segmentation from imaging modalities face challenges due to the renal compartment within the kidney, similarities in the intensities of kidney with adjacent organs such as liver and the kidney shape variations [10].

Some of the literatures that presented deep learning segmentation techniques for the analysis of images in medical applications have been thoroughly studied. In [11], histology image based deep contour-aware network (DCAN) that could be used to segment histological images is presented by the authors. The training was based on contour and appearance features such as color and texture. Tumors that occurs in brain were segmented using a deep neural network (DNN) and it was presented in [12]. The network learns both local and global features simultaneously while in [13] segmentation of the tumor was experimented with a convolutional neural network (CNN). The researchers experimented a U-Net model for the segmentation of lungs in [14]. Pancreas segmentations has also been done using deep learning techniques. In [15], advanced richer feature convolutional network (RFCN) is employed whereas in [16] a multi-level deep CNN has been used for the same. Automated kidney segmentation using deep learning techniques have also been explored by researchers. In [17–19] CNN has been used while in [20] a pre-trained VGG-16 model on ImageNet [21] dataset along with boundary distance regression network and pixel classification network is used for the kidney segmentation.

The author of [22] has presented some of the frequently used deep learning segmentation models such as CNN, FCN, U-Net, CRNs, RNNs and LSTM, their challenges and achievements in medical field. The purpose of this work is the assessment of performance acquired by pre-trained U-Net model [23] using various backbones for kidney segmentation for easier, fast and efficient kidney segmentation from 2D US images. The backbones considered here are Residual neural network-34 (ResNet-34) [24], Visual Geometry Group-16 (VGG-16) [25], Squeeze-and-Excitation [26] ResNet-18 (Se-ResNet-18) and MobileNet [27]. The kidney segmentation framework for experimentation is illustrated in Fig. 1 for a precise understanding. The remaining paper is sectioned into various sections mentioned. The U-Net model that is been used is briefed in Sect. 2 followed by specifications of pre-trained U-Net model in Sect. 3. The interpretation of performance metrics used for segmentation analysis is done in Sect. 4, thereafter, the results and discussions of the work done is mentioned in Sect. 5 with Sect. 6 as the concluding section.

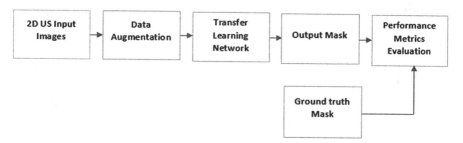

Fig. 1. Schematic representation of kidney segmentation framework

2 U-Net

A deep learning segmentation model developed using CNNs for medical applications is the U-Net model. The model was formulated for segmentation of biomedical imaging data. The architecture was developed by the researchers of the University of Freiburg, Germany [23]. Fully convolutional networks (FCN) [28] constitutes the U-Net architecture and as the name indicates, the architecture takes the 'U' structure as pictured in Fig. 2. The deep learning architecture comprises mainly of two sections, namely an encoder and a decoder. The encoder section is otherwise called as down-sampling path or contracting path and it consist of 4 blocks. Each block consist of two 3 × 3 convolutional layers together with ReLU activation function followed by a max pooling layer. Batch Normalization is used in the ReLU activation function while the size is 2 × 2 for the max pooling layer. The need for the encoder is to acquire the context of a given image such that segmentation is made possible.

Decoder section or otherwise called as up-sampling path or else an expansion path even consist of 4 blocks. Each block comprises of a deconvolution layer that uses stride of 2, skip connections and finally, two convolutional layers of size 3 x 3 along with ReLU activation function using batch normalization. The skip connections consist of the concatenation of cropped feature maps from the contraction path with the corresponding output of transposed convolution layer in the up-sampling path and this is done to obtain accurate locations. With the precise capture of contextual and localization information from down-sampling and up-sampling path respectively, effective segmentation map prediction can be acquired by the combination of both. The main advantage of U-Net is that the network depends only on the kernel size and as a result the input images could be of any size.

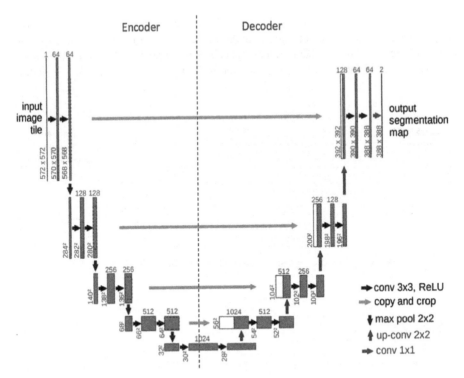

Fig. 2. U-Net architecture illustration

3 Pre-trained U-Net

As already mentioned, U-Net consist of an encoder and decoder. The U-Net architecture for kidney segmentation can be trained in two ways. Either the model can be trained from scratch or by using transfer learning. Training a model from scratch is tedious and the amount of data required is quite huge hence pre-trained U-Net is used for the same. In the pre-trained U-Net segmentation model [29], the encoder part will be substituted by a specified pre-trained weights of an already trained model also known as a backbone model and this technique is known as transfer learning. The backbone model is used as a feature extractor without the dense layers. Here, the decoder is built depending on the specified internal features of the backbone selected. The four backbones used for evaluation as stated earlier are ResNet-34, VGG-16, SeResNet-18, MobileNet.

4 Performance Metrics

The performance measurement of the U-Net segmentation is determined using the confusion metrics [30] and a schematic representation for the determination of various segmentation errors is demonstrated in Fig. 3.

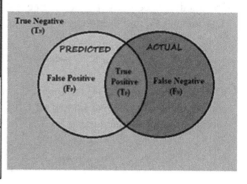

Fig. 3. Segmentation errors representation

The segmentation error parameters are defined as follows:

- True positive (T_P): Case where the foreground pixels in ground truth overlaps with the foreground pixels in predicted image.
- True Negative (T_N): Case where the background pixels in ground truth overlaps with the background pixels in predicted image.
- False positive (F_P): Instance where the background pixels are falsely segmented as foreground. This also called as Type 1 error.
- False Negative (F_N): Instance where the foreground pixels are falsely segmented as background. This also called as Type 2 error.

Based on the above parameters, several performance metrics can be defined for evaluation of the segmentation. The metrics considered for evaluation is briefly explained below.

1. Accuracy: Segmentation accuracy is expressed as the extent to which the predicted mask coincides with the ground truth mask [31] and Eq. (1) expresses the same.

$$Accuracy = \frac{T_P + T_N}{T_P + T_N + F_P + F_N} \tag{1}$$

2. Recall: Recall of segmentation is determined by calculating the ratio of correctly segmented foreground to the sum of all foreground in the ground truth [32]. It is represented using Eq. (2).

$$Recall = \frac{T_P}{T_P + F_N} \tag{2}$$

3. Precision: Segmentation precision can be defined as the ratio of correctly segmented foreground to the total foreground segmented [32]. Precision is expressed as Eq. (3).

$$\Pr ecision = \frac{T_P}{T_P + F_P} \tag{3}$$

4. Specificity: Specificity is the degree of background that have been correctly determined [33] and is expressed using Eq. (4).

$$Specificity = \frac{T_N}{T_N + F_P} \qquad (4)$$

5. F1-score: F1-score [30, 34] is expressed as the harmonic mean/average of precision and recall. It is otherwise known as DICE coefficient or boundary F1 score (BF score) and is represented using Eq. (5).

$$F1 - score = 2 \times \frac{Recall \times Precision}{Recall + Precision} \qquad (5)$$

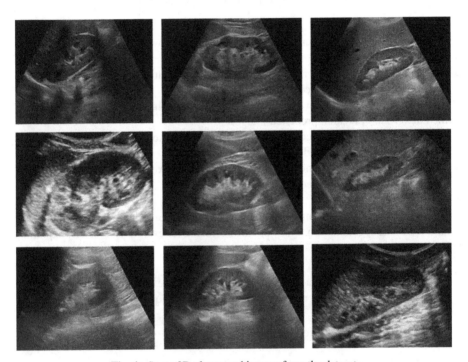

Fig. 4. Some 2D ultrasound images from the dataset

6. Jaccard Index: The ratio of intersection between the actual and the predicted to the union between the same [35, 36] is represented as Jaccard index otherwise known as the intersection over union (IoU). It is numerical expressed as in Eq. (6).

$$IoU = \frac{DICE}{2 - DICE} \qquad (6)$$

For all the performance metrics the values ranges from 0 to 1 or 0 to 100%. Higher the performance metrics values more better the predicted segmentation will be.

5   Results and Discussions

Segmentation using pre-trained U-net model was experimented on about 560 2D US kidney images taken in the longitudinal plane. The images were acquired from different scan centres across India. The dataset is separated as training, validation and testing sets in the ratios 80:10:10, respectively. The dataset was previously pre-processed to obtain a despeckled, inpainted and region of interest (ROI) selected dataset. The dimensions of the images within the dataset is 768×512, some of the images from the dataset is displayed in Fig. 4 for reference. The images within training set is augmented for the construction of a robust and precise segmentation model. Data augmentation for the same was carried out using traditional augmentation methods [37].

Segmentation was done on U-Net models with ResNet-34, VGG-16, Se-ResNet-18 and MobileNet backbones, respectively. The performance metrics was calculated and tabulated in Table 1 for each model mentioned. The segmented output mask along with the original image and corresponding ground truth mask for some randomly picked images from the test dataset using each model is shown in Fig. 5. The ground truth masks were segmented by experts to obtain precise results.

Table 1. Performance metrics of segmentation models experimented

Performance metrics	U-Net with ResNet-34	U-Net with VGG-16	U-Net with Se-ResNet-18	U-Net with MobileNet
Accuracy	0.86	0.89	0.85	0.83
Recall	0.76	0.81	0.80	0.84
Precision	0.61	0.63	0.50	0.38
Specificity	0.87	0.92	0.86	0.84
F1 score	0.72	0.75	0.65	0.50
IoU	0.60	0.62	0.51	0.33

In this work, all the U-Net models with various backbones were pre-trained on ImageNet dataset. The U-Net model training was done in 100 epochs with a batch size of 16. The activation function used was softmax function. The performance metrics results from Table 1 shows that all the U-Net models have performed reasonably well. Tabulation clearly exhibits that the U-Net model with VGG-16 as the backbone has outperformed the other models with an average accuracy of 0.89, recall of 0.81, precision of 0.63, specificity of 0.92, F1 score of 0.75 and IoU of 0.62 followed by ResNet-34 model. Even though the U-Net model with MobileNet gave an overall accuracy of 0.83, the precision and IoU was obtained was poor. U-Net model with Se-ResNet-18 performed better than U-Net model with MobileNet backbone.

Further work could be done by altering and analyzing the predicted results using different number of epochs, activation function etc. More number of backbones for U-Net model could also be considered. The acquired results could be further improvised with implementation of some boundary distance regression network or by the inclusion

Input	Ground truth	ResNet-34	VGG-16	Se-ResNet-18	MobileNet

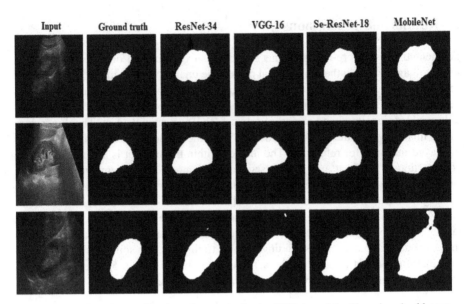

Fig. 5. Representative predicted results acquired using U-Net model with various backbones

of nested dense skip pathways [38]. By using a pre-trained model for segmentation or any other task could always ease the work and improvise the results of the researcher even with less number of data.

6 Conclusion

One of the important and crucial step in medical imaging analysis is segmentation. Automated kidney segmentations from 2D ultrasound images face a lot of challenges hence, deep learning techniques for segmentation was introduced. Deep learning techniques fails to perform effectively when the dataset is small. To overcome this problem, transfer learning technique was used in experimentation. The work was explored on 560 2D ultrasound images pictured in the longitudinal plane of size 768 × 512 pixels each. Kidney segmentation was done using U-Net model with 4 types of backbone models namely, ResNet-34, VGG-16, Se-ResNet-18 and MobileNet and the results were tabulated. The U-Net model with VGG-16 as the backbone have performed better with 0.89 overall accuracy and a modest 0.75 F1-score for the same. Further works is done towards the improvisation of the results obtained by the incorporation of some boundary distance regression network or by the inclusion of nested dense skip pathways and by using an appropriate post processing technique.

References

1. Chartrand, G., Cheng, P.M., Vorontsov, E., Drozdzal, M., Turcotte, S., Pal, C.J., Kadoury, S., Tang, A.: Deep learning: A primer for radiologists. Radiographics **37**, 2113–2131 (2017). https://doi.org/10.1148/rg.2017170077

2. Angelov, P., Sperduti, A.: Challenges in deep learning. In: ESANN 2016 - 24th European Symposium on Artificial Neural Networks. pp. 489–496. i6doc.com publication (2016)
3. Razzak, M.I., Naz, S., Zaib, A.: Deep learning for medical image processing: overview, challenges and the future. In: Dey, N., Ashour, A.S., Borra, S. (eds.) Classification in BioApps. LNCVB, vol. 26, pp. 323–350. Springer, Cham (2018). https://doi.org/10.1007/978-3-319-65981-7_12
4. Shorten, C., Khoshgoftaar, T.M.: A survey on image data augmentation for deep learning. J. Big Data 6(1), 1–48 (2019). https://doi.org/10.1186/s40537-019-0197-0
5. Mikołajczyk, A., Grochowski, M.: Data augmentation for improving deep learning in image classification problem. In: 2018 International Interdisciplinary PhD Workshop, IIPhDW 2018, pp. 117–122. IEEE (2018). https://doi.org/10.1109/IIPHDW.2018.8388338
6. Ravishankar, H., et al.: Understanding the mechanisms of deep transfer learning for medical images. In: Carneiro, G., et al. (eds.) LABELS/DLMIA -2016. LNCS, vol. 10008, pp. 188–196. Springer, Cham (2016). https://doi.org/10.1007/978-3-319-46976-8_20
7. Huang, Z., Pan, Z., Lei, B.: Transfer learning with deep convolutional neural network for SAR target classification with limited labeled data. Remote Sens. 9 (2017). https://doi.org/10.3390/rs9090907
8. Pal, N.R., Pal, S.K.: A review on image segmentation techniques. Pattern Recogn. 26, 1277–1294 (1993). https://doi.org/10.1016/0031-3203(93)90135-J
9. Sharma, N., et al.: Automated medical image segmentation techniques. J. Med. Phys. 35, 3–14 (2010). https://doi.org/10.4103/0971-6203.58777
10. Torres, H.R., Queirós, S., Morais, P., Oliveira, B., Fonseca, J.C., Vilaça, J.L.: Kidney segmentation in ultrasound, magnetic resonance and computed tomography images: a systematic review. Comput. Methods Programs Biomed. 157, 49–67 (2018). https://doi.org/10.1016/j.cmpb.2018.01.014
11. Chen, H., Qi, X., Yu, L., Dou, Q., Qin, J., Heng, P.A.: DCAN: deep contour-aware networks for object instance segmentation from histology images. Med. Image Anal. 36, 135–146 (2017). https://doi.org/10.1016/j.media.2016.11.004
12. Havaei, M., et al.: Brain tumor segmentation with Deep Neural Networks. Med. Image Anal. 35, 18–31 (2017). https://doi.org/10.1016/j.media.2016.05.004
13. Thaha, M.M., Kumar, K.P.M., Murugan, B.S., Dhanasekeran, S., Vijayakarthick, P., Selvi, A.S.: Brain tumor segmentation using convolutional neural networks in MRI images. J. Med. Syst. 43(9), 1–10 (2019). https://doi.org/10.1007/s10916-019-1416-0
14. Ait Skourt, B., El Hassani, A., Majda, A.: Lung CT image segmentation using deep neural networks. Procedia Comput. Sci. 127, 109–113 (2018). https://doi.org/10.1016/j.procs.2018.01.104
15. Fu, M., et al.: Hierarchical combinatorial deep learning architecture for pancreas segmentation of medical computed tomography cancer images. BMC Syst. Biol. 12 (2018). https://doi.org/10.1186/s12918-018-0572-z
16. Roth, H.R., et al.: DeepOrgan: multi-level deep convolutional networks for automated pancreas segmentation. In: Navab, N., Hornegger, J., Wells, W.M., Frangi, A.F. (eds.) MICCAI 2015. LNCS, vol. 9349, pp. 556–564. Springer, Cham (2015). https://doi.org/10.1007/978-3-319-24553-9_68
17. Sharma, K., et al.: Automatic segmentation of kidneys using deep learning for total kidney volume quantification in autosomal dominant polycystic kidney disease. Sci. Rep. 7 (2017). https://doi.org/10.1038/s41598-017-01779-0
18. Thong, W., Kadoury, S., Piché, N., Pal, C.J.: Convolutional networks for kidney segmentation in contrast-enhanced CT scans. Comput. Methods Biomech. Biomed. Eng. Imaging Vis. 6, 277–282 (2018). https://doi.org/10.1080/21681163.2016.1148636

19. Jackson, P., Hardcastle, N., Dawe, N., Kron, T., Hofman, M.S., Hicks, R.J.: Deep learning renal segmentation for fully automated radiation dose estimation in unsealed source therapy. Front. Oncol. **8** (2018). https://doi.org/10.3389/fonc.2018.00215

20. Yin, S., et al.: Automatic kidney segmentation in ultrasound images using subsequent boundary distance regression and pixelwise classification networks. Med. Image Anal. **60** (2020). https://doi.org/10.1016/j.media.2019.101602

21. Deng, J., Dong, W., Socher, R., Li, L.-J., Li, K., Fei-Fei, L.: ImageNet: a large-scale hierarchical image database. In: IEEE Conference on Computer Vision and Pattern Recognition, pp. 248–255. IEEE (2009). https://doi.org/10.1109/cvprw.2009.5206848

22. Hesamian, M.H., Jia, W., He, X., Kennedy, P.: Deep learning techniques for medical image segmentation: achievements and challenges. J. Digit. Imaging **32**(4), 582–596 (2019). https://doi.org/10.1007/s10278-019-00227-x

23. Ronneberger, O., Fischer, P., Brox, T.: U-Net: convolutional networks for biomedical image segmentation. In: Navab, N., Hornegger, J., Wells, W.M., Frangi, A.F. (eds.) MICCAI 2015. LNCS, vol. 9351, pp. 234–241. Springer, Cham (2015). https://doi.org/10.1007/978-3-319-24574-4_28

24. He, K., Zhang, X., Ren, S., Sun, J.: Deep residual learning for image recognition. In: Proceedings of the IEEE Computer Society Conference on Computer Vision and Pattern Recognition, pp. 770–778 (2016). https://doi.org/10.1109/CVPR.2016.90

25. Chatfield, K., Simonyan, K., Vedaldi, A., Zisserman, A.: Return of the devil in the details: delving deep into convolutional nets. In: BMVC 2014 - Proceedings of the British Machine Vision Conference 2014 (2014). https://doi.org/10.5244/c.28.6

26. Hu, J., Shen, L., Sun, G.: Squeeze-and-excitation networks. In: Proceedings of the IEEE Conference on Computer Vision and Pattern Recognition, pp. 7132–7141 (2018). https://doi.org/10.1109/CVPR.2018.00745

27. Howard, A.G., et al.: Mobilenets: efficient convolutional neural networks for mobile vision applications. arXiv Prepr. arXiv:1704.04861 (2017)

28. Long, J., Shelhamer, E., Darrell, T.: Fully convolutional networks for semantic segmentation. In: Proceedings of the IEEE Conference on Computer Vision and Pattern Recognition, pp. 3431–3440 (2015). https://doi.org/10.1109/CVPR.2015.7298965

29. Yakubovskiy, P.: Segmentation models. GitHub Repos. (2019)

30. Kumar, S.N., Lenin Fred, A., Ajay Kumar, H., Sebastin Varghese, P.: Performance metric evaluation of segmentation algorithms for gold standard medical images. In: Sa, P.K., Bakshi, S., Hatzilygeroudis, I.K., Sahoo, M.N. (eds.) Recent Findings in Intelligent Computing Techniques. AISC, vol. 709, pp. 457–469. Springer, Singapore (2018). https://doi.org/10.1007/978-981-10-8633-5_45

31. Csurka, G., Larlus, D., Perronnin, F., Meylan, F.: What is a good evaluation measure for semantic segmentation? In: Proceedings British Machine Vision Conference, p. 2013 (2013). https://doi.org/10.5244/C.27.32

32. Sokolova, M., Japkowicz, N., Szpakowicz, S.: Beyond accuracy, F-Score and ROC: a family of discriminant measures for performance evaluation. In: Sattar, A., Kang, B.-h. (eds.) AI 2006. LNCS (LNAI), vol. 4304, pp. 1015–1021. Springer, Heidelberg (2006). https://doi.org/10.1007/11941439_114

33. Thanh, D.N.H., Prasath, V.B.S., Hieu, L.M., Hien, N.N.: Melanoma skin cancer detection method based on adaptive principal curvature, colour normalisation and feature extraction with the ABCD rule. J. Digit. Imaging **33**(3), 574–585 (2019). https://doi.org/10.1007/s10278-019-00316-x

34. Thanh, D.N.H., Sergey, D., Surya Prasath, V.B., Hai, N.H.: Blood Vessels Segmentation Method for Retinal Fundus Images Based on Adaptive Principal Curvature and Image Derivative Operators. Int. Arch. Photogramm. Remote Sens. Spat. Inf. Sci. (2019). https://doi.org/10.5194/isprs-archives-xlii-2-w12-211-2019

35. Thanh, D.N.H., Erkan, U., Prasath, V.B.S., Kumar, V., Hien, N.N.: A skin lesion segmentation method for dermoscopic images based on adaptive thresholding with normalization of color models. In: IEEE 2019 6th International Conference on Electrical and Electronics Engineering, pp. 116–120. IEEE (2019). https://doi.org/10.1109/ICEEE2019.2019.00030

36. Taha, A.A., Hanbury, A.: Metrics for evaluating 3D medical image segmentation: analysis, selection, and tool. BMC Med. Imaging **15**, 29 (2015). https://doi.org/10.1186/s12880-015-0068-x

37. Mikołajczyk, A., Grochowski, M.: Data augmentation for improving deep learning in image classification problem. In: 2018 International Interdisciplinary PhD Workshop (IIPhDW), pp. 117–122. IEEE (2018). https://doi.org/10.1109/IIPHDW.2018.8388338

38. Zhou, Z., Rahman Siddiquee, M.M., Tajbakhsh, N., Liang, J.: UNet ++: a nested U-Net architecture for medical image segmentation. In: Stoyanov, D., et al. (eds.) DLMIA/ML-CDS 2018. LNCS, vol. 11045, pp. 3–11. Springer, Cham (2018). https://doi.org/10.1007/978-3-030-00889-5_1

Development of Hierarchical Attention Network Based Architecture for Cloze-Style Question Answering

Fahad Alsahli$^{(\boxtimes)}$ and Andri Mirzal

Department of Information and Computer Science,
King Fahd University of Petroleum and Minerals, Dhahran, Saudi Arabia
{g201221720,andri.mirzal}@kfupm.edu.sa

Abstract. Recently, researchers have been addressing Question Answering (QA) by utilizing deep learning architectures. Architectures include Recurrent Neural Networks (RNNs), Convolutional Neural Networks (CNNs), and attention mechanism. QA has several variants, for example, document-based QA and cloze-style QA. In general, QA tasks could be addressed via similar approaches. This is due to the nature of QA which needs a context and a question to be analyzed so that an answer is retrieved. We are tackling cloze-style QA. In such task, a context and a query are given. Query is a sentence that is missing a piece of information (e.g., a word). The missing information should be inferred based on the given context. We develop a Hierarchical Attention Network (HAN) model to tackle cloze-style QA. Because HAN models employ hierarchical attention, HAN models are suitable for this task. We utilize two publicly available cloze-style data. The datasets are two instances of Children's Book Test (CBT), namely, Named Entity (CBT-NE) and Common Nouns (CBT-CN). CBT-NE data includes 108,719 training, 2,000 validation, and 2,500 test samples. CBT-CN data includes 120,769 training, 2,000 validation, and 2,500 test samples. We conduct experiments to compare our model against a baseline model which is HAN pointer sum attention. Comparison is based on inference time (i.e., time needed to process a single sample) and accuracy score. Results show that our model outperforms baseline model in both criteria. Our model achieves an average inference time of 0.0476 s and an average accuracy score of 70.47% in CBT-NE test data, and achieves an average inference time of 0.049 s and an average accuracy score of 67.5% in CBT-CN test data. On the other hand, the baseline model achieves an average inference time of 0.115 s and an average accuracy score of 68.99% in CBT-NE test data, and an average inference time of 0.105 s and an average accuracy score of 67.12% in CBT-CN test data.

1 Introduction

Natural Language Processing (NLP) aims to represent semantics and syntactics features of natural languages to a computer program. As a result, time consuming tasks could be automated. Such tasks include searching or translating

© ICST Institute for Computer Sciences, Social Informatics and Telecommunications Engineering 2020
Published by Springer Nature Switzerland AG 2020. All Rights Reserved
M. H. Miraz et al. (Eds.): iCETiC 2020, LNICST 332, pp. 196–213, 2020.
https://doi.org/10.1007/978-3-030-60036-5_14

documents. There exist NLP tasks that do not require semantic processing such as finding stop words or extracting numbers form text. There are NLP problems that do not need to process whole documents, and this includes suggesting a better phrasing of a sentence or finding grammatical mistakes. These tasks do not need to understand the whole document. Finally, some other NLP tasks require processing of documents as in the case of providing a summary of a document or answering a question based on a context within a document. Such tasks need to process documents and understand interactions between words and sentences. Those NLP tasks are currently being solved via applying deep learning architectures such as Recurrent Neural Networks (RNNs) and Convolutional Neural Networks (CNNs). One NLP task that is recently being solved with deep learning is Question Answering (QA).

QA is where a computer program (or a system) is given a question, and the goal is to provide an answer. There are several variants of such systems. For example, there are systems that provide answers based on Knowledge Bases (KBs). Some other systems are given questions paired with corresponding input documents, and their task is to answer questions based on input documents. In addition, QA systems could be classified by the types of questions they are answering. For instance, some systems answer multiple choice questions. Other systems consider short-answer questions. Also, there exist systems that answer cloze-style questions. In such systems, a document (context) and a sentence with missing information (e.g., a name) are provided, and the task is to infer the missing piece of information.

All these classes of QA systems utilize similar deep learning techniques. This is due to the nature of the problem. For instance, every QA system should analyze a question based on a context then provide an answer. Hierarchical Attention Network (HAN) architecture [1] is suitable for QA tasks since HAN based models process text in a hierarchical approach to extract its semantics and syntactics properties. In this research, we are considering task of cloze-style QA using HAN architecture.

2   Problem Statement

We develop HAN [1] model to address cloze-style QA. HAN architecture processes text in a hierarchical manner that allows it to focus (e.g., via attention mechanism) on key information. So it is suitable for QA tasks. There are several aspects of HAN architecture that can be improved. For example, HAN models use two layers of recurrent text encoding. We argue that one layer of text encoding is sufficient for a HAN model to learn interactions of words in a given context such as cloze-style QA. This is because HAN uses pre-trained Glove embeddings [2] which already capture meaning of words. Also, having a single layer of text encoding would improve inference time (i.e., time to process and answer a single sample) as recurrent text encoding is time consuming (e.g., recurrent networks process text sequentially). In this research, we aim to improve HAN models for cloze-style QA task by developing a HAN model with a single layer of text encoding. The following are the research questions that will be addressed in this research:

- Q1: What effect does one-layer text encoding have on HAN's inference time compared to two-layer text encoding?
- Q2: What effect does one-layer text encoding have on HAN's accuracy score compared to two-layer text encoding?

Corresponding hypotheses are formalized as:

- H_{01}: One-layer text encoding HAN model and two-layer text encoding HAN model have the same average inference time.
- H_{11}: One-layer text encoding HAN model and two-layer text encoding HAN model have different average inference times.
- H_{02}: One-layer text encoding HAN model and two-layer text encoding HAN model have the same average accuracy score.
- H_{12}: One-layer text encoding HAN model and two-layer text encoding HAN model have different average accuracy scores.

3   Literature Review

Some related work in cloze-style QA systems and some general approaches towards QA tasks will be briefly reviewed in this section. In addition, four common cloze-style question datasets will be discussed.

3.1   Cloze-Style Approaches

HAN was developed by Yang et al. [1] with the goal to perform text classification. Since then HAN architecture has been applied in many NLP applications including QA modeling. In cloze-style QA task, Alpay et al. [3] proposed two cloze-style QA models based on HAN architecture that utilizes Bi-directional Recurrent Gated Units (BiGRUs) to encode input sequences. The main difference between the two models is in the final layer where the first model used a soft-max based classifier to generate the output and the second model used pointer sum attention to generate the output. In this work, the authors used Glove embeddings [2] to convert the input text into vector spaces and Children's Book Test (CBT) data to validate their models. Accuracy scores of the first model on validation and test sets of CBT Named Entity (CBT-NE) data were 62.9% and 57.7% respectively, and its scores on validation and test sets of CBT Common Nouns (CBT-CN) data were 60.4% and 56.4% respectively. Accuracy scores of the second model on validation and test sets of CBT-NE data were 75.5% and 69.9% respectively, and its scores on validation and test sets of CBT-CN data were 69.1% and 67.7% respectively.

Fu et al. [4] proposed a model to answer cloze-style questions. The model was based on BiGRU and intra-attention. Intra-attention was used to model long-term dependencies. The output (e.g., an answer) was provided via inter-attention mechanism. The authors utilized CBT data to validate their model.

The model achieved accuracy scores of 77.7% and 74.2% on validation and test sets of CBT-NE data respectively, and 75.9% and 74.5% on validation and test sets of CBT-CN data respectively.

Fu and Zhang [5] developed a model that addresses cloze-style questions. The model utilized multiple latent semantic spaces to process queries and documents. Also, the model utilized a bit-level attention instead of token-level attention. Fu and Zhang argued that bit-level attention is more effective than token-level attention. The authors validated their model using CBT data. The model achieved accuracies of 78.1% on validation and 73.1% on test sets of CBT-NE and 73.9% on validation and 71.5% on test sets of CBT-CN.

Dhingra et al. [6] proposed a Gated Attention (GA) and BiGRU based model for cloze-style question answering. Gates in attention mechanism instructed the attention whether to apply summation, concatenation, or multiplication of the output provided by BiGRUs. The model had 4 layers of BiGRUs and GA. The researchers validated their model on CBT-NE and CBT-CN. The model achieved accuracy scores of 78.5% and 74.9% on validation and test sets of CBT-NE data and 74.4% and 70.7% on validation and test sets of CBT-CN data.

Kadlec et al. [7] proposed an ensemble model based on attention mechanism and BiGRU to provide answers for cloze-style questions. The model was validated on CBT data and achieved 76.2% and 71% accuracy scores on validation and test sets of CBT-NE data, and 72.4% and 67.5% accuracy scores on validation and test sets of CBT-CN data.

Hermann et al. [8] proposed an attention mechanism and bidirectional long short-term memory (BiLSTM) based model for cloze-style questions. They developed two instances of the model. The first instance, Attentive Reader, applies attention on context and query after they were fully encoded; and the second instance, Impatient Reader, applies attention every time a query token was encoded. The instances were validated on data from CNN and Daily Mail websites collected by the authors. The Attentive Reader achieved accuracy scores of 61.6% and 63% on validation and test sets of CNN data, and 70.5% and 69% on validation and test sets of Daily Mail data. And the Impatient Reader achieved accuracy scores of 61.8% and 63.8% on validation and test sets of CNN data, and 69% and 68% on validation and test sets of Daily Mail data.

Shen et al. [9] proposed an attention mechanism and BiLSTM based model to address cloze-style questions. The authors introduced some reinforcement learning techniques to dynamically instruct the model when to stop reading a document. The model was validated on CNN and Daily Mail data with accuracies of 72.9% and 74.7% on CNN validation and test sets, and 77.6% and 76.6% on Daily Mail validation and test sets.

The presented work shows that there are several deep learning approaches towards cloze-style QA systems. Although HAN based models are relatively simple and provide good results, only one model—proposed by Alpay et al. [3]— was based on HANs. As a result, HANs are not sufficiently studied for cloze-style QA. In this research, we improve the application of HAN models on cloze-style QA by studying effects of text encoding layers on HANs' inference times and accuracy scores. Table 1 summarizes presented literature. For accuracy scores, we included the highest achieved score by a model on a test set.

Table 1. Summary of approaches towards cloze-style QA.

Reference	Attributes		
	Architecture	Data	Accuracy scores
Alpay et al. [3]	HAN and BiGRU	CBT-NE	69.9%
Fu et al. [4]	BiGRU and intra-attention	CBT-CN	74.5%
Fu and Zhang [5]	Latent semantic spaces and bit-level attention	CBT-NE	73.1%
Dhingra et al. [6]	Gated Attention and BiGRU	CBT-NE	74.9%
Kadlec et al. [7]	Attention mechanism and BiGRU	CBT-NE	71%
Hermann et al. [8]	Attention mechanism and BiLSTM	Daily Mail	69%
Shen et al. [9]	Attention mechanism and BiLSTM	Daily Mail	76.6%

3.2   General Approaches

There are several approaches that have been used to design QA systems. The following discusses some of recent work that is related to this research.

Du et al. [10] proposed a biomedical QA system consisting of four layers. The first layer contains pre-trained Bidirectional Encoder Representation Transformers (BERT) [11], the second layer Bidirectional Long-Short Term Memory (BiLSTM), and the third layer an attention mechanism. The fourth layer is the output layer. Since BERT was pre-trained, the authors fine-tuned it with the BioASQ [12] dataset to improve its performance. The dataset had 1,799 questions related to the biomedical field. The model was then tested using a biomedical related dataset containing 1,799 questions and achieved a strict accuracy score of 0.33 and a Mean Reciprocal Rank (MRR) score of 0.38.

Li et al. [13] developed a Recurrent Neural Network (RNN) and Convolutional Neural Network (CNN) based encoders QA system. The model was trained on the NLPCC2016 which is a chinese language dataset containing training and testing sets [14]. The training set has 181,882 question and answer pairs. The testing set has 122,531 question and answer pairs. The model achieved a Mean Average Precision (MAP) score of 0.844, an MRR score of 0.845, and a precision of 77.1%.

Xiao et al. [15] proposed a QA system that utilizes both BiLSTMs and attention mechanism. The input text was converted into vector space using Glove word embeddings [2]. Some features were added to the encoded paragraphs such as

Part of Speech (POS) and named entity tags. The authors used Stanford Question Answering Dataset (SQuAD) [16] to train their model. The model achieved an F1 score of 79.7% and an Exact Match (EM) score of 71.4% on that dataset.

Peng and Liu [17] proposed an attention-based CNN model for QA tasks. The main goal of the model is to re-rank candidate answers and remove factoid answers. This task was accomplished by obtaining word-level and phrase-level interactive. The model then generates probabilities to re-rank candidate answers. The model was trained on TrecQA [18] which has 4,718 training examples, 1,148 validation examples, and 1,517 testing examples. The model achieved an MAP score of 0.688 and an MMR score of 0.773 on this dataset.

As discussed above, there are different approaches to build deep learning based systems for QA tasks. However, attention mechanism seems to be the common approach as it allows models to ignore irrelevant information. Table 2 summarizes presented literature. For accuracy metrics, we included the highest achieved value.

Table 2. Summary of general approaches towards QA.

Reference	Attributes		
	Architecture	Data	Accuracy metrics
Du et al. [10]	BERT and BiLSTM	BioASQ	MRR score of 0.38
Li et al. [13]	RNN and CNN	NLPCC2016	MRR score of 0.845
Xiao et al. [15]	Attention mechanism and BiLSTM	SQuAD	F1 score of 79.7%
Peng and Liu [17]	Attention mechanism and CNN	TrecQA	MMR score of 0.773

3.3   Cloze-Style Questions Datasets

Three commonly used cloze-style data are Children's Book Test (CBT), Cable News Network (CNN), and Daily Mail datasets. Recently they have been utilized to train and validate deep learning based models to answer cloze-style questions. The following discusses some information about these datasets.

CBT was collected from children books, and Hill et al. [19] argued that children books provide a clear narrative structure. Each example in the data has a 20-sentence context, a 1-sentence query with a missing word, 10 candidate answers, and 1 true answer. Missing words in query sentences could be one of two types which are named entities and common nouns. So, CBT has two instances namely Named Entity (CBT-NE) and Common Nouns (CBT-CN) where the first has 108,719 training, 2,000 validation, and 2,500 test examples; and the second has 120,769 training, 2,000 validation, and 2,500 test examples.

The other two datasets, CNN and Daily Mail, were collected by Hermann et al. [8] from Cable News Network[1] and Daily Mail[2] websites. The authors noticed that articles in CNN and Daily Mail websites are followed by bullet point summaries. So, by removing an entity from one of the bullet points and having the other points as queries, the researchers could construct a document-query-answer triple data. CNN data consists of 380,298 training examples, 3,924 validation examples, and 3,198 testing examples; and Daily Mail data 879,450 training examples, 64,835 validation examples, and 53,182 testing examples.

Three common cloze-style data are CBT, CNN, and Daily Mail datasets. They have been utilized recently to train and validate deep learning based models to answer cloze-style questions. Table 3 provides a summary of these datasets.

Table 3. Summary of cloze-style question datasets.

Data	Attributes		
	Training examples	Validation examples	Testing examples
CBT-NE	108,719	2,000	2,500
CBT-CN	120,769	2,000	2,500
CNN	380,298	3,924	3,198
Daily Mail	879,450	64,835	53,182

4 Proposed Model

We describe proposed model in some details. We discuss overall operations of the model. Then, we illustrate first and second level attentions. We do not provide mathematical details in this section. Instead, we present them in the appendix section.

4.1 Model Description

Our proposed model is based on Hierarchical Attention Network-pointer sum attention (HAN-ptr) model for cloze-style developed by Alpay et al. [3]. Figure 1 shows a block diagram of the proposed model. Colored boxes indicate inputs or outputs, and white boxes indicate operations. Dashed arrow going from a Bidirectional Gated Recurrent Unit (BiGRU) indicates all hidden states of that BiGRU, and solid arrow going from a BiGRU indicates last hidden state of that BiGRU.

First, context sentences and query are encoded word by word using two separate BiGRUs. Then, attention is performed on all hidden states of encoded sentences and last hidden state of encoded query. This results in an attended

---

[1] www.cnn.com.

[2] www.dailymail.co.uk.

context vector (context after attention is performed on it) that has relevant information to query. Another attention is performed on the encoded query and attended context. This enhances the attended context vector because the operation reduces values of irrelevant information compared to relevant. Then, first and second attention scores are multiplied which results in word scores. After that, attention sum [7] is performed on candidate answers (e.g., a list of 10 possible answers) and word scores.

Attention sum just adds scores of a word. To illustrate, a context could have repeated words, and scores of these words might be different depending on their locations in context. As an example, if a context has the word "school" 3 times with scores 0.05, 0.1, and 0.07, then score of "school" would be 0.22. The output of HAN is the word with maximum score, and it is predicted to be the answer to query.

4.2 First Attention

First attention is illustrated in Fig. 2. Inputs to the operation are encoded context and encoded query. Encoded context is a matrix with shape $(sequence, OS * 2)$ where $sequence$ is the number of words in a context, and OS is the output space of a GRU unit. It is multiplied by 2 because we concatenate outputs of 2 GRUs. Encoded query is a vector with shape $(1, OS * 2)$. Dot product is applied between encoded query and every row in encoded context. The result is

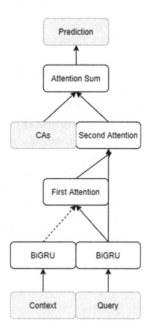

Fig. 1. A block diagram of the proposed model where CAs stands for Candidate Answers.

a vector of size (*sequence*, 1), and a soft-max operation is applied on this vector. Soft-max operation produces attention scores of words. For example, row$_i$ in attention scores vector has the score of ith word in input context. Finally, each row in encoded context is multiplied by the corresponding score using element-wise multiplication which gives attended context. As indicated by colored boxes in Fig. 2, outputs of first attention are attention scores and attended context.

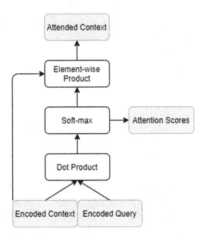

Fig. 2. A block diagram of first attention.

4.3   Second Attention

Operations of second attention are similar to first attention and are shown in Fig. 3. Inputs are attended context, encoded query, and attention scores (input attention scores). Dot product is applied between encoded query and every row in attended context. The result is a vector of size (*sequence*, 2∗*d*), and a soft-max operation is applied on this vector to get attention scores (obtained attention scores). After that, element-wise multiplication is performed between obtained attention scores and input attention scores. Although the operation reduces values of input attention scores, it decreases values of irrelevant words much more since values of these words will be multiplied by small values compared to values that correspond to relevant words. The output of second attention is the result of element-wise multiplication which is word scores vector.

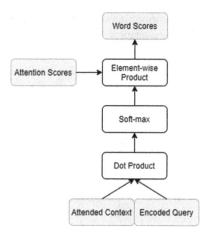

Fig. 3. A block diagram of second attention.

5   Developments of Models

We develop two Hierarchical Attention Network (HAN) models. Models are implemented using TensorFlow[3]. First model (proposed model) is implemented as described in Sect. 4. Second model is baseline model, and we implement it as described by Alpay et al. [3].

We carry out training process on a High Performance Computing (HPC) cluster provided by Information and Communication Technology Center[4] at King Fahad University of Petroleum and Minerals (KFUPM). The cluster has 20 Central Processing Units (CPUs) of type Intel(R) Xeon(R) CPU E5-2680 v2 @ 2.80 GHz. The cluster provides a disk space of 11 Terabytes (TBs) and a Random Access Memory (RAM) of size 125 Gigabytes (GB). Training is done in batches each of size 32 samples. Models are evaluated every 200 batches. Training process is terminated if a model's accuracy on validation set does not improve for 5 consecutive evaluations.

6   Data

We utilize Children's Book Test (CBT) [19] data. We are considering CBT-Named Entity (CBT-NE) and CBT-Common Noun (CBT-CN) data. Each example of both datasets has 21 lines. The first 20 lines are context sentences, the 21st line has three parts which are a query, true answer, and a list of 10 candidate answers. The three parts are separated by tabs instead of spaces.

Figure 4 shows distributions of true answers of CBT-NE training, validation, and testing data. True answers are not equally distributed, so the datasets are not

---

[3] https://www.tensorflow.org/.

[4] http://www.kfupm.edu.sa/centers/itc/default.aspx.

balanced. Total numbers of unique answers of training, validation, and testing data are 5234, 317, and 427 respectively.

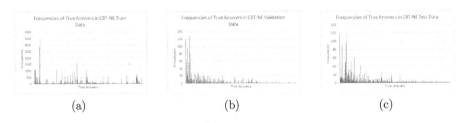

Fig. 4. Distribution of true answers of CBT-NE (a) train data, (b) validation data, and (c) test data.

Similarly, Fig. 5 shows distributions of true answers of CBT-CN training, validation, and testing data. CBT-CN's true answers are also not equally distributed, so the CBT-CN is not balanced. Total numbers of unique answers of training, validation, and testing data are 4753, 533, and 722 respectively.

7   Data Pre-processing

Children's Book Test (CBT) data is well organised. Hence, data pre-processing is minimal. We process data line by line as the following. For each line, we remove line numbers and new line character (e.g., n). After that, we store each word of the line in a Counter data structure[5]. Each entry in the structure is a tuple consisting of a word and its frequency. The frequency of a word is updated as the processing progresses. For example, if a word in some line has a frequency of 2, then its entry in the Counter data structure would be 2. If the same word appears in another line with a frequency of 3, then its frequency would be updated to be 5 (e.g., 2 + 3). At the end of this process, Counter has entry for each word in the data and its corresponding frequency.

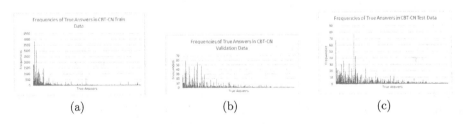

Fig. 5. Distribution of true answers of CBT-CN (a) train data, (b) validation data, and (c) test data.

---

[5] https://docs.python.org/2/library/collections.html#collections.Counter.

We utilize these frequencies to sort words from the most common to the least common. This allows us to assign Identification (ID) numbers to words. IDs ranged from 0 to (max − 1) where max is the total numbers of words in a data set (e.g., CBT-Named Entity (CBT-NE) or CBT-Common Nouns (CBT-CN)). ID of 0 is assigned to the most common word in a dataset, and ID of (max − 1) is assigned to the least common word in the dataset. Then, we convert data files from text to integers by replacing each word by its ID. This step is not necessary, but it results in smaller file sizes. For instance, the original size of CBT-NE training data is 237 Megabyte (MB), while the size of the corresponding ID file is 168 MB. In addition, working with integer values is generally simpler than working with string values.

After we read ID files, we convert them into vector space using pre-trained Glove [2] embedding matrix. Originally, embedding matrix is indexed by words row-wise. For instance, row_i has the vector representation of $word_i$. So, we replaced word indices by the corresponding IDs.

8 Results

Tests are performed by evaluating proposed and baseline models on batches of 32 samples from test data. We consider two criteria which are inference times and accuracy scores. Inference time is expressed in seconds, and it is the time needed by a model to process a single test sample. Accuracy is computed as the total number of correctly identified answers divided by the total number of predictions. Following subsections discuss results obtained from CBT-NE and CBT-CN test data.

8.1 Test Results on CBT-NE Data

CBT-NE test data has 2500 examples. Proposed model gets an average inference time of 0.0476 s and an average accuracy score of 70.47%. Baseline model gets an average inference time of 0.106 s and an average accuracy score of 68.99%. Results show that proposed model has inference time reduction of 55.26% and accuracy increase of 2.14%. Results are presented in Table 4.

Table 4. Test results of CBT-NE data.

Model	Results	
	Average inference time	Average accuracy score
Proposed model	0.0476 s	70.47%
Baseline model	0.106 s	68.99%
Reduction in inference time	55.26%	-
Increase in accuracy	-	2.14%

8.2   Test Results on CBT-CN Data

CBT-CN test data has 2500 examples. Proposed model achieves an average inference time of 0.049 s and an average accuracy score of 67.5%. Baseline model achieves an average inference time of 0.105 s and an average accuracy score of 67.12%. Results show that proposed model has inference time reduction of 53.6% and accuracy increase of 0.572%. Results are shown in Table 5.

Table 5. Test results of CBT-CN data.

Model	Results	
	Average inference time	Average accuracy score
Proposed model	0.049 s	67.5%
Baseline model	0.105 s	67.12%
Reduction in inference time	53.6%	-
Increase in accuracy	-	0.572%

9   Statistical Analysis

We conduct statistical tests on obtained results of models. Statistical tests are needed to show whether obtained results of proposed and baseline models have the same distribution (e.g., both results are the same), or they have different distributions. We utilize Shapiro test [20] to test normality of our results. Test shows that most of results are not normally distributed. Consequently, we conduct a non-parametric test to test hypotheses, and test is Mann–Whitney U test [21]. For normally distributed results, we use t-test. Following subsections discuss statistical tests of results obtained from CBT-NE and CBT-CN test data.

9.1   Statistical Test of CBT-NE Results

Shapiro test indicates that inference times of proposed model are normally distributed with a p-value of 0.13, and inference times of baseline model are normally distributed with a p-value of 0.145. Regarding accuracy scores, test indicates that accuracy scores of proposed model are normally distributed with a p-value of 0.0674, and accuracy scores of baseline model are not normally distributed with a p-value of $2.19 * 10^{-15}$. Table 6 summarizes outcomes of Shapiro test of CBT-NE's results.

We perform statistical tests to test first and second hypotheses. We use T-test for inference times since results of both models are normally distributed. The test shows that inference times of both models are from different distributions with a p-value of $5.04 * 10^{-68}$. For accuracy scores, scores for proposed model are normally distributed, whereas scores of baseline model are not. As a result, we utilize Mann–Whitney U test for accuracy scores. The test indicates that accuracy scores of both models are from different distributions with a p-value of 0.04089. Since inference times and accuracy scores of models have different distributions, hypotheses H_{01} and H_{02} are rejected, and there are evidences (e.g., statistical tests of inference time and accuracy scores) that one-layer text encoding HAN model and two-layer text encoding HAN model have different average inference times and different average accuracy scores.

Table 6. Summary of Shapiro test results of CBT-NE data.

Model	Shapiro test's p-value	
	Inference times	Accuracy scores
Proposed model	0.13	0.0674
Baseline model	0.145	$2.19 * 10^{-15}$

9.2 Statistical Test of CBT-CN Results

Shapiro test shows that inference times of proposed model are not normally distributed with a p-value of 0.0163, and inference times of baseline model are normally distributed with a p-value of 0.394. Test also indicates that accuracy scores of proposed model are normally distributed with a p-value of 0.231 and accuracy scores of baseline model are not normally distributed with a p-value of $7.55 * 10^{-14}$. Table 7 summarizes outcomes of Shapiro test of CBT-NE's results.

We performed Mann–Whitney U test to test first and second hypotheses. Test indicates that inference times of both models are from different distributions with a p-value of $2.13 * 10^{-27}$, and accuracy scores of both models are from the same distribution with a p-value of 0.371. Since inference times of models have different distributions, hypothesis H_{01} is rejected, and there is evidence that one-layer text encoding HAN model and two-layer text encoding HAN model have different average inference times. In addition, hypothesis H_{02} is not rejected, and there is evidence that one-layer text encoding HAN model and two-layer text encoding HAN model have different average accuracy scores.

Table 7. Summary of Shapiro test results of CBT-CN data.

Model	Shapiro test's p-value	
	Inference times	Accuracy scores
Proposed model	0.0163	0.231
Baseline model	0.394	$7.55 * 10^{-14}$

10   Discussion

Results presented in Sect. 8 show that developed model performs better than baseline model in terms of inference time and accuracy score for both data sets. In addition, statistical tests discussed in Sect. 9 show that proposed and baseline models do not have the same average inference times. On the other hand, average accuracy scores of both models are comparable. Although Mann–Whitney U test indicates that accuracy scores of models on CBT-NE data have different distributions, its p-value is close to 0.05. Hence, developed model outperforms baseline model in terms of inference time, and it maintains accuracy scores. Consequently, the answer to the first research question is "one-layer text encoding HAN provides, on average, 54.4% decrease on inference time compared to two-layer text encoding HAN". The answer to the second research question is "one-layer text encoding HAN maintains accuracy score of two-layer text encoding HAN".

Regarding validity of experiments, experiments do not have construct validity because models are sufficiently trained (e.g., training process is terminated if a model does not improve on 5 consecutive validations). Experiments do not have internal validity because, for each experiment, only second layer of text encoding is changed while other factors are fixed. To illustrate, the only difference between developed model and baseline model is that developed model does not have a second layer of text encoding while baseline model does. As a consequence, observed behaviours of models are caused by this difference. Regarding external validity, experiments have this type of threat since models are trained and tested on two datasets, so results of experiments cannot be generalized.

11   Conclusion

Question Answering (QA) has gained researchers' attention recently. One reason is the advancement of deep learning architectures. Cloze-style QA is a QA task where a model is fed a context and a query as inputs. The model should infer an answer to the query based on the context. As a candidate model, Hierarchical Attention Network (HAN) model could be utilized for such task. We develop a HAN model with a single layer of text encoding. We address 2 research questions to compare our proposed model against a baseline model having two-layers of text encoding. The questions are "What effect does one-layer text encoding have on HAN's inference time compared to two-layer text encoding?" and "What effect does one-layer text encoding have on HAN's accuracy score compared to two-layer text encoding?".

To answer research questions, we design and run experiments. Experiments show that the answer to the first question is that one-layer text encoding HAN results in 54.4% decrease on inference time compared to two-layer text encoding HAN. The answer to the second question is that one-layer text encoding HAN gives the same average accuracy score as two-layer text encoding HAN. So, proposed model has better inference times, and it maintains accuracy scores.

Appendix

In the appendix section, we illustrate mathematical details of proposed and baseline models. Both models have two layers of attention. First layer of both models have two Bi-directional Recurrent Gated Units (BiGRUs) and an attention operation. These operations are defined mathematically as:

$$encoded\_doc = all\_states(BiGRU(doc)) \tag{1}$$

$$encoded\_query = last\_state(BiGRU(query)) \tag{2}$$

$$dot\_product = encoded\_query^T \cdot encoded\_doc \tag{3}$$

$$attention\_level_{1i} = \frac{exp(dot\_product_i)}{\sum_{j=1}^{sequence} exp(dot\_product_j)} \tag{4}$$

$$attended\_doc_i = attention\_level_1 \cdot encoded\_doc_i \tag{5}$$

where doc stands for document, i in Eq. 4 corresponds to i^{th} element of vector $attention\_level_1$, and $sequence$ in Eq. 4 is the size of vector $dot\_product$ which equals to the maximum number of words in all documents. It should be noted that Eq. 1 returns concatenated hidden states of BiGRU. Consequently, $encoded\_doc$ is a matrix of dimension $(sequence, output\_space * 2)$ where $output\_space$ is the output dimension of a GRU unit. Equation 2 returns concatenated last state of BiGRU. So, $encoded\_query$ is a vector of dimension $output\_space * 2$. Equation 3 performs dot product between transpose of $encoded\_query$ and $encoded\_doc$ which results in a vector of dimension $sequence$. Equation 4 performs a soft-max operation on vector $dot\_product$. Finally, Eq. 5 performs element-wise product between $attention\_level_1$ and i^{th} row of $encoded\_doc$. The result of Eq. 5 is matrix $attended\_doc$ with dimension $(sequence, output\_space * 2)$ (e.g., as the dimensionality of $encoded\_doc$).

For second layer, proposed model does not have text encoding operation, while baseline model does. So, proposed model proceeds by performing the following set of operations:

$$dot\_product = encoded\_query^T \cdot attended\_doc \tag{6}$$

$$attention\_level_{2i} = \frac{exp(dot\_product_i)}{\sum_{j=1}^{sequence} exp(dot\_product_j)} \tag{7}$$

$$word\_scores = attention\_level_2 \cdot attention\_level_1 \tag{8}$$

$$attention\_sum = \sum_{word \in CA} \sum_{j=1}^{sequence} ((word\_scores_j) and (word == doc_j)) \tag{9}$$

$$prediction = CA(index\_of\_argmax(attention\_sum)) \tag{10}$$

where CA in Eq. 9 stands for candidate answers, and it is a list of 10 possible answers. Equation 6 performs dot product between transpose of $encoded\_query$ and $attended\_doc$. The resulted vector $dot\_product$ has a dimensionality of *sequence*. Equation 7 computes second level attention vector $attention\_level_2$ with dimensionality of *sequence*. Equation 8 computes word scores by performing element-wise product between $attention\_level_2$ and $attention\_level_1$. Vector $word\_scores$ has a dimension of *sequence*. Equation 9 performs attention sum operation by summing all scores of a word $\in CA$. Consequently, $attention\_sum$ has 10 entries. Each entry is a score that the corresponding word in CA is the answer to query. Equation 10 takes index i of maximum score and predicts CA_i as the answer to query.

Regarding baseline model, it performs the following set of operations:

$$encoded\_doc = all\_states(BiGRU(attended\_doc)) \tag{11}$$

$$dot\_product = encoded\_query^T \cdot encoded\_doc \tag{12}$$

$$attention\_level_{2i} = \frac{exp(dot\_product_i)}{\sum_{j=1}^{sequence} exp(dot\_product_j)} \tag{13}$$

$$word\_scores = attention\_level_2 \cdot attention\_level_1 \tag{14}$$

$$attention\_sum = \sum_{word \in CA} \sum_{j=1}^{sequence} ((word\_scores_j)and(word == doc_j)) \tag{15}$$

$$prediction = CA(index\_of\_argmax(attention\_sum)) \tag{16}$$

Equation 11 performs text encoding, and $encoded\_doc$ is concatenation of hidden states of BiGRU, and it is a matrix of dimension $(sequence, output\_space*2)$. Description of Eqs. 12–16 follow exactly the same description of Eqs. 6–10. It should be noted that Eq. 6 performs dot product between transpose of $encoded\_query$ and $attended\_doc$, whereas Eq. 12 performs dot product between transpose of $encoded\_query$ and $encoded\_doc$.

References

1. Yang, Z., Yang, D., Dyer, C., He, X., Smola, A., Hovy, E.: Hierarchical attention networks for document classification. In: Proceedings of the 2016 Conference of the North American Chapter of the Association for Computational Linguistics: Human Language Technologies, pp. 1480–1489. Association for Computational Linguistics, San Diego, June 2016
2. Pennington, J., Socher, R., Manning, C.D.: Glove: global vectors for word representation. In: EMNLP (2014)
3. Alpay, T., Heinrich, S., Nelskamp, M., Wermter, S.: Question answering with hierarchical attention networks, July 2019
4. Fu, C., Li, Y., Zhang, Y.: ATNet: answering cloze-style questions via intra-attention and inter-attention, pp. 242–252, March 2019
5. Fu, C., Zhang, Y.: EA reader: enhance attentive reader for cloze-style question answering via multi-space context fusion. In: Proceedings of the AAAI Conference on Artificial Intelligence, vol. 33, pp. 6375–6382, July 2019

6. Dhingra, B., Liu, H., Yang, Z., Cohen, W., Salakhutdinov, R.: Gated-attention readers for text comprehension. In: Proceedings of the 55th Annual Meeting of the Association for Computational Linguistics (Volume 1: Long Papers), pp. 1832–1846. Association for Computational Linguistics, Vancouver, Canada, July 2017

7. Kadlec, R., Schmid, M., Bajgar, O., Kleindienst, J.: Text understanding with the attention sum reader network. In: Proceedings of the 54th Annual Meeting of the Association for Computational Linguistics (Volume 1: Long Papers), pp. 908–918. Association for Computational Linguistics, Berlin, August 2016

8. Hermann, K.M., et al.: Teaching machines to read and comprehend. In: Proceedings of the 28th International Conference on Neural Information Processing Systems - Volume 1, NIPS 2015, pp. 1693–1701. MIT Press, Cambridge (2015)

9. Shen, Y., Huang, P.-S., Gao, J., Chen, W.: Reasonet: learning to stop reading in machine comprehension, September 2016

10. Du, Y., Pei, B., Zhao, X., Ji, J.: Deep scaled dot-product attention based domain adaptation model for biomedical question answering. Methods (2019)

11. Devlin, J., Chang, M.-W., Lee, K., Toutanova, K.: BERT: pre-training of deep bidirectional transformers for language understanding. In: Proceedings of the 2019 Conference of the North American Chapter of the Association for Computational Linguistics: Human Language Technologies, Volume 1 (Long and Short Papers), pp. 4171–4186. Association for Computational Linguistics, Minneapolis, June 2019

12. Balikas, G., Krithara, A., Partalas, I., Paliouras, G.: BioASQ: a challenge on large-scale biomedical semantic indexing and question answering. In: Müller, H., Jimenez del Toro, O.A., Hanbury, A., Langs, G., Foncubierta Rodríguez, A. (eds.) Multi-modal Retrieval in the Medical Domain. LNCS, vol. 9059, pp. 26–39. Springer, Cham (2015). https://doi.org/10.1007/978-3-319-24471-6_3

13. Li, W., Li, W., Wu, Y.: A unified model for document-based question answering based on human-like reading strategy. In: AAAI (2018)

14. Qiu, X., Qian, P., Shi, Z.: Overview of the NLPCC-ICCPOL 2016 shared task: chinese word segmentation for micro-blog texts. In: Lin, C.-Y., Xue, N., Zhao, D., Huang, X., Feng, Y. (eds.) ICCPOL/NLPCC 2016. LNCS (LNAI), vol. 10102, pp. 901–906. Springer, Cham (2016). https://doi.org/10.1007/978-3-319-50496-4_84

15. Xiao, L., Wang, N., Yang, G.: A reading comprehension style question answering model based on attention mechanism, pp. 1–4, July 2018

16. Rajpurkar, P., Zhang, J., Lopyrev, K., Liang, P.: SQuAD: 100,000+ questions for machine comprehension of text. In: Proceedings of the 2016 Conference on Empirical Methods in Natural Language Processing, pp. 2383–2392. Association for Computational Linguistics, Austin, November 2016

17. Peng, Y., Liu, B.: Attention-based neural network for short-text question answering, pp. 21–26, June 2018

18. Wang, M., Smith, N.A., Mitamura, T.: What is the Jeopardy model? A quasi-synchronous grammar for QA. In: Proceedings of the 2007 Joint Conference on Empirical Methods in Natural Language Processing and Computational Natural Language Learning (EMNLP-CoNLL), pp. 22–32. Association for Computational Linguistics, Prague, June 2007

19. Hill, F., Bordes, A., Chopra, S., Weston, J.: The goldilocks principle: Reading children's books with explicit memory representations, November 2015

20. Shapiro, S.S., Wilk, M.B.: An analysis of variance test for normality (complete samples). Biometrika **52**(3/4), 591–611 (1965)

21. Wilcoxon, F.: Individual comparisons by ranking methods. In: Kotz S., Johnson N.L. (eds.) Breakthroughs in Statistics. Springer Series in Statistics (Perspectives in Statistics), pp. 196–202. Springer, New York (1992)

An ARIMA-LSTM Correlation Coefficient Based Hybrid Model for Portfolio Management of Dhaka Stock Exchange

Rafatul Alam, Raisul Islam Arnob[✉], and Alvi Ebne Alam

BRAC University, 66 Mohakhali, Dhaka 1212, Bangladesh
rafatul.alam@gmail.com, rislam.arnob@gmail.com,
t88.alam@gmail.com

Abstract. This paper proposes the forecasting of correlation coefficients of the Dhaka Stock Exchange (DSE) market assets required for portfolio optimization using an ARIMA-LSTM hybrid model. DSE dataset contains a mix of linear and nonlinear data, where linearity means a direct relationship between the dependent and the independent variables and vice-versa for non-linear data. In relatable papers we came across, either linearity or non-linearity was handled within the dataset but none dealt with the combination of both. Our proposed model encompasses both linearity and non-linearity within the datasets of the DSE assets. This cannot be accomplished using other conventional statistical models. We have filtered the linear components in the datasets using the ARIMA model and passed the residuals obtained onto the LSTM model which deals with the non-linear components and random errors. We have compared the empirical results of this model with several other traditional statistical models used in portfolio management namely the Single Index model, Constant Correlation model, and Historical Model. We have also predicted the correlation coefficients using the ARIMA model to see how one of the models in our hybrid performs individually. The experimental results demonstrate that the hybrid model outperforms the other models in terms of accuracy and indicates that the ARIMA-LSTM hybrid model can be an effective way of predicting correlation coefficients required for portfolio optimization.

Keywords: ARIMA · Dhaka Stock Exchange · Hybrid · Linear · LSTM · Non-linear · Portfolio

1 Introduction

The stock market is volatile and stochastic in nature, the investors' main interest lies in maximizing the profitable return on investment and reducing the risk. In stock market asset analysis, a group of monetary assets consisting of stocks, commodities, currencies, and cash equivalents along with mutual, exchange-traded, closed funds, and other items is termed as a portfolio. Correlation coefficients can be found between the stock market

© ICST Institute for Computer Sciences, Social Informatics and Telecommunications Engineering 2020
Published by Springer Nature Switzerland AG 2020. All Rights Reserved
M. H. Miraz et al. (Eds.): iCETiC 2020, LNICST 332, pp. 214–226, 2020.
https://doi.org/10.1007/978-3-030-60036-5_15

companies based on certain parameters like closing price, opening price, high price, and low price. We chose to work with the closing price of each day to eliminate price fluctuations throughout the day. These coefficients are used to define strong or weak relations between the pair of companies. A portfolio serves as a guide for potential return and risk in investment.

In 1952, Markowitz proposed the Modern Portfolio Theory in his paper 'Portfolio Selection' [1]. This theory shows how investors can form a portfolio that will give them maximum returns for a certain level of risk. It suggests that a group of optimal portfolios termed as 'Efficient Frontier' can be built which offers maximum possible return depending on investor's desired level of risk. The Modern Portfolio Theory contends that the traits of an investment's risk and return should be assessed based on how the investment affects the overall portfolio's risk and return. Finding correlations between company pairs helps to find an investment's merit in context to the entire portfolio. A lower or negative correlation means the companies are loosely related. So, investors averse to risk can form portfolios with companies having lower or negative correlation. On the other hand, high risk can reward the investor with greater returns. Building a portfolio with positively correlated companies would be preferable for such investors. For better portfolio optimization, the correlation coefficients in the near future need to be forecasted well enough and this can be done using the historical data. Several statistical methods are used for predicting correlations, but few of the most commonly used statistical models for forecasting the correlation coefficients between the stocks in a portfolio are Single Index model, Constant Correlation model, and Historical Model. These are traditional models that were employed to forecast the stock prices before the advent of more robust neural networks [2, 3]. Besides the traditional models, several other different models such as the ARIMA and Recurrent Neural Network (RNN) have the potential to work better on forecasting correlation coefficient values between stock prices. This can be justified given that the models have proven to work well on forecasting short term as well as long term stock market data [4, 5].

We aim to propose an ARIMA-LSTM hybrid model to forecast the correlation coefficients between stock market assets. For this research, we have used 15 registered companies from DSE. After that, we analyzed and compared the performance of our proposed model with the traditional statistical models along with the widely used ARIMA model. Even though such models have been used in other time series data, forecasting stock market correlation coefficients with this model is still relatively a new thing.

The rest of the paper is structured as follows. Background Study has been discussed in Sect. 2. System Architecture and explanation regarding its effectiveness, capabilities, and scope have been represented in Sect. 3. Experimental Results and Analysis in Sect. 4 discusses the performance evaluation of our model.

2 Background Study

Several researchers have studied and found that the majority of the developed countries' stock markets exhibit random walk movement, which means that the future price or movement of stock or market cannot be forecasted from its past price. It has been found that the inefficiency of any emerging market happens due to the market's size, the thinness of trading and the authentication of the information disclosed. Early studies performed on the Dhaka Stock Exchange for examining the weak form efficiency were found to be inconclusive [4].

Chakraborty [5] performed a comparative study on analyzing and predicting the stock market trend movement amongst the companies in Dhaka Stock Exchange using ARIMA model and LSTM model, respectively. They used the historical stock market data and split it into train and test sets. They used the training set to identify an appropriate ARIMA model for forecasting the stock price of a chosen company for the next 60 days approximately. They used the same training dataset to train the LSTM model and perform the prediction for the same number of future days.

Alam et al. [6] investigated the performance by performing an empirical case study on Dhaka Stock Exchange to test its market efficiency. They used a dataset of 3209 daily observations from a period of 1994 to 2005 to analyze risk and return ratio followed by CAPM modeling to find the risk-return relationship in the market. They deduced that there was not enough liquidity in the stock market data and the market is of weak form inefficient evidently.

Hengjian [7], performed a study on determining the prediction accuracy of LSTM networks on stock markets' prices particularly on high, low, open, or close prices, respectively. He used the open source dataset of Google's daily stock market data ranging from the 1st of January 2005 till the 31st of December 2015. He split the resultant dataset into train and test sets. Instead of feeding the whole train dataset on the proposed neural network at once, the length of the dataset was segmented into several portions, each of size 256 lengthwise. The dataset was trained on an optimal neural network of 100 epochs, the batch size of 20 samples, and a value of 0.001 on Adam optimizer. The accuracy of the model was deduced in the form of calculating the RMSE (Root Mean Squared Error) on a varying range of layers followed by a different number of units on each layer. The model's performance was also compared to a simplified neural network.

Salem and Kent [8] tested the learning performance of the various forms of LSTM types. The different types of LSTM cells were embedded within a proposed neural network to test for its performance. The LSTM variants within the custom neural network model were tested with several forms of activation functions in them such as Tanh, Linear, Sigmoid, Rectified Linear Unit (ReLu), etc. The learning rate of the LSTM variant cells, together with their validation accuracy and loss, were measured after iterating them up to 100 epochs precisely.

Zhang et al. [9] investigated the forecasting performance of a custom-made model by combining ARIMA and ANN. This model was then compared with an individual ARIMA model and an ANN model, respectively. He used three different types of datasets to investigate the performance of his proposed model and measured its accuracy in the form of calculating Mean Squared Error (MSE) and Mean Absolute Deviation (MAD) values. In every dataset experimentation, his proposed hybrid model has performed significantly well enough to identify the trending patterns from the data.

Roondiwala et al. [10] used LSTM only to make predictions of certain features of stock market data, particularly on the stock market return of Nifty50 company. They trained and predicted for features using a custom LSTM model. This model is made up of a sequential input layer followed by 2 layers of LSTM. To add more, a ReLU activation enabled dense layer was included. Finally, as an output, a dense layer with a linear activation function was added. After performing several iterations with a different number of pricing types and epochs, the LSTM model has performed better on 4 features mainly High, Low, Open, and Close prices, respectively with an epoch value of around 500 and achieved less value on Root Mean Squared Error (RMSE).

Hossain et al. [11] proposed to develop a predictive model for forecasting the General Index of the DSE market over the desired timeframe. The general index, also known as the market index, can simply be defined as an aggregate value found by combining several stocks or investment vehicles and expressing their total value against a base value from a particular date. These indexes can help to provide an overview of the way a specific group of stock performs against other groups of stock. They used the data of DSE general index ranging from 3rd of January, 2010 till the 30th of September, 2013. They derived a set of different ARIMA models that best fit their proposed predictive model and found ARIMA (2, 2, 1) to be the most suitable one. To add more, they took the volatility of their time series data into consideration and tested the same dataset against several conditional covariance models. In the end, they deduced that eGARCH (1, 1) (Generalized AutoRegressive Conditional Heteroskedasticity) was the best covariance model that met the requirement. Therefore, they concluded that the mean ARIMA model, together with the conditional covariance model eGARCH (1, 1), was found to be the most competent model for predicting the volatility of index data and forecasting future values for the desired period.

Zou and Qu [12] predicted stock returns on the next trading day using the time series model ARIMA and three forms of the deep learning model LSTM namely Single LSTM, Stacked LSTM, and Attention Based LSTM. Based on the predictions they proposed two trading strategies and compared results produced following their strategies with the market benchmark. From their experimental results, they found the Attention Based LSTM to show superior results to the other two forms of LSTM and ARIMA. From their results, they also concluded that the Single LSTM performed better than the Stacked LSTM model despite the latter having a more complex structure potentially due to overfitting of data.

3   System Architecture

Our hybrid ARIMA-LSTM model entails separate processing of the data. The data we obtained is first preprocessed to remove gaps in the data to make it continuous before it is given as an input to our model. After preprocessing, the data is given as an input to the ARIMA model where the precise order of the model is determined and parameters are identified.

The residual values from the ARIMA model mostly consist of nonlinear data. This residual value acts as an input for the LSTM model where the input layer gates pass the data to the hidden layers. Both the forget gate and the input candidate gate within each LSTM cell manipulates the data and propagates it through the cells of each layer. Finally, we compared the accuracy of the results of our model with prevalent traditional model values using statistical error checking measures like Mean Squared Error (MSE) and Mean Absolute Error (MAE). Figure 1 outlines the steps of our system architecture.

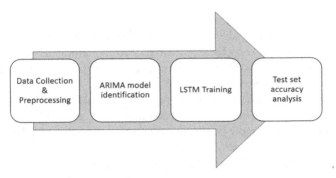

Fig. 1. Workflow

3.1 Data Fetching

We have scraped off daily market data of 356 registered companies of the Dhaka Stock Exchange by building a Python script. DSE provides data in its official website archive and also through third party websites such as AmarStock.com which uses data for plotting and visualization. However, the DSE archive does not contain data before the 1st of July 2017 and hence we collected the rest of the data from AmarStock.com. We collected data from January 2000 till February 2019. The scrapped off data was then stored in an online real time database provided by the Google Firebase.

For our purpose we have collected daily index data under the parameters *Opening price, Closing price, High price, Low price,* and *Trading volume,* respectively. The collected data was originally fetched in UNIX time format, which was later converted to the human-readable date-time format. The data is of varying time range starting as early as January 2000 till February 2019.

3.2 Data Preprocessing

Before feeding the data to the hybrid model we have built, we needed to preprocess it as the initial datasets of companies were inconsistent. In this section, we discussed the steps and procedures we went through to turn the scrapped data into a dataset suitable for our model.

In this paper, we used *the 'Close price'* data of the DSE companies. Though we had collected data from 356 companies, all companies were not listed in DSE at the same time. So, to create an equal dataset of the companies we decided to select those which have data from January 2007 onwards. We found 44 companies that met the requirement. Next, we filled in the missing data by imputing values at time t with t−1 values for selected assets. Out of these complete datasets we selected 15 companies at random. We took pairs of the companies and calculated the correlation coefficient between the imputed datasets with a 100-day rolling time window. We got $15C_2$ or 105 possible pairs and that with a 100-day stride results to 10500 sets of data each containing 24-time steps. In the final step of preprocessing, we built the train, test1, and test 2 datasets with 10500 × 24 data.

3.3 ARIMA Modelling

To deal with the linear components of the datasets we went through the ARIMA process. ARIMA is a regressive model used for the detection of linearity in stationary data. It is expressed as (p, q, d) where p, q determines the definite order of Auto Regressive (AR) and Moving Average (MA) models and d specifies the number of times differentiation required to make input data stationary. Mathematically ARIMA can be modelled as,

$$x_t = c + {}_1x_{t-1} + {}_2x_{t-2} + \cdots + {}_px_{t-p} - \theta_1 \in {}_{t-1} - \theta_2 \in {}_{t-2} - \ldots - \theta_q \in {}_{t-q} \tag{1}$$

Symbol c is constant and the coefficients k, θ_1, belong to x_{t-k} of AR and ϵ_{t-1} of MA. ϵ_{t-1} denotes loss term encompassing zero mean and unvaried variance.

We discussed in detail the steps of this process and how the residual values help in the forecast. Besides, as performance metrics - MSE and MAE values are used in the analysis of the experimental results, to indicate the performance of other models with our model. After optimizing the data for the 20-times step model we got a new dataset with a dimension of 525 $\times$ 24. Then we divided the data into train, test1, and test2 datasets. The train set was formed with columns of indices 1–21, test1 set with indices 2–22, and test2 set with indices 3–23.

We transposed the datasets which give us 525 columns and 20 rows for each dataset. For each of the columns, we first determined whether the set is stationary or not and applied differencing accordingly. A unit root statistical test called Augmented Dickey Fuller (ADF) test helped us in this regard. We noticed that most of the columns required to be differenced once to make them stationary.

ADF follows a null hypothesis which states that a series is probably defined by a trend if it can be represented by a unit root i.e. it is not stationary and contains time dependent structure. On the other hand, if this null hypothesis is rejected, the series does not have a unit root. This means that the time series is stationary and contains no time dependent structure. In the ADF statistics, the null hypothesis is rejected if the p-value is less than 0.05, or else we accept the null hypothesis [4]. The more negative the ADF statistic value is, the more likely the series is stationary.

Figure 2 (a) shows a graph of one of the columns within the train dataset which is non-stationary initially and requires differencing. Figure 2 (b) shows the pattern of the same series after differencing once. In the first graph, the p-value is 0.3285 which is greater than 0.05 and so does not reject the null hypothesis. After differencing, the p-value changes to 0.000015. Thus, it can be said that the series rejects the null hypothesis and is stationary.

We have found that the majority of the columns in the train, test1 and test2 datasets required differencing. To make them stationary, we have decided to differentiate all the columns once. Then by plotting the Auto Correlation Function (ACF) and Partial Auto Correlation Function (PACF) plots on random columns from each dataset we have tried to figure out the possible orders of the ARIMA model that best fit those series of data within each column. During this process the models which we found multiple times were (p, d, q) = (0, 1, 1), (0, 1, 0), (1, 1, 1), (1, 1, 0), (2, 1, 1) which represents the AR(p), MA(q) and I(d) terms.

Figure 2 (c), (d) shows the ACF and PACF plots of order (0, 1, 1). We can derive the p terms from the PACF plot while the q terms are derived from the ACF plot. The ACF

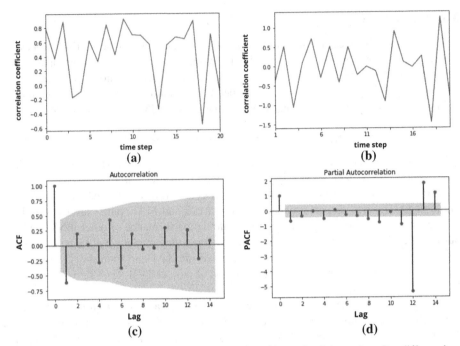

Fig. 2. (a) represents graph of non-stationary series, (b) graph of the series after differencing once, (c) ACF plot of order (0, 1, 1), (d) PACF plot of order (0, 1, 1). (Color figure online)

plot shows a significant spike at lag 1 while the rest of the spikes are within the 95% confidence zone as represented by the blue region in Fig. 2 (c). But in the PACF plot, we do not notice any significant spikes at lag 1 in Fig. 2 (d). Hence, we can conclude that this data series has 1 p term but no q terms. The rest of the models were found similarly from the corresponding ACF and PACF plots of the different columns.

We fitted the four models with our train, test1 and test2 datasets and compared their Akaike Information Criterion (AIC) values for each column of the datasets. We found the ARIMA model of order (0, 1, 1) to be the best fit for the majority of the datasets as it generated the least AIC value for most of the columns in the train, test1, and test2 datasets. In total, the train, test1, and test2 datasets contain 1575 columns. Model (0, 1, 1) was found to be best fit for 1291 columns, model (1, 1, 1) was found best for 229 columns, model (0, 1, 0) for 51 columns and model (2, 1, 1) for 4 columns.

In the model fit, we have used the Maximum Likelihood Estimator (MLE) to compute the log likelihood function. AIC works on the amount of information lost by a model, the less the better. AIC deals with balancing between the goodness of fit and simplicity of the model and reduces the risk of overfitting and underfitting.

For each of the columns in the train, test1, and test2, we made predictions and calculated the residual values. The residual values were obtained by subtracting the forecasted ARIMA values from the original time series values. After that, we have calculated the MSE and MAE values from the forecasted and original datasets. For the (0, 1, 1) model the MSE and MAE values are as represented in Table 1.

Table 1. MSE and MAE values for ARIMA model (0, 1, 1)

Sets	MSE	MAE
Train	0.4661	0.5779
Test1	0.4560	0.5713
Test2	0.4539	0.5682

The error values of MSE and MAE gradually improved for both predicted outcomes of test1 and test2 compared to train set though the improvement is slight.

A normal distribution is plotted to analyze the residual values left behind after ARIMA processing. Figure 3 represents the data point distribution curve that appeared to be normally distributed without showing a significant amount of skewness to the left or right with a mean value near to zero.

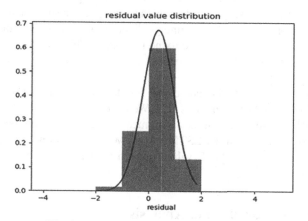

Fig. 3. Normal distribution of residual values

3.4 LSTM Modeling

Through the ARIMA model, we removed any linear tendencies present in our dataset. The residuals contain mostly of non-linear components and random errors. The ARIMA process is not capable of dealing with non-linear data. For this, the obtained residuals are passed on to the LSTM process for analyzing the non-linear portion of the datasets [13].

The residual values obtained from the ARIMA model are reshaped and used to form the Train X and Y, Test1 X and Y and Test2 X and Y datasets respectively. Each, X dataset is comprised of 525 rows of data with 20-time steps and each Y dataset contains the corresponding expected Y output. The splitting of the Train, Test1 and Test2 together with their X and Y components are given as - Train X: index 0–19, Test1 X: index 1–20, Test2 X: index 2–21, Train Y: index 20, Test1 Y: index 21 and Test2 Y: index 22.

For training the model, we built the neural network layers with an instance of the sequential class and used 50 LSTM units. For outputting the prediction, we used 1 dense layer. The model contains an input shape of 20-time steps and 1 feature. We fitted the model with an optimal batch size of 105 samples. Within this LSTM cell, we added a dropout value of 0.4. To prevent issues associated with the overfitting problem, we reduced the neuron interdependency within each LSTM unit by applying the dropout method to deactivate neurons with a certain value of probability. We have tried building with no dropouts and another dropout size of 0.2. However, with these initial values, we faced issues with overfitting over the train dataset.

We have experimented with a double tanh activation function for the model. Double tanh function is simply an activation function multiplied by a factor of 2. However, the results were not satisfactory as the pair of test datasets performed poorly. As an option, we used the ReLu function which is used widely for time series analysis nowadays. In the end, the default tanh activation function performed better than the other two in the case of our datasets. To further assist with the overfitting problem, we used Lasso regularization (L1) and Ridge regularization (L2). The regularization techniques kept the weight values from growing too large which in turn alters the data in the neural layers causing loss of information and vanishing gradient problem. However, during the trial and error run with our model, we have found that our model with Ridge regularization (L2) had the best output. The Ridge regularization had a value of 0.1 for our LSTM model.

Other details of the model include compiling the model with ADAM optimization algorithm, and MSE and MAE metrics [13]. We iteratively ran our LSTM model up to around 80 epochs. An epoch is an arbitrary measurement of the number of times the whole sample is used to train the LSTM model. We aimed to find the optimal epoch number where the MSE and MAE values of both test1 and test2 datasets converged closer to the train set.

4   Experimental Results and Analysis

For evaluating the ARIMA-LSTM hybrid model, we compare its performance against some of the traditional statistical models, together with the ARIMA model, often used in portfolio optimization. The walk forward validation method is used generally to build any model involving the use of a neural network at every time step. However, using this procedure is time-consuming computationally. Instead of building a single model on every time step, we train our hybrid model on the first-time step from the train set and test it directly against the test1 and test2 datasets respectively, or in other words against the two different time steps.

Our criteria for evaluating and comparing the model was to find its MSE and MAE values. We calculated the MSE and MAE values for the other traditional statistical models and the ARIMA model as well. We ran our model on a different number of epochs numerically up to around 80 and determined the optimal epoch number where the MSE and MAE values converged to an acceptable value. From around 40 epochs, the MSE and MAE values started to converge as shown in Fig. 4. We made the use of an equation to derive the optimal epoch selection. The equation sums up the overfitting metric and the performance metric to give the outcome of the resultant epoch. The overfitting metric is a normalized value found by performing subtraction between the MSE difference of the train set and the mean of any of the test1 or test2 dataset's MSE difference and dividing it by the standard deviation of the train set's MSE difference. On the other hand, the performance metric is another normalized value found by calculating the difference between the sum of the train set's MSE and the mean of any of the test1 or test2 dataset's MSE sum and dividing it by the standard deviation of the train set's MSE sum as shown in Eq. 2. We then add up both the overfitting metric and the performance metric to round up and find the Criterion value which is the value of the optimal epoch. This is where MSE values between the train, test1 and test2 datasets converged at a significant tolerance level. The equation used to find the criterion for the optimal epoch number is shown below [13].

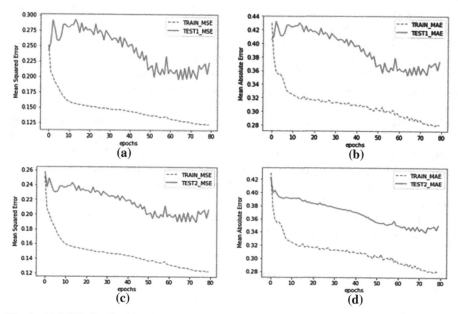

Fig. 4. (a) MSE distribution of train and test1 dataset, (b) MAE distribution of train and test1 dataset, (c) MSE distribution of train and test2 data, (d) MAE distribution of train and test2 dataset

$$Criterion = \frac{\Delta MSE - \mu(\Delta MSE)}{\sigma(\Delta MSE)} + \frac{\sum MSE - \mu\left(\sum MSE\right)}{\sigma\left(\sum MSE\right)} \qquad (2)$$

We performed 2 iterations to find out the optimal epoch number for our ARIMA-LSTM hybrid model. In the first iteration, we calculated both the performance metric and the overfitting metric and then deduced the overall Criterion value as per the equation, using the train set and test1 set only. In the second iteration, we calculated the same metric values but using the train set and test2 set only. For the first iteration, the Criterion value or the value of the optimal epoch is found to be approximately 65th epoch shown in Fig. 4 (a), (b). For the second iteration, the Criterion value is found to be approximately 55th epoch shown in Fig. 4 (c), (d). We then determine the mean optimal epoch, mean (Criterion$_{train\text{-}test1}$, Criterion$_{train\text{-}test2}$) to give the optimal value of the epoch to be approximately equal to the 60th epoch. Figure 4 (a), (b), (c) and (d), respectively represent the learning curve pattern of our ARIMA-LSTM hybrid model where we compared the forecasting accuracy of our model against the train set, test1 set, and test2 set, respectively in terms of measuring their MSE and MAE values at a certain epoch number.

Our custom model produced the MSE and MAE pairs of values of 0.205, 0.361, 0.197, and 0.350 from test1 and test2 datasets respectively. Then we tested against the same train set at around 60th epoch number. The small variations among the values support the claim that the values have been generalized sufficiently. To add more, we have performed a comparison study to justify the accuracy of our hybrid model. For the same dataset, we have calculated their MSE and MAE values. When implemented on traditional statistical models and the renowned ARIMA model Table 1 shows that the accuracy comparison of our model against ARIMA as well as other statistical models in stock market asset coefficient estimation for portfolio analysis and management.

The ARIMA-LSTM model's MSE and MAE values on test1 and test2 are similar though test2 values were slightly better. The nearest competitor from the traditional models was the Constant Correlation model but still had a significant difference in MSE and MAE values from both test1 and test2 datasets. The other two traditional models namely Historical Model and Single Index Model showed larger deviations in their respective MSE and MAE values compared to the hybrid ARIMA-LSTM model. Lastly, the ARIMA model alone performed worst against all the enlisted models. This proved that the ARIMA model did not handle nonlinearity in time series data and was reflected on the comparable large error values in MSE and MAE. Therefore, our model showed the best accuracy in forecasting correlation coefficients for a set of stock assets in a portfolio with the least error (Table 2).

Table 2. Accuracy comparison of ARIMA-LSTM hybrid model against standard statistical models

Models	MSE	MAE
ARIMA-LSTM-Test1	0.205	0.361
ARIMA-LSTM-Test2	0.197	0.350
Constant Correlation-Test1	0.225	0.422
Constant Correlation-Test2	0.265	0.395
Historical Model-Test1	0.426	0.528
Historical Model-Test2	0.355	0.484

(*continued*)

Table 2. (*continued*)

Models	MSE	MAE
Single Index Model-Test1	0.338	0.488
Single Index Model-Test2	0.305	0.450
ARIMA-Test1	0.456	0.571
ARIMA-Test2	0.453	0.568

5 Conclusion

Although our hybrid model established the fact that it outperformed all the traditional models including the ARIMA model alone, there were some limitations to our study. As different companies were enlisted for stock trading at different times, the range of data available was not equal for all companies. For this inconsistency, we could not find correlations between companies that had a huge difference in data. Therefore, we had to remove companies from the research that did not have data starting from our desired time frame. Furthermore, there was a good amount of data missing for some company datasets that we selected. We had to fill the missing values with previous values in the dataset. If the data was consistent, we could have optimized our model more. For future work, we plan to make a program capable of scraping daily stock index data in real time and store it in our online repository. In this way, we will be able to build an API containing data of stock prices and overtime construct a consistent dataset. In this paper, our goal was to find how the hybrid model performs compared to the other models. We did not build company portfolios here. For future research, we plan to cluster the correlation coefficients obtained from our model and group companies based on the correlation between them. For this, we will take several time ranges into consideration and separate the companies based on data availability. Furthermore, we only worked with DSE data in this paper but in the future, we are aiming to work with Chittagong Stock Exchange (CSE) data as well to develop a comprehensive cross stock exchange market asset portfolio to encompass any deviation in the correlation between same assets in different stock markets. If there is any deviation, we would like to investigate the effect of averaging the correlation in cross-market against an individual market to better understand portfolio optimization.

Acknowledgment. We want to acknowledge the contributions of Dr. Jia Uddin, Assistant Professor of Technology Studies Department, Endicott College, University of Woosong, South Korea for his valuable time during the preparation of the draft by guiding, commenting and reviewing.

References

1. Markowitz, H.: Portfolio selection. J. Finan. **55**(1), 77–91 (1952). https://doi.org/10.1111/j.1540-6261.1952.tb01525.x

2. Sarker, M.R.: Comparison among different models in determining optimal portfolio: evidence from Dhaka Stock Exchange in Bangladesh. J. Bus. Stud. **36**(3), 39–56 (2015). http://fbs-du. com/news_event/15053071733.pdf

3. Rout, A.K., Dash, P.K., Dash, R., Bisoi, R.: Forecasting financial time series using a low complexity recurrent neural network and evolutionary learning approach. J. King Saud Univ. Comput. Inf. Sci. **29**(4), 536–552 (2017). https://doi.org/10.1016/j.jksuci.2015.06.002

4. Haider, A.S.M.S., Kabir, M.R.: Forecasting Dhaka Stock Exchange (DSE) return an AutoRegressive Integrated Moving Average (ARIMA) approach. North South Bus. Rev. **3**(1), 36–54 (2009). http://www.researchgate.net/publication/298971617_FORECASTING_DHAKA_STOCK_EXCHANGE_DSE_RETURN_AN_AUTOREGRESSIVE_INTEGRATED_MOVING_AVERAGE_ARIMA_APPROACH

5. Chakraborty, P.: Forecasting market movement in Dhaka Stock Exchange: LSTM vs. ARIMA. Dspace Bracu (2018). http://dspace.bracu.ac.bd/xmlui/bitstream/handle/10361/12335/18175001.pdf. Accessed 4 July 2019

6. Alam, M.M., Alam, K.A., Uddin, M.G.S.: Market depth and risk return analysis of dhaka stock exchange: an empirical test of market efficiency. ASA Univ. Rev. **1**(1), 93–101 (2007). http://arxiv.org/ftp/arxiv/papers/1702/1702.01354.pdf

7. Hengjian, J.: Investigation into the effectiveness of long short-term memory networks for stock price prediction. arXiv (2016). http://www.arxiv.org/pdf/1603.07893.pdf. Accessed 5 July 2019

8. Salem, F., Kent, D.: Performance of the three slim variants of the long short-term memory (LSTM) layer. arXiv (2019). http://www.arxiv.org/pdf/1901.00525.pdf. Accessed 5 Aug 2019

9. Zhang, G.P., Patuwo, B.E., Michael, Y.H.: A simulation study of artificial neural networks for nonlinear time-series. Comput. Op. Res. **28**(4), 381–396 (2001). http://www.sciencedirect.com/science/article/abs/pii/S0305054899001239

10. Roondiwala, M., Patel, H., Varma, S.: Predicting stock prices using LSTM. Int. J. Sci. Res. (IJSR) **6**(4), 1754–1756 (2017). http://www.researchgate.net/publication/327967988_Predicting_Stock_Prices_Using_LSTM

11. Hossain, M.M., Imtiaz, I., Hasan, M.R.: Forecasting the general index of Dhaka Stock Exchange. Int. Res. J. Finan. Econ. **171**, 20–37 (2019). http://www.researchgate.net/publication/331563444_Forecasting_the_General_Index_of_Dhaka_Stock_Exchange

12. Zou, Z., Qu, Z.: Using LSTM in Stock prediction and Quantitative Trading. CS230 (2020). http://cs230.stanford.edu/projects_winter_2020/reports/32066186.pdf. Accessed 2 July 2020

13. Choi, H.K.: Stock Price Correlation Coefficient Prediction with ARIMA-LSTM Hybrid Model. arXiv (2018). http://www.arxiv.org/pdf/1808.01560.pdf. Accessed 10 July 2019

The Combination of Attention Sub-convnet and Triplet Loss for Pulmonary Nodule Detection in CT Images

Khai Dinh Lai[1]([⊠]), Thanh Minh Cao[1], Nhan Hoang Thai[2,3], and Thai Hoang Le[2,3]

[1] Faculty of Information Technology, Saigon University, Ho Chi Minh City 70000, Vietnam
laidinhkhai@sgu.edu.vn
[2] Faculty of Information Technology, University of Science, Ho Chi Minh City 70000, Vietnam
lhthai@fit.hcmus.edu.vn
[3] Vietnam National University, Ho Chi Minh City 70000, Vietnam

Abstract. This paper proposed models based on CNN to detect lung cancer tumors in CT images. More details, three models combined multiple Convolutional Attention Networks were generated: (1) ATT (Attention-Triplet-Triplet) used triple loss in training and testing; (2) ASS (Attention–Softmax–Softmax) used Softmax loss in training and testing; (3) AST (Attention–Softmax–Triplet), AST (Attention-Softmax–Triplet) used ASS as a pre-trained model in training and triplet loss in testing. Theoretical and empirical analyses were discussed to demonstrate the efficacy of the AST model in comparison with ATT and ASS. The feasibility of the AST model is also confirmed when compared to other methods on the same dataset (AST obtained has a specificity of 98.9%).

Keywords: Attention convolutional network · Triplet loss · Nodules detection

1 Introduction

Lung cancer is the leading cause of death from cancer for both men and women [1]. Computer-aided diagnosis (CAD) can help doctors interpret medical images, making for a more sensitive and accurate cancer diagnosis which is crucial for patients [2]. The tumor identification system consists of the main stages shown in Fig. 1 including: preprocessing the images, localizing candidates and classifying candidates as positive or negative.

In the scope of our research, we focused on the second stage is how to classify the nodule candidates as positive or negative. Deep Learning has progressed rapidly in recent years, especially in image processing problems. Many works applied deep learning in medical imaging processing, a large area of this are CT images. The two broad types of methods are used to classify the nodule candidates into nodules and non-nodules: (i) traditional feature-based classifiers and (ii) convolutional neural networks (CNNs). We would like to present a summary of some related research that used CNN for pulmonary nodule detection. The multiview convolutional network-based lung nodule

M. H. Miraz et al. (Eds.): iCETiC 2020, LNICST 332, pp. 227–238, 2020.
https://doi.org/10.1007/978-3-030-60036-5_16

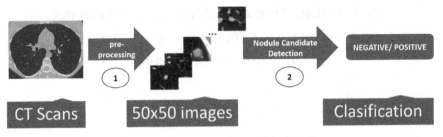

Fig. 1. Show the architecture of tumor identification system

detection system was proposed by Setio et al. [3]. This method obtained by combining three candidate detectors specifically designed for solid, subsolid, and large nodules. Their method reaches high detection sensitivities of 85.4% and 90.1% at 1 and 4 false positives per scan, respectively. Authors in [3] need high cost to have a dataset which classified subsolid nodules, solid nodules, large subsolid nodules. Besides, the training for each detection is quite time-consuming. On the other hand, the cost of mix-fusion detection and operating the system is high.

A lung nodule detection system based on deep CNNs was proposed by Ding et al. [4]. The application of a region-based CNN to detect nodules on slides of the image was involved their system. More over, a 3-D CNN to reduce FPs was employed in this system. It was evaluated using the Lung Nodule Analysis Challenge (LUNA16) dataset and achieved a high sensitivity (94.4%) with only four FPs/scans. Authors took advantage of VGG 16 and used the regional proposal network to attain high efficiency, but the expense of developing the area proposal network is not low.

In recent times, the author [5] studies tumor identification process based on 50×50 pixels images. This model has a precision of 89.3%, recall of 71.2% and specificity of 98.2%. However, this model [5] has not exploited the specific characteristics of medical images. To address the drawbacks we suggested the model was defined in Fig. 2 within the scope of this paper. This was called the Nodule Candidate Detection in general.

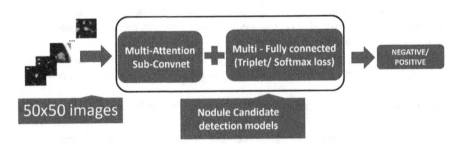

Fig. 2. The position of nodule candidate detection model in identification system

Based on the structure of the model in Fig. 2, three models were generated as in Figs. 4, 5 and 6 in Sect. 3. In more details, all of these models consisted of many SubConvnets combined using the attention mechanism which took into account the specific characteristics of data. We also considered selecting a softmax or triplet loss for the classification stage. On the same dataset, the models are compared with each other on performance, precision, recall and specificity, then best one will be selected. The final model chosen is compared with the one in [5]. The results show the feasibility of the proposed models. The order of our work is as follows: (1) we built a model with Attention convolutional layers with double Triplet functions for both training and validation. So we call it ATT model; (2) possibly the ATT, except the triplet loss was replaced with Softmax loss in the classification stage, meaning we've used the softmax loss both for training and validation. This is ASS model; (3) we trained a model with the name is AST that used ASS model as a pre-trained model and validated it with the triplet loss on the validating dataset; (4) we trained the model which was the best of all, on both training and validating subsets.

The following sections of the paper are organized as follows, Sect. 2 describes background of paper. Section 3 describes in detail how the data used and the architectures of the proposed models are created. In Sect. 4, we present how to evaluate the models as well as the results obtained through the models. We also discuss and pick the best model for our problem of concern.

2 Background

2.1 Attention Mechanism

In 2017, Jie Hu et al. [6] proposed an attention mechanism in order to improve the accuracy of image classification deep networks. The motivation is that inside a feature map with C channels, not all C are crucial to the final decision of a deep network. In which, there are some important ones that should be focused on. Therefore, it needs an attention (self-attention) mechanism so as to emphasize to those essential ones. Authors proposed a block (as ResNet block [7]), called Squeeze-and-Excitation block. This block can be built upon a transformation F_{tr} to map the input feature
$X \in R^{H' \times W' \times C'}$ to output feature $U \in R^{H \times W \times C}$. Then, the output feature is squeezed by applying a Global Average Pooling operation to form a vector $z_c = F_{sq}(U) \in R^{1 \times 1 \times C}$. Subsequently, the vector z_c is nonlinearly transformed by a Fully-connected layer, which maps z_c to $s = \sigma(F_{ex}(z_c, W)) \in R^{1 \times 1 \times C}$. In which, $W \in R^{C \times C}$ is the weight of the Fully-connected layer, and σ is the sigmoid function. The final sigmoid function constraints the value rage of the vector s within [0, 1]. Here, s can be seen as the attention gate. More specifically, each element s_i corresponds to a channel U_i. If the value of s_i is close to 1, the channel U_i is more important. After obtaining the attention gate s, the attentioned output feature can be computed as: $\hat{X} = s \times U$. By multiplying the output feature U with the vector s, less crucial channels will be suppressed, while other important ones will be remained.

2.2 Loss Function: Triplet Loss and Softmax Loss

a. Triplet Loss

The main purpose of Triplet loss [8] is to distinguish identities by minimizing the distance between an anchor and a positive, both of which have the same identity, and maximizing the distance between the anchor and a negative of a different identity. Thus, desirable criteria is

$$L = \sum_{i}^{N} \left[\left\| f(x_i^a) - f(x_i^p) \right\|_2^2 - \left\| f(x_i^a) - f(x_i^n) \right\|_2^2 + \alpha \right]_+ , \tag{1}$$

Where x_i^a is an anchor image, x_i^p is a positive image and x_i^n is a negative image. α is a margin that is made compulsory between a pair of positive and negative. The loss is computed with the formula (1), where N is number of candidates in training set.

b. Softmax Loss

Softmax loss takes a vector of K real numbers elements as its input, which normalizes it into a probability distribution made up of K probabilities equal to the exponential origin values [9]. That is, prior to applying softmax, some vector components could be random numbers; and might not sum to 1; but after applying softmax, each component will be in the interval (0, 1) and sum to 1. Softmax loss with a cross-entropy loss that has the form:

$$L_i = -\log\left(\frac{e^{f y_i}}{\sum_j e^{f_j}}\right) \tag{2}$$

Where f_j mean the j-th element of the vector of class scores f.

2.3 The Model in [5]

Swetha Subramanian [5] posted on github.com a network model used to detect tumors from CT images (see in Fig. 3), we considered this model as a reference model.

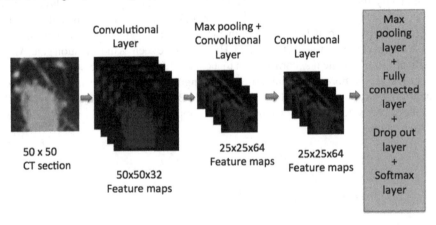

Fig. 3. An overview of the Swetha Subramanian's proposed CNN that used a 3 convolutional layers in the architecture.

3   Proposal Methods

3.1   Attention SubConvnet

As described above, the "attention" approach was used to improve the precision of the image classification in deep-networks. The channels were chosen in the feature maps which were useful. We developed a small convolution network called Attention subConvnet. Its architecture is mentioned in Table 1.

Table 1. An overview of the Attention subConvnet architecture included: layers, input size, output size and parameters

Layer	Input size	Output size	Parameter
Input	H × W × C'		
Convolution	H × W × C'	H × W × C	Kernel K × K
Average Pooling	H × W × C	1 × 1 × C	Kernel H × W
Fully connected	1 × 1 × C	1 × 1 × C	
Sigmoid	1 × 1 × C	1 × 1 × C	
Multiply	H × W × C, 1 × 1 × C	H × W × C	
Output	H × W × C	H × W × C	

3.2   ATT Model

In this scenario, we used three Attention SubConvnets. Concurrently, for both training and validating, we took Triplet loss. To eventually obtain the 512 neurons, we used double fully connected layers (see in Fig. 4).

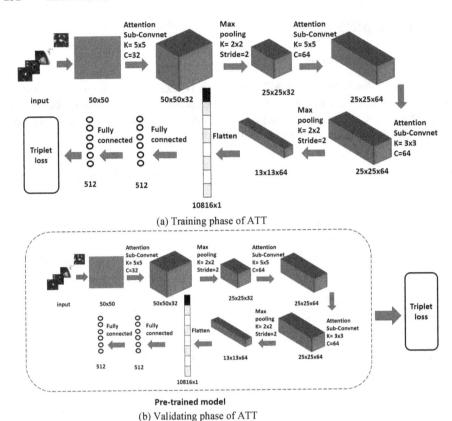

(a) Training phase of ATT

Pre-trained model

(b) Validating phase of ATT

Fig. 4. The architectures of ATT

3.3 ASS Mode

We used attention subConvnet for convolution layers, as well as ATT. The softmax loss is used for the training. Instead, we again used the softmax loss to validate and test (see in Fig. 5).

3.4 AST Model

ASS model was used as pre-trained model. we used the triplet loss to adjust the parameters of the model. Finally, the triplet loss was used once again for testing (see in Fig. 6).

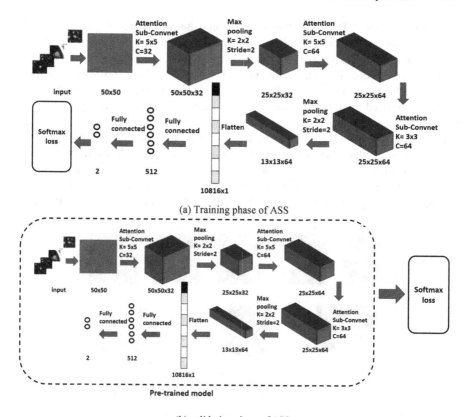

(a) Training phase of ASS

(b) validating phase of ASS

Fig. 5. The architectures of ASS

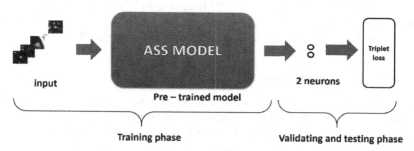

Fig. 6. The architectures of AST

4 Experimental Results

4.1 Datasets

Image data is taken from the Association for Research on Infectious Diseases and Lung Database [(LIDC/IDRI)] [10]. We use the reformatted version, LUNA16 [11]. This dataset includes 888 CT scans with notes describing the coordinates of the nodule region and whether or not the image is labeled as a nodule. Each CT scan has a size of 512 × 512 × n, where n is the number of scans, there are about 200 images in each CT scan.

There are 551065 annotations totaling. 1351 are labeled as a positive in all these notes, often known as a nodule, while the rest are labeled as negative, not a nodule. The author [5] cropped the images around the coordinates provided in the captions for the new images were created with a size of 50 × 50 pixels in gray scale to train, validate and test the CNN model. However, the data is out of balance because the number of images containing the tumor is too small for the entire data. The solution to this problem was that the author [5] made a rotation of 90° and 180° to create more images with the tumor (see in Fig. 7). The last dataset that the author [5] as well as we used in this study includes 8106 images with 50 × 50 pixel size divided into 3 directories, in particular:

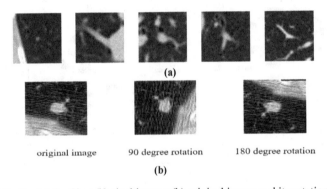

(a)

original image   90 degree rotation   180 degree rotation

(b)

Fig. 7. (a) the 50 × 50 pixel images (b) original image and its rotations

The training folder includes 5187 images, with 845 positive labels and 4342 negative labels. The validating folder includes 1297 images with 224 positive labels and 1073 negative labels. The testing folder contains 1622 images, with 282 positive labels and 1340 negative labels. Therefore, the ratio for the two classes is 20:80.

4.2 Environment for Experiments

Models were implemented in the same environment, in particular the same training, evaluation and testing datasets, were calculated on the same computer system. Initializing a set of weights based on a Guassian distribution with mean of zero, std (standard deviation) as 0.02, bias as zero. To optimize stochastic objective functions based on gradient, we chose an algorithm using adaptive estimates of lower-order moments in Adam [12]. This method requires little memory, is simple to implement, has computational efficiency, is invariant to diagonal rescaling of the gradients. We used Adam with learning rate is 1e−4 and weight decay is 1e−6. For each case, we performed about 50,000 steps corresponding to 50 epochs with a batch size of 8 images. We implemented early stopping technique for our convolutional neural networks. This helps us not only to avoid spending time training after the performance has converged but also help avoid overfitting.

4.3 Evaluation

We used the Holdout method to evaluate models. To get objective results, we splitted the data into three independent directories with ratio between training set, validating set and testing set, respectively 64%, 16% and 20%. We performed as follows on each model sequentially, with four different steps. Firstly, to use data from training to identify parameters and create models. Second, to use cross-validation method to determine the accuracy of the models. If the validation accuracy is poor, then the back-propagation method should change it. After the final model has been obtained, an accuracy test will be conducted with the testing data.

We determined the results were split into four groups in confusion matrix when conducting the test move. They were true positive (TP), false positive (FP), true negative (TN), and false negative (FN), respectively. The measurements we used for our comparative analyses were precision, recall, specificity, AUC, loss of validation [13].

4.4 Experimental Results

After implementing these models in the Sect. 3, the results were obtained visually in the diagrams and matching tables (see in Fig. 8 and Table 2, 3). Observing the results in the tables, it was clear that for all the comparison measures ATT has yielded worse results than ASS and AST. We have some clarity why at the Sect. 4.5. Experiments showed that AST, the proposed softmax network trained with a combination of multi-Attention subconvnets with double fully connected and validated by triplet loss gave us the best result. Therefore, we decided to re-train the AST model, but this time on both the training and validating datasets. We calculated the area under the ROC- in the final model, scoring as high as 0.9923 (see in Fig. 9). The FP value dramatically decreased whereas the TP and TN ratio deals better. We matched our results with the results of [5], as they are performed in the same datasets and comparison results are shown in Table 4.

4.5 Discussion

The aim of the training phase is to change the parameters to achieve the optimational function according to the training data and to be highly efficient when tested. For classification point, ATT used the triplet loss by minimizing the distance between it and the co-label samples and maximizing the distance between it and other samples. If the samples with the same label are identical in form, the evaluation of the model by a triplet loss is simple and highly efficient. Unfortunately, the peculiarities of the nodule dataset are very complex, the samples are not the same. This variation appears in images of both nodule and non-nodule. That is, while two samples containing the same label are positive, their form is quite different. In other words, the distance between co-labeled samples is not even short. Therefore, when conducting training by using a triplet loss may fall into the case of overfitting, the explanation is that the triplet attempts to change the parameters to match the training dataset the best. In fact, the nodule images are so complicated as mentioned above, so that the system can easily make mistakes during the test process. Additionally, the data is so complex that target value is hard to reach, which is why ATT has the highest loss in the models. Nevertheless, the use of the triplet

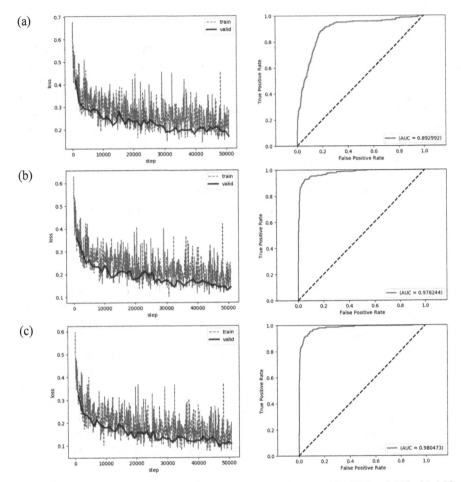

Fig. 8. These models were stopped at step 50000 (a) ATT, loss = 0.17; AUC ≈ 0.892, (b) ASS, loss = 0.15; AUC ≈ 0.978, (c) AST, loss = 0.12; AUC ≈ 0.980.

Table 2. The confusion matrix determined specific values for TP, FP, TN and FN.

Model	TP	FP	FN	TN
ATT	200	82	59	1281
ASS	259	23	49	1291
AST	261	21	56	1284

Table 3. Displays results for precision, recall, specificity of models

Model	Precision	Recall	Specificity
ATT	0.710	0.773	0.933
ASS	0.917	0.840	0.984
AST	0.924	0.823	0.986

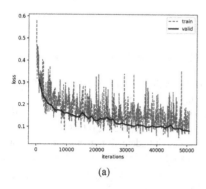
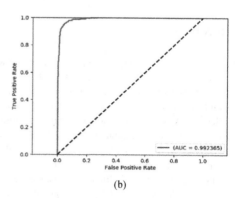

(a)　　　　　　　　　　　　　　　(b)

Fig. 9. The diagrams displays the results of the final chosen model with (a) loss $= 0.08$; (b) AUC ≈ 0.992

Table 4. The comparation between the method in [5] with our method

Model	Precision	Recall	Specificity
[5] method	0.893	0.712	0.982
Our method	0,950	0,864	0,989

was successful in the testing phase, as the two classes were now explicitly partitioned. Softmax is flexible in weight adjustment as long as the input is provided into classes without depending on the data characteristics. The ability to prevent overfitting by softmax loss is evaluated in the papers [14]. In specific applications, a suitable loss will be chosen in order to obtain the highest performance.

5 Conclusions

In this paper, we are interested in classifying whether a candidate is a nodule or not as a nodule in the problem of identifying nodules in the lung. We have proposed the general model include many attention convolutional layers. From the general model, we generated 3 models ATT, ASS, AST using Attention sub-convnet. The choice of softmax loss or triplet loss has demonstrated the effectiveness of each model through both experimental and theoretical assessments. Therefore, it is proposed to select the most effective AST model for the nodule detection problem on LUNA16. Our final result has a precision of 95%, recall of 86.4% and specificity of 98.9%. The comparation of our proposed model with the model in [5] on the same dataset showed the effectiveness and feasibility of our model.

Acknowledgements. This research is funded by Saigon University under grant number CS2018-58.

References

1. Lung Cancer Statistic Homepage. https://www.wcrf.org/dietandcancer/cancer-trends/lung-cancer-statistics. Accessed 15 Oct 2019
2. Ignatious, S., Joseph, R.: Computer aided lung cancer detection system. In: Global Conference on Communication Technologies (GCCT), Thuckalay, pp. 555–558 (2015)
3. Setio, A.A.A., et al.: Pulmonary nodule detection in CT images: false positive reduction using multi-view convolutional networks. IEEE Trans. Med. Imaging **35**(5), 1160–1169 (2016)
4. Ding, J., Li, A., Hu, Z., Wang, L.: Accurate pulmonary nodule detection in computed tomography images using deep convolutional neural networks. In: Descoteaux, M., Maier-Hein, L., Franz, A., Jannin, P., Collins, D.Louis, Duchesne, S. (eds.) MICCAI 2017. LNCS, vol. 10435, pp. 559–567. Springer, Cham (2017). https://doi.org/10.1007/978-3-319-66179-7_64
5. GitHub Swethasubramanian Page. https://git.io/Jf9Og. Accessed 15 Aug 2019
6. Hu, J., Shen, L., Albanie, S., Sun, G., Wu, E.: Squeeze-and-excitation networks. In: The IEEE Conference on Computer Vision and Pattern Recognition (CVPR), pp. 7132–7141 (2018)
7. He, K., Zhang, X., Ren, S., Sun, J.: Deep residual learning for image recognition. In: IEEE Conference on Computer Vision and Pattern Recognition (CVPR), Las Vegas, NV, pp. 770–778 (2016)
8. Schroff, F., Kalenichenko, D., Philbin, J.: FaceNet: a unified embedding for face recognition and clustering. In: IEEE Conference on Computer Vision and Pattern Recognition (CVPR), Boston, MA, pp. 815–823 (2015)
9. Elfadel, I.M., Wyatt Jr, J.L.: The softmax nonlinearity: derivation using statistical mechanics and useful properties as a multiterminal analog circuit element. In: Cowan, J., Tesauro, G., Giles, C.L. (eds.) Advances in Neural Information Processing Systems, vol. 6, pp. 882–887. Morgan Kaufmann, San Mateo (1994)
10. LIDC-IDRI Homepage. https://wiki.cancerimagingarchive.net/display/Public/LIDC-IDRI. Accessed 10 May 2019
11. LuNa Homepage. https://luna16.grand-challenge.org/. Accessed 20 Sep 2019
12. Kingma, D.P., Ba, L.J.: Adam: a method for stochastic optimization. In: International Conference on Learning Representations (ICLR), 13 p. (2015)
13. Branco, P., Torgo, L., Ribeiro, R.: A survey of predictive modeling on imbalanced domains. ACM Comput. Surv. **49**(2), 1–50 (2016). Article 31
14. Li, X., Wang, W.: Learning discriminative features via weights-biased softmax loss (2019). arXiv preprint arXiv:1904.11138. Accessed 12 Feb 2020

A Review on Steel Surface Image Features Extraction and Representation Methods

Mohammed W. Ashour[1]([✉]) [ID], Fatimah Khalid[2] [ID], Alfian Abdul Halin[2] [ID],
Samy H. Darwish[3] [ID], and M. M. Abdulrazzaq[4] [ID]

[1] Faculty of Information Technology, Majan University College, Muscat, Sultanate of Oman
eng.m.ashour@gmail.com
[2] Faculty of Computer Science and Information Technology, University Putra Malaysia,
Seri Kembangan, Malaysia
[3] Faculty of Engineering, Pharos University, Alexandria, Egypt
[4] International Islamic University Malaysia, Gombak, Malaysia

Abstract. This paper extensively explores and highlights the main issues, concepts and trends related to steel surface image features extraction and representation methods. These methods are widely used in the past years to identify the surface texture and surface detects in several industrial fields. The different analysis techniques used to extract features from steel surface images for the purpose of classification are also explored. Furthermore, this study aims to identify the research gap in steel surface inspection domain by reviewing the previous related works of visual inspection methods and exploring their main outcomes, limitations and how they are solved in their fields.

Keywords: Image analysis · Feature extraction · Feature representation · Steel surface classification

1 Introduction

Machining processes is a manufacturing term that deals with shaping a previously formed raw material (workpiece) by removing a tiny layer of its surface in order to improve a surface finish, surface tolerance or to form a product (Liang and Shih 2015). In manufacturing of specific steel materials, the various machining processes involved yield surfaces with varying textures. Each of these surfaces require inspection that is traditionally performed by human operators. The inspection serves as quality assurance to ascertain manufacturing parameters such as cutting apparatus kinematics and geometries are met, as well for identifying machining irregularities. From the stand-point of reverse-engineering, the ability to perform such inspections using a semi or fully automated computer system would be highly beneficial as drawbacks relating to human inconsistencies involving fatigue, subjectivity and judgement oversights, can be avoided. In recent times, computer vision systems with in-built artificial intelligence have been explored for automatic inspection. Each of these systems share two components in common: (1) a vision-based feature (surface properties) extraction component, and (2) a

© ICST Institute for Computer Sciences, Social Informatics and Telecommunications Engineering 2020
Published by Springer Nature Switzerland AG 2020. All Rights Reserved
M. H. Miraz et al. (Eds.): iCETiC 2020, LNICST 332, pp. 239–250, 2020.
https://doi.org/10.1007/978-3-030-60036-5_17

decision making engine that classifies inspected materials into its respective class/type. Brief descriptions about each component are given in the following:

(1) **Feature extraction:** This step employs low-level image processing techniques to extract the discriminative and characteristics features of an input image. Such features can be (i) global: obtained from the entire image, or (ii) local: extracted form specific regions within the image. Xu et al. (2015) for example extracted global features from the DST-KLPP's (Discrete Shearlet Transform with Kernel Locality Preserving Projection) Mean and Variance data. In other cases, researches extract both features types, such as by Chu et al. (2017), Song and Yan (2013) and Song et al. (2014). They obtained local statistical shape distance and linear binary patterns LBP were extracted. Other approaches might only consider global features, such as Xiao et al. (2017) where they used the gray-level co-occurrence matrix, Unified LBP, histogram of oriented gradients, gray-level histogram, and the Gabor filter. Chondronasios et al. (2016) made use of Gradient-only co-occurrence matrices (GOCM) as well as the four derived GOCM properties namely Homogeneity, Correlation, Contrast and Energy. Vimalraj et al. (2014) used the Energy sub-bands frp, the Discrete Wavelet Transform (DST) to extract the single frequency domain feature.

(2) **Decision making engine:** Most of the works rely on supervised machine learning (SML) algorithms. Generally, SML necessitates the availability of a labeled image dataset in order to optimally train (fit) and test/validate the algorithm. Specifically, each SML algorithm employed are trained on the specific features being extracted. Popular algorithms in steel strip classification include (but are not limited to) multi-class Support Vector Machine (SVM) (Chu et al. 2017; Song et al. 2014; Song and Yan 2013), Bayes classifier (Song et al. 2014; Song and Yan 2013) and artificial neural networks (Zhou et al. 2017; Chondronasios et al. 2016; Song et al. 2014)

As illustrated from the given examples, various feature extraction methods are employed as well as decision making (classification engines) algorithms. This paper attempts to track the current innovations of vision systems in different steel surfaces processing through the review of published literature in recent years.

2 Surface Texture

According to Hudson (2013), surface texture can be defined as any system with an abrupt change of system properties, which includes density, crystal structure and orientation, and chemical composition. Deriving from this definition, one can say that surface texture is a profile explaining waviness or roughness. An expansion of that description can also add the concept pf lay, hence lay, surface roughness, and waviness (DeGarmo et al. 1997). Texture in particular, exhibits and comprises local surface deviations from the perfectly flat plane. As an illustration, surface texture can best be visualized in Fig. 1.

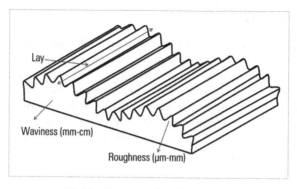

Fig. 1. Structure of surface texture

3 Digital Image Processing and Analysis

In most of the existing systems, the image processing and step involve taking in an input image, applying some form of processing, and producing a desired output. This is a crucial step as it is the first phase in identifying relevant patterns relevant to the inspection task at hand. This is akin to produce a numeric representation to facilitate further processing of the contained information for the specific vision systems (Gonzalez et al. 2007). Commonly, image processing and analysis can be divided into three types, namely: low-level, intermediate-level (or mid-level) and high-level. It is arguable whether these specific divisions are bounded, but they do act as intuitive separating frameworks when developing computer vision-based systems. Specifically, low-level processing requires virtually no form of computational intelligence. Ping Tian (2013) gives a good low-level processing example in image acquisition. Here, a sensor and digitizer works in tandem to produce a digital image from an analogue source. Specifically, a physical sensor sensitive to a specific band of the electromagnetic spectrum senses responses from the analogue source, producing output in the form of an electrical signal. For the most part, the most popular sensor are solid-state arrays such as the charge coupled device (CCD) complementary metal oxide semiconductor (CMOS) sensors. The second element in the acquisition process is the digitizer (also referred to as a frame grabber or a video capture card). This digitizer normally interfaces a camera to a host workstation (or personal computer) to capture the image data to be converted into digital form. When a digital representation is obtained, further preprocessing or processing of the image can be more easily performed. Preprocessing for example, is when necessary enhancements are made to the image in order to prepare it for the main task of the vision system. The gist of this step is to elicit any salient details or to highlight aspects that were originally hidden in the image. Common preprocessing techniques include image registration, edge detection, atmospheric correction and topographic correction and radiometric calibration (Lu and Weng 2007). In the field of automated manufacturing materials inspection, preprocessing typically involves contrast enhancement, noise elimination/removal and region of interest (ROI) isolation.

3.1 Feature Extraction

Features extraction is one example of intermediate-level processing. Several types of visual features are commonly extracted in image analysis such as texture, shape and color. Note however that this list is non-exhaustive where other types of features can be extracted or even derived based on the task at hand. For most image recognition/classification systems, these features serve as input data; training and validation data in supervised learning algorithms. As previously mentioned, features can broadly be categorized into global and local. The upcoming subsections will present more details about related work on features extraction.

3.2 Texture Feature

Texture features cannot be measured in isolation, but instead requires values from neighboring pixels (unlike color). This is because image texture characteristics deals with changes in directions with scale. One however needs to be careful when calculating texture features as some information can be lost, such as during image shifts, scaling or rotation (Milanese and Cherbuliez 1999). Among the most popular texture features are wavelets by Ortega et al. (1998), Co-occurrence matrix by Haralick et al. (1973) and multidirectional Gabor Filter features by Turner (1986). A more recent feature that is also commonly used is the Discrete Shearlet Transform (DST) by Guo and Labate, which is multiscale and multidirectional.

Texture features are categorized into spatial and spectral/frequency domains. Spatial domain features are obtained though pixel statistics or finding local structures in the image itself. The latter domain on the other hand operates in the frequency domain. Both spatial and frequency domain features have advantages and limitations, where readers can be directed to the work Ping Tian (2013) of for more detail. In this paper, a summarized version of Ping Tian's (2013) work is provided in Table 1.

Table 1. Spatial versus frequency domain

Texture method	Advantages	Limitations
Spatial domain	- Easier to comprehend - Minimal information loss - Extractable from any shape	- Noise and distortions sensitive - Scale and rotation invariant
Frequency domain	- Robust - Requires less computation - Multiscale and multidirectional	- Lack semantic meaning -Requires sufficiently-sized square regions

3.3 Shape Feature

The main purpose of shape features is to represent the whole geometrical information of image objects, which are independent on the variation of object orientation, scale or location. The description of those features depends on dividing input images into objects or regions. Mainly, the shape can be segmented into two types; region dependent, which uses the overall shape region and boundary dependent, which uses the object boundary information only (Zhang and Lu 2004). Local Binary Pattern (LBP), and Speed Up Robust Features (SURF) descriptors are significant types of shape features due to their ability to work on localized cells, where this in turn permits upholding invariance to both photometric and geometric transformations, except the object orientation. Those variations appear in large spatial regions only. LBPs are feature descriptors that are widely utilized in both image processing and computer vision fields. It has many merits, such as insensitivity to light, invariance in rotation and simplicity in calculation (Ojala et al. 2002). SURF utilizes the scale and rotation invariance characteristic to facilitate objects identification, regardless of rotating or resizing the representation around a certain axis in the image (Bay et al. 2006).

3.4 Color Features

Color features extraction can be done from various color spaces, such as Red Green and Blue (RGB), Hue Saturation and Lightness (HSL) and Hue Saturation and Value (HSV) (Sural et al. 2002). Various researches have been conducted to find the most optimal color space that take into account the impact of certain factors, such as light conditions and viewing positions (Milanese and Cherbuliez 1999). Color spaces simplify the recognition of image colors under changeable conditions. However, some spaces might result in a loss of main color information. In surface images, the color involvement is restricted since the majority of surface images are in grayscale.

3.5 Global and Local Features

Generally, local features of images which are block-based representation can be extracted by dividing the image into small blocks of pixels (Ping Tian 2013). Those features are essential, especially when coping with partial visibility. In comparison with global features, local features offer more details concerning images (Datta et al. 2005). Thus, local features result in enhanced classification results in several domains (Paredes et al. 2001). Global features of images offer description that represent the entire image content. The main benefit of using "global features" is the rapidity of extracting and using them to find a match among images (Glatard et al. 2004). However, those features cannot offer information concerning image details. So features representation of an image can be a combination of booth global and local representation.

3.6 Features Reduction

Choosing the most suitable features (i.e. feature engineering) is extremely crucial in the implementation of a highly accurate image classification systems (Lu and Weng 2007). Feature reduction is the second main step of the intermediate-level processing coming after features extraction. It is typically the process of removing the redundant and irrelevant noisy data from the large features vector that representing a particular image, and thus returning a subset of the extracted features' set rather than creating new features. Feature reduction techniques are often used in vision systems for multiple reasons such as simplifying the model and reducing its complexity, shortening training time, enhancing generalization by reducing overfitting which may cursedly affect the final classification accuracy (Guyon and Elisseeff 2003; Bay et al. 2008; Vinay et al. 2015). While this is true from an engineering point of view, recent interdisciplinary research has emphasized how feature reduction achieves intelligent generalization, within short times, by allocating the amount of information to the computational capacity available for solving classification tasks (Hamid 2015).

Recently, numerous researchers attempted to find optimal solutions to reduce the high dimensional image feature vector. It was observed that reducing those high dimensional vectors effectively requires applying several "dimensionality reduction" techniques over an image vector (Guyon and Elisseeff 2003). Examples of some researches that benefited from the use of dimensionality reduction approaches are; Vinay et al. (2015), proved that the use of PCA for dimensionality reduction of features extracted by Gabor Wavelet transform is superior to other techniques such as K-PCA. They used the reduction techniques of Linear Discriminant Analysis (LDA) and Kernel-Linear Discriminant Analysis KLDA to reduce extracted features by Gabor filter for in face recognition system. These features reduction approaches have the advantage of capturing linear holistic features but ignore the localized features. Xu et al. (2015) used PCA to reduce features extracted by Shearlet transform of different steel surface images. They proved that the use of this technique allowed to achieve higher accuracy in defect classifications.

4 Summary of Related Work

A wide variety of experiments on feature extraction methods have identified single or several types of features in order to classify different surfaces. Table 2 reviews the previous studies that are specifically related to steel surface problems.

Table 2. Summary of features extraction and classification methods for steel surface images

Source	Features extraction	Classifier	Dataset type	Achieved results
Ashour et al. (2019)	Combined DST & GLCM features	SVM	Hot-rolled steel strips	Accuracy 96.0%
Abu-Mahfouz et al. (2017)	Continuous Wavelet Transform (CWT)	SVM	Machined steel surface textures	Accuracy 81.2%
Chu et al. (2017)	Shape distance & LBP operators	Twin multi-class SVM	NEU hot-rolled steel dataset	Accuracy 98.0%
Zhou et al. (2017)	–	CNN	NEU hot-rolled steel dataset	Accuracy 99.0%
Xiao et al. (2017)	ULBP, GLCM, Gabor Filter	SVM along with Bayes	NEU hot-rolled steel dataset	Accuracy 97.4%

(*continued*)

Table 2. (*continued*)

Source	Features extraction	Classifier	Dataset type	Achieved results
Chondronasios et al. (2016)	• Gradient-only • Co-occurrence matrices (GOCM) • GLCM	2-Layers feed-forward Artificial Neural Network (ANN)	Aluminium alloy surface defect (145) gray-scale images	Accuracy rates for each method are: • GLCM 79.5% • GOCM 98.6%
Simunovic et al. (2016)	Statistical features	Neuro-fuzzy inference system (ANFIS)	Machined steel surface textures	Accuracy 93.0%
Chondronasios et al. (2016)	Gradient-only co-occurrence matrices (GOCM)	ANN	Aluminium alloy surface defects (blisters and scratches)	Accuracy 98.6%
Xu et al. (2015)	• Discrete shearlet transform with Kernel locality preserving projection (DST-KLPP) • Curvelet-KLPP • Contourlet-KLPP • Wavelet • GLCM	SVM with (RBF) kernel	Three datasets: • Casting slabs 496 samples • Hot-rolled steel 1273 samples • Aluminium sheets 480 samples	• Achieved accuracy for three datasets by DST-KLPP: • Casting Slabs (94.3%) • Hot-rolled steel (95.7%) • Aluminium sheets (92.5%)
Samtaş et al. (2014)	Binary image representation	ANN	Machined steel surface textures	Accuracy 99.9%
Singhka et al. (2014)	• Geometric Features: 1. Pixel 2. Euler-number 3. Equivalent Diameter 4. Eccentricity 5. Perimeter • Gray - Scale Features: 1. Mean 2. Variance 3. Skewness 4. Kurtosis • Textural features: 1. Contrast 2. Entropy	3-Layers feed-forward Artificial Neural Network (ANN)	• Steel strips surface images	• Accuracy rates per defect type are: • Water Droplets: • Accuracy = 89.8% • Blisters: • Accuracy = 90.7% • Scratches: • Accuracy = 92.6% • Total Accuracy = 91.0%
Song et al. (2014)	Scattering Convolution Network (SCN)	NNC, and SVM	NEU hot-rolled steel dataset	Accuracy 98.6%
Vimalraj et al. (2014)	Discrete Shearlet Transform (DST)	Multi-level thresholding	Alloy steel surface images	Accuracy 99.6%

The outcomes of the previous studies related to steel surface images listed in Table 2 demonstrate that a single feature method in one domain only i.e. spatial or frequency can work well with small datasets and with few types of defects. Moreover, ignoring the significance of the directional features extracted in the frequency domain as presented in the studies introduced by Simunovic et al. (2016) and Singhka et al. (2014) can produce lower accuracy rates in classification. Another observation was also reported that those researchers who used GLCMs as a feature extraction method i.e. Xiao et al. (2017) could achieve higher accuracy by making use of multilevel classifier approach. Additionally, the work produced by Chondronasios et al. (2016) which used GLCM descriptors along with ANN classifier could not achieve high accuracy rates since the features were less descriptive and insufficient for discrimination. Finally, the remaining researches listed in Table 2 that used an integrated set of both spatial domain and frequency domain features have achieved better accuracy than the other aforesaid studies.

4.1 Global and Local Features Representation

In the literature, several researchers designed their extracted features in different forms i.e. global, local or in both ways. Table 3 summarizes researches from different domains and show the extracted types of features. Alqoud et al. (2016), utilized the advantage of combining Global and local features also in breast tissues classification. Sub-band image features were extracted by Gabor Filters in multi-scales and two orientations (45°, 90°), then the parameters (means, standard deviation, and skewness) were calculated and combined with other local features generated by the Local Binary Patterns. This method also showed a noticeable accuracy rate achievement of 98.78%. Ignat et al. (2015) extracted frequency domain multi-scale features in multi-directions using Discrete Wavelet Transform (DST) and Gabor Filter (GF) methods, then the extracted features have been integrated for the purpose of discrimination between texture images of Brodatz album. Gabor filter banks were also used by Khan et al. (2015) for breast cancer detection where features from different scales and orientation were utilized. The features were extracted globally then locally based on SMGR (Statistical Magnitude Gabor Response) and WSMGR (Widows-based SMGR) respectively. The maximum accuracy rate achieved by this method was very promising (100%) which indicates the significance of using Gabor filters in different orientations and scale. In addition, Tsai et al. (2009) utilized global, local and region-based feature combinations in order to represent their images. They concluded that global and local features showed best performance when used together. Furthermore, Mikolajczyk et al. (2005) investigated the use of various feature detectors in parallel and proposed the effect of using more than one type of features on enhancing the image recognition process. On the other hand, Li et al. (2013) investigated in the use of a combination of multiple global and local features and proposed a novel system to interactively and precisely retrieve item images.

Hence, it can be observed from the aforementioned methods that the combination of multi-types and multi-level features may offer higher discriminative properties for images, while the use of only one type of features may not be always sufficient to describe an image content effectively. This can be due to the reasons; (i) Lack of enough information with the use of global features only. (ii) Lack of information about the whole

Table 3. Global and Local Features

Source	Global features adopted	Local features adopted
Chu et al. (2017)	Histogram, statistical features, and shape distance	LBP operators
Alqoud et al. (2016)	Gabor filters	Local Binary Patterns (LBP)
Ignat et al. (2015)	Discrete Wavelet Transform (DWT) in 3 directions (H, V, D) Gabor Filter (GF) in 6 directions, and 3 scales	Gini index
Khan et al. (2015)	Statistical Magnitude Gabor Response (SMGR)	Windows Statistical Magnitude Gabor Response (WSMGR)
Tian et al. (2012)	HSV color histogram	HSV solor moments, Gabor wavelets texture and sobel shape
Tsai et al. (2009)	HSV color moments, four levels of Daubechies-4 wavelet decomposition	HSV color moment, four levels of Daubechies-4 wavelet decomposition
Lisin et al. (2005)	LBP and shape index	SIFT

image structure with the use of local features only. (iii) The precise description of image properties may depend on extracting several future types in different ways.

4.2 Defect Detection Using Deep Learning

The advent of Deep Learning (DL) has seemingly driven computer vision to a whole new level with solutions to many complex image and object recognition problems, which includes steel surface defect detections (Luo et al. 2020). DL has gained much popularity and attention due to its supremacy in terms of accuracy when trained with huge amounts of data (Czimmermann et al. 2020). Furthermore, DL has also eliminated (or greatly lessened) the need for feature engineering where most works now focus on learning the necessary features. Wang et al. (2018), highlighted the DL capabilities in smart manufacturing showing how DL changed the future trends in industry. A number of relevant studies have also been published recently that highlighted the role of DL in steel manufacturing field such as Psuj 2018, Zhao et al. 2019, Yang et al. 2020, Tabernik et al. 2019. The recent study by Yang et al. (2020) proposed a DCNN-based system for detecting and classifying defects occurred during laser welding in battery manufacturing. The study has also presented a novel model named Visual Geometry Group (VGG) in order to improve the defects classification efficiency. With 8,000 tested samples and an accuracy up to 99.87%, they demonstrated that the pre-trained VGG architecture had a lower false positive rate and took lesser time to train and make predictions. This makes such a system highly appropriate for real-world quality inspection systems. Succeeding the evolution of the industrial applications, there is always an explicit need for advanced machine learning algorithms to solve complex challenges to control the products quality.

5 Conclusion

Image processing and computer vision technology has tremendous benefits in automating tasks related to the steel manufacturing processes. According to the World Steel Association (WSA), steel can be divided into several essential market sectors such as; buildings and infrastructure, mechanical equipment, automotive, metal products, domestic appliances and Electrical equipment. Automatic visual inspection systems of machined steel surfaces during manufacturing can help ensure high production quality while potentially reducing machining costs, which is a crucial concern for modern-day production. Color, texture and shape are the main used features by those systems in describing contents of steel surface images. These features can be represented either globally, locally or with both, where several techniques are used in extracting them. The overall review carried out highlighted the importance of extracting features in both spatial and frequency domains for a better surface recognition. Finally, the produced automated visual inspection systems have reached a good level of maturity for steel surfaces classification and defects detection problem, especially with the use of deep learning approaches which seem to be very promising in the near future. However, all these approaches are required to be properly adaptable for the particular industrial application.

References

Abu-Mahfouz, I., El Ariss, O., Esfakur Rahman, A.H.M., Banerjee, A.: Surface roughness prediction as a classification problem using support vector machine. Int. J. Adv. Manuf. Technol. **92**, 803–815 (2017). https://doi.org/10.1007/s00170-017-0165-9

Ashour, M.W., Khalid, F., Halin, A.A., Abdullah, L.N., Darwish, S.H.: Surface defects classification of hot-rolled steel strips using multi-directional shearlet features. Arab. J. Sci. Eng. **44**(4), 2925–2932 (2019)

AlQoud, A., Jaffar, M.A.: Hybrid gabor based local binary patterns texture features for classification of breast mammograms. Int. J. Comput. Sci. Netw. Secur. (IJCSNS) **16**(4), 16 (2016)

Bay, H., Ess, A., Tuytelaars, T., Van Gool, L.: Speeded-up robust features (SURF). Comput. Vis. Image Underst. **110**(3), 346–359 (2008)

Bay, H., Tuytelaars, T., Van Gool, L.: SURF: speeded up robust features. In: Leonardis, A., Bischof, H., Pinz, A. (eds.) ECCV 2006. LNCS, vol. 3951, pp. 404–417. Springer, Heidelberg (2006). https://doi.org/10.1007/11744023_32

Chondronasios, A., Popov, I., Jordanov, I.: Feature selection for surface defect classification of extruded aluminum profiles. Int. J. Adv. Manuf. Technol. **83**(1-4), 33–41 (2016). https://doi.org/10.1007/s00170-015-7514-3

Chu, M., Gong, R., Gao, S., Zhao, J.: Steel surface defects recognition based on multi-type statistical features and enhanced twin support vector machine. Chemometr. Intell. Lab. Syst. **171**, 140–150 (2017)

Czimmermann, T., et al.: Visual-based defect detection and classification approaches for industrial applications—a survey. Sensors **20**(5), 1459 (2020)

Datta, R., Li, J., Wang, J. Z.: Content-based image retrieval: approaches and trends of the new age. In: Proceedings of the 7th ACM SIGMM International Workshop on Multimedia Information Retrieval, pp. 253–262. ACM (2005)

DeGarmo, E.P., Black, J.T., Kohser, R.A., Klamecki, B.E.: Materials and Process in Manufacturing. Prentice Hall, Upper Saddle River (1997)

Glatard, T., Montagnat, J., Magnin, I.E.: Texture based medical image indexing and retrieval: application to cardiac imaging. In: Proceedings of the 6th ACM SIGMM International Workshop on Multimedia Information Retrieval, pp. 135–142. ACM (2004)

Gonzalez, R.C., Woods, R.E., Czitrom, D.J., Armitage, S.: Digital Image Processing, 3rd edn. Prentice Hall, United States (2007)

Guo, K., Labate, D.: Optimally sparse multidimensional representation using shearlets. SIAM J. Math. Anal. **39**(1), 298–318 (2007)

Guyon, I., Elisseeff, A.: An introduction to variable and feature selection. J. Mach. Learn. Res. **3**, 1157–1182 (2003)

Haralick, R.M., Shanmugam, K.: Textural features for image classification. IEEE Trans. Syst. Man Cybern. **6**, 610–621 (1973)

Hamid, O.H.: A model-based Markovian context-dependent reinforcement learning approach for neurobiologically plausible transfer of experience. Int. J. Hybrid Intell. Syst. **12**(2), 119–129 (2015)

Hudson, J.: Surface Science: An Introduction. Elsevier, Amsterdam (2013)

Ignat, A.: Combining features for texture analysis. In: Azzopardi, G., Petkov, N. (eds.) CAIP 2015. LNCS, vol. 9257, pp. 220–229. Springer, Cham (2015). https://doi.org/10.1007/978-3-319-23117-4_19

Khan, S., Hussain, M., Aboalsamh, H., Bebis, G.: A comparison of different Gabor feature extraction approaches for mass classification in mammography. Multimed. Tools Appl. **76**(1), 33–57 (2015). https://doi.org/10.1007/s11042-015-3017-3

Liang, S., Shih, A.J.: Analysis of Machining and Machine Tools. Springer, Boston (2015)

Li, H., Wang, X., Tang, J., Zhao, C.: Combining global and local matching of multiple features for precise item image retrieval. Multimed. Syst. **19**(1), 37–49 (2013)

Lisin, D.A., Mattar, M.A., Blaschko, M.B., Learned-Miller, E.G., Benfield, M.C.: Combining local and global image features for object class recognition. In: IEEE Computer Society Conference on Computer Vision and Pattern Recognition-Workshops. CVPR Workshops 2005, pp. 47–47. IEEE (2005)

Lu, D., Weng, Q.: A survey of image classification methods and techniques for improving classification performance. Int. J. Remote Sens. **28**(5), 823–870 (2007)

Luo, Q., Fang, X., Liu, L., Yang, C., Sun, Y.: Automated visual defect detection for flat steel surface: a survey. IEEE Trans. Instrum. Meas. **69**(3), 626–644 (2020)

Mikolajczyk, K., et al.: A comparison of affine region detectors. Int. J. Comput. Vis. **65**(1–2), 43–72 (2005)

Milanese, R., Cherbuliez, M.: A rotation, translation, and scale-invariant approach to content-based image retrieval. J. Vis. Commun. Image Represent. **10**(2), 186–196 (1999)

Ojala, T., Pietikainen, M., Maenpaa, T.: Multiresolution gray-scale and rotation invariant texture classification with local binary patterns. IEEE Trans. Pattern Anal. Mach. Intell. **24**(7), 971–987 (2002)

Ortega, M., Rui, Y., Chakrabarti, K., Porkaew, K., Mehrotra, S., Huang, T.S.: Supporting ranked Boolean similarity queries in MARS. IEEE Trans. Knowl. Data Eng. **10**(6), 905–925 (1998)

Paredes, R., Pérez, J.C., Juan, A., Vidal, E.: Local representations and a direct voting scheme for face recognition. In: Proceeding of Workshop on Pattern Recognition in Information Systems, Setúbal, Portugal, pp. 71–79 (2001)

Ping Tian, D.: A review on image feature extraction and representation techniques. Int. J. Multimed. Ubiquit. Eng. **8**(4), 385–396 (2013)

Psuj, G.: Multi-sensor data integration using deep learning for characterization of defects in steel elements. Sensors **18**, 292 (2018)

Samtaş, G.: Measurement and evaluation of surface roughness based on optic system using image processing and artificial neural network. Int. J. Adv. Manuf. Technol. **73**, 353–364 (2014). https://doi.org/10.1007/s00170-014-5828-1

Simunovic, G., Svalina, I., Simunovic, K., Saric, T., Havrlisan, S., Vukelic, D.: Surface roughness assessing based on digital image features. Adv. Prod. Eng. Manage. **11**(2), 93 (2016)

Singhka, D.K.H., Neogi, N., Mohanta, D.: Surface defect classification of steel strip based on machine vision. In: 2014 International Conference on Computer and Communications Technologies (ICCCT), pp. 1–5. IEEE (2014)

Song, K., Yan, Y.: A noise robust method based on completed local binary patterns for hot-rolled steel strip surface defects. Appl. Surf. Sci. **285**, 858–864 (2013)

Song, K., Hu, S., Yan, Y.: Automatic recognition of surface defects on hot-rolled steel strip using scattering convolution network. J. Comput. Inf. Syst. **10**(7), 3049–3055 (2014)

Sural, S., Qian, G., Pramanik, S.: Segmentation and histogram generation using the HSV color space for image retrieval. In: Proceedings 2002 International Conference on Image Processing, vol. 2, pp. II-589–II-592). IEEE (2002)

Tabernik, D., Šela, S., Skvarč, J., Skočaj, D.: Segmentation-based deep-learning approach for surface-defect detection. J. Intell. Manuf. **31**(3), 759–776 (2019). https://doi.org/10.1007/s10 845-019-01476-x

Tian, D., Zhao, X., Shi, Z.: Support vector machine with mixture of kernels for image classification. In: Shi, Z., Leake, D., Vadera, S. (eds.) IIP 2012. IAICT, vol. 385, pp. 68–76. Springer, Heidelberg (2012). https://doi.org/10.1007/978-3-642-32891-6_11

Tsai, C.F., Lin, W.C.: A comparative study of global and local feature representations in image database categorization. In: 2009 Fifth International Joint Conference on INC, IMS and IDC, NCM 2009, pp. 1563–1566. IEEE (2009)

Turner, M.R.: Texture discrimination by Gabor functions. Biol. Cybern. **55**(2), 71–82 (1986)

Vimalraj, N., Giriraj, B.: Classification and segmentation of alloy steel surface based on discrete shearlet transform and thresholding approaches. Asian J. Sci. Res. **7**, 66–75 (2014)

Vinay, A., Shekhar, V.S., Murthy, K.B., Natarajan, S.: Face recognition using Gabor wavelet features with PCA and KPCA - a comparative study. Procedia Comput. Sci. **57**, 650–659 (2015)

Wang, J., Ma, Y., Zhang, L., Gao, R.X., Wu, D.: Deep learning for smart manufacturing: methods and applications. J. Manuf. Syst. **48**, 144–156 (2018)

Xiao, M., Jiang, M., Li, G., Xie, L., Yi, L.: An evolutionary classifier for steel surface defects with small sample set. EURASIP J. Image Video Process. **2017**(1), 1–13 (2017). https://doi.org/10.1186/s13640-017-0197-y

Xu, K., Liu, S., Ai, Y.: Application of Shearlet transform to classification of surface defects for metals. Image Vis. Comput. **35**, 23–30 (2015)

Yang, Y., et al.: A high-performance deep learning algorithm for the automated optical inspection of laser welding. Appl. Sci. **10**, 933 (2020)

Zhang, D., Lu, G.: Review of shape representation and description techniques. Pattern Recogn. **37**(1), 1–19 (2004)

Zhou, S., Chen, Y., Zhang, D., Xie, J., Zhou, Y.: Classification of surface defects on steel sheet using convolutional neural networks. Materiali in tehnologije **51**(1), 123–131 (2017)

Zhao, Z.Q., Zheng, P., Xu, S.T., Wu, X.: Object detection with deep learning: a review. IEEE Trans. Neural Netw. Learn. Syst. **30**, 3212–3232 (2019)

Parameterization of an Agent-Based Model of Spatial Distribution of Species

João Bioco[1,2,4(✉)] ⓘ, Paulo Fazendeiro[1,2,4] ⓘ, Fernando Cánovas[3] ⓘ, and Paula Prata[1,2,4] ⓘ

[1] Universidade da Beira Interior, UBI, Covilhã, Portugal
joaobioco@gmail.com
[2] C4 - Centro de Competências em Cloud Computing (C4-UBI), Universidade da Beira Interior, Rua Marquês d'Ávila e Bolama, 6201-001 Covilhã, Portugal
[3] Facultad de Ciencias de la Salud, Universidad Católica San Antonio de Murcia, Murcia, Spain
[4] Instituto de Telecomunicações (IT), Aveiro, Portugal

Abstract. Agent-based models (ABMs) have been widely applied in several fields such as ecology, biology, climate changes, engineering and many other fields. In ABMs approach, the behaviour of a system is determined by the local interactions between its individuals (agents), and the interactions between these individuals with the environment where they exist. Due to its interactions at the individual's level, ABMs can produce quite realistic results regarding to the models behaviour. Therefore it is necessary to perform several analysis from the point of view of the models parametrization. In this paper we perform a parametric study in ways to analyze the implications of models parameterization in the models output, by implementing an agent-based model to simulate spatial distribution of species in an heterogeneous environment. The models output resulting from several parameters combination are compared and discussed.

Keywords: Agent-based modeling · Parameterization · Computer simulation · (Biological)Spatial distribution · Discrete agents

1 Introduction

Agent-based models (AMB) describe individuals (agents) as a unique and autonomous entities that normally interact with each other and their environment [13]. ABMs are considered computational models that show how the

This work was supported by operation Centro-01-0145-FEDER-000019 - C4 - Centro de Competências em Cloud Computing, co-financed by the European Regional Development Fund (ERDF) through the Programa Operacional Regional do Centro (Centro 2020), in the scope of the Sistema de Apoio à Investigação Científica e Tecnológica - Programas Integrados de IC&DT. This work was also funded by FCT/MCTES through the project UIDB/50008/2020.

© ICST Institute for Computer Sciences, Social Informatics and Telecommunications Engineering 2020
Published by Springer Nature Switzerland AG 2020. All Rights Reserved
M. H. Miraz et al. (Eds.): iCETiC 2020, LNICST 332, pp. 251–260, 2020.
https://doi.org/10.1007/978-3-030-60036-5_18

dynamics of a system have emerged, from the interactions of its entities (agents) in a shared environment [1]. ABM has been applied in several areas such as ecology, biology, engineering, climate change, and many other fields [2,10,11]. Agents have their own behaviours and act in order to accomplish a purpose. In the ecological modeling field, agent-based models (individual-based models in ecology [13]) are simulation models that consider agents or individuals as unique and discrete entities with proprieties that change during its life cycle [7]. Normally, four classification criteria are taken into account to distinguish classical models and agent-based models in ecology: (1) the individuals life cycle reflected in the model, (2) the considered resources (like food, habitat quality), (3) the representation of population size, (4) the variability of individuals of the same age that is considered [17]. Agent-based model (ABM) brings to the ecological modelling field the ability to simulate ecological phenomena (such as distribution of species) in more realistic ways [3], allowing management and conservation of species more suitable. Several studies have shown how ABM have helped ecological modelers to create and simulate species distribution models in a certain study area analyzing and comparing its results [12,14,15]. However, uncertainty related to the ABMs outputs and the production of more realistic models output remains a challenge for modelers [2].

This paper presents the results of the analyses performed to study the effects that model parameters have on the behavior of an agent-based modeling approach which has been designed to study spatial distribution of species in real and predicted environmental scenarios. With that purpose, a series of simulations are run to define accuracy and performance of this model by modifying colonization scenarios in a simple heterogeneous environment.

The remaining of this paper is organized as follows: In the second section the description of the model is addressed; In the third section the results of the study are addressed; In the fourth section the discussion of the study is presented, followed by the concluding section.

2   Methods

In our model, the agents interact with their environment (habitat units or grid cell) in a way that a percentage of agents in each iteration is transferred to their neighbouring cells. Agents tend to survive and reproduce more widely in locations (cells) considered suitable. In the locations less suitable agents tend to disappear. The model description follows the ODD (Overview, Design concepts, Detail) protocol [4–6]. The main components are briefly presented in the following.

2.1   Purpose

The purpose of this model is to analyze the spatial distribution of species in an heterogeneous habitat. It is intended here to perform a parametric study, before drawing conclusions regarding the behavior of the model.

2.2 Entities, State Variables and Scales

This study considers an agent as a colony of individuals (instead of one particular individual or species), that depends on the suitability of the environment to establish itself. Suitable environment can be seen as places (habitat units) with appropriate environmental conditions and enough resources for the specie to survive and reproduce. The environment consists of habitat units or cells characterized by their location (x, y) coordinates, the quantity of species in that location, and a suitability value of the cell. The suitability value of each cell has values between zero and one. Cells with values close to one are more suitable for the specie to survive an reproduce. An artificial environment was set, with a dimension of 200×200 (grid).

2.3 Process Overview

The goal of the agents (species) is to move and establish itself (survive and reproduce) in more suitable places, where the suitability values are closer to one. In this process three main parameters are taken into account: birth rate, death rate and the spread rate. These three parameters (birth rate, death rate and spread rate) are independent of each other. However, the composite effect of these parameters on the model's output is observed. Underlying the model it is assumed that there is a description of the suitability of the environment, its determination (a modeller's task) is outside the scope of this article. After setting the parameters of the model, the environment is initialized with the map of suitability. Similarly, the population of species is initialized. In that specific case, a random number of species is set in a random chosen cell. In each iteration (tick) is applied a birth and death rate for each quantity of species in each cell. The birth and death rate are affected by the suitability of the cell. Therefore, the quantity of species in suitable places (higher suitability) grows in greater quantities compared to the places with low suitability at same birth rate. Likewise, the death rate has a higher incidence in less suitable places. After that, the species tries to expand and colonize the neighbours cells. Each neighbour cell will receive a percentage of the quantity of species (spread rate).

2.4 Design Concepts

The species life cycle consists of three main steps: (1) at each time (tick) the species reproduce according to the birth rate and the conditions of its cell (suitability value); (2) an amount of species dies according to the death rate and the suitability of the cell (low suitability, more death); and (3) neighbours cells receive each one an amount of species according to the spread rate, see Fig. 1 and Algorithm 1. Reproduction is dependent on the suitability of the cell according to the mathematical expression of line 3 of Algorithm 1. Likewise, mortality is dependent on the suitability of the cell according to the mathematical expression of line 5 of Algorithm 1.

Algorithm 1. Species life cycle

1: **procedure** LIFE CYCLE($self, birth\_rate, death\_rate, spread\_rate, neighbours$)
2:     #*reproduction phase*
3:     $self.quantity+ = self.quantity * birth\_rate * self.suitability$
4:     #*death phase*
5:     $self.quantity- = self.quantity * death\_rate * (2 - self.suitability)$
6:     #*expansion phase*
7:     **for** *neighbour in neighbours* **do**
8:         $neighbour.quantity+ = self.quantity * spread\_rate$
9:         $self.quantity- = self.quantity * spread\_rate$
10:     **end for**
11:     *limit the quantity of species*
12: **end procedure**

2.5   Initialization

Only one cell in the environment is initialized, with a random quantity of species. The location of the cell is also random but chosen between the cells with suitability values close to one (places where species have more probability to survive and reproduce). The model considers 1000 as the maximum quantity of species in each cell. The model runs according to the number of ticks defined by the modeler.

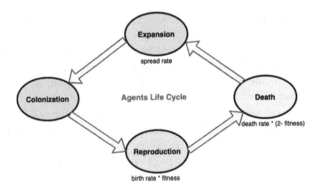

Fig. 1. Species life cycle.

2.6   Input Data

The model use as input data a grid of cells called map of suitability that represents the suitability of each habitat unit (cell) in the map, see Fig. 2.

2.7   Parameterization

Before drawing any conclusions regarding the model's behavior, several parameters combination will be tested and then its results will be compared with the map of the environment Fig. 2. Combinations are made between birth rate, death rate and spread rate. For the birth and death rates the following values were chosen: 0.1, 0.3, 0.5, 0.7 and 0.9, and for the spread rate: 0.03, 0.05, 0.07, 0.09. That gives a total of 100 combinations. Table 1 shows the number of average ticks that each parameters combination takes until the stabilization. Normally, parameters combination with a small quantity of ticks presented the worst results. Parameters combination that presented better results ran at least 340 iterations.

Table 1. Number of ticks for each parameters combination. In the header br represents birth rate, dr stands for death rate.

dr\br	Spread rate: 0.03					Spread rate: 0.05					Spread rate: 0.07					Spread rate: 0.09				
	0.1	0.3	0.5	0.7	0.9	0.1	0.3	0.5	0.7	0.9	0.1	0.3	0.5	0.7	0.9	0.1	0.3	0.5	0.7	0.9
0.1	20	2890	1030	1080	1070	20	1360	880	980	850	20	1190	670	780	520	20	920	600	620	500
0.3	10	20	30	850	680	10	20	800	580	700	10	10	20	470	410	10	10	540	540	340
0.5	10	10	20	20	1000	10	10	10	30	30	10	10	10	10	570	10	10	10	360	450
0.7	10	10	10	20	20	10	10	10	10	10	10	10	10	10	10	10	10	10	10	10
0.9	10	10	10	10	20	10	10	10	10	10	10	10	10	10	20	10	10	10	10	10

3 Selected Experiments and Results

Due to the high number of simulated scenarios (100 scenarios or parameters combinations), only some results are presented in Fig. 3. As can be seen in Fig. 3, species tend to establish themselves in locations where the environment conditions are suitable to them to survive and reproduce. Excluding the scenarios where the species cannot survive neither reproduce, model outputs often follow the same pattern, although the capacity of species to expand varies according to the three parameters (birth rate, death rate and spread rate).

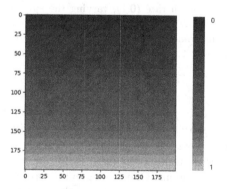

Fig. 2. Environment map. The color scale represents the suitability of the environment. At values close to one, species are more likely to reproduce (Color figure online).

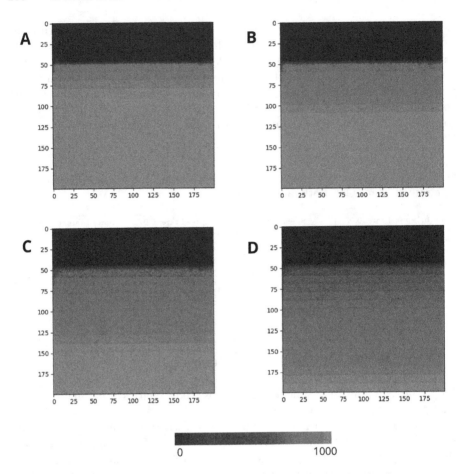

Fig. 3. Distribution of the species in the environment. The scale of color represents the abundance of the species in each cell. This scale varies from 0 to a limit of 1000 individuals in each cell. In this figure we show four simulations scenarios with the same birth rate (0.7) and death rate (0.1), varying the spread rate for values equals to (A) 0.03, (B) 0.05, (C) 0.07 and (D) 0.09. The simulation starts with a random quantity of individuals in a random cell and then the model evolves according to their life cycle. These results refer to the moment when the system reaches stability (Color figure online).

In a first approach, doing a visual comparison between these results (Fig. 3) and the environment map (Fig. 2), it is possible to verify similarities between maps. Model output follows the transition (gradation) presented in the environment map. However a visual comparison is not enough to draw conclusions related to the model's behaviour. One fundamental aspect related to the simulation of the model was the exact time to stop each simulation (stop criteria). We run several simulations in order to find the interval where the system reached the stabilization. We analyzed the differences between two sequential states of the system (time t and time $t - 1$). In our model, the difference between one state of the system and another, lies in the quantity of species presented in each cell. Thus, we calculate the sum of the Cell-by-Cell differences in these sequential states of the system. The goal was to stop the simulation when this difference is maintained below a small threshold for several ticks. Figure 4 shows the variation of these differences until reach of the stabilization point.

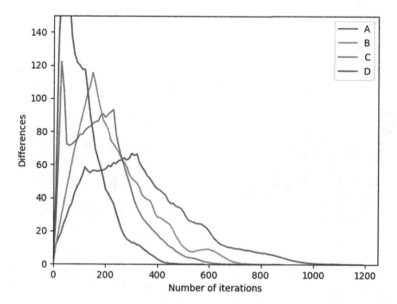

Fig. 4. Stabilization of the model for the four simulation scenarios. (A) Spread rate equal to 0.03, (B) spread rate equal to 0.05, (C) spread rate equal to 0.07 and (D) spread rate equal to 0.09.

Observing the Fig. 4 we notice that at the beginning of the simulation the difference between two sequential states of the system is small. This happens because we initialize the simulation adding a random quantity of species in just one cell randomly chosen. For this reason we verify the increase of the difference until a certain number of iterations and then these differences starts to decrease to the point that it stabilizes. Often, species did not survive when the values of birth rate and death rate are equal, and in scenarios where the value of birth rate is less than death rate. In order to analyze the output of the model in these different parameters combination, Fig. 5 depicts the comparison of the model's output in all scenarios with the map of suitability (see the environment map in Fig. 2).

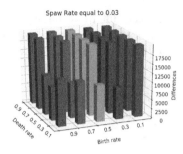

Spaw Rate equal to 0.03

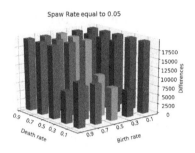

Spaw Rate equal to 0.05

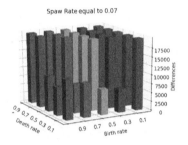

Spaw Rate equal to 0.07

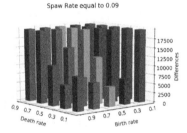

Spaw Rate equal to 0.09

Fig. 5. Normalized Cell-by-Cell comparison between model output and the environment map. For each spreading rate scenario the vertical bars depicts the result for a particular tuple (Death rate, Birth rate) of parameters.

We convert the model output in the same scale (0, 1) of the environment map to facilitate comparison. The overall comparison technique, adapted from [8] was performed for each model output. In Fig. 5 it is possible to observe the scenarios with the lowest differences. The combination (birth rate = 0.5, death rate = 0.1, spread rate = 0.09) presented the lowest difference, followed by the combination (0.9, 0.3, 0.09), and the combination (0.5, 0.1, 0.07) in the same order of the rates. According to Fig. 5 at death rate greater than 30% species do not reproduce neither survive. For values of death rate greater or equal than 50% even with a birth rate of 90% the chances of the species to survive are remote. On the other hand, at a birth rate less than 20% species have few chances to survive and expand. The model presented better results for higher spread rates.

4   Discussion

Model behaviour and model outputs are strictly related to their parameters. The parameters of the reported model are completely independent of each other in the sense that any adjustment made to any parameter does not affect the value of the remaining parameters. However any small change in a subset of parameters can result in drastic changes on the overall behavior of the model. Before starting drawing any assumption related to the model's behaviour it is necessary to perform a thorough parameter analysis. A comprehensive analysis of the output to input variability is an important step during the development of an agent-based model [9]. Model parameterization allows the model to give more realistic results [16]. Parameters analyzed in our study have each one its effect in the model. Although, we cannot consider only these parameters individually but the effect that the combination of the different parameters have in the model's output. Discarding the effect of either one of the parameters will jeopardize the ability to explain the output of the model. One of the aspects to taking into account is the distinction between birth rate and death rate. If we want our species to survive and reproduce, it is important to have a significant distinction between birth rate and death rate, fixing the values of birth rate always greater than death rate. This is the only case that the species can survive and reproduce. However, without spread rate there is no way for the species to expand (colonize) in other cells in the neighbourhood.

The results of our model depend on the values that were chosen for the parameters. That means that the choice of parameters will always constraint the desired results. Several scenarios have to be analyzed until the parameters combination that answer the purpose of the reference model is found.

5   Conclusion

In this study we analyzed the effects of model's parameters in the model's output, by implementing an agent-based model to simulate the spatial distribution of species in an heterogeneous environment. We performed a parametric study in order to find the parameters combination that fits the purpose of our model. The results showed that in addition to the environmental conditions, the combination of the model parameters has a significant impact on its results. Our study is limited in the sense that the environment of our model was not real.

In the future we intend to apply our model to real environments aiming at predicting the geographical distribution of biological species with economical interest in a setup of deep environmental uncertainty.

References

1. Abar, S., Theodoropoulos, G.K., Lemarinier, P., O'Hare, G.M.: Agent based modelling and simulation tools: a review of the state-of-art software. Comput. Sci. Rev. **24**, 13–33 (2017)
2. An, L., Grimm, V., Turner, B.L.: Meeting grand challenges in agent-based models. J. Artif. Soc. Soc. Simul. **23**(1), 1–13 (2020)
3. Grimm, V.: Ten years of individual-based modelling in ecology: what have we learned and what could we learn in the future? Ecol. Model. **115**(2–3), 129–148 (1999)

4. Grimm, V.: A standard protocol for describing individual-based and agent-based models. Ecol. Model. **198**(1–2), 115–126 (2006)

5. Grimm, V., Berger, U., DeAngelis, D.L., Polhill, J.G., Giske, J., Railsback, S.F.: The odd protocol: a review and first update. Ecol. Model. **221**(23), 2760–2768 (2010)

6. Grimm, V., et al.: The odd protocol for describing agent-based and other simulation models: a second update to improve clarity, replication, and structural realism. J. Artif. Soc. Soc. Simul. **23**(2), 1–7 (2020)

7. Huston, M., DeAngelis, D., Post, W.: New computer models unify ecological theory: computer simulations show that many ecological patterns can be explained by interactions among individual organisms. Bioscience **38**(10), 682–691 (1988)

8. Kuhnert, M., Voinov, A., Seppelt, R.: Comparing raster map comparison algorithms for spatial modeling and analysis. Photogram. Eng. Remote Sens. **71**(8), 975–984 (2005)

9. Ligmann-Zielinska, A., et al.: One size does not fit all: a roadmap of purpose-driven mixed-method pathways for sensitivity analysis of agent-based models. J. Artif. Soc. Soc. Simul. **23**(1), 1–6 (2020)

10. Macal, C.M.: Everything you need to know about agent-based modelling and simulation. J. Simul. **10**(2), 144–156 (2016)

11. Marvuglia, A., Rege, S., Gutierrez, T.N., Vanni, L., Stilmant, D., Benetto, E.: A return on experience from the application of agent-based simulations coupled with life cycle assessment to model agricultural processes. J. Clean. Prod. **142**, 1539–1551 (2017)

12. Pepin, K.M., Davis, A.J., VerCauteren, K.C.: Efficiency of different spatial and temporal strategies for reducing vertebrate pest populations. Ecol. Model. **365**, 106–118 (2017). https://doi.org/10.1016/j.ecolmodel.2017.10.005. http://www.sciencedirect.com/science/article/pii/S0304380017304349

13. Railsback, S.F., Grimm, V.: Agent-Based and Individual-Based Modeling: A Practical Introduction. Princeton University Press, Princeton (2019)

14. Reuter, H., Kruse, M., Rovellini, A., Breckling, B.: Evolutionary trends in fish schools in heterogeneous environments. Ecol. Model. **326**, 23–35 (2016)

15. Sheehan, K.L., Esswein, S.T., Dorr, B.S., Yarrow, G.K., Johnson, R.J.: Using species distribution models to define nesting habitat of the eastern metapopulation of double-crested cormorants. Ecol. Evol. **7**(1), 409–418 (2017)

16. Thiele, J.C., Kurth, W., Grimm, V.: Facilitating parameter estimation and sensitivity analysis of agent-based models: a cookbook using NetLogo and R. J. Artif. Soc. Soc. Simul. **17**(3), 11 (2014)

17. Uchmański, J., Grimm, V.: Individual-based modelling in ecology: what makes the difference? Trends Ecol. Evol. **11**(10), 437–441 (1996)

Emerging Technologies in Engineering Education and Sustainable Development

A Survey on the Use of e-Portfolios as a Form of Assessment in Online Computer Science Courses

Nkaepe Olaniyi[(✉)] [iD]

Kaplan Open Learning, Leeds LS1 2NS, UK
nkaepe.olaniyi@kaplan.com

Abstract. Online learning is a growing field, offering the required flexibility in learning in this modern age. Higher education institutions are now developing online undergraduate and postgraduate degree courses. These courses reach a larger and more diverse student body. The use of e-portfolios in various institutions across the globe has increased, with many providing evidence of a positive impact on student outcomes and with generally positive student views. There is positive feedback from employers on the use of these e-portfolios for gauging the suitability of an applicant.

The question then arises as to how this tool fares in an online degree course, particularly one where portfolios, in general, are not normally used. Through a survey of the literature, it is evident that there are many examples of the use of e-portfolios on degree courses as a valid form of assessment. Its use in online undergraduate and postgraduate computing courses needs increased focus. This paper will provide information on how to develop an e-portfolio assessment for an online course, as part of curriculum development, as well as how to determine its effectiveness.

Keywords: e-Portfolio · Higher education · Online learning · Constructive alignment · STEM

1 Introduction

Computer Science professionals are in ever-increasing demand across the globe: the US Bureau of Labor and Statistics [1] predicts a faster than average rise of 16% between 2018 and 2028. In Europe, STEM roles are expected to increase by 16% between 2016 and 2033 [2]. Almost simultaneously, there is an increase in the number of Massive Open Online Courses (MOOCs) in various Computing fields, some of which are accredited or offered by well-known higher education institutions [3]. This, in part, has been driven by the need for greater flexibility in study patterns [3].

The provision of online undergraduate (UG) and postgraduate (PG) courses by brick-and-mortar HE institutions is currently on the rise for similar reasons [4–6]. Notable institutions such as the University of Oxford, University of Essex, University of Liverpool, Curtin University, Stockholm University, John Hopkins University and New York

© ICST Institute for Computer Sciences, Social Informatics and Telecommunications Engineering 2020
Published by Springer Nature Switzerland AG 2020. All Rights Reserved
M. H. Miraz et al. (Eds.): iCETiC 2020, LNICST 332, pp. 263–277, 2020.
https://doi.org/10.1007/978-3-030-60036-5_19

University now offer UG and PG courses in various disciplines. The opportunity to gain a (higher) degree qualification (from a known institution) is a key driver for many learners as this is usually looked upon favorably by employers [1].

Another aspect of learning generally well-received by employers is the portfolio [7–9]. In fact, the use of portfolios in obtaining jobs after graduation has been a key driver in their use in higher education (HE) institutions [10–12]. A portfolio is defined as "a purposeful collection of student work that exhibits the student's efforts, progress, and achievements" [13]. Students have the opportunity not only to collect and organize their learning content but also to reflect on it, taking on feedback from academics and their peers. Hence portfolios can be used to support learning [6].

It is only in more recent years that portfolios have made the move to being electronic [14, 15]. e-Portfolios can have various uses in a course. They have been identified as a form of authentic assessment [10] that causes students to be more dynamic participants in their learning journey [15, 16]. In general, this is because portfolios rely on several pieces of evidence rather than one. Therefore, the e-portfolio represents a student's ability more accurately [17].

Portfolios, in general, have seen their use extended recently from art and design disciplines into more technical fields of study like Engineering and Computer Science [10, 18–21]. In the United States, a significant number of institutions now use e-portfolios on their campuses [18, 22]. Several universities are also developing institution-wide e-portfolio programmes that encompass a student's entire university career [23].

Currently, there is a lack of empirical data on the effect of e-portfolios on student academic outcomes in courses offered by HE institutions [22, 23]. This could be down to the eager adoption of new practices prior to assessing is effectiveness, which is a regular practice in the field of education [23].

This paper reviews the development and use of e-portfolios by HE institutions as a form of assessment in online UG and PG Computer Science courses. The author chose to focus on works traditionally utilized by HE institutions in the development of HE practices. Hence, the survey includes peer reviewed articles and institutional reports only. Considering the limited research in the development of e-portfolios in Computer Science courses, the survey will take into account research in this area involving various disciplines, including other technical\STEM courses.

Accordingly, the rest of this paper is organized as follows: Sect. 2 reviews e-portfolio use in higher education (postgraduate and undergraduate courses), reviewing its validity as a form as assessment, its impact on student outcomes and highlighting student views. Section 3 provides an overview of the use of e-portfolios in technical HE courses, practical implementation, as well as student views. Section 4 considers employers' views on e-portfolios. Section 5 looks at the development and use of e-portfolios in online PG computer science courses, a development plan for this assessment tool, and reviews the limitations of this survey. Section 6 concludes the paper.

2   e-Portfolios in Higher Education

An e-portfolio can be defined as a personalized, web-based collections of work that describe and document "a person's achievement and learning" [24]. So, e-portfolios are user (student)-centered as they are used to share work and plans with others and to provide evidence of lifelong learning [17]. The use of e-portfolios in higher education has increased in the past decade [25]. They are generally seen as tools to help students monitor, evaluate and reflect on their learning journey [15].

2.1   Drivers for the Use e-Portfolios

The Jisc toolkit [26] states that the diversity of purpose is one reason that e-portfolios have the potential for institution-wide impact. The toolkit goes further to report on the key reasons e-portfolios are used in higher education. These cover educational gains where institutions see improved attainment and the development of lifelong learning in students [11, 17, 19]. Being digital also means that students can enhance their digital skills in the process of developing their e-portfolio [18].

A second gain is in employability [10, 11, 27]. Ensuring that students can apply their learning to real-world situations and experiences is a key goal for many institutions. It helps to meet the increasing demand for universities to produce graduates that are ready for the workplace. There is also a drive to integrate the personal development planning process into the curriculum and the e-portfolio seems to be the most reliable vehicle for that process [20].

In terms of "integrative learning", students can now develop a wider perspective on their learning as they include volunteering activities to prove acquisition or development of key skills [8]. This can therefore help HE institutions to attract and retain students from non-traditional backgrounds (widening participation) [10].

2.2   e-Portfolio Development and Content

In designing an e-portfolio for use in a course, it is important to determine how it will be implemented. Consequently, as a starting point for ensuring a successful implementation of an e-portfolio, some key questions need to be considered in the development process [10, 24, 26, 28]:

- What is the purpose of the e-portfolio?
- Who will own the e-portfolio?
- What items (including artifacts) are required/acceptable?
- How should the items be organized?
- How will the e-portfolio be introduced?
- How will the e-portfolio be assessed?
- What support is needed (for students and staff)?

The Jisc toolkit [26] gives further practical guidance on these principles for the successful implementation of e-portfolios. This is based on various case studies covering extra-curricular to inter-institutional use. The five key principles are:

1. The purpose of the e-portfolio needs to be aligned to learning outcomes to maximize benefits. This refers to constructive alignment between course learning objectives and assessments. Hence, this purpose must be made transparent to students.

2. Learning activities need to be designed to suit the purpose of the e-portfolio. Staff will need to be familiar with the e-portfolio tool. There also needs to be a scaffolding of certain learning activities for students in order to successfully convey the purpose of the e-portfolio to students [29].
3. Processes need to be supported technologically and pedagogically. An effective technical support team is needed, as well as pedagogic support such as example portfolios and peer review.
4. Ownership needs to be student-centered. Even though the e-portfolio is made available to peers and staff during the course, it ultimately belongs to the student and should be available/transferred to them once the course is completed.
5. Transformation (or disruption) needs to be planned for. Each instance of an e-portfolio in a course might be classed as a "new practice" point for the students. This needs to be taken into consideration during curriculum development, in terms of student guidance and support - it is best not to assume "full familiarity" with the tool and process when developing the second, third, (etc.) instance of the e-portfolio.

These are in line with the criteria that can be applied to the construction and successful use of e-portfolios in a course, as reviewed by Butler [10]. These include introducing students to the purpose of the e-portfolio and its connection to the curriculum; ensuring student ownership of the portfolio; ensuring student buy-in by showcasing past examples and demonstrating how effective they are in the learning process; ensuring academic buy-in by highlighting strong, supportive leadership and appropriate resources; and ensuring sufficient infrastructure (resources, knowledge and commitment) are available for the e-portfolio.

One criterion not extensively covered in literature, probably due to the relative novelty, is the issue of data privacy and the right to be forgotten as specified by the General Data Protection Regulation (GDPR) [30]. This can be an issue whether the University creates its own tool or decides to use facilities from a third-party. In both instances, it is fair to say that students taking ownership of their e-portfolio is a key requirement. In the latter scenario, the University has a duty to ensure that the third-party vendor follows GDPR guidelines **before** engaging their services. Hence, once the students have graduated, their interaction will be with the third-party vendor and standard GDPR procedures in that respect will apply. If the tool used is created by the University, it will be in line with the GDPR procedures used by the University; the information is to be held as long as is deemed necessary (particularly if an appeal is brought against the University after the student has graduated) [31] and is only to be used for the agreed purposes [32]. Regardless of the tool used, the student must be made aware of the applicable GDPR procedures at the start of the course and reminded of those procedures when they complete the course.

In order to support the students effectively, there is a need to consider the variety of skills within the student body in terms of their technical abilities This can be accomplished by ensuring that the necessary pedagogic and technical support mechanisms are provided to students [26, 33]. This should include the use of peer communities to aid that support framework [33].

e-Portfolios are used for formative feedback, summative assessment, employment applications, professional accreditation, and recording personal and/or professional growth [10, 14, 17, 27, 28]. Hence, e-portfolios tend to have varying structures. Jisc [34] provides exemplars of e-portfolios used in various contexts and on various platforms.

Even with the varied purposes of e-portfolios, there are some elements that are common to all e-portfolios [10, 24, 27, 28]:

- Author's information (including contact details)
- Layout information
- Selected artifacts
- Reflection (which includes the description of the artifacts and their context in the e-portfolio)
- Relationships between parts of the e-portfolio

Some additional items are specific to the type of e-portfolio being used. For example, if the purpose is for professional development, the e-portfolio would include a professional development plan and CV [28]. The reflections would aid the development of the plan. For outcome-based e-portfolio, the rubric used to assess the e-portfolio would be necessary [27].

2.3 Use of e-Portfolios as a Form of Assessment

In an earlier paper [35], the essential ingredients for better student academic outcomes was reviewed. It showed the need for constructive alignment between course and module learning outcomes and assessment criteria, as well as the need for student-centered learning and timely feedback. So, it can be said that any form of assessment must meet the intended learning outcome of the course, as well as encourage deep learning [20].

In terms of pedagogy, e-portfolios are based on constructivism [10, 20]; the alignment between learning outcomes, teaching and learning activities, and assessments in a course. Social scientists like David Baume class the e-portfolio as a suitable form of assessment because [28, 36]:

- students have to achieve at least one learning outcome of the course, making the e-portfolio a valid assessment task,
- the process of assessing the e-portfolio is also valid if the assessor is judging the work against those learning outcomes,
- the assessment of the e-portfolio can be judged as reliable if the students are given clear instructions on the tasks to be undertaken, as well as the assessment criteria.
- the use of personalized elements (such as reflection and artifact commentaries) and work-integrated learning in e-portfolios are seen as ways of ensuring and improving academic integrity [29, 37].

Hence, ideally, an e-portfolio should have a limited number of artifacts, commentary from the students on how each artifact demonstrates the selected learning outcome of the course, and a reflective piece [17, 36, 38–40]. This would provide an effective alignment between the assessment and the module or course learning outcomes. Thereby ensuring better student academic outcomes at the end of the module or course [35]. In determining the content of the e-portfolio, a balance needs to be struck between student creativity and institution requirements. This would also aid in the assessment of the portfolio, particularly if clear guidelines and a rubric are used [24, 26].

The active involvement of students in creating and maintaining their e-portfolio has been seen by many institutions to encourage that deep learning [15, 20]. This is because the e-portfolio is a process for students to construct knowledge through participatory activities, which help them internalize their learning [41]. Hence, to a large extent, the creation of an e-portfolio does involve the student's use of higher-order cognitive skills (such as critical thinking), meta-cognitive control (self-regulatory) strategies, as well as collaborative learning strategies [33, 42]. Meta-cognitive strategies refer to a student's strategy to plan and monitor their approach to learning. This brings to the fore the deep learning aspect to developing and maintaining an e-portfolio.

It should be noted that some students may need to be aware of such strategies to effectively construct their e-portfolio [42]. This is particularly detrimental if the e-portfolio is a high-stakes assessment, acting as the sole or highest weighted assessment for a module [38]. This should be considered during curriculum development (when constructing e-portfolios as a form of assessment) so as not to impede learning. This would also mean that a clear set of guidelines and assessment criteria need to be provided to students from the outset [35], as well as academic support throughout the e-portfolio development process [10, 26].

Effect on Student Academic Outcomes. A few papers have been published which provide empirical data on the impact e-portfolios have on students' academic outcomes at the end of a course. In 2013, Bryant and Chittum [23] published an extensive survey of literature for empirical support for the use of e-portfolios in course. It was found that e-portfolios "can plausibly make great contributions to student learning when properly implemented". The authors acknowledged a gap in peer-reviewed literature regarding empirical data on student outcomes. Only a few papers identified in the review presented data on academic outcomes and only two papers evaluated these outcomes using reliable measures and a control/comparison group [23].

In an example from a Computer Science course [43], portfolios were used in four undergraduate units, creating various iterations of the portfolio assessment. Subsequent iterations were based on staff reflections and students' performance. The final iteration saw a clarity in guidance and assessment criteria. This reduced the amount of time staff spent assessing the portfolio and they recorded higher student grades. The views of student and staff in this example is shared by their peers using e-portfolios [38].

In recent years, Handel et al. [15] carried out an empirical field study on the influence of e-portfolio use on exam performance. This was based on a group of undergraduate Educational Psychology students. The study indicated that students who used the e-portfolio during the course seemed to attain higher exam performance. The reason for this could be due to the continuous use of the e-portfolio rather than the actual e-portfolio elements. It should be noted that the groups in this study (test and control) were determined by the students, rather than assigned by the researchers. This is because student participation was voluntary, with "a little exam bonus" as the incentive.

Therefore, Bryant and Chittum's [23] statement on the plausible benefits of e-portfolios on student' academic outcomes still stands. However, there is still a need for more empirical data on this aspect of e-portfolio use.

Students Views on e-Portfolios. As introduced in Sect. 2.2, it is important to ensure that the purpose of the e-portfolio and its connection to the curriculum is made evident to students from the outset. Therefore, it is essential to gauge their views on the use of e-portfolios as assessments in their courses, regardless of the weighting of these assessments.

e-Portfolios are commonly used in educational technology, education, health, literacy, arts, music and architecture [23]. This is at both undergraduate and postgraduate levels. This sub-section will focus on various disciplines in order to provide an understanding of its current use in HE.

Previous research has shown the students' views on the e-portfolio was not very encouraging [17, 39]. This was due confusion about the required materials and organization of the e-portfolio. The students also found the development of the e-portfolios time-intensive, with some not having a clear vision of the purpose of the e-portfolio. Other authors mentioned in the Contreras-Higuera et al. study [39] saw that if students were provided with clear instructions and support during the development process, they responded positively to its use. One author in that same study saw that students in classes where the e-portfolio had a greater assessment weighting rated it highly, as well as "its ability to boost competencies". It should be noted that in determining the weighting of the e-portfolio assessment, consideration must be given to the level of risk associated with that weighting [20, 38, 39].

In some areas of applications, the students' view on e-portfolios is determined by its use. Strivens et al. [40] reports on e-portfolios used for accreditation purposes on postgraduate vocational Law courses. The students were satisfied with the use of the e-portfolio to support their job applications. However, they were wary of using the e-portfolio to reflect on any areas of improvement during the course due to the fierce competition they face in the sector. The students were also concerned about privacy and wanted to ensure they were able to choose the levels of access to their e-portfolios.

In the same report [40], there is an example of e-portfolios used for professional development in an undergraduate Education course at Portsmouth University. Here, students' initial reaction was one of reluctance to share views/work with their peers. This was seemed to be due to a lack of confidence in their work. This contrasts with students on a postgraduate course at Northumbria University who were comfortable with the peer review process from the outset [40]. So, the level of study seems to have an impact on students' perception of the e-portfolio.

The digital format of the e-portfolio has resulted in an entirely positive student view. [33]. This may be because expectations on the use of e-portfolios is set from the outset; students are expected to construct and develop an e-portfolio at various points in the course. The study by Wuetherick and Dickinson [33] involved students from Residential Interiors, Fine Arts and Writing and Editing courses, all in continuing education courses. The authors highlighted that most students rate the portability of the e-portfolio highly, especially when they have completed their course. Two other significant factors that was rated highly by students was the ability to demonstrate their learning to others and the importance of reflection in their learning journey. The authors did find that students under the age of 30 were more comfortable and more experienced with using the required technology for their e-portfolio. Hence, the need for adequate pedagogical support for a diverse student body.

3 Use of e-Portfolios in Technical HE Courses

The drivers described in Sect. 2.1 have meant institution-wide interest in its use across various fields of study. One key success criterion for the use of e-portfolios in technical courses is the merge in student and academic expectations. Students view the e-portfolio as an aid in gaining employment while academics view it in terms of proof of attaining learning outcomes and incorporating professional development in the curriculum [10]. In a technical course, both goals can be achieved with the right artifacts that reflect the student's technological skills, as well as improvement, for the duration of the course. These are commonly referred to as Learning e-portfolios [28]. Integrating the learning with professional development, as most curricula do, would make it a Learning and Development e-portfolio [10, 28]. Due to the nature of the artifacts used, these e-portfolios can easily be transferred to Presentation e-portfolios, showcasing the relationship between, for example, code written, professional certifications/degree qualification and employment history [17, 28].

Implementation. Ideally, most institutions would prefer to use off-the shelf e-portfolio systems that can be adapted to their needs [44]. However, this is not always the case, particularly with Computer Science courses. Many tend to use their own web-space databases and tools (or open source tools) and create comprehensive instructions to guide students [8, 23, 38, 40, 44, 45].

In terms of assessing the e-portfolio, many institutions have adopted rubrics. One of the reasons for using rubrics in conjunction with e-portfolios is that it helps students better understand the assessment, making it more transparent [20, 39]. The rubrics must be in line with the learning outcomes of the applicable module or course to ensure this transparency, achieving constructive alignment [8, 20, 26, 43, 46]. This should result in a more efficient marking process, with valid and reliable results [20].

Students Views on e-Portfolios in Technical Courses. Introducing e-portfolios to technical students can present certain issues. Due to the nature of technical/STEM courses, students find it difficult to reflect. This is possibly due to the abstract nature of the task and the cultural background of the students [29]. Hence, the need to scaffold learning, particularly for undergraduate students who might not be equipped with the life skills to undertake this task. Students should also be presented with the opportunity to reflect in a variety of formats which are formatively assessed [29].

One New Zealand experience involving Computer Science and Engineering students [19] shows that making participation in the e-portfolio voluntary can result in incomplete e-portfolios, even though its development was described to students as encouraging lifelong learning. The students who did complete the e-portfolio stated that the process of developing the e-portfolio did help them understand lifelong learning. The authors mention that one reason for the low completion rates could be the time-intensive nature of e-portfolio development. However, none of the responses received from students confirmed this hypothesis.

On the other hand, a recent study found that undergraduate computing students in a UK University were more likely to accept the use of e-portfolios on their courses if they understood its usefulness [6]. This was determined by the students perceived ease of use and enjoyment factors. The authors called for "education sessions" to help students understand the usefulness of e-portfolios. The students should also be involved in the implementation process and their perceptions assessed during this process so that any amendments can be made accordingly. There should also be pedagogical support provided to students to ensure ease of use.

In a study conducted at the University of Lincoln with undergraduates from a technology-based course, Beresford and Cobham [45] found that students enjoyed personalising their e-portfolios. The students also indicated that the e-portfolios helped them "learn by doing" as they focused on themselves and their work. This is in line with Kolb's experiential cycle learning theory [47]. Students are then able to take ownership of their learning.

The Business Information Systems department at one University created an undergraduate module to integrate Personal Development Planning in their various curricula [20]. Quantitative and qualitative methods were used to monitor student achievement. Also, making the e-portfolios summative ensured student engagement. In general, the students were happy with the e-portfolio, seeing it as an effective tool in assessing their learning and underpinning their knowledge. This sentiment was shared by amongst undergraduate students on another Computing course [44]. This group of students also understood its usefulness in finding employment in technical fields [44]. For the academic staff from the Clark and Adamson study [20], the main challenge was with the first-year module, where the students may lack confidence in their own ability. Hence, reiterating the need for scaffolding of learning activities to ensure that learning is not hindered.

A final opinion that seems to be shared by technical students is regarding the privacy issue in e-portfolio use. Many students were not concerned with having their portfolio publicly available to people they did not know [44, 48]. However, this may depend on the tools used to develop the e-portfolio [8].

4 Employer Perspectives

Many students are aware that the e-portfolio is a useful aid in seeking employment after graduation [8]. The AACU [9] found that more than 4 out of 5 employers said that an e-portfolio would be useful to them. One student using a teaching portfolio mentioned that the e-portfolio helped draw attention to their job application [12].

One review found that engineering students find that their e-portfolios are well-received by employers [7]. In that study, the employers interviewed liked the portability of the e-portfolio and the ease of access to information. It helped to assess the potential fit of the student with the company. One employer even stated that the calibre of the e-portfolio could be the deciding factor for an interview.

In a different study, one employer wanted to see examples of other activities which helped to enhance key stills [19]. In that study, all the employers interviewed (from Engineering and IT disciplines) appreciated the time it took to create an e-portfolio and recognized the importance of reflection on artifacts.

In the recruitment process, it is essential for students to ensure they provide information that is relevant to the role/company [7]. Weber [7] gives an example of an engineering students portfolio which had a specific section entitled "Professional". This served as a landing page for employers to view the resume, awards and achievements. This aspect of the portfolio is key as it also addresses the privacy issue that is of concern to some students. Some HE institutions now provide further information to students on the content that employers prefer to see in e-portfolios [49–51].

5 e-Portfolios and Online Computer Science Courses

One key reason for studying a degree online is for the desired flexibility of studying part-time while still being able to work full-time [3, 4]. Many use the advanced, postgraduate degree to climb up the employment ladder, securing higher positions or moving into a different field of practice [1, 52].

The skills students need to have mastered by graduation can be quite demanding - being creative, reflective and communicative [19, 23]. So, the e-portfolio will be the ideal way for a graduate to show a potential employer the in-depth, and advanced, knowledge and understanding acquired during their course, as well as their critical awareness of current issues in the field. Its impact on student learning, particularly in developing the lifelong learner, is a clear driver at this level of learning. This, therefore, establishes the need to use e-portfolios in online undergraduate and postgraduate Computing courses.

The lack of research publications on the use of e-portfolios (as a form of formative or summative assessment) in online computing courses shows that this is a key area of research for HE institutions. Hence, the focus for the remainder of this section is on determining a format for an e-portfolio that can be used in an online UG or PG computing course.

5.1 Proposed e-Portfolio Development Plan for Online Computer Science Courses

Teaching and assessing a technical subject online pose some significant challenges which need to be taken into consideration during course development. This is based primarily on Human-Computer Interaction. In a programming module, for example, students can feel particularly isolated when dealing with problems and have to deal with the lack of immediate feedback [4].

Hence, in developing assessments for these online courses, consideration must be given to the importance of group work and group learning in the development of desirable soft skills [48, 53]. This also addresses the establishment of peer communities to support students [33]. There is also a need to use a variety of assessment formats to cater to a diverse student body [4].

The use of industry tools should be taken into consideration as this will help graduates settle quickly into a role in industry. For example, Feliciano et al. [48] used GitHub to foster group interaction and peer review as a software development tool in two software engineering courses. The use of this industry tool aids professional development as students can demonstrate skills and practices relevant to the industry [48].

Based on the various studies in this paper, the e-portfolio can be a versatile tool that captures all these aspects of assessment design. Thereby aiding the development of a successful online course.

Preferably, an e-portfolio for an online computing course would need to be Learning and Development portfolio (as identified in Sects. 3 and 4). Therefore, it should contain the following aspects [10, 24, 27, 28]:

- Author's information (including contact details)
- Layout information, describing the relationships between parts of the e-portfolio
- Selected artifacts
- Reflection (which includes the description of the artifacts and their context in the e-portfolio)
- Professional Development Plan (based on a set of skills applicable to industry, links to activities that prove the skill development and a corresponding action plan)
- A landing page for employers (*Professional Showcase* page) to highlight industry-specific skills and applicable projects

The development of this e-portfolio would take into account the highlighted areas of good practice for e-portfolio development identified in this survey. These include [8, 20, 26, 39, 43]:

- Introducing the e-portfolio as a form of assessment **early** in the course
- Helping students understand the benefits of the e-portfolio, via teaching sessions, discussion groups, etc.
- Gaining student buy-in by getting them involved in the development of the system and/or showcasing examples of good portfolios.
- Providing clear assessment guidelines (e.g. rubrics and instructions)
- Encouraging staff buy-in by improving their skills on the e-portfolio platform
- Providing continuous technical and pedagogical support to student and staff throughout the course.
- Providing a mechanism for ensuring the e-portfolio can be fully owned by the student on completion of the course.
- Ensuring students are aware of the applicable GDPR procedures before utilizing the e-portfolio tool and once the course is completed.

In order to determine its effectiveness in a course, it is necessary to [23]:

- ensure there is qualitative data on the outcome of the project by carrying out focus group sessions and interviews with students, as well as staff.
- have a control or comparison group to determine if any positive student outcomes are as a result of the e-portfolio rather than course design. This can take the form of comparing e-portfolio use in one module of the course with another in the same course where the e-portfolio does not feature.
- collate empirical data on the impact on students' learning based on academic achievement and improvements in skills.

Limitations. In putting forward this development and implementation design for the e-portfolio as a form of assessment on an online UG and PG computer science course, the limitations of this survey must be reviewed. The sampling of literature took place over a year and was focused on peer-reviewed journal articles and institutional reports. Hence, the survey may not address all possible pieces of work on e-portfolios use as a form of assessment in technical subject. Where a comprehensive literature reviews have been carried out previously, the aim of this survey was to provide a summary of the findings rather than delve into the applied methodology.

There is also an issue with the age of the research covered in this survey. Most studies in e-portfolios took place in the early 2000s and current research is limited. The author aimed to use more recent research to supplement (or contradict) the findings from older pieces of research, where applicable. Therefore, further surveys will be necessary, and will need to encompass seminal pieces of work which may have been published in recent years.

6 Conclusion

E-learning has been on the rise, globally in recent years [6]. This has led to an increase the use of various tools to support student learning, one of which is the e-portfolio. Almost simultaneously, there has been an increase in online learning opportunities offered by HE institutions across the globe [25]. One key driver bringing online learning and e-portfolios together is the need to embed professional development in the curriculum [10] and to help students gain employment after graduation [8]. This is particularly useful for technical degree courses where the knowledge and skills gained by the student can be showcased effectively.

e-Portfolios can take various forms, depending on their use [26] and are seen to be valid forms of assessment [20]. Student views on this use of e-portfolios as assessment pieces tends to vary, depending on the course, the purpose of the e-portfolio and how it is implemented.

Although there are a limited number of peer-reviewed publications on the effect that e-portfolios have on student academic outcomes, the evidence presented in this review points to a plausible positive effect [23]. Hence, the need for more empirical research in this area.

Research on e-portfolio use in online computing courses is also lacking. The reason for this is not clear but may be due to an eagerness to adopt a process seen as a "silver bullet" without first establishing its effectiveness or appropriate use, particularly with regards to student views and assessment risks [23]. However, this review goes some way to establishing the e-portfolio as a valid form of assessment which tends to receive positive reviews from students and staff, particularly when used in computer science courses.

Hence, the need to develop and review an e-portfolio format that can be applied to online UG and PG computer science courses as a form of assessment. A format is proposed in this survey, as well as a development structure for such e-portfolios. This is based on shared areas of good practice. The paper also provides a process for gathering empirical evidence of its impact on student outcomes.

In conclusion, Mason et al's [17] comments on the e-portfolio sums up its versatility and validity; it is a method of assessment that "builds independence and learning-to-learn skills". These are indeed essential building blocks for the development of a lifelong learner, a core aim of any HE institution when offering an online computer science course.

References

1. U.S. Bureau of Labor and Statistics Occupational Outlook Handbook. https://www.bls.gov/ooh/computer-and-information-technology/computer-and-information-research-scientists.htm. Accessed 26 Jan 2020
2. Arregui Pabollet, E., et al.: The changing nature of work and skills in the digital age. In: Gonzalez Vazquez, I., et al. (eds) Publications Office of the European Union, Luxembourg (2019). https://doi.org/10.2760/679150
3. Al-Rahmi, W., Aldraiweesh, A., Yahaya, N., Kamin, Y., Zeki, A.: Massive Open Online Courses (MOOCs): data on higher education. Data Brief **22**, 118–125 (2019)
4. Gulatee, Y., Brown, J., Combes, B.: Factors that influence successful online teaching and learing programs in technical computer science subjects. In: Proceedings of the EDU-COM 2008 International Conference. Sustainability in Higher Education: Directions for Change, pp. 212–224. Edith Cowan University, Perth, Western Australia (2008)
5. Palvia, S., et al.: Online education: worldwide status, challenges, trends, and implications. J. Global Inf. Technol. Manage. **21**(4), 233–244 (2018). https://doi.org/10.1080/1097198X.2018.1542262
6. Abdullah, F., Ward, R., Ahmed, E.: Investigating the influence of the most commonly used external variables of TAM on students' Perceived Ease of Use (PEOU) and Perceived Usefulness (PU) of e-portfolios. Comput. Hum. Behav. **63**, 75–90 (2016). https://doi.org/10.1016/j.chb.2016.05.014
7. Weber, K.: Employer perceptions of an engineering student's electronic portfolio. Int. J. ePortoflio **8**(1), 57–71 (2018)
8. Jovanovic, V., Mize, M., Rodrigo, R., Verma, A.: Use of ePortfolio as integrated learning strategy in computer integrated manufacturing online course. In: 2016 ASEE Annual Conference and Exposition, pp. 1–12. ASEE, New Orleans. https://doi.org/10.18260/p.27116 (2016)
9. American Association of Colleges and Universities (AACU) and Hart Research Associates: It Takes More than a Major: Employer Priorities for College Learning and Student Success. Association of American Colleges and Universities, Washington, DC. https://www.aacu.org/sites/default/files/files/LEAP/2013_EmployerSurvey.pdf. Accessed 26 Jan 2020
10. Butler, P.: A Review of the Literature on Portfolios and Electronic Portfolios. eCDF ePortfolio Project, Palmerston North (2006)
11. Moores, A., Parks, M.: Twelve tips for introducing E-Portfolios with undergraduate students. Med. Teacher **32**(1), 46–49 (2010). https://doi.org/10.3109/01421590903444414451
12. Reese, M., Levy, R.: Assessing the future: E-Portfolio trends, uses and options in higher education (Research Bulletin). EDUCAUSE Centre for Applied Research, Boulder (2009)
13. Paulson, F., Paulson, P., Meyer, C.: What makes a portfolio a portfolio? Educ. Leadership **48**(5), 60–63 (1991)

14. Jisc(a): The e-portfolio implementation toolkit: Purposes for e-portfolios. https://epip.pbw orks.com/w/page/49130192/Purposes%20for%20e-portfolios. Accessed 15 Jan 2020

15. Händel, M., Wimmer, B., Ziegler, A.: E-portfolio use and its effects on exam performance – a field study. Stud. Higher Educ. **45**(2), 258–270 (2018). https://doi.org/10.1080/03075079. 2018.1510388

16. Kimball, M.: Database e-portfolio systems: a critical appraisal. Comput. Composition **22**(4), 434–458 (2005)

17. Mason, R., Pegler, C., Weller, M.: E-Portfolios: an assessment tool for online courses. British J. Educ. Technol. **35**(6), 717–727 (2004). https://doi.org/10.1111/j.1467-8535.2004.00429.x

18. Lorenzo, G., Ittelson, J.: An overview of e-portfolios. Educause Learning Initiative, Louisville (2005)

19. Rayudu, R., Heinrich, E., Bhattacharya, M.: Introducing ePortfolios to computer science and engineering students: a new zealand experience. In: TENCON 2009 – 2009 IEEE Region 10 Conference, pp. 1-6. IEEE, Singapore (2009). https://doi.org/10.1109/tencon.2009.5396260

20. Clark, W., Adamson, J.: Assessment of an ePortfolio: developing a taxonomy to guide the grading and feedback for personal development planning. Practitioner Res. High. Educ. **3**(1), 43–51 (2009)

21. Kilgore, D., Sattler, B., Turns, J.: From fragmentation to continuity: engineering students making sense of experience through the development of a professional portfolio. Stud. Higher Educ. **38**(6), 807–826 (2012). https://doi.org/10.1080/03075079.2011.610501

22. Rhodes, T., Chen, H., Watson, C., Garrison, W.: Editorial: a call for more rigorous ePortfolio research. International Journal of ePortfolio **4**(1), 1–5 (2014)

23. Bryant, H., Chittum, J.: ePortfolio effectiveness: A(n Ill-fated) search for empirical support. Int. J. ePortfolio **3**(2), 189–198 (2013)

24. University of British Columbia Office of Learning Technology. http://etec.ctlt.ubc.ca/510 wiki/Electronic_Portfolio_Uses_and_Content. Accessed 21 Jan 2020

25. Wakimoto, D., Lewis, R.: Graduate student perceptions of eportfolios: used for reflection, development, and assessment. Internet High. Educ. **21**, 53–58 (2014). https://doi.org/10.1016/j.iheduc.2014.01.002

26. Jisc(b): The e-portfolio implementation toolkit: Why should we use e-portfolios?, https://epip. pbworks.com/w/page/44803388/Why%20should%20we%20use%20e-portfolios. Accessed 15 Jan 2020

27. Jwaifell, M.: A proposed model for electronic portfolio to increase both validating skills and employability. Procedia – Soc. Behav. Sci. **103**, 356–364 (2013)

28. Quality and Curriculum Authority (QCA): e-Assessment: Guide to Effective Practice. QCA, London (2007). https://www.e-assessment.com/wp-content/uploads/2014/08/e-assess ment_-_guide_to_effective_practice_full_version.pdf. Accessed 18 Jan 2020

29. Chng, S.: Incorporating reflection into computing classes: models and challenges. Reflective Practice **19**(3), 358–375 (2018). https://doi.org/10.1080/14623943.2018.1479686

30. Information Commissioner's Office: Guide to Data Protection. https://ico.org.uk/for-organi sations/guide-to-data-protection/. Accessed 04 Apr 2020

31. Information Commissioner's Office: Principle on Storage Limitation. https://ico.org.uk/ for-organisations/guide-to-data-protection/guide-to-the-general-data-protection-regulation-gdpr/principles/storage-limitation/. Accessed 04 Apr 2020

32. Information Commissioner's Office: Principle on Purpose Limitation. https://ico.org.uk/ for-organisations/guide-to-data-protection/guide-to-the-general-data-protection-regulation-gdpr/principles/purpose-limitation/. Accessed 04 Apr 2020

33. Wuetherick, B., Dickinson, J.: Why ePortfolios? student perceptions of ePortfolio use in continuing education learning environments. Int. J. ePortfolio **5**(1), 39–53 (2015)

34. Jisc(c): Exemplars taster of e-portfolio use. https://epip.pbworks.com/w/page/40459056/Exe mplars%20taster%20of%20e-portfolio%20use. Accessed 15 Apr 2020

35. Aluko-Daniels, O., Olaniyi, N.: Outcome based assessments: essential ingredients. J. Assessment, Learn. Teach. Int. Educ. **1**(1), 111–128 (2019). https://doi.org/10.34255/jaltie.v1i 1.25

36. Baume, D.: A briefing on assessment of portfolios. learning and teaching support network, New York (2001). https://blogs.shu.ac.uk/teaching/files/2016/09/No6abriefingontheassessm entofportfolios_6_.pdf. Accessed 18 Jan 2020

37. Egan, A.: Improving Academic Integrity through Assessment Design. Dublin City University National Institute for Digital Learning (NIDL), Dublin (2018)

38. Strivens, J.: Efficient Assessment of Portfolios: A Report. Advance HE, New York (2006)

39. Contreras-Higuera, W., Martínez-Olmo, F., Rubio-Hurtado, M., Vilà-Baños, R.: University students' perceptions of e-portfolios as combined assessment tools in education courses. J. Educ. Comput. Res. **54**(1), 85–107 (2016). https://doi.org/10.1177/0735633115612784

40. Strivens, J., Baume, D., Owen, C., Grant, S., Ward, R., Nicol, D.: The Role of e-portfolios in formative and summative assessment practices: Report of the Jisc-Funded Study (2009)

41. Klenowski, V., Askew, S., Carnell, E.: Portfolios for learning, assessment and professional development in higher education. Assessment Eval. High. Educ. **34**(3), 267–286 (2007). https://doi.org/10.1080/02602930500352816

42. Cheng, G., Chau, J.: Exploring the relationship between students' self-regulated learning ability and their ePortfolio achievement. Internet High. Educ. **17**, 9–15 (2013)

43. Cain, A.: Developing assessment criteria for portfolio assessed introductory programming. In: Proceedings of 2013 IEEE International Conference on Teaching, Assessment and Learning for Engineering (TALE), pp. 55–60. IEEE, Bali (2013). https://doi.org/10.1109/tale.2013.665 4399

44. Ritzhaupt, A., Singh, A.: Student perspectives of ePortfolios in computing education. In: Proceedings of the 47st Annual Southeast Regional Conference, pp. 152–157. ACM-SE, Melbourne, Florida, USA (2006). https://doi.org/10.1145/1185448.1185483

45. Beresford, W., Cobham, D.: Undergraduate students: interactive, online experiences and ePortfolio development. In: IEEE 3rd International Conference on Communication Software and Networks (ICCSN), pp. 272–275. IEEE, Xi'an, China (2011). https://doi.org/10.1109/ iccsn.2011.6013825

46. Cain, A., Woodward, C.: Toward constructive alignment with portfolio assessment for introductory programming. In: Proceedings of IEEE International Conference on Teaching, Assessment, and Learning for Engineering (TALE), pp. H1B-11-H1B-17. IEEE, Hong Kong (2012). https://doi.org/10.1109/tale.2012.6360322

47. Kolb, D.: Experiential Learning: Experience as the Source of Learning and Development. Prentice-Hill, London (1984)

48. Feliciano, J., Storey, M., Zagalsky, A.: Student experiences using GitHub in software engineering courses; a case study. In: 2016 IEEE/ACM 38th International Conference on Software Engineering Companion (ICSE-C), pp. 422–431. IEEE, Austin, USA (2016)

49. College of Charleston Library Guides. https://libguides.library.cofc.edu/c.php?g=865405& p=6207696. Accessed 20 Jan 2020

50. The Open University Help Centre. https://help.open.ac.uk/create-a-professional-portfolio-for-when-you-are-applying-for-jobs. Accessed 06 Feb 2020

51. University of Waterloo Writing and Communication Centre. https://uwaterloo.ca/writing-and-communication-centre/resources-eportfolios-purpose-composition. Accessed 06 Feb 2020

52. QAA Characteristics Statement: Master's Degree. https://www.qaa.ac.uk/docs/qaa/quality-code/master's-degree-characteristics-statement.pdf?sfvrsn=6ca2f981_10. Accessed 21 Jan 2020

53. Rovai, A., Downey, J.: Why some distance education programs fail while others succeed in a global environment. Internet High. Educ. **13**(3), 141–147 (2010)

Design for Medical Simulation: Guidelines and Visioning for a New Model of Education

Stefania Palmieri(✉), Mario Bisson, Martino Zinzone, and Alessandro Ianniello

Politecnico di Milano, 20153 Milan, Italy
{stefania.palmieri,mario.bisson,martino.zinzone,
alessandro.ianniello}@polimi.it

Abstract. In complex design contexts, which require horizontal management of vertical knowledge, design is taking on roles increasingly distant from those that originally distinguished it. Strategic visions and methodologies conceive the figure of the designer as a mediator between actors and knowledge with highly different background and great intercommunication and design difficulties; and as a catalyst for the processes around innovation.

This paper was born from first research, contextualized to the present, which focused on the development of guidelines for the creation of tools and environments, in order to improve the simulation techniques used to provide training to medical professionals and students, that act in contexts of urgency and emergency.

Having defined the design direction to follow in the aforementioned research, it is necessary to go for a visioning operation projecting the medical simulation in the near future (2030), where the scientific and technological progress allows to hypothesize a remarkable innovation in the system already proposed. This process is fundamental in order to anticipate and propose innovative ways to use innovative technologies.

This research is developed by an open-source and cooperative network composed of SIMNOVA, a medical simulation center based in Novara, LogosNet, a company that works in the field of virtual reality and the Design Department of the Politecnico di Milano with its project and management skills, with the aim of creating tools and guidelines for a new model of medical education.

Keywords: Medical training · Medical simulation · Extended reality · Next internet generation · Integrated design

1 Introduction

Starting from previous studies and research [1, 2], the following discussion will define a new standard for medical simulation, contextualising the reference scenario in the near future, carrying out a foresighting operation.

The simulation in 2025 will allow a full and multisensorial immersion. This will be possible thanks to studies in progress to date: relating to haptic perception[1], which will

---

[1] It is the process of recognizing objects through touch.

© ICST Institute for Computer Sciences, Social Informatics and Telecommunications Engineering 2020
Published by Springer Nature Switzerland AG 2020. All Rights Reserved
M. H. Miraz et al. (Eds.): iCETiC 2020, LNICST 332, pp. 278–287, 2020.
https://doi.org/10.1007/978-3-030-60036-5_20

therefore allow to return tactile feedback, still not perfectly achieved with the instruments currently available; neuroscientific studies and the creation of neurodevices that will help users to create an interaction with analogical and digital machines[2], developing not static scenarios, editable in real time by the ones who are monitoring the operations, and therefore highly useful for training problem solving skills. Most likely any form of analog tool will disappear, as can be the dummies[3], replaced by purely digital elements.

A focal feature will be the access to the tools, which will become fundamental for training in every medical branches: if the tools used will be available for a large number of people, progress in managing emergency situations will be global and very fast.

Another important goal will be the coding of a normative that everyone will have to follow in order to perform with high efficiency; this will be possible through the understanding of the movements and actions that are done by the users and through the analysis of the data obtained, in order to identify the correct practices to be performed, depending on the kind of emergency that teams have to deal with.

2 Strategic Role in Innovation

Nowadays designers are increasingly called upon to design solutions that derive from careful and multidisciplinary research, which is, therefore, capable of integrating and translating the needs that come from the various areas involve [3].

In this regard Mozota [4] defines four fundamental design behaviors, the characteristics that create value to the act of design itself. Not only in the research field, but even in the strategic and management field it is recognized this value to design.

Some authors clarify the importance of the involvement of external stakeholders, who they call performers, whose aim is to ignite disruptive innovation [5]. Manzini [6] states that Design can bring on different skills in a context of co-design, both as an activator of the innovation process and as a facilitator of co-creation activities.

In the literature of the sector it is repeatedly emphasized that the value of Design is fundamental to innovate sectors other than the reference one: for example, companies and organizations that have been able to use typical design tools to innovate their business sectors [7, 8].

This paragraph show the strategic design characteristics, aims and methodology, highlighting its central role as a catalyzer of the design process in a field of complex and multidisciplinary projects, where every actors have peculiar skills and languages, allowing the best exchange of information within the co-planning network established.

---

[2] Artificial intelligence studies whether and how the most complex mental processes can be reproduced through the use of a computer. This research develops along two complementary paths: on the one hand the a.i. tries to bring the functioning of computers closer to the capabilities of human intelligence, on the other hand it uses computer simulations to make assumptions about the mechanisms used by the human mind.

[3] Mannequins are simulators used for training methods in the medical field. They are capable of reproducing physiological behaviors and reactions of the human body. The most performing are equipped with software to modify certain vital parameters and reactions, based on the type of scenario that will be simulated.

3 Medical Simulation Today

Simulation can be defined as a technique or method for artificially reproducing the conditions of a phenomenon. The fundamental characteristic of the simulation is therefore that of being able to verify in real time the consequences of the actions of the subjects. The training simulations are designed to teach subjects the fundamental elements of a system, observing the results of the actions or decisions made, through a feedback process generated by the simulation itself [9].

The simulation-based teaching methodology is the most engaging among the active methodologies, since it requires subjects to recite firsthand the management of phenomena and/or complex relationships [10].

The active methodology is a didactic method, deepened in the pedagogical and formative field, which consists in presenting the contents of the teaching as concrete problems to be solved, providing the learner with all the information and means necessary to manage the situation.

It is based on the principle of learning by doing and experimenting with situations or activities that stimulate the reflection of both the individual and the group. It is therefore a process based on interaction with the group through a continuous exchange of outputs and feedback [11].

The simulation, therefore, creates a protected environment, within which it is possible to learn and teach using errors as resources for action; it also involves sensory perceptions, like all the situations regarding psycho-bodily involvement [12].

For this reasons the simulation became a useful and established technique both for teaching and for the training of those professions in which continuous training is required to enhance the awareness that the mistakes made can result in loss of life or cause serious damage to organizations [13].

The Johns Hopkins Medicine Simulation Center[4] represents one of the excellence among the simulation centers for the health professions, incorporating within its spaces five different types of activity: standardized patient, practice on human simulator, virtual reality, management practice, computer simulation.

These centers are set up with different equipment and tools, determined by the type of simulation that has to be performed: clinical, extra-clinical or managerial. High fidelity and medium fidelity human simulators, capable of simulating physical and physiological reactions, thanks to the use of interactive software, are fundamental: they can open and close the eyes, breath expanding the ribcage, they can be auscultated in different parts of the body, have veins in which drugs can be injected, offer the possibility to change organs (male or female) and they can speak.

Virtual scenario simulators, with which learners can train soft skills and management skills, especially in the context of maxi-emergencies, are also used within this center,

---

[4] The medical simulation center of the Johns Hopkins University in Baltimore, Maryland is a fully accredited state-of-the-art medical training facility, whose aim is to improve safety within patient care. Current and future health care professionals "practice on plastic" honing their skills, refining advanced techniques and learning valuable social interactive tools for delivering important news to patients. Homepage: https://www.hopkinsmedicine.org/simulation_center Last access 15 March 2020.

and every clinical instruments useful for the rescue, surgery or other type of hospital practice, can be also found within it.

4 SIMNOVA

The Interdepartmental Center for Innovative Education and Simulation in Medicine and Health Professions (SIMNOVA)[5] is established to carry out higher education, research and service activities within the medicine area, showing strong attention to simulation techniques as tools to create innovative educational training, in order to improve the abilities of every professionals in delivering cares, reducing clinical risk and increasing patient safety.

It was design in order to erogate training through the use of immersive scenarios, which are able to reproduce the typical environments in which the different actions of the medical processess take place, and where students and professionals can deal with the typical practices that they will have to perform during the real operations and rescues.

The human simulators are the tools used in order to simulate the real patients. Different kind of mannequins exist, which can be used for different types of training, and in regard of the procedures that have to be performed. The simulators can imitate the physical and physiological characteristics of the human body, they can give feedbacks when stimulated, and they can undergo surgical operations, all through a dedicated software.

In 2017 SIMNOVA started to collaborate with LogosNet[6], a company that delivers services based on the use of virtual and augmented realities system. The collaboration led to the creation of a multisensorial and immersive environment, inside SIMNOVA's spaces, which is composed of three rooms and where the training activities can be carried out.

5 Enabling Technologies

Nowadays we can talk about three different types of technological realities: virtual reality, augmented reality and mixed reality. Virtual reality represents a simulated space, thanks to various technologies and techniques, which create scenarios where the users are capable of performing actions and receiving feedbacks and information from it. Who lives this kind of experience can look around, move and interact with the features or objects present within the scene.

Watching its state of art, both in terms of applied research and development, it is clear that virtual reality is capable of creating high immersive environments, but it is also true that, compared to augmented and mixed realities it presents higher system complexity and costs.

Augmented reality is the overlapping of digital elements on the real spaces and objects, which can be increased or modified, through the use of software-based technologies [14]. It is designed with a simpler system because it generates images or data on the real environment without the need of creating it.

---

[5] SIMNOVA homepage: https://www.simnova.unipo.it Last accessed 15 March 2020.
[6] LogosNet homepage: https://www.logosnet.org Last access 15 March 2020.

However, the possibility of generating immersive scenarios are reduced, because the "feature" of the real environment can't be changed.

Mixed reality creates a new environment and a new visualization, thanks to the coexistence of both physical and digital contents, which are able to interact with themselves in real time. It is the most recent and innovative technology in this field of application [15].

It can be seen as an evolution of augmented reality, and, in fact, it has the same advantages of it compared to virtual reality, but it is still in development, so it has a lower reliability. In the near future it can for sure become the best technology to design this kind of immersive environments, but, in the present, the best choice should be the virtual reality.

The Internet of Things can be seen as an implementation of the Web [16]: objects become smart and are able to communicate data and informations with each other. The aim of the Internet of things is to create a digital picture of the phenomenal world, by electronically identify objects, places and people in the spaces.

MEMS is the acronym of Micro Electro-Mechanical Systems, which are produced by microfabrication. They can vary from simple or really complex systems. They can be used to monitor and control different environmental features.

The integration of the aforementioned technology within the simulated training tools system, can be for sure helpful in achieving the goal of designing a behavioural and performative regulation which should be used to create a common normative regarding the medical practices. The challenges that this integration brings on will regard the level of reality achieved through the extend realities and the capability of sensorial stimulations.

6   Design Guidelines for the Present

The goal is to develop different tool-kits to design a highly performing simulation center, given the technological development in different fields.

In a first phase of research different contributes have been taken into account. The first proposed concept was designed to satisfy the request of the professional in the field of medicine, but it did not seem to meet the demand.

The main highlighted issue after this first phase was the necessity for shifting from user needs to system needs: the designed model must, therefore, be accessible, exportable and reproducible, in order to implement an open net, based on principles of democracy, defined by the designed guidelines.

The simulation room is the centerpiece of the space, the environment where training simulation activities take place, following the learning by doing methodology, through the use different tools.

Through the integration of different types of technologies and software, and the simulation of scenarios in immersive multisensorial environments, hard and soft skills can be learnt and trained.

The environment must achieve different request, so that the training is truly efficient and educational. It should permit a practice that is as similar as possible to the actual rescue operations to be carried out in the field.

The simulation of both simple and complex scenarios must be possible, through the integration of digital and physical features, to allow learners to train on a large number of cases and, for this reason, it must also be easily reconfigurable in based on simulation needs.

The activities and practices which take place internally must be controlled and analyzed, in order to obtain a high quantity of data which, once analyzed, will let to understand which are the best practices, or to that set of rules and actions to be performed to ensure that rescue operations can be extremely effective [17].

Finally, this space must be connected to the other rooms, through an IoT system, in order to automatize the control of some features of the it and obtain real-time data from them [18].

The highly immersive simulation room -white room- measures nine square meters of surface, has three continuously painted white walls and is divided from the control room through a surface which lets instructors to supervise the practice without being seen. The dimension of the room is optimized for the practice of 3–5 people.

Different solution packages can be installed in the room; for the moment the implemented ones are "basic simulation", "medical simulation", "environmental simulation" and "tracking".

The control room, an environment is deeply needed by the instructors in order to supervise the team work during the simulation session, and to defined an objective methodology of training based on the data acquired.

The control room measures six square meters. The space must, like the previous one, respect certain standards, in order transmit with efficiency the notions.

It must allow observing what is happening in the simulation room, in order to avoid possible errors due to performance anxiety disorders.

Collection of different kind data from the sessions must be possible in order to be analyzed and used to generate standard action protocols.

It must allow the placing and management of elements in the scenario to increase the degree of difficulty of the simulations and allow more effective learning of hard and soft skills.

Given the possibility of changing the environmental parameters of the simulation room, the control room must allow observation and monitoring of the status of the first, in order to be able to act quickly in the event of malfunctions.

It must allow direct communication with the simulation room and the supervision of the checklists of actions and objectives by scenario, so that the progress of the training session is immediately clear to the instructors. Finally, it must be connected to the other environments of the space, through an IoT system.

Every package is made of different objects and devices, so in the control room there will be present the ones that manage and control the installed in the simulation room.

The debriefing space is the room where the learners and supervisors will talk about the practice, watching the recordings and trying to share thoughts about the results achieved, the errors performed and other important issues.

The requirements that the room must satisfy, in order for the practice to really have an instructive-didactic effect, are being a comfortable environment, which facilitates sharing and constructive discussion, a fundamental element for understanding the mistakes made and therefore being able to improve.

It must allow another two other teams who are not practicing to attend the simulation session in progress, as observing a busy team can have the same value as being those who are training.

It must allow viewing of the session just ended, so that practitioners can personally see where and when they have demonstrated gaps or strengths.

It must provide interactive tools for the activities carried out within it and didactic tutorials related to the errors committed, useful for a better management of the teaching practice. Like other environments, it must be connected to them, via an IoT system. The room is nine square meters and is set up to let inside up to 14 people. It can be used as a white room.

After the creation of the first Center it will be possible to build up the horizontal network. Through the network and its tools it will be possible to let information, scenarios and data flow inside it and to monitor the different practices. This will allow the implementation of guidelines which must be innovative, but unambiguous.

During the 2018 it was activated an Interdepartmental Center within the Politecnico di Milano, which has the goal of nurturing innovation in the field of simulation. It was created by the Department of Design, by the Department of Chemical Engineering and Materials, by the Department of Electronics Engineering and the Department of Mechanical Engineering, SIMNOVA and LogosNet.

7   Scientific Contamination

The mixed reality is undergoing a strong development and implementation, with major investments by IT and technology companies [19]. This suggests that well before 2025, given the exponential innovation curve, it could become the universal tool for simulation, given its great versatility. It will therefore become more usable, less invasive and more efficient than today's solutions. Neurosciences are disciplines that deal with conducting studies on the nervous system.

In particular, the most interesting areas for the project addressed are systemic neuroscience[7] [20], which investigate the anatomical and physiological functioning of neural systems, in order to understand the behavioral and sensory sphere; and, to a lesser extent, cognitive neuroscience[8].

Various studies are underway, aiming at understanding aspects such as perceptual integration, and how it can be influenced by external stimulations [21]; the generation of somatosensory feedback obtained in paraplegic patients, thanks to haptic devices, which allow the perception of the soil and virtual limbs [22]; the creation of visual feedback in blind patients, through sound and tactile patterns [23].

If we move from the theoretical, research and academic field, there are neurodevices on the market, such as Epoch and Insight, produced by Emotiv[9], which allow the user to

---

[7] The branches of neuroscience that study the functions of circuits and neural systems.

[8] A branch of neuroscience that studies the brain bases of thought, and allows to highlight the changes in the brain associated with the main evolutionary turning points.

[9] Emotiv homepage: https://www.emotiv.com Last access 25 March 2020.

monitor the brain activity in real time according to some parameters; to mentally control physical and virtual objects, making them move in real and virtual space; to carry out market surveys focused on personalization and user experience.

Another very interesting tool is Hiro III [24], a touch screen system, consisting of a robotic arm, which is able to simulate the touch of virtual objects, receiving feedback. The touch-screen uses a 3D display to generate the visual stimulus, while the physical hand is connected to the robotic hand, which returns texture, size and weight.

Observing the opportunities given by these worlds and knowledge, and projecting them to a ten-year development, it is clear that the visionary scenario that is opened up turns out to be a totally immersive simulated experience; it will be dynamic and therefore real, thinking about the neural devices that allow the users to imagine simulated scenarios that change in real time, based on the variables that will also influence the actual rescue operations.

8 Concept

The mission will be the excellent training of rescue teams, through increasingly advanced simulation techniques, and the constant updating of action protocols, through collaboration between the network actors and the sharing of useful data. An essential point will be to allow the simulation to any structures used for medical training, whether it is a hospital, a university, or a sort of traveling simulations, and, more generally, to any sector in which it may be necessary to resort to simulation techniques, both for training and for other purposes, obviously in line with ethical and moral principles.

The vision will be a totally immersive simulation experience, which will recreate the physical and mental conditions of the real experiences, involving all the user's senses. A simulation accessible to anyone will need to use this type of methodology, in an easy way in any context.

Going into detail of the concept conceived, it essentially consists of two different tools for interacting with the simulated elements; one dedicated to those who will carry out the simulation, another one for those who will supervise and manage it; and a device to generate the mixed reality, which must be transportable, in order to bring the simulation in as many environments as possible. The first object consists of two lenses, which will act as an interface between the mixed reality and the subject and will be active, managing to see what happens during the simulation and to feel the simulated elements, sending stimuli to an apparatus of miniaturized actuators on the body user. In this way he/she will be equipped with a sensory system dedicated to simulated reality, connected to the body itself and, therefore, in communication with it, through an artificial neural network.

The device designed for the trainers is a neuro-tool that will allow the user to dynamically modify the simulation, in order to make it more truthful, managing to recreate the evolution of a rescue operation, and to increase the level of difficulty for the simulators, inserting always different variables. It will also be able to collect and process sensitive data and to generate action protocols, based on the results obtained during the various simulations. The ergonomic and fruition improvements made, attributable to a highly immersive and adherent to reality experience, are understandable through the choice of using a set of non-invasive and much more functional tools. The development of a global and shared network of medical simulation could represent an important improvement for safety management, at least in the matter of interest, no longer fragmented and not univocal, but discussed, accepted and followed, in a global communion of intent.

9 Conclusions

The evolution and innovations are absolutely positive factors for the correct progress of the society, and therefore they are developed, in their first phases, in highly specific sectors, before going established and spread. The project addressed falls within these cases: the application is designed for the medical field, with a highly positive and functional purpose, which could allow this development to find possible applications in different fields. Unfortunately, once an innovation develops and spreads globally, the uses can be manifold, and could also include highly improper ones. The more disruptive the innovation is, the more serious the negative implication can be: by addressing issues related to neuroscience is fundamental to try to design also with an aim in limiting the possibility of improper uses. Going to design in such a specific context even if data collection operations are carried out, they are so peculiar and linked to the specific scenario, that they do not arouse ethical questions about this operation; however, if, as hypothesized on several occasions, the tool designed can be used in different sectors, the question about Big Data can become a topic of relevance to be addressed. There is absolutely no denying the enormous usefulness that massive data collection can have, as it can significantly improve different aspects of daily, social and economic life; however, precisely because huge quantities of data are processed and are accessible and usable by many subjects, it is necessary that the operations that can be performed on them are regulated by institutions.

There must also be structures capable of managing the acquisition, scanning and interpretation of these data, which must ensure the protection of the privacy of the people involved.

The visioning work, the design of the training system in 2030[10], is an increasingly necessary design operation, if someone wants to be able to achieve outputs that are truly valid, innovative and, therefore, long-lasting. Secondly, it is necessary to understand the essential nature of such a process: a founding brick of a design methodology, which tries to evaluate the present to solve typical and today's problems, and to anticipate needs and processes that can manifest themselves in a longer period of time.

References

1. Volontè, F., Ianniello, A., Bisson, M., Ingrassia, P.L.: La simulazione medica del futuro: un tentativo di visioning. J. Ital. Med. Educ. **75**, 3401–3406 (2017)
2. Bisson, M., Ianniello, A., Ingrassia, P.L.: Guidelines to set up a simulation center. In: III International Conference on Environmental Design 2019, MDA, vol. 3, pp. 485–490. Delettera WP (2019)

---

[10] We choose 2030 to give us the possibility to conceptualize some social and technological features of the project through the hypothesis of their innovation; also, we choose this year keeping in mind the contents of the "2030 agenda" by ONU.

3. Dorst, K., Cross, N.: Creativity in the design process: co-evolution of problem solution. Des. Stud. **22**(5), 425–437 (2001)
4. Mozota, B.B.: The four powers of design: a value model in design management. Des. Manag. Rev. **17**(2), 44–53 (2006)
5. Norman, D.A., Verganti, R.: Incremental and radical innovation: design research vs. technology and meaning change. Des. Issues **30**(1), 78–96 (2014)
6. Manzini, E.: Design When Everybody Designs. MIT Press, Cambridge (2015)
7. Martin, R.L.: The Design of Business: Why Design Thinking is the Next Competitive Advantage. Harvard Business Press, Boston (2009)
8. Yee, J., et al.: Transformations: 7 Roles to Drive Change by Design. BIS Publishers, Amsterdam (2017)
9. Aggarwal, R., et al.: Training and simulation for patient safety. Qual. Saf. Healthc. **19**(2), 34–43 (2010)
10. Schmidt, E., et al.: Simulation exercises as a patient safety strategy. Ann. Intern. Med. **158**(5.2), 426–432 (2013)
11. Ingrassia, P.L., et al.: Nationwide program for education for undergraduates in the field of disaster medicine: development of a core curriculum centred on blended learning and simulation tools. Prehosp. Disaster Med. **29**(5), 508–515 (2014)
12. McGaghie, W.C., et al.: A critical review of simulation-based medical education research. Med. Educ. **44**(1), 50–63 (2010)
13. Ziv, A., et al.: Simulation-based medical education: an ethical imperative. Acad. Med. **78**, 783–788 (2003)
14. Knaflewski, J.: 10 revolutionary augmented reality apps that you should know about (2019). https://dzone.com/articles/10-revolutionary-augmented-reality-apps-that-you-s. Accessed 25 Mar 2020
15. Watson, T.: What is mixed reality: examples and development features (2019). Web Article. https://skywell.software/blog/what-is-mixed-reality-examples-and-development-features/. Accessed 25 Mar 2020
16. Jayavardhana, G., et al.: Internet of things: a vision, architectural elements and future directions. Future Gener. Comput. Syst. **29**(7), 1645–1660 (2013)
17. Makary, M.A., Daniel, M.: Medical error: the third leading cause of death in the US. BMJ **353**, 2139–2145 (2016)
18. Amir, M.R., et al.: Exploiting smart e-Health gateways at the edge of healthcare Internet-of-Things: a fog computing approach. Future Gener. Comput. Syst. **78**(2), 641–658 (2018)
19. Bezegová, E., et al.: Virtual Reality and Its Potential in Europe. Ecorys, Bruxelles (2017)
20. Felten, D.L., et al.: Netter's Atlas of Neuroscience, 3rd edn. Elsevier, Amsterdam (2015)
21. Stonkus, R., et al.: Probing the causal role interregional synchrony for perceptual integration via tACS. Sci. Rep. **6**, 1–13 (2016)
22. Shokur, S., et al.: Assimilation of virtual legs and perception of floor texture by complete paraplegic patients receive artificial tactile feedback. Sci. Rep. **6b**, 1–14 (2016)
23. Stiles, N.R.B., Shimojo, S.: Auditory sensory substitution is intuitive and automatic with texture stimuli. Sci. Rep. **5**, 1–14 (2015)
24. Takahamura, E., et al.: Five-fingered haptic interface robot: HIRO III. IEEE Trans. Haptics **4**(1), 14–27 (2010)

Design and Implementation of an E-Notice Board Using a NodeMCU

Md. Bakhtiar Abid[1]([✉]), Mamunur Rashid Rumon[1], Tasnuba Sraboni[1],
Romaiya Hossain[1], Farah Ahmed[1], and Jia Uddin[2]

[1] CSE Department, BRAC University, 66 Mohakhali, Dhaka, Bangladesh
abid.bu16@gmail.com, mamunurrumon@gmail.com,
tasnuba.sraboni97@gmail.com, romaiyahossain@gmail.com,
amifarah2016@gmail.com
[2] Technology Studies, Endicott College, Woosong University, Daejeon, South Korea
jia.uddin@wsu.ac.kr

Abstract. Notice board is the most consistent and main appliances in every university, school, or public place location such as bus stations, train stations, parks. But fixing and updating specific instructions on every day is a difficult operation. Wireless electronic notice boards are a faster alternative to conventional pin-up type notice boards. The main goal of this project is to design a wireless notice board to displays notifications that are received from a smartphone user. In this paper, the development of a simple and low-cost Android-based wireless notice board is presented. A prism-shaped device, having a portable circuit inside and an LCD outside is a solution for displaying any messages or notices immediately. A user can type a message in the app and the message will be displayed on the notice board instantly. It is a convenient substitute for a traditional noticeboard where written papers are pinned on the board. Other than institutional purposes, the same technology can be used in traffic signals, railway stations, bus stands, shopping malls, and in every public place where people can get messages or emergency alerts. The wireless notice board display is configured using NodeMCU, 16 × 02 LCD Display, I2C Adapter for 16 × 02 LCD Display, Buzzer, Mini Breadboard, Jumper Wires, and PVC Boards. As the electronic notice board is wireless so it minimizes the hassles of wires as well as it is very easy to operate and consumes less power.

Keywords: Node-MCU · LCD display · I2C adapter · Android application

1 Introduction

Over the past few years, wireless technology has tremendous progress in every sector. As a means of communication, notice boards can be widely used in schools, colleges, universities, hospitals to major organizations [1]. Wireless notice boards tackle the global problem of deforestation by conveying messages at large without the use of paper. The notice boards we usually see are fixed and to convey a message it needs the involvement

M. H. Miraz et al. (Eds.): iCETiC 2020, LNICST 332, pp. 288–295, 2020.
https://doi.org/10.1007/978-3-030-60036-5_21

of some additional people to do tasks like printing it in the paper, distributing those papers, and attaching them on the board. So, it requires more effort as well as in case of emergency manual notice board is time-consuming and it also takes more space where we hang the notice. To minimize the complexity, a wireless notice board display is proposed which can instantly display any message or alert sent by a user without having the assist of any additional people [2]. The main objective of this system is to make it as simple and convenient as possible for the user to access and update notice from anywhere and also save paper. In this paper, wireless display technology is used to make the notice board portable and this important task is getting done by I2C Adapter. The NodeMCU is programmed to receive the message coming from the app and display it. And the buzzer is connected so that the user gets the confirmation when the NodeMCU receives a message. All the components are assembled in such a way that the code makes them work as a smartboard.

The other parts of the paper are organized as follows: Sect. 2 contains the literature review and comparison between some relevant works, Sect. 3 illustrates the general idea of the proposed model and how does it work. Experimental setup and result analysis are shown in Sect. 4. And finally, Sect. 5 concludes the paper.

2 Literature Review

Notice boards are one of the widely used ones ranging from primary schools to major organizations to convey messages at large. If we want to share some information or emergency alert to people in that case notice board is very effective but for that notice, a lot of paper is being used and which is later wasted by the organizations [3]. The process leads to a lot of deforestation thus leading to global warming [4]. The elderly system conveying the important message in the notice board needs a burdensome number of attempts to transport information if the school, college, universities, and other institutions are distance-separated. Moreover, this method is defined as the dependable responsibility for myriad staff to deliver the notification system which is determining as converse to the one centralized heading system. Adhering different notices every day is a troublesome procedure. To keep away from a large portion of these disadvantages of this regular strategy, a lot of ways to deal with digitize the techniques have just been proposed and actualized such as Liquid Crystal Displays (LCD) and Light Emitting Diode (LED) screens spreading over a specific area. A couple of the pre-existing techniques incorporate the utilization of Global System for Mobile Communication (GSM) network systems with smaller scale microcontrollers, for example, ATmega32 [5], GSM modem [6] with Short Messaging Service (SMS) for notice information and microcontrollers, for example, ARM-LPC2148 attached with visual representations [7]. The structure proposed by Darshankumar C. Dalwadi et al. [5] and Yash Teckchandani et al. [6] either figure out how to show a solitary notification message at a given time or just fit for sees which are just textual in nature with a 160-character limit requirement forced by Short Messaging Service (SMS) technique utilized for notice generation. As referenced in Yash Teckchandani *et al.* [6], the technique utilized by Nivetha S. R. *et al.* [7] utilizes a 16 × 2-character LCD which has a permeability disservice as the viewers required to close to the screen to peruse the notification data being shown on the screen. All the above suggested and actualized systems have some pivotal disadvantages or are not attainable in application with regards to genuine execution. In that case, the implementation of this project can bring enormous change on the environmental issues as well as improving by utilizing technology. To implement this project NodeMCU and an android application are must require connected via web server [8].

Various types of notice boards are used in various institutes to display notices and these boards are managed manually. It is a long process to put up notices on the notice board. This wastes a lot of resources like paper, printer ink, manpower, and also loss of time [9]. Other notice boards are LED indicators used at railway stations for displaying the information of arriving trains. But LEDs are currently more expensive and require heat sinking for a long life. Some other types of notice boards are notice displayed in buses and malls using an LCD screen. These notices are previously feed in the memory of the displaying unit and the notice cannot be changed easily and it is time-consuming process [10].

To overcome the limitations of the state of art models, in this project LCD display is used which is cheaper than an LED indicator as well as saves our valuable time because it can also be changed anytime when the important message is needed to show in the display.

3   Proposed Model

The following sub-sections represents the different components associated with the proposed model.

3.1   Components

In this project, the entire model is based on the NodeMCU with each component placed meticulously on the breadboard. NodeMCU is chosen because of its main properties ideal for this project - simple, low cost, and programmable. Its work similar to Arduino and also is Wi-Fi enabled which is best for the IoT application process [13, 14]. I2C adapter is required to connect NodeMCU with the LCD display. NodeMCU uses 4 pins to connect with the display. We are using a 16×2 LCD to display the notice. The basic LCD requires 3 control lines as well as 4 or 8 I/O lines for the data bus. The user may select whether the LCD is to operate with a 4-bit data bus or an 8-bit data bus. This LCD is sufficient to display. But we can connect JUMBO LCD also. A buzzer is used to notify the user whether notice is sent to display or not. Figure 1 shows the block diagram for this model.

3.2   Circuit Details

A simple block model has been used in the project. In this model, we have to connect the NodeMCU with a power supply. This power can be supplied by any power source. After connecting the NodeMCU with the power supply, NodeMCU will show a message that input an IP address. To input an IP address, we have to connect the NodeMCU with a hotspot. After connecting the NodeMCU with the hotspot there will be an IP address screening on the NodeMCU. Figure 2 shows the circuit diagram for this model.

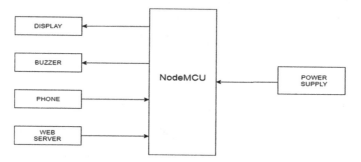

Fig. 1. Block diagram of proposed architecture

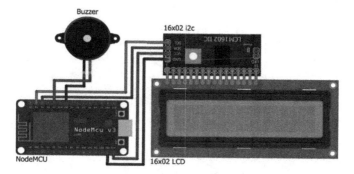

Fig. 2. Circuit diagram of proposed architecture

3.3 Working Principle

Firstly, initializing the NodeMCU as well as webserver and app by supplying power the display will show an unset IP address. By creating a personal hotspot, the NodeMCU will receive the established connection and showing an IP address on the display. However, often using multiple access from different persons from the different connection of phones, laptops, and other devices this must be connected to the same personal hotspot to show the convey a message. After doing this, there is also an app that is used for making the connection between a NodeMCU and a phone. After connecting the phone with the following IP address, the phone will be directly connected to the android app. By using this android app, we can write a notice and it will directly go to the NodeMCU.

Whenever NodeMCU receives a notice, the buzzer will give a beep sound, and a notification message will be shown on the display. If there is a problem between connecting an android and following IP address which means no matching for both IP addresses showing in the NodeMCU and the app the message will not be shown in the display. In that case, the procedure must be restarted to assemble the whole process to work again with principles as well. Figure 3 shows the working principle for this model.

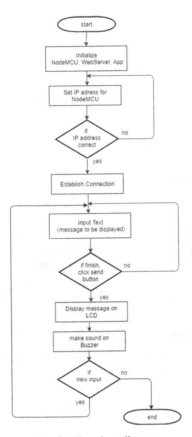

Fig. 3. Flowchart diagram

4   Experimental Setup and Result Analysis

In this project, we are going to send the data in the 16 × 02 LCD Display without using any wire. The list of the components is NodeMCU esp8266, I2C Adapter for 16 × 02 LCD Display, 16 × 02 LCD Display, Mini Breadboard, Jumper Wires, PVC Board, Buzzer [11, 12]. NodeMCU esp8266 Wi-Fi model it works as a server in this project. By using its driver port 16 × 02 LCD Display shows the data has sent. Firstly, we set the GND of I2C Adapter to GND of NodeMCU esp8266. After that, we set the VCC of I2C Adapter to Vin of NodeMCU esp8266. Then the SDA of I2C Adapter set to D2 of NodeMCU esp8266 and SCL of I2C Adapter set to D1 of NodeMCU esp8266. Another GND and D4 of NodeMCU esp8266 set to Buzzer. Lastly, we have to connect a 1-16 pin of I2C Adapter with a 16 × 02 LCD Display. The model is now capable of display any notice through the proper use and changes in code and application. Figure 4 shows some samples of the experimental circuit setup and the final device of this model.

After all the circuit construction we have given some sample input for analyzing the result. Table 1 presents the experimental result of our project. Table 1 shows the action done by the mobile application to the notice board via a web server. Initially, the IP was

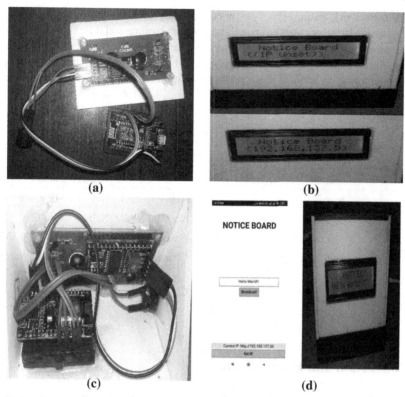

Fig. 4. Step by step detailed implementation of the project (a) circuit implementation, (b) display IP address, (c) architecture implementation, (d) GUI of the project.

not set. So, the notice board was not connected. When we have connected the device to the notice board, we have ensured by testing that if we give the wrong IP address then the device will be connected to the Notice Board. After setting the connection we input some text in the device as a sample message and we have checked that our project worked fine and display the message to the notice board that we want. For developing this software that is being used in this project, we followed the software development cycle. First, we find out every functional and non-functional requirement such as the client will have the option to compose notice in the wake of associating with the IP address, User Interface is easy to use but the framework will have various clients, etc. Second, we developed a detailed specification of the software like how the application will connect to the hardware, and so on. Third, we use an agile method to design and develop the software. Fundamentally we concentrated more on coding than structuring, attempt to decrease overheads in the product procedure and react rapidly to change the necessities. Fourth, we use the MIT app inventor to design the application. Fifth, we performed testing for assuring the quality of the application. For, functional we performed unit testing and system testing. We have detached each piece of the product and indicated that each part is associated. After that, we performed testing the entire programming which is a piece of framework testing. For, non-functional we performed performance testing. In performance testing, we checked speed, capacity, scalability, stability. But we have some limitations in our project. Be that as it may, we have a few restrictions on our task. At this moment by utilizing this undertaking we can't pass numerous notifications at once. We are attempting to address these restrictions and make this undertaking stunningly better.

Table 1. Analysis of the operation for different signals

Experiment no.	Web server IP address	Given IP address	Operation	Given message	Display of notice board
1	Null	Null	Not connected	Null	IP unset
2	192.168.43.73	192.168.10.19	Not connected	Null	Null
3	192.168.137.5	192.168.137.5	Connected		192.168.137.5
4	192.168.137.5	192.168.137.5	Connected	Hello World!!!	Hello World!!!
5	192.168.43.73	192.168.43.73	Connected	Testing	Testing

5 Conclusion and Future Scope

In this modern era of technology is helping us to reduce human work. The proposed project can decrease the workload and human dependency. It is proposed to design a display toolkit that can be used from an authorized app. The display boards are one of the most important media for transferring information to the maximum number of end-users. With the advancement in technology, the display board systems are migrating from normal hand-written displays to the digital display. A user can send a message from anywhere in the world. Being a user-friendly, long-range, and speedy means of conveying information are major characteristics of this system. The system is basic, low cost and it is easy to use that interacts directly with expected users. The program can be used in various applications such as the banking sector, colleges, and restaurants, offices, hospitals, sports scoreboards, etc. The voice calling that calls. The suggested framework could be incorporated as a further option for improved usage of the network system in train, airport, or bus stations.

References

1. Bento, A.C.: IoT: NodeMCU 12e X Arduino Uno, results of an experimental and comparative survey. Int. J. **6**(1), 1–12 (2018)
2. Ilha, P., Schiesari, L., Yanagawa, F.I., Jankowski, K., Navas, C.A.: Deforestation and stream warming affect body size of Amazonian fishes. PloS One **13**(5), 1–20 (2018)
3. http://www.forbes.com/sites/kateharrison/2018/08/27/cant-go-paperless-try-this-paper-light-approach-and-save-a-fortune

4. Kashyap, M., Sharma, V., Gupta, N.: Taking MQTT and NodeMCU to IOT: communication in internet of things. Proc. Comput. Sci. **132**, 1611–1618 (2018)
5. Dalwadi, D.C., Trivedi, N., Kasundra, A.: Wireless notice board our real-time solution. In: National Conference on Recent Trends in Engineering and Technology (2011)
6. Teckchandani, Y., Perumal, G.S., Mujumdar, R., Lokanathan, S.: Large screen wireless notice display system. In: 2015 IEEE International Conference on Computational Intelligence and Computing Research (ICCIC), pp. 1–5. IEEE (2015)
7. Nivetha, S.R., Pujitha, R., Preethi, S., Yashvanthini, S.M.: SMS based wireless notice board with monitoring system. Int. J. Adv. Electr. Electron. Eng. **2**(3), 58–62 (2013)
8. Meenachi, A., Kowsalya, S., Kumar, P.P.: Wireless E-Notice board using wi-fi and bluetooth technology. J. Netw. Commun. Emerg. Technol. (JNCET) **6**(4), 14–20 (2016)
9. Merai, B., Jain, R., Mishra, R.: Smart notice board. Int. J. Adv. Res. Comput. Commun. Eng. **4**(4), 105–107 (2015)
10. Reddy, G.G.: IoT Based Real Time Digital Led Notification Display Board using Node MCU via Telegram Messenger App (2018)
11. Ling, Z., et al.: Review on thermal management systems using phase change materials for electronic components, Li-ion batteries and photovoltaic modules. Renew. Sustain. Energy Rev. **31**, 427–438 (2014)
12. Khera, N., Shukla, D., Awasthi, S.: Development of simple and low-cost Android based wireless notice board. In: 2016 5th International Conference on Reliability, Infocom Technologies and Optimization (Trends and Future Directions) (ICRITO), pp. 630–633 (2016)
13. Rahman, A., Rahman, T., Ghani, N.H., Hossain, S., Uddin, J.: IoT based patient monitoring system using ECG sensor. In: 2019 International Conference on Robotics, Electrical and Signal Processing Techniques (ICREST), Dhaka, Bangladesh, pp. 378–382 (2019)
14. Alam, A.I., Rahman, M., Afroz, S., Alam, M., Uddin, J., Alam, M.A.: IoT enabled smart bicycle safety system. In: 2018 Joint 7th International Conference on Informatics, Electronics & Vision (ICIEV) and 2018 2nd International Conference on Imaging, Vision & Pattern Recognition (icIVPR), Kitakyushu, Japan, pp. 374–378 (2018)

A Study of the Impacts of Technological Innovations on Cooperation Cases

Martin Holubčik, Oliver Bubelíny[(⊠)], and Milan Kubina

Faculty of Management Science and Informatics, University of Zilina, Univerzitna 8215/1,
010 26 Žilina, Slovakia
oliver.bubeliny@fri.uniza.sk

Abstract. The research problem is the involvement of companies in the alliance to obtain additional benefits in the form of synergy effects in the technological environment. The aim of the article is to confirm that the creation of cooperation relations of the company can support the creation of synergistic effects in the technological environment. One of the basic synergy effects is also building the online reputation of cooperating alliances. Through technology, stakeholders can not only disseminate information and communicate, but a new element is also building an online reputation. The result of the analyzed case studies are selected positive synergy effects, which were created by this cooperation and caused an increase in the positive reputation of individual actors in the alliance. In the discussion, we want to highlight the importance of technological innovation, the synergic results of cooperative acts of the various market stakeholders. Today, the involvement of innovative technologies for the building of a positive reputation and management is important for achievement of the greater competitiveness and customer and public loyalty.

Keywords: Technology innovation · Big data · Reputation · Reputation management · Cooperation management · Synergy effects · Case studies

1 Introduction

Information technology has become a standard part of business management. Within individual management processes, these technologies are used for better planning, organization, staffing, leading, and controlling. A significant advantage of using these technologies is also decision-making based on the obtained data that the company can use. These technologies have even penetrated the marketing management of individual companies. Communication with customers has moved to the online environment. The online environment offers benefits to businesses that can better target advertising while providing products and services of interest. For customers, the online environment offers a wide range of products and services. Customers often select products based on reviews from other users. Given this fact, companies must be able to manage their reputation. With Big data, a company can analyze its current market position and influence its reputation.

M. H. Miraz et al. (Eds.): iCETiC 2020, LNICST 332, pp. 296–303, 2020.
https://doi.org/10.1007/978-3-030-60036-5_22

Reputation management can be valuable for many businesses. It is the involvement in the alliance that creates a positive synergy effect concerning the reputation of individual stakeholders. For customers, membership in companies can be a guarantee of quality. For companies, membership brings many benefits and in addition to a positive reputation, it is possible to observe many others, such as lower costs, increased market share and access to new markets.

The method of obtaining, processing, and evaluating information was used to process the document. The method of content analysis was used to collect information. The following documents were primarily analyzed:

- scientific articles focused on Big Data, online reputation, reputation management, collaborative management,
- case studies focused on the cooperation of individual companies.

Secondary sources were used to process the article, which are articles by companies focused on digital marketing and cooperation of individual alliances. Deduction was used to formulate conclusions and results of cooperation relations.

2 Theoretical Research

Nowadays, many businesses use Big Data. The main topics currently discussed are data privacy and security in the context of effective use. [1] Increase customer experience is challenging. The Gartner survey shows that in 2019 more than 75% of companies increased customer experience technology investment through artificial intelligence, virtual customer assistants and chatbots [2].

Big Data can use various areas such as [3]: Banking and security, communication, media, entertainment, health care, education, production, and natural resources, government, policy holding, retail, transport and energy.

Many businesses already use the Big Data solutions and capabilities. The number of connected devices will have an upward tendency in the future, and thus the volume is already large enough to increase. Big Data is important for businesses and should therefore search for Big Data providers and solutions. The number of case studies [4] demonstrates the positive effects of the implementation of the Big Data solutions to the company and based on them think about the same step.

Because of the increasing potential of IoE and thus generating large amounts of data and the use of a large number of heterogeneous applications, it is necessary to facilitate and establish communication between such applications by implementing the integration platform into the company. Business managers should capture this trend and implement it if they want to achieve [5, 6]:

- that their business proceeds,
- is competitive,
- effectively set up processes and communication between individual departments,
- global reach,

- effective solutions for solving problems,
- generating a higher profit.

The integration platform has more ways to deal with, and the information technology segment is very dynamic, so it is necessary to continually monitor their development and look for the best way to deal with the company. Currently, there is an unpopular method of integrating the iPaaS platform. IPaaS is a cloud-based integration platform with no need for hardware. In implementing and correctly selecting an integration platform, managers need to identify, know and well determine the following criteria [7, 8]:

- company size,
- willingness to invest,
- what processes are inefficient in the company,
- subject of improvement,
- business goals.

After learning about these criteria, it is time to analyze alliances in which technological innovations are taking place and require the involvement of an integration platform. In this step, it is very important to find the solution that will best suit the requirements of the alliances. In conclusion, it can be stated that the implementation of the integration platform into the alliance becomes more competitive and increases the potential for better and faster technological innovation. For companies that work with large amounts of data and multiple applications, tracking and developing integration platforms is a goal for the future.

3   Analysis of Case Studies from Selected Alliances

This analysis is a cross-section of the main bases, which are characteristic of the selected alliances. This analysis mainly identifies technological innovations that have been implemented to improve cooperative activities and strengthen the reputation of the alliance.

One World
The Joint venture of American Airlines, British Airways, Iberia and Finnair are members of the World Alliance of One World. The aim is to work together on transatlantic flights to strengthen global competitiveness in the market. The alliance has set itself the task of creating better conditions for customers, employees, shareholders, and the community. The content of this cooperation is the definition of common pricing, transport capacity, coordination of flight pricing and income interests. These activities have been filled through technological innovation. A reservation system was an important solution. A single transparent reservation system which is characterized by a combination of sales force (greater offers of flights for customers, more affordable tickets), cross-sales (sale tickets of competitors) and alignment of flight routes. For communication and collaboration with customers it uses modern technology and software (smartphones, applications).

This technology solution has helped in global support within the resorts and addressing customer problems (interconnection requirements), also brought about cost savings into the broader supply (coverage) of flights, which creates a better offer for travelers.

Aerospace Valley

Aerospace Valley is a French aeronautical engineering cluster that brings together several diverse entities. The primary goal of the cluster is the sharing of knowledge, technology, and know-how (cluster is contributing to supporting that members' competitiveness are development in science and research, production and education in the form of knowledge transfer between companies, institutions together with knowledge of aviation and aerospace). The cluster has a non-profit character. It is currently one of the European and world leaders in employment in the field of aerospace. The main actors are small, medium, and large companies, state and regional administrations, universities, education and research centers. This large and diverse alliance is about creating technological innovations. The alliance serves as a breeding ground for various businesses and individuals. However, these entities belong to the field of aviation and cosmonautics. The cluster offers a wide range of services from searching for offers to submitting proposals and calls for its members, taking into account their abilities and interests. This is supported by the following activities: a) joint development of capabilities and technologies; b) creation of a steering committee for obtaining and providing information (market insight, cluster development); c) promoting strategic cooperation in the cluster, supported by the logistical proximity of companies. This alliance has a well-established complex internal organizational structure, in which several governing bodies act, such as the mentioned steering committee, strategic management, and others. It is this structure that provides support to small and medium-sized companies (collaborating on projects with industry leaders, attracting investors, and providing them with access to research organizations). The cluster's expertise resulted in obtaining advice on future improvements and a higher number of technological innovations. Characteristic cooperation with competing clusters within Europe or the whole world ensures higher competitiveness and a stronger position of the European aerospace industry on the world market.

Danish Food Cluster

Danish Food Cluster is a member of non-profit organization for businesses, research institutions and public authorities operating in the food and agricultural sector in Denmark. Maximizing the sector's potential for global growth, fostering innovation in the sector, promoting knowledge sharing and cooperation. The cluster focuses on organizing events, creating contacts and expanding cooperation in this sector. The goals of the cluster include: supporting innovation, strengthening competitiveness or attracting new businesses and investments. The increasing turnover and increasing production of this cluster is of great importance in the food and agricultural sector of Denmark. Due to a good reputation, the visibility and growth of members on a global level is increasing. This alliance is characterized by: a) Research, development, and innovation activities are important for all members of the cluster and are closely related to the process of promoting the cluster; b) Support for research and development in the food industry; c) Promotion of the cluster at the international level (communication, awareness); d) Providing an environment for cooperation of cluster members (establishing contacts, cooperation, organization of conferences and meetings, networking); e) Ensuring an environment for knowledge sharing (use and dissemination of acquired knowledge, building the image of a reliable partner for cooperation or investment); f) Building attractiveness by targeting new customers, members, professionals, and investors; g) networking between cluster members, support for cooperation; h) Technology and Innovation Sharing (Development Center).

Chery Jaguar Land Rover Automotive Company

A British-Chinese joint venture called the Chery Jaguar Land Rover Automotive Company. The cooperation between the car manufacturer Chery Automotive Company and the automotive company Jaguar Land Rover ensures the production of cars and engines as well as a research center and a center for the design of new models. The intention is to increase sales abroad by creating a distribution network in China. Their task is to search for and use new and advanced technologies and innovations while maximizing lean production (flexibility, automation) while maximizing sales will be met. However, the basis was the acquisition of a strong technological and development background. JLR is trying to find a capable partner in the Chinese market who will provide production capacity for these brands, thereby reducing production costs and significantly improving the availability of JLR cars in the Chinese market. They adapted management and marketing tools in the new market in the following activities: increased customer focus, examined market consumer behavior, began to build and expand distribution channels, strengthened socially responsible business (emissions, recyclability) and sought investment.

4 Conclusion

The article points out the formed alliances of individual companies, the merger of which brought benefits for all stakeholders. The formation of an alliance is conditioned by the emergence of an advantage from which all stakeholders can benefit. Membership in such a group is multifaceted. The benefits come from the development of synergy effects, which bring, for example, increased competitiveness, access to new markets, cost-sharing, etc. One of the synergy effects is the improvement of the reputation of the entities involved in the alliance. Reputation management is currently moving primarily to the online environment. The reason is the continually improving technological environment. A lot of marketing activities have moved to the online environment.

In these cases, we can observe that building a reputation depends on technological innovation and the emergence of synergies in the following activities.

- Creating new value for the customer in the form of a unified service (for example: technological innovation within the reservation system).
- Creating new technological innovations based on the increasing professional level of cooperating entities (for example: by creating a common shared environment in which entities can operate).
- Increasing global competitiveness in order to strengthen brands, increase awareness and visibility of their activities (for example: attractiveness in targeting to attract new members).

- Increasing the growth of members (for example: create contact databases).
- Improving people's living conditions (for example: work environment).
- The use of modern, leading technologies that bring energy and cost savings, increase quality.

These activities build a positive reputation and move towards better relationships with all stakeholders in the market, while we can see the increasing customer loyalty that ensures the sustainability of the business. Maintaining and increasing market share is also a very important part of it.

5 Discussion

Cooperation between companies and the subsequent emergence of synergy effects also supports the very reputation of individual companies. [9, 10] It is mainly about improving the position on the market, increasing customer loyalty, the position of the brand itself on the market, etc. Building a reputation as such is currently tied to technologies that can manage it directly in the online environment. Dijkmans argues that the very role of online reputation management is to interact with people in the online environment, create shared content, follow the views of other stakeholders, address negative content, etc. [11, 12] A perceived problem in managing a company's reputation is mainly the fact that there are many websites, blogs, forums, social networks, which in turn makes management much more complicated. Online reputation research points directly to two sources of reputation.

The first source is search engines. Search engines are the gateway that directs all stakeholders, including customers, business partners, or competitors, to the websites in question. The second important source is social networks, where subjects can receive information and also perform searches. [13–15] In relation to search engines, the reputation management tool is SEO - search engine optimization. SEO is a set of techniques that improves website traffic from organic search results. Search results are often displayed through a Google search. The position of pages in search results depends on the relevance of the page to the search term. [17, 18] The primary goal of this optimization is mainly to get the company's website among the first in the list to be displayed to the interested party. In addition to web views themselves, the companies must create analytical and statistical reports about the traffic of the site and the reputation of the company. They have a high value as they show the management of the company where there are differences between expectations and reality. They create space for improving the very reputation management in the company.

A secondary resource is social networks, where virtual assistants can be used to manage reputation. It can be assumed that the sheer speed of introducing new technologies will cause a clear separation between people and devices. Interactions arise: human vs. human (H2H), machine vs. machine (M2M), human vs. machine (H2M), machine vs. human (M2H). [19, 20] Virtual assistants play an important role in building the company's online reputation. ChatBots can answer customer questions directly on the web or via social networks. ChatBot can be defined as a program that simulates a conversation ("chatting") through text or voice interactions. At present, these Chatbots can replace a simple dialogue between a customer and a business (B2C) or between two companies [21, 22].

Advantages of virtual assistants are:

- saving of human capital costs,
- 24/7 available,
- building the company's online reputation,
- customers are motivated to purchase.

However, it is necessary to emphasize that some chatbots work only based on rules, which represents a cost-saving in implementation.

On the other hand, this type of assistant may rather fail or fail to understand customer requirements. Another type are ChatBots using artificial intelligence, which learn from each reaction and thus improve over time. However, this solution is much more complex and also more expensive. More than 80% of companies worldwide will use virtual robots this year (2020) [23, 24].

The online environment will ensure that the company can have a large amount of data, which is a primary or secondary source of reputation. This data is another opportunity for the company to use it for further analysis to get value-added data for the business. An important key in Big Data is the ability to interpret this data and use it to gain a competitive advantage. Big data sources include content generated by users through blogs, social media, and online reviews. The data obtained in this way and correctly interpreted are of high value for further use in targeted advertising, relationship management with customers and companies [16].

Currently, the use of Big Data for reputation management has a big impact on the success of the business. If a company does not use Big Data, it can quickly become unsuccessful. Working with Big Data for Reputation Management is possible in several areas:

- data analysis for measuring brand performance (sentiment analysis),
- data analysis to detect real-time conversations,
- data analysis with an orientation on industry trends,
- data analysis with a focus on monitoring competition and other stakeholders).

Acknowledgements. This paper was supported by the Slovak republic scientific grant VEGA: 1/0533/20 Online reputation management: Tools and methods.

References

1. Surbakti, F.P.S., Wang, W., Indulska, M., Sadiq, S.: Factors influencing effective use of big data: a research framework. Inf. Manag. **57**(1) (2020)
2. Omale, G.: Improve Customer Experience with Artificial Intelligence. https://www.gartner.com/smarterwithgartner/improve-customer-experience-with-artificial-intelligence/. Accessed 25 Apr 2020

3. Jain, V.K.: Big Data and Hadoop. Khanna Book Publishing, India (2017)
4. Quinto, B.: Next Generation Big Data, 1st edn. Apress, Australia (2018)
5. Jayaratne, M., et al.: A data integration platform for patient-centered e-healthcare and clinical decision support. Future Gener. Comput. Syst. **92**, 996–1008 (2019)
6. O'Reilly, T.: Hardware, software, and infoware. Commun. ACM **40**(2), 33–34 (1997)
7. Pathak, R.C., Khandelwal, P.: A model for hybrid cloud integration with a case study for IT service management (ITSM). In: 6th IEEE International Conference on Cloud Computing in Emerging Markets (CCEM), pp. 113–118. IEEE, New York (2017)
8. Ebert, N., Weber, K., Koruna, S.: Integration platform as a service. Bus. Inf. Syst. Eng. **59**(5), 375–379 (2017). https://doi.org/10.1007/s12599-017-0486-0
9. Wikaningrum, T., Ghozali, I., Nurcholis, L., Widodo, Nugroho, M.: Strategic partnership: how important for reputation of small and medium enterprise? Quality-Access Success **21**(174), 35–39 (2020)
10. Zraková, D., Kubina, M., Koman, G.: Influence of information-communication system to reputation management of a company. Proc. Eng. **192**, 1000–1005 (2017)
11. Dijkmans, C., Kerkhof, P., Beukeboom, C.J.: A stage to engage: social media use and corporate reputation. Tour. Manag. **47**, 58–67 (2015)
12. Varmus, M., Kubina, M., Koman, G., Ferenc, P.: Ensuring the long-term sustainability cooperation with stakeholders of sport organizations in Slovakia. Sustainability **10**(6), 1–19 (2018)
13. Seker, S.E., Eryarsoy, E.: Generating digital reputation index: a case study. Proc. Soc. Behav. Sci. **195**, 1074–1080 (2015)
14. Calin, M.A., Enache, A., Florea, D., Militaru, G.: Empowering business through sentiment analysis, state-of-the-art models, trends, and applications. In: 9th International Conference of Management and Industrial Engineering, Management Perspectives in the Digital Transformation, pp. 652–663. Editura niculescu, Romania (2019)
15. Vodák, J., Soviar, J., Kubina, M.: Cooperation management - software support solution. In: 16th International Scientific Conference on Globalization and Its Socio-Economic Consequences, pp. 2377–2382. University of Zilina, Zilina (2016)
16. Koman, G., Kundríková, J.: Application of big data technology in knowledge transfer process between business and academia. Proc. Econ. Finance **39**, 605–611 (2016)
17. Baye, M.R., De Los Santos, B., Wildenbeest, M.R.: Search engine optimization: what drives organic traffic to retail sites. J. Econ. Manag. Strat. **25**(1), 6–31 (2016)
18. Sheffield, J.P.: Search engine optimization and business communication instruction: interviews with experts. Bus. Prof. Commun. Q. **83**(2), 153–183 (2020)
19. Kaczorowska-Spychalska, D.: How chatbots influence marketing. Management **23**(1), 251–270 (2019)
20. Varmus, M., Kubina, M., Soviar, J.: Cooperation on sport market – reasons and ways how to improve it. Proc. Econ. Finance **23**, 391–395 (2015)
21. Peras, D.: Chatbot evaluation metrics: review paper. In: 36th International Scientific Conference on Economic and Social Development (ESD) - Building Resilient Society. Varazdin Development & Entrepreneurship Agency, Croatia (2018)
22. Lokman, A.S., Ameedeen, M.A.: Modern chatbot systems: a technical review. In: Arai, K., Bhatia, R., Kapoor, S. (eds.) FTC 2018. AISC, vol. 881, pp. 1012–1023. Springer, Cham (2019). https://doi.org/10.1007/978-3-030-02683-7_75
23. Louie, A.: 79 Critical Chatbot Statistics: 2020 Data Analysis & Market Share. https://financesonline.com/chatbot-statistics/#link7. Accessed 25 Apr 2020
24. Smutny, P., Schreiberova, P.: Chatbots for learning: a review of educational chat-bots for the Facebook messenger. Comput. Educ. **151** (2020)

Possibilities of Building Company's Reputation with the Support of Digital Marketing Tools – A Case Study

Gabriel Koman, Jakub Soviar, and Irina Ďaďová$^{(\boxtimes)}$

Faculty of Management Science and Informatics, University of Zilina, Univerzitna 8215/1, 010 26 Zilina, Slovakia
irina.dadova@fri.uniza.sk

Abstract. The online environment has become increasingly important for companies and their activities recently, and nowadays due to the pandemic. Thanks to the constant development of ICT there are so many possibilities of using tools accessible online. For their better application, there are specific tools of digital marketing that can be very useful and even necessary for building a company's reputation. This article aims to present how important it is for the company to build its' reputation in the online environment. The reputation represents any associations, opinions, or views that customers make on the base of interactions in connection with the company. The reputation in a certain way allows customers to determine the attractiveness of the company, product, or brand. The problem that has appeared recently is an enormous movement of the customers to the online environment. In this environment company's marketers should be able to manage correctly all the activities in the field of digital marketing and apply appropriate tools. Data for writing this article were obtained in charge of ongoing research focused on building an online reputation and thanks to the analysis of the case study with the focus on building the company's reputation with the support of online marketing tools. The result is the presentation of possibilities of building the company's reputation in the online environment. Also, it points to the specific tools of digital marketing according to the analyzed case study. Described digital marketing tools can marketers apply similarly to the support of building the reputation of their company in the online environment. Some general limitations for application of selected tools in companies should be the necessity of additional training courses for employees, most marketers, because of the understanding and the importance of functioning and online marketing as a whole. In the future, it could be essential to provide similar research with the focus on the evaluation of the tools of digital marketing that should have a more radical impact on building a reputation in the online environment.

Keywords: Online reputation · Digital marketing · Digital marketing tools

M. H. Miraz et al. (Eds.): iCETiC 2020, LNICST 332, pp. 304–317, 2020.
https://doi.org/10.1007/978-3-030-60036-5_23

1   Introduction

Due to the development of information and communication technologies, customer buying behavior is constantly changing. Purchase decisions are no longer influenced only by offline advertising tools, but mostly by the activities of companies in the online environment, which have been currently supported by a global pandemic. Customer buying behavior is more oriented to the online environment than ever before. For these reasons, companies need to adapt their marketing activities and develop their activity within digital marketing. At the same time, it is important to build up the company's reputation in the online environment, as the customer does not have the opportunity to test the product physically. Reputation represents any association or opinion about a company and its' products, that customers have formed based on inter-actions in connection with the company. In this point of view reputation allows customers to determine the attractiveness of the company, product, or brand itself. To ensure the proper functioning of the company in moving customer's behavior to the online environment, as we can currently observe, it is necessary to properly manage activities related to digital marketing and use appropriate tools in the online environment. For the reasons mentioned above, the article focuses on the possibilities of building a reputation in the online environment, while reflecting on the tools of digital marketing according to a case study.

2   Materials and Methods

Data for this article has been obtained through ongoing research in the field of building a company's reputation with the support of digital marketing tools. The research is carried out by identifying and analyzing available information from the online environment and available literature at the theory level. The subject of the research was also carried out case study, which provides a broader view of the usability of digital marketing tools for the needs of building a company's reputation in the online environment. The obtained data were evaluated qualitatively on the basis of the knowledge and experience of the authors of this article and quantitatively on the basis of available quantitative indicators of the Google Analytics platform.

3   Theoretical Background

The company's reputation is a strong accelerator of the company's activities. Because it has been already proved to be true that one unfavourable event can deprive the company of the number of customers. Several authors in this field of study agree that reputation is a summary of attitudes, expectations and judgments of relevant subjects for the company. This means that these attitudes and judgments of stakeholders directly affect the business activities of the company. [1, 2] Reputation is also presented as information that directly affects the formation of judgment about the company or its part. [2–4] A positive reputation supports the company in the competition while it can affect company's market value. [5] According to [9], reputation is a more perfect synonym for image, although the means and forms of realization may not be the same as are in the case of image creation [5, 6]. The present is characterized by the development of technology, especially the invention of the Internet, which has caused moving globalization to a completely different level. Thanks to the Internet, customers have become globally connected, thanks to this service they are able to connect with anyone anywhere in the world (almost anywhere), and also it has opened up completely new opportunities for marketing. The online environment allows the company to obtain data for possible business opportunities [7, 8, 10]. From this moment on, the individual brands have began to gradually move to the online environment and create advertising campaigns directly oriented to online platforms and online customers. These steps affected, that nowadays, there are many companies that have grown and gained many new customers thanks to existence of digital marketing tools. It is possible to observe a number of successful stories in the area of digital marketing, which, thanks to its almost limitless possibilities, can be more beneficial for building up a company's reputation than with the application marketing tools outside the online world. Undoubtedly, the decisive factors for success are overall strategy and the correctly set goals, which necessarily need to be monitored and evaluated for the managers of the company. Then the managers can assess the fulfillment of the given goals and subsequently, if necessary, change selected steps. In the physical world, the company would determine the methods of measurement and the specific intervals of continuous inspections. Subsequently, the measurements would be performed at an exact time. In the online world, it works on the same principle, however, there is a specific tool called web analytics that allows companies to implement it. The most used platform in the field of web analytics is Google Analytics [11, 12].

In an online environment, if the goals are not defined and the basic data is not tracked, the company may succeed and gain new visitors or new customers, but company's managers will not know exactly how they have succeeded, so it will be difficult to try for further success in the future. In this case, Google Analytics is an imaginary compass. In summary, Google Analytics is a digital marketing tool in the form of a web analytics service offered by Google, which aims to track and report website traffic, currently as a brand within the Google Marketing Platform [13].

3.1 Basic Settings and Understanding of Google Marketing Platform

When initially setting up a profile on this platform, it is necessary to identify the users. These users can be owners of the company, marketing employees or other employees. They will have an access to the profile and thus to the important data. The platform allows users to set user rights. It is possible to set up user rights only for reading as well as it is possible to allow all users to edit campaign, goals, individual statistics, even add or subtract rights to the other users. Proceeding with caution in the setting rights is crutial because the more users can edit and interfere in statistics and targets, the higher is the threat of chaos that may arise. Ideally, one or few users should be able to intervent in the platform and the rest should have the rights only for reading. Google Analytics anticipates that a single brand has multiple pages that have to be managed, so there is the option to add multiple pages and categorize them. When adding pages, other than the URL link, it is possible to set the category in which the company fits. The most important thing is to get a tracking code (also called a UA code), which has to be inserted into the code of the website so that Google Analytics can track "traffic" on the site. Also it is useful to apply Google Tag Manager, which allows users to track all the elements required on a given website. This is especially useful for multiple tracking use. It is also important to set up blocking of employees or administrators of the site for Google Analytics, so that traffic data on the site is not distorted. If the blocking is not set, the statistics shows more visitors than truly visit the website, while administrators who regularly check the site or edit something on it are also included [14, 15].

Before launching the platform itself, it is important to understand the importance of linking Google Analytics and Google Ads. Since the appearance of the online customer, one specific metric has been changing over time, it's path. The term path refers to the individual steps that potential customer performs before getting on th desired website. In the past, these paths were relatively legible and standardized, while today they are so complex that we can no longer even think of a standard path. In effect it is not possible to find two paths that are the same. [16, 17] Customers today are very demanding and require relevant information throughout their path and this way they make significant challenges for marketing departments. The company needs to identify the basic locations where potential customers can be located and what they currently need to know in given time and place. It is important to include such critical points correctly because the competition is big enough and if the company is not there, several other competitors will definitely be waiting there and then they can easily take over a potential customer. [16, 18] Current paths could also be defined as multi-step or curious. This behavior of users on the Internet environment creates a number of diverse paths even for one particular product. One customer can go through several web pages before making a purchase, and it will take him or her few days to make a purchase. Another customer can visit three times more web pages, read some reviews, and take a month to make a purchase. Only the company that is on the right time, at the right place and with the right information will gain advantage - getting a customer. According to a Google study, up to 88% of customers like brands that provide helpful information throughout the path from their research to purchase. Simply said the way to ensure a customer experience is to make the right link between the analytics and the advertising. With Google Analytics, a company can find out what customers prefer, what is their path. And marketing department can communicate right, personalize information to the customers through Google Ads (the ad can be searchable through Google, or as a content ad on other sites, applications, or social networks). Then it is possible to monitor how customers respond to particular ads that can be adapted and optimized operationally [18].

Linking Google Analytics and Google Ads allows the company to gain a clear view which ads are generating conversions and how to adjust them to be most appropriate. It is also possible to identify the most important segment and then target personalized advertising on it. Thanks to this collaboration, it is possible to optimize bids in SEM optimization, where the company can identify the key-words that generate the most conversions and bring to the company the most of the benefits. Because of this, it is possible for the company to increase its' bid to make its' ad more likely to appear higher in search. On the other hand, it is also possible to find keywords where the company's bid is too high because the costs outweigh the benefits. The company can thus consider lowering the bid or completely eliminating such a keyword. In summary, the combination of Google Analytics and Google Ads will allow to the marketers to view online activity comprehensively and uniformly. The platform can track the impact of each click or conversion and understand visitors in more detail. As well as it gain valuable information about the performance of ad campaigns. Mentioned approach allows to marketers to make better decisions and create more compelling and creative campaigns. Based on this data, it is also possible to build positive feedback at the same time thanks to compliance with customer requirements and their satisfaction. And this has a direct impact on building the company's reputation.

3.2 Google Marketing Platform Parameters Important for the Support of Building the Company's Reputation in the Online Environment

Within the Google Marketing Platform service, to be more specific directly in the internet application of Google Analytics, it is advisable to monitor several parameters in the support of building up the company's reputation in the online environment.

The data from these parameters can later be used for building a positive reputation of the company by constant evaluation of the data and modification of the advertising and its products to the needs and requirements of customers. In the case of satisfying the customer's needs, there is an assumption based on the initial summarised theory, that in the customer's mind will arise a positive association with the company or product and it will significantly affect the creation of a positive reputation of the company. The parameters that should be monitored include the following [14, 19–23]:

– Conversions are the elements triggering the desired actions. These elements allow to the marketers to identify what are the potential customers interested in and thus optimize the site. Conversions can also be very useful for measuring the performance and effectiveness of online campaigns, so conversions allow to the users to use metrics to quantify their business benefits. Business goals should be set before the marketers decide to track the conversions. Then they should determine in Google Analytics which conversions will allow them to track set business goals. A conversion is basically a measurable action that the marketers of the company need a customer to take, thereby meeting set business goals. Thus, for example, if the company's goal is to improve its reputation, then the conversion will be a number of positive public feedback. Other examples of conversions include filling out a contact form, downloading key files, playing an important video, subscribing to news, clicking on links on a page (these can be hyperlinks to other sites, social networks, or even paid affiliate links). Then it is necessary to define on what specific places on the page the conversions will be placed. This step is extremely important, as there appears a high probability of receiving skewed data if the conversion tracking code was improperly placed on the page. For example, if company's business goal is not increasing clicking on a page, then it is not necessary to put tracking code on its' homepage. This code needs to be placed on a page that will be displayed to the user only after performing the required action. For example, in the case of a contact form, the company is not interested in how many people view the form, but how many people fill it out, so the conversion code is needed on the page that appears when you fill out the form (such as a thank you for filling it out).

- Traffic is the number of visitors on the website. It is a simple statistics that brings an informative value about the success of online operations. An enterprise can track changes in the number of visitors over a period of time to determine easily whether a web site's traffic has increased or not. Subsequently, appropriate steps need to be taken to promote traffic in relation to one of the business goals.
- Identification of company's customer - with the help of this platform the marketers can identify their customers or potential customers much more closely. Google Analytics provides information about visitors in three basic categories: demographics, interests, and geo-location. Demographics transmit information about the age composition of visitors and their gender. This information can be useful for campaign management when user can target certain campaigns to a specific gender or age group and monitor if these metrics will change during the campaign. Campaigns can be targeted on the most widespread groups and support them this way, or they can be targeted on a specific segment that is underdeveloped and needs to be increased. Interests are likely to be slightly more valuable than demographics because Google Analytics creates different categories of visitors, which it divides into two groups: liking groups and market segments.
- Liking groups represent categories of visitors who are interested in a particular topic or hobby and also they have had certain behavior typical for it over a certain period of time. Market segments, on the other hand, represent groups of potential customers who are interested in purchasing products or services from a particular area. This category can therefore tell the company what interest groups are visiting the web site and what is their percentage share. Again, this is advantageous for more accurate targeting of online campaigns, or for setting up products and brands so that it is possible to create a positive reputation on the part of customers. The third interesting category is geo-location, which is an essential part of companies focused on certain specific areas and markets. Google Analytics provides an interactive map where a company can track their potential customers to know from what countries, locations, and web sites they come from and how many are they. On this interactive map, it is also possible to find out from what specific places they visit the given page. This information can be used to target advertising to the right geographic locations, or international companies can tailor content to individual countries and their languages and cultural backgrounds. It is also possible in case of negative reactions on the company, brand, or product identified in specific locations take corrective action in a short time to prevent building a negative reputation in a specific location.
- The origin of the visitors – it is important to know from where individual visitors come on the website. For the "tracking" of visitors of the company's website, it is necessary to set the so-called tracking lines that allow this. These links contain UTM parameters, which are simply certain tags (data) that are added sequentially to the end of the URL adress. These parameters are made up of four types of data. The first parameter is the source and tells user from which page the visitor came. It can be a social network or an email. This parameter provides important information about from what platforms the most potential customers come from. This information is useful for the marketers, while it can be used for future campaigns, when they as users decide for the best option. It can also be used for identification of the weaknesses, for instance, what marketing channels need to be improved and optimized. The second parameter is the

so-called "Medium" or carrier that provides information on the type of traffic. This makes it possible to find out whether visitors came to the website from an organic search or from paid advertisement. This is valuable information for determining the performance of individual ads. The third parameter is the campaign. This parameter provides information about which campaign brought how many visitors to the page. The marketers are thus able to compare the success of online campaigns. The fourth parameter is content, which is one of the most important parameters because it provides to the marketers information whether specific contribution or specific content ad brought potential customers to the website. For example, the company can determine whether image, text, or video ads are more successful. Based on this, it is possible to customize the further advertising content according to what users like best.

– Visitor activities – useful for monitoring what content customers prefer and like most. At the same time, we can find out how much time visitors spend on the site and what areas they are most interested in and what exactly they do on the website. In addition, it is also interesting for the company in what area and part of their searching potential customers are leaving the website. It is important for the company to know whether they will leave immediately from the home page or continue by clicking on the next one. If the company also has an e-shop within its website, the essential information about the leaving the page is in connection with the number of completed orders, that is how many customers leave without putting something in the basket, how many of them put the products in the basket and leave, and how many of them leave just before the completion of the order. This is very important information that can help the company to identify weaknesses and try to identify the reasons for early leaving and, based on that, optimize the areas and then monitor whether the individual variables monitored are better. In such cases, it is very appropriate to choose re-marketing, which consists in reaching potential customers who have gone somewhere during buying process and try to attract them back to the website. An interesting technique, such as attracting customers who have already added products to the basket, is to address them with a content advertisement in the form of a discount on a product for which they have already shown an interest.

– Use of various devices – is important because of obtaining information about what devices potential customers use. Probably one customer has several devices that he actively uses (such as a mobile phone, tablet, laptop, desktop computer, or even a smart TV) and the customer uses them for his/her activities in the online environment. For the proper functioning of the website and customer satisfaction (increasing reputation), it is necessary to adjust the web page for these devices applying a responsive design. Once the company has solved this, it is important to start tracking the customer's path also in terms of the equipment used. Since one customer has several devices at his/her disposal and it is possible to assume the use of several of them. The customer's path will likely consist of passing through different devices. For example, the customer may start searching for information on a mobile phone, and when the customer decides to make a purchase, he/she should be using a computer. Or, if the customer's path lasts several days, one day he/she can use a tablet, the next day a desktop computer, and a third mobile phone. The availability of different devices and their compatibility is one of the main reasons why the path to the same product is never the same today. By careful tracking the customer's path, also from the point of view of the equipment used, the company's marketers can adapt the content for individual devices to provide a greater customer experience. For example: If, by the analysis, marketers finds out that most of the customers' purchases start with searching for an information via a mobile phone and then they complete their purchase via a laptop, then thanks to this crutial information marketers can target their online activities and ads for smarthphone purchase.

4   Case Study

The case study was carried out in a company operating in the Slovak business environment. The line of the business is selling paints. As the company wants to be anonymous, it will be referred to as Color XY in this article.

The company's problem was the absence of the using of online digital marketing tools, while the sale took place primarily in the network of it's retail stores. The company's marketers have created a profile in the Google my business. This is very important for the company, as it has retail stores, so that it can also be displayed on Google maps and customers should able to find the store without any problem. One of the options offered by Google Analytics in the field of geo-location is the evaluation of the number of path requests from individual places where the company has stores (Fig. 1). This platform also has the advantage in the case of searching for a company by potential customers from a certain city in Slovakia, the customer will be shown the store branch that is closest to him/her according to customers' location, even if it will not be the "most successful" store branch. This case could be demonstrated to a potential customer from the village of Jarovnice who would be interested in Color XY products and their purchase in a retail store. In the search, customer would suggest a store in the village of Chminianska Nová Ves, despite the fact that the store in Prešov is more visited.

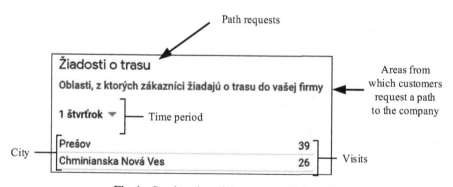

Fig. 1. Geo-location of the company Colour XY

The importance of the company's presence on Google maps can also be demonstrated by the following analysis in Fig. 2, which presents an overview of where potential customers get to Color XY from. It is possible to see in the picture that until March, customers were informing about the company, they were using a search engine and they were almost equally working with the maps. However, the situation changed in April, when the number of new customers coming from maps fell, which could be due to a global pandemic. The pandemic limited retail stores and reduced the free movement of customers. However, in the period before the pandemic, it is possible to see how essential it was for a given company to be active on Google maps.

Fig. 2. How customer search for company Color XY

Another important element is the ability to track what is happening on the website. Google Analytics can provide important data about the visitors' activity on the website over time. As can be seen in Fig. 3, the activity has increased since the beginning of February, with an increase recorded mainly in the area of visits to the website itself and in the area of calls to the company, but the path requests have decreased significantly (impact of the mentioned pandemic). This information tells the marketers that it is necessary to prepare for increase in customer calls, to which they can respond by strengthening customer service. However, these are still relatively low numbers, so even current employees can do it.

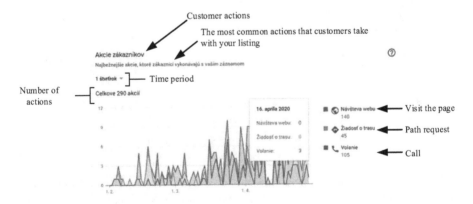

Fig. 3. Actions took by the customers of Color XY

In terms of the mentioned phone calls, for the company's employees to be able to prepare and respond better, there are also statistics on what days customers call most often. This data can be seen in Fig. 4, where it is clear that the busiest day is Thursday, with Sunday being zero, and Saturday and Wednesday are less frequented. Thanks to this information, the company's marketers know when it is necessary to strengthen customer service and when it is not.

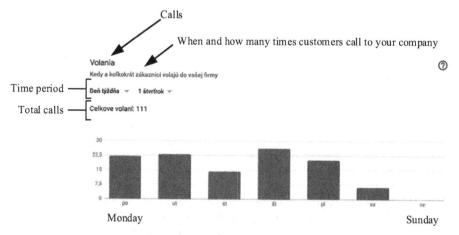

Fig. 4. Frequency of calls to the company during the week

The company also has its' own photos of products or stores added to Google. The Google Analytics platform also provides an overview of success in this way. This should be seen in Fig. 5, where photos of Color XY are displayed up to 23.3% more than photos of similar companies. It is even possible to see advice from this tool for a company to publish more photos, thus maintaining its advantageous position.

Color XY is an example of the right response to unexpected situations, which in this case is a coronavirus pandemic that has affected global markets, as well as the Slovak market. To protect the health of citizens, the government has put in place measures against the rapid spread of the virus in the form of massive closure of the stores. However, the company has had implemented a digital strategy already before the pandemic, so this company was ready to attract customers online as well. The success of the strategy of Color XY is evident by favorable rising numbers, which means an increasing interest in the company while creating a positive reputation as the company has adapted to the situation and thus satisfied the needs and requirements of customers by using digital marketing tools.

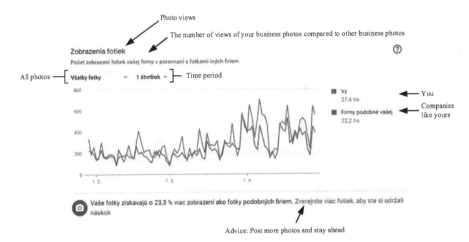

Fig. 5. The number of views of Color XY photos compared to similar companies

5   Results

Google Analytics can be considered as very beneficial and useful in the field of digital marketing and building up a company's reputation in the online environment. A basic prerequisite for the proper implementation of the activities associated with building the company's reputation in the online environment is an exhaustive analysis. To be able to start building a reputation in the online environment with a close connection to digital marketing, it is necessary to take any steps in marketing, to know the customer, and define the customer precisely. It is important to find out customers' interests, demographics, and buying behavior. While in the physical world it is quite a demanding process, in the digital world Google Analytics practically does most of this work. One of the things that need to be done is to set up the pages and tracking codes correctly, ideally to create URLs supplemented by UTM parameters. Subsequently, it is still necessary to keep the website active and after a certain time, the result will be achieved in the form of detailed statistics as customers' paths, demographic features, search sites, or even categorization according to their interests. Thanks to this, it is possible to set suitable goals for marketing activities with the focus on building a reputation in the online environment, which will target the company's customers directly and create interesting and creative campaigns. At the same time, the Google Analytics platform allows users to measure the performance of their campaigns based on set goals through conversion analysis. Users gradually find out which ads bring them more customers and which elements on the page are most effective for triggering the desired action. This is essential information for the marketers that can customize website content and paid advertising to be as effective as possible and eliminate those that generate more costs than revenue. In principle, on the basis of this data, it is possible to indirectly measure the company's reputation at the level of a specific location or customer segment and then implement the necessary measures or strengthen existing advertising campaigns with an emphasis on building up the company's reputation.

6 Discussion

Despite the huge number of benefits and opportunities resulting from the use of Google Analytics, it is possible to find certain shortcomings that can partially jeopardize the operation of the company and building its reputation in the online environment. The biggest shortcomings for the platform are the so-called "Ad blocking" programs or extensions that are capable of deleting or altering online advertisements on websites and applications. Examples are the NoScript web extension or the Disconnect Mobile application. These software solutions are able to block the tracking code, so that certain data cannot be collected and included in the statistics and thus the data is distorted. The threat to Google Analytics is to block the use of cookies, which are an important part of collecting information. If cookies are rejected, the given website visit will not be captured and it will be lost. This should be addressed by the setting of the website itself. Because of that on the webpage should be a friendly environment as well as publishing privacy policy information to encourage the visitors not to reject cookies [13, 15].

Providing enough data to carry out marketing activities in connection with building an online reputation, despite the before mentioned shortcomings of the Google platform, can be achieved to some extent by combining several Google services. The most important thing is the connection with the Google Ads tool, which is a practically necessary part of the given platform if the company really wants to succeed in the digital world. This link allows the marketers to know the customer and his path comprehensively and create online marketing campaigns and measure their performance. Subsequently, a link to Google Tag Manager is suitable, while it creates an environment for easier and more intuitive management of the code intended for tracking pages or conversions. At the same time, for a more efficient online operation, the free Campaign URL Builder tool is recommended, which creates URL addresses supplemented by specified UTM parameters. In addition to the tools already mentioned, it is worth mentioning Google Keyword Planner and Google Trends. These tools provide information for optimizing paid advertising in search through SEM optimization.

7 Conclusion

The article presents the Google Analytics platform and the possibilities of its use for building the company's reputation in the field of digital marketing with a reflection on the parameters of digital marketing, which can be considered as crucial in building the company's reputation in the online environment. By analyzing the case study, it is possible to make a conclusion that the tool is currently the most used tool for web analytics and provides data for building a company's reputation in the online environment. This tool is suitable for small companies starting their own business or starting their operations in the online world, as well as for large multinational companies. This is ensured by the fact that the tool works correctly at different levels of its use and thus creates conditions for any range of use and functionalities. This tool is practically essential for the companies in the online world, as it provides choices of the range and depth of data that companies need to know in order to successfully manage their activities in the online environment. It allows company's marketers to identify the customers and their paths, which ads are most preferred, which are unsuccessful, what devices they use. With the help of the results of analysis and using the correct evaluation to make the following steps better, e.g. in the case of building a company's reputation in the online environment. While the Google platform has some shortcomings, there are limitations that other web analytics tools face as well.

Acknowledgement. This article is the outcome of the project VEGA: 1/0533/20 Online reputation management: Tools and methods.

References

1. Klučka, J.: Goodwill is difficult to obtain and easy to lose (Dobré meno sa ťažko získava a ľahko stráca) (in Slovak). https://www.etrend.sk/podnikanie/dobre-meno-sa-tazko-ziskava-a-lahko-straca.html. Accessed 15 Aug 2019
2. Gattiker, U.E.: Brand versus reputation: Jeff Bezos, Richard Branson, Josef Ackermann and Pat Russo. http://commetrics.com/articles/branding-versus-reputation-jeff-bezos-richard-branson-josef-ackermann-and-pat-russo-to-the-rescue/. Accessed 17 Aug 2019
3. Farmer, F.R., Glass, B.: Building Web Reputation Systems. O'Reilly Media, Newton (2010)
4. Zrakova, F., Ferenc, P., Polackova, K., Kubina, M.: Reputation management using online and offline communication tools. In: Marketing Identity, pp. 277–289 (2017)
5. Argenti, P.A., Druckenmiller, B.: Reputation and the corporate brand. Corp. Reput. Rev. **6**(4), 368–374 (2004)
6. Adamik, R., Varmus, M., Kubina, M.: The impact of social media on the reputation of the sports club. In: Marketing Identity, pp. 16–23 (2017)
7. Ferenc, P., Varmus, M., Vodak, J.: Stakeholders in the various field and relations between them. In: Bujnak, J, Guagliano, M. (eds.) 12th International Scientific Conference of Young Scientists on Sustainable, Modern and Safe Transport, High Tatras, Slovakia, vol. 192, pp. 166–170 (2017)
8. Holubcik, M.: Theoretical knowledge in terms of forming cooperation. In: Bektas, C. (ed.) Selected Papers of 5th World Conference on Business, Economics and Management, BEM-2016, Antalya, Turkey, pp. 88–95 (2017)
9. Svoboda, V.: Public Relations, 2nd edn. Grada, Prague (2009)
10. Stokes, R.: eMarketing: The Essential Guide to Marketing in a Digital World. Quirk eMarketing Ltd. (2008)
11. Plaza, B.: Google Analytics for measuring website performance. Tour. Manag. **32**(3), 477–481 (2011)
12. W3Techs: Usage statistics of traffic analysis tools for websites. https://w3techs.com/technologies/overview/traffic_analysis. Accessed 02 June 2020
13. Google Marketing Platform. https://marketingplatform.google.com/about/. Accessed 04 June 2020
14. Ledford, J.L., Tyler, J.: Google Analytics 2.0. Wiley, Hoboken (2007)
15. Google Analytics Support (in Slovak). https://support.google.com/analytics/answer/1008015?hl=sk&ref_topic=3544906. Accessed 05 June 2020
16. Think with Google: How search enables people to create a unique path to purchase. https://www.thinkwithgoogle.com/feature/path-to-purchase-search-behavior/. Accessed 05 June 2020
17. Upadhyay, U.D., Jovel, I.J., McCuaig, K.D., Cartwright, A.F.: Using Google Ads to recruit and retain a cohort considering abortion in the United States. Contraception: X 2, 100017 (2020)

18. Meltzer, J.: Solution Guide: Linking analytics and ads. https://services.google.com/fh/files/misc/analytics_ads_guide.pdf. Accessed 03 June 2020
19. Analytics Help. https://support.google.com/analytics/answer/3124493?hl=en. Accessed 20 May 2020
20. Pollitt, H.: How to get international insights from Google Analytics. https://www.searchenginewatch.com/2019/04/10/international-insights-google-analytics/. Accessed 22 May 2020
21. Campaign URL Builder. https://ga-dev-tools.appspot.com/campaign-url-builder/. Accessed 22 May 2020
22. Clifton, B.: Advanced Web Metrics with Google Analytics. Wiley, Hoboken (2012)
23. Use your Remarketing Audiences in Google Ads. https://support.google.com/analytics/answer/2611291?hl=en&ref_topic=2611283. Accessed 25 May 2020

Developing an Interactive Mathematical Learning Media Based on the TPACK Framework Using the Hawgent Dynamic Mathematics Software

Tommy Tanu Wijaya$^{(\boxtimes)}$ (iD), Jianlan Tang, and Aditya Purnama

Guangxi Normal University, Guilin, China
tommytanu@foxmail.com

Abstract. The integration of technology in education has grown rapidly in the 21st century. The ability to use technology in teaching materials has become an important skill for mathematics teachers and is an important topic in the current research. This is why as a rookie teacher; it is important to have the ability to develop an ICT based learning media. The purpose of this research is to design an interactive mathematical learning media based on the TPACK framework using the Hawgent dynamic mathematics software. There were 30 students divided into five groups for this research and each group consisted of six students. Each group conducted a research to find out the difficulties faced by the teachers in school when they are explaining mathematics concept and will then design a learning media based on their observation using Hawgent dynamic mathematics software. This research is a merged descriptive and quasi-experiment research aimed to describe students' creativity in developing an interactive learning media using the HAWGENT Dynamic Mathematics Software. This result shows students' creativity in designing a mathematics learning media using Hawgent dynamic mathematics software on various topics and different levels. Hawgent dynamic mathematics software has been proved to improve the students' creativity when the researchers designed a learning media based on the needs of the teachers and students in school using Hawgent dynamic mathematics software. Other than that, using Hawgent dynamic mathematics software with a TPACK framework can help teachers in explaining an abstract mathematics concept so that it would be easier for the students to understand.

Keywords: Hawgent dynamic mathematics software · TPACK · Students' creativity

1 Introduction

Generally, technology in the education field can be used as an effective learning media to improve the students' mathematics ability [1]. Technology can also make students be more interested and enthusiastic to learn mathematics compared to the traditional

M. H. Miraz et al. (Eds.): iCETiC 2020, LNICST 332, pp. 318–328, 2020.
https://doi.org/10.1007/978-3-030-60036-5_24

teaching method [2, 3]. This learning condition can potentially make students be more active and self-confident when learning a certain topic [4]. Based on the current problems an ICT based learning media can help teachers in guiding students to find the basic concept and the core of learning [5]. According to De Porter's research results, humans are able to absorb a material by as much as 70% if they actively and practically engage in doing the work, 50% of if they only hear and see, while from what he saw only 30% of the information is retained, then by only hearing only 20% and from 10% by just reading. This kind of activity can help improve students' mathematics ability [6].

In reality, there are a lot of researchers that have shown that the students' mathematics ability especially ability of mathematics communication [7, 8], mathematics connection ability [9], problem-solving ability [10] and mathematics critical thinking ability are still not optimal. A lack in the students' mathematics understanding of the basic concepts causes their mathematics ability to fall behind.

Technological Pedagogical Content Knowledge (TPACK) is a framework to know the teachers' technological, pedagogical, and content knowledge [11–13]. TPACK can be used to design a technology-based learning media that can be combined with a learning method to help students understand the basic concept of a topic and how the technology that is designed can help the students [14]. Various studies have shown that the innovation of an ICT-based learning media that utilizes a-TPACK framework can help students in understanding a certain concept [15–17]. An ICT-based learning media could guide the students to figure out the primary concept of mathematics as opposed to recalling equations [18–20]. The learning media can also help students to truly understand an abstract concept [21].

Hawgent dynamic mathematics software is a learning media designed according to the needs in the 21st century. Hawgent dynamic mathematics software has a lot of features that are flexible and easy to use [22]. Hawgent can be used to teach various mathematical topics such as calculus, three-dimensional figure, algebra, probability, etc. Hawgent can also be used with in both a computer or a tablet. The practicality and efficiency of using Hawgent dynamic mathematics software can help improve students' mathematical ability [22–25].

The purpose of this research is to increase college students' creativity in developing mathematics learning media using Hawgent dynamic mathematics software based on the TPACK framework. Firstly, college students went to schools to observe the difficulties faced by teachers when explaining a mathematical topic. They also interviewed some students to know the difficulties faced by students when they are learning mathematics. Based on this information, the college students then designed a learning media using Hawgent dynamic mathematics software to meet the teachers' and students' needs. Lastly, college students were helped by their lecturer to evaluate the learning media before being implemented in school.

2 Method

This research merged descriptive and quasi-experiment research aimed to describe the teacher's expectation towards the students' creativity when designing an interactive learning media based on the TPACK framework using Hawgent dynamic mathematics software. The students have learned the basic knowledge of Hawgent dynamic mathematics software. There were 30 students divided into 5 groups for this research and each group consisted of 6 students. Each group did research to find out the difficulties faced by the teachers in school when they are explaining a mathematical concept.

2nd semester mathematics education college students have learned how to use technology in education. This time, the students used Hawgent dynamic mathematics software to make a learning media. After the students became familiar with the software, they did field research so that the learning media that they were making will be able to help teachers and students when teaching and learning mathematics. Before designing the learning media, every group had the freedom to observe any grade in elementary school or junior high school. The college students observed the difficulties faced by teachers and students that are difficult to understand.

Surface area of a cone = area of the base + the curved surface area

$$L = \pi . r^2 + \pi . r . s$$

$$L = A = \pi . r . (r. s)$$

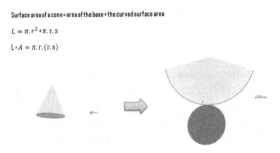

Fig. 1. Animation on the surface area of a cone

The second group made a proof on the surface area of a cylinder. Students found that the surface area of a cylinder is a combination of the area of the circle in the cylinder with the area of the rectangle that wraps the side of the cylinder. The length of the rectangle is the same as the circle's circumference. After designing the proof of the formula, Students added an animation to the learning media. The formula proof of a cylinder's surface area can be seen in Fig. 2.

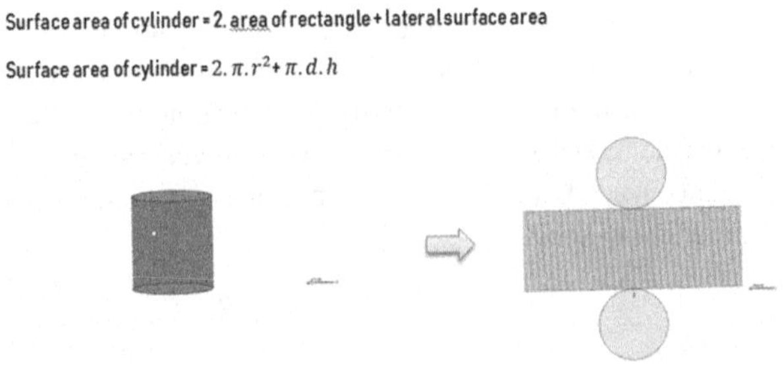

Surface area of cylinder = 2. area of rectangle + lateral surface area

Surface area of cylinder = 2. $\pi . r^2 + \pi . d . h$

Fig. 2. Animation on the surface area of a cylinder

The third group made a proof formula for algebra $(a + b)2$ by using two squares with the length of a and b. With this, we can proof that $(a + b)2 = a2 + 2ab + b2$ and we can see it in Fig. 3 below.

$$(a+b)^2 = a^2 + 2ab + b^2$$

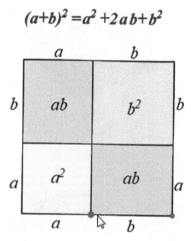

Fig. 3. Third groups' formula proof for algebra

Group 4 made a formula proof of the algebra $(a + b)^3$ by using 2 cubes with the length a and b each, 3 rectangles with length of $a^2.b$, and 3 rectangles with the length of $a.b^2$. This way, we can proof that $(a + b)^3 = a^3 + 3a^2b + 3a.b^2 + b^3$ as shown in Fig. 4.

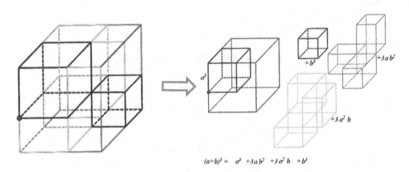

Fig. 4. Fourth groups' formula proof for algebra

The fifth group made a learning media to proof the number of cube sides and to proof the surface area of a cube as can be seen in Fig. 5.

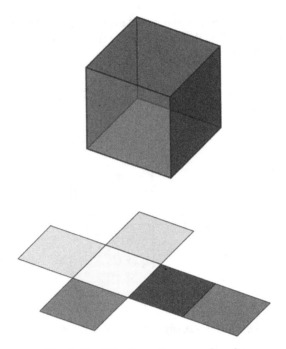

Fig. 5. Proof for the surface area of a cube

3 Results and Discussion

Each group designed a learning media using Hawgent dynamic mathematics software based on their observation. The numerical range in Table 1 is classified to indicate subjective levels of difficulty.

Table 1. Difficulty categories on the learning material

Interval	Category
3.60–4.00	Very hard
2.60–3.59	Hard
1.60–2.50	Average
0.00–1.59	Easy

Based on the teachers' and students' observation results in Table 2, we can see that the average rating score on addition and subtraction is 1.25 and the teachers' rating score is 1.0 which suggest that teachers most likely don't have problems explaining the operation of addition and subtraction. The students' rating on this topic is 1.5 which means that students also don't experience difficulties mastering the operation of addition and subtraction. The average rating score on the fraction is 2.4 and the teachers' rating score is 2.2 which shows that teachers are still able to explain the basic concept of the fraction. While the students' rating on the fraction is 2.6 which suggests that students don't have a problem in understanding the fraction. The teachers' rating score for multiplication and division is 2.1 which shows that teachers are still able to explain the concept to the students while the students' score is 2.4 which shows that students are still able to understand the teacher's explanation on the topic.

Table 2. Initial observation in school.

Topic that are difficult	Teachers' observation result	Students' observation result	Average rating score	Difficulty
Two-dimensional figure	3.2	3.8	3.5	Hard
Three-dimensional figure	3.8	3.4	3.6	Very hard
Algebra	4.6	4.8	4.7	Very hard
Operation of addition and subtraction	1.0	1.5	1.25	Easy
Fraction	2.2	2.6	2.4	Average
Operation of multiplication and division	2.1	2.4	2.25	Average

There are 3 topics that are considered hard to understand by the students and hard to explain for the teachers which are algebra, three-dimensional figures, and two-dimensional figures. The average rating score for two-dimensional figures, three-dimensional figure and algebra are 3.5, 3.6, and 4.7 respectively which falls into the hard, very hard, and very hard category. Based on the interview with the teachers for two-dimensional figures and three-dimensional figures, the teachers teach using cardboard so that students can be more active in doing the experiment and better understand the concept of two-dimensional figure and three-dimensional figure. However, based on the teacher's experience, the class time is often not sufficient or there is a need for extra time to be able to understand the concept of two-dimensional and three-dimensional figures. While for algebra, teachers often use the whiteboard to explain the formula of algebra.

In the development stage, the first group made a learning media on three-dimensional figure based on the TPACK framework. According to the college students' observations, students often find it difficult when calculating the surface area and volume in three-dimensional figures. The 1st group students' thinking process can be seen in Fig. 6.

Firstly, the college students made a circle which is the area of the base. Then, students added the curved surface area. After designing the proof of the formula, the college students created an animation so that the cone in the media could move. The formula proof of the cone's surface area can be seen in Fig. 1.

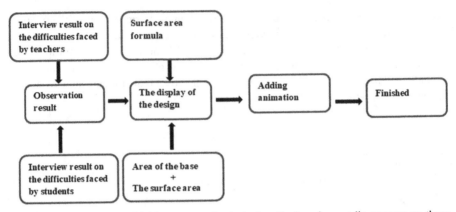

Fig. 6. Students' creative thinking process in designing the learning media process on three-dimensional figure.

To be able to make a learning media based on the needs of the teachers and students is not easy. The college students need to think on how to design a learning media that is easy for the teachers to use given that some of them can't operate the computer very well. Other than that, in the animation step, college students need to make a learning media that will help students to understand the basic concept and are interesting. These two steps need the students' creative thinking skills. The students' creative thinking process when they made a learning media on the cube's surface area can be seen in Fig. 7.

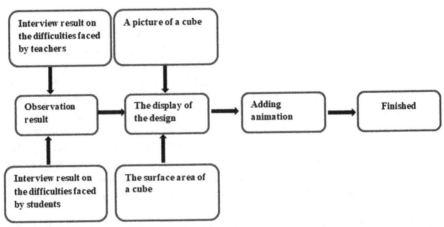

Fig. 7. Students' creative thinking process in designing the learning media on the cube's surface area.

After each group designed a learning media using Hawgent dynamic mathematics software, each group went back to school to implement and also evaluate the learning media that has been designed by each group. The students' response towards Hawgent dynamic mathematics software according to the TPACK framework can be seen in Table 3.

Table 3. Students' respond and suggestion on the learning media.

Students' abilities	Respond	Suggestion
High abilities	1. It helps a lot for me to understand the mathematical concept	Add an interesting sound
	2. Mathematical concepts are easier to understand	
	3. I want to try to make a learning media using Hawgent myself	
Moderate abilities	1. Can understand better compared to when the teacher just explains the formula	Make writing and more interesting 3-D design
	2. I now know where the algebra formula comes from	
	3. It's very interesting to learn with Hawgent dynamic mathematics software	
Low abilities	1. I don't feel sleepy anymore during mathematics class	I wish I can learn more with the help of Hawgent dynamic mathematics software
	2. After I understand the concept, I don't need to memorize mathematical formulas anymore	

Based on the students' response in school towards the learning media, Hawgent dynamic mathematics software got a good feedback from both the teachers and students. From Table 3, we can see the students state that Hawgent dynamic mathematics software is very interesting and able to guide students to understand the basic concept of mathematics.

According to the analysis made for the learning media using Hawgent dynamic mathematics software, researchers found out that the college students are working together to create a piece of work that can help teachers in the school to explain mathematical concepts. Researchers also found that Hawgent dynamic mathematics software can improve the students' creativity when designing a unique and interesting learning media but still consist of the basic concept of mathematics that should be mastered by students. Creative thinking is a process to make something from involving elements and experiences that exist to be processed in the brain in order to create a new thing.

4   Limitations of the Study and Recommendations for Future Study

The limitation of this study is that learners' achievement was measured by the marks obtained on the Development only, while not addressing other factors that are needed for learners to achieve, such as motivation.

This research can serve as an instrument for the coming studies. For example, the research may be concluded to examine how to improve student's mathematical ability using Hawgent dynamic mathematics software in various of circumstances inside and outside the classroom.

Further research shall be directed on the strength of Hawgent dynamic mathematics software in teaching and learning mathematics in diverse stage of learning and to explain diverse mathematics materials, also in variant learning fields.

The researchers further suggested more qualitative studies to evaluate the students' impression on the usage hawgent dynamic mathematics software and other software in learning mathematics. The experiment should as well evaluate teachers' perspective and view point on the usage and combination of ICTs into the teaching of mathematics.

5   Conclusion

Hawgent dynamic mathematics software gives various possibilities to help students obtain an intuitive feeling and to adequately visualize mathematical processes. The use of this hawgent dynamic mathematics software's tools allows students to explore a wider range of function types, and provides students the opportunity to make the connections between symbolic, visual, and numeric representations. Students should learn new techniques and should be able to model and evaluate a situation that is challenging, more interesting, and real.

Hawgent dynamic mathematics software has been shown to improve students' creativity when using technology in education. Other than that, using Hawgent dynamic mathematics software with a TPACK framework can help teachers in explaining abstract mathematical concepts making it easier for the students to understand. From the students' point of view, Hawgent dynamic mathematics software can help them to be more active and confident when learning mathematics in class. Recommendations that were conveyed based on the research result is that other mathematical topics requires a learning media such as Hawgent dynamic mathematics software to help teachers in explaining the basic concept.

References

1. Zhang, J., Meng, L., Jing, Q.: ICT supported instructional innovative practice and diffusion mechanism of K-12 in China. In: Huang, R., Kinshuk, P.J. (eds.) ICT in Education in Global Context. LNET, pp. 17–56. Springer, Heidelberg (2016). https://doi.org/10.1007/978-3-662-47956-8_2
2. Goldhammer, F., Gniewosz, G., Zylka, J.: ICT engagement in learning environments. In: Kuger, S., Klieme, E., Jude, N., Kaplan, D. (eds.) Assessing Contexts of Learning. MEMA, pp. 331–351. Springer, Cham (2016). https://doi.org/10.1007/978-3-319-45357-6_13

3. Newhouse, C.P.: STEM the boredom: engage students in the Australian curriculum using ICT with problem-based learning and assessment. J. Sci. Educ. Technol. **26**(1), 44–57 (2016). https://doi.org/10.1007/s10956-016-9650-4

4. Pierce, R., Stacey, K., Barkatsas, A.: A scale for monitoring students' attitudes to learning mathematics with technology. Comput. Educ. **48**(2), 285–300 (2007). https://doi.org/10.1016/j.compedu.2005.01.006

5. Zaranis, N., Exarchakos, G.M.: The use of ICT and the realistic mathematics education for understanding simple and advanced stereometry shapes among university students. In: Mikropoulos, T.A. (ed.) Research on e-Learning and ICT in Education, pp. 135–152. Springer, Cham (2018). https://doi.org/10.1007/978-3-319-95059-4_8

6. Chotimah, S., Bernard, M., Wulandari, S.M.: Contextual approach using VBA learning media to improve students' mathematical displacement and disposition ability. J. Phys.: Conf. Ser. **948**(1) (2018). https://doi.org/10.1088/1742-6596/948/1/012025

7. Pertiwi, I., Wahyudin: Analysis of elementary student's mathematical connection and communication ability. J. Phys.: Conf. Ser. **1521**(3) (2020). https://doi.org/10.1088/1742-6596/1521/3/032092

8. Rahmawati, D., Budiyono, Saputro, D.R.S.: Analysis of student's mathematical connection ability in linear equation system with two variables. J. Phys.: Conf. Ser. **1211**(1) (2019). https://doi.org/10.1088/1742-6596/1211/1/012107

9. Sari, D.N.O., Mardiyana, M., Pramudya, I.: Analysis of the ability of mathematical connections of middle school students in the field of algebra. J. Phys.: Conf. Ser. **1469**(1) (2020). https://doi.org/10.1088/1742-6596/1469/1/012159

10. Franestian, I.D., Suyanta, Wiyono, A.: Analysis problem solving skills of student in Junior High School. J. Phys.: Conf. Ser. **1440**(1) (2020). https://doi.org/10.1088/1742-6596/1440/1/012089

11. Valtonen, T., Leppänen, U., Hyypiä, M., Sointu, E., Smits, A., Tondeur, J.: Fresh perspectives on TPACK: pre-service teachers' own appraisal of their challenging and confident TPACK areas. Educ. Inf. Technol. **25**(4), 2823–2842 (2020). https://doi.org/10.1007/s10639-019-10092-4

12. Castéra, J., et al.: Self-reported TPACK of teacher educators across six countries in Asia and Europe. Educ. Inf. Technol. **25**(4), 3003–3019 (2020). https://doi.org/10.1007/s10639-020-10106-6

13. Kadıoğlu-Akbulut, C., Çetin-Dindar, A., Küçük, S., Acar-Şeşen, B.: Development and validation of the ICT-TPACK-science scale. J. Sci. Educ. Technol. **29**(3), 355–368 (2020). https://doi.org/10.1007/s10956-020-09821-z

14. Utami, P., Pahlevi, F.R., Santoso, D., Fajaryati, N., Destiana, B., Ismail, M.E.: Android-based applications on teaching skills based on TPACK analysis. IOP Conf. Ser.: Mater. Sci. Eng. **535**(1) (2019). https://doi.org/10.1088/1757-899X/535/1/012009

15. Pusparini, F., Riandi, R., Sriyati, S.: Developing technological pedagogical content knowledge (TPACK) in animal physiology. J. Phys.: Conf. Ser. **895**(1) (2017). https://doi.org/10.1088/1742-6596/895/1/012059

16. Sukaesih, S., Ridlo, S., Saptono, S.: Development of biology teaching management textbooks based on competency and conservation to maximize Pedagogical and Content Knowledge (PCK) the prospective teachers. J. Phys.: Conf. Ser. **1321**(3) (2019). https://doi.org/10.1088/1742-6596/1321/3/032114

17. Widowati, A.: The innovative framework for developing science teacher education: NOS within TPACK. J. Phys.: Conf. Ser. **1233**(1) (2019). https://doi.org/10.1088/1742-6596/1233/1/012091

18. Mainali, B.R., Heck, A.: Comparison of traditional instruction on reflection and rotation in a Nepalese high school with an ICT-rich, student-centered, investigative approach. Int. J. Sci. Math. Educ. **15**(3), 487–507 (2015). https://doi.org/10.1007/s10763-015-9701-y

19. Rohaeti, E.E., Bernard, M.: The students' mathematical understanding ability through scientific-assisted approach of GeoGebra software. Infinity J. **7**(2), 165 (2018). https://doi.org/10.22460/infinity.v7i2.p165-172

20. Rohaeti, E.E., Bernard, M., Primandhika, R.B.: Developing interactive learning media for school level mathematics through open-ended approach aided by visual basic application for excel. J. Math. Educ. **10**(1), 59–68 (2019). https://doi.org/10.22342/jme.10.1.5391.59-68

21. Agyei, D.D.: From needs analysis to large-scale implementation: using collaborative design to support ICT integration. In: Pieters, J., Voogt, J., Pareja Roblin, N. (eds.) Collaborative Curriculum Design for Sustainable Innovation and Teacher Learning, pp. 305–328. Springer, Cham (2019). https://doi.org/10.1007/978-3-030-20062-6_17

22. Cunhua, L., Ying, Z., Qunzhuang, O., Wijaya, T.T.: Mathematics course design based on six questions cognitive theory using hawgent dynamic mathematic. J. Educ. **02**(01), 36–44 (2019)

23. Wijaya, T.T., Ying, Z., Purnama, A.: The empirical research of hawgent dynamic mathematics technology integrated into teaching. J. Cendekia: Jurnal Pendidikan Matematika **04**(01), 144–150 (2020)

24. Wijaya, T.T., Ying, Z., Purnama, A.: Using hawgent dynamic mathematics software in teaching trigonometry. Int. J. Emerg. Technol. Learn. **15**(10), 215–222 (2020). https://doi.org/10.3991/ijet.v15i10.13099

25. Suan, L., Ying, Z., Wijaya, T.T.: Using hawgent dynamic mathematics software in teaching arithmetic operation. Int. J. Educ. Learn. **2**(1), 25–31 (2020). https://doi.org/10.31763/ijele.v2i1.97

Author Index

Printed in the United States
By Bookmasters